TRAVELS IN THE
CONFEDERATE STATES
A BIBLIOGRAPHY

TRAVELS IN THE CONFEDERATE STATES

A BIBLIOGRAPHY

BY E. MERTON COULTER

LOUISIANA STATE UNIVERSITY PRESS

Baton Rouge and London

Copyright © 1948 by the University of Oklahoma Press. Reprinted by arrangement with the
    University of Oklahoma Press
All rights reserved
Manufactured in the United States of America

Louisiana Paperback Edition, 1994
03   02   01   00   99   98   97   96   95   94   5   4   3   2   1

Library of Congress Cataloging-in-Publication Data

Coulter, E. Merton (Ellis Merton), 1890–
    Travels in the Confederate States : a bibliography. — Louisiana
paperback ed.
        p.   cm.
    Includes bibliographical references (p.) and index.
    ISBN 0-8071-1952-0 (p : alk. paper)
    1. Confederate States of America—Description and travel—
Bibliography.   I. Title.
Z1251.S7C68   1994
[F214]
016.917504'7—dc20   94-17847
                                                 CIP

The paper in this book meets the guidelines for permanence and durability of the Committee on
Production Guidelines for Book Longevity of the Council on Library Resources. ∞

To Colonel J. Alton Hosch

DEAN OF THE UNIVERSITY OF GEORGIA SCHOOL OF LAW
WHO, HAD HE LIVED DURING THE CIVIL WAR,
WOULD DOUBTLESS HAVE LEFT A TRAVEL NARRATIVE
WORTHY TO BE INCLUDED IN
THIS BIBLIOGRAPHY

EDITOR'S FOREWORD

This is the first of several Southern volumes to be published in the American Exploration and Travel Series. Professor E. Merton Coulter has examined a large quantity of personal and descriptive material of the Civil War period, and has analyzed it effectively and concisely. He took the pains to chart on maps, where possible, the routes followed by each author, and to pass on this information to his reader in his annotations. Neither Professor Coulter nor the editor assumes that this volume is a complete coverage of material of this type for the years 1861–1865. Both of us are familiar with the contents of the voluminous *Bibliography of State Participation in the Civil War, 1861–1865,* published by the War Department in 1913, and recognize that even it, with its all but unlimited space, is far from comprehensive. Professor Coulter's bibliography does, however, represent a thoughtful analysis of a major portion of the more significant Civil War travel sources.

The compiler has adjudged this selection of material on the basis of its descriptive values. His main questions were: What was the South like during the war years? *and* How did its people respond to war conditions? Equally important was the effect of war on the region. What destruction did the territory suffer? What was the reaction of federal soldiers to prison life? What were their reactions to the destruction, carnage, and pillage of war? In addition to the soldier reaction was that of nonmilitary observers. Among these were journalists, foreigners, visitors, and innocent victims caught within the grip of war. This volume has approached the subject of travel and description with the intent of evaluating a major block of material without being too much concerned with why the authors were traveling. Soldiers did not necessarily give up their powers of observation just because they were being moved about as involuntary travelers under the dictates of military discipline.

We hope that this bibliography will make a contribution in the field of travel and description. Also, we hope it will serve to indicate the important reflections of the postwar American mind, both North and South. These memoirs and reminiscent accounts of the war constitute a significant personal chapter in the process of national reunion. The historian can hardly understand the pyrotechnics of "Bloody Shirt" politics, or the panegyrics of the Southern cause, without dipping heavily into this important resource.

Technically, in the preparation of this bibliography we have attempted to follow the most widely accepted methods of citation. In only one instance have we made a significant departure. Book sizes given are those of title pages rather than of outside covers. We have used this standard of measurement with the feeling that it comes nearest to being an accurate physical description of the book itself.

The whole intent of the projected Southern volumes in the American Exploration and Travel Series is to analyze the greater portion of the vast body of descriptive material relating to the South, and, eventually, to make some of the more representative titles available in a carefully edited form. Travel accounts have constituted major sources of information in many types of historical studies. To date these important first-hand observations as a whole have not been evaluated. When this project was first conceived, the plan was to prepare approximately fourteen volumes of travel accounts with full editorial notes and appraisal for republication, but, before this could be carried out, it was realized that no one knew either the extent or comparative values of travel accounts relating to the South. Thus it was deemed imperative to prepare first a critical bibliographical study of the entire field of Southern travel, 1606–1946. At the present time the remainder of this material is being prepared for publication.

The Rockefeller Foundation, through Mr. David H. Stevens, director of the Division of Humanities, generously made available funds with which to finance preparation of these studies. President H. L. Donovan and Comptroller Frank D. Peterson of the University of Kentucky graciously assumed administrative responsibility for the funds. The University of Kentucky has been exceedingly generous with its library and staff facilities in preparing the manuscript for publication. Miss Jacqueline Bull, University Archivist, checked the technical points of the bibliographical entries, and gave freely of her time in attempting to determine whether or not the titles published in this volume were representative of the whole field of war memoirs and personal histories.

For material assistance in the publication of this series we are deeply indebted to Mr. Guy A. Huguelet, president of the Southeastern Greyhound Lines. Mr. Huguelet's intelligent interest in Southern travel is academic as well as commercial, and he and the Southeastern Greyhound

Lines have given genuine encouragement to this study. Also, we wish to acknowledge the assistance of William H. Townsend, Lexington attorney and historian. Finally we wish to thank Mr. Savoie Lottinville of the University of Oklahoma press for the sound advice and assistance given this undertaking from the moment of its inception.

Thomas D. Clark

University of Kentucky

COMPILER'S PREFACE

Not again until the twentieth century, if then, were there as many travelers in the South or in any other part of America as during the Civil War; for soldiers, who made up the vast majority, were travelers even though they did not have the opportunities for observation nor the viewpoints which characterize peacetime visitors. And never have as many travel accounts been written dealing with so short a period of American life as appeared on the Confederacy.

Of course, not all of these visitors were soldiers, nor were all of the soldiers Federals, for most Confederates moved widely enough over the South to assume the character of travelers as much as did the Northerners. True enough, the Confederates had the attitudes neither of the enemy they were fighting nor of peacetime travelers, but they were nonetheless travelers, and their observations are equally important. For example, a Texan passing through Virginia was as keenly impressed by what he saw there as was a New Yorker, though doubtless with not the same reactions. And, indeed, a Virginian traveling in his own state gained impressions which differed, perhaps, from those of a Texan or a New Yorker, but they are no less significant in evaluating that part of the South.

Although soldiers, or other persons related to the war in some respect, composed the great mass of travelers in the South during the Civil War, they were not the only visitors. There were some foreigners who made their way into the Confederacy as true travelers, carrying on the traditions of the prewar years. Most of these, as previously, were English, but there were a few of other nationalities, such as Germans, Scotch, Hungarians, Frenchmen, and Swedes.

The value and reliability of the travel narratives written by these visitors vary widely, depending on the writer, the time when he wrote, and the nature of his account. As to the writers, those who were divorced from any connection with the war, and who, therefore, by the very nature of the situation, were almost entirely foreigners, should as a class be placed first in the value and significance of their narratives. What bias and prejudice they may have had were more than counterbalanced by the freshness of their point of view, as well as by the fact that these foreigners would probably report incidents which might be considered commonplace and, therefore, unworthy of notice by Americans, whether Northerners or Southerners. Therefore, for unusual glimpses, familiar enough to all but strangers, their narratives must be consulted.

Of the foreigners who visited the South, less than two dozen wrote accounts of their travels, and practically all were in sympathy with the Confederacy, its institutions, and its fight for independence. This is not surprising, for they came either to join the Confederate Army or to observe its operations and wartime conditions in the South. Only that uncertain character Bela Estvàn wrote a hostile account. In addition to the soldiers like Heros von Borcke, there were such others as the newspaper correspondent William H. Russell, the military observer Colonel Fremantle, the schoolmistress Catherine C. Hopley, the blockade-runner Hobart Pasha, the merchant William C. Corsan, and the clergyman William W. Malet.

As for soldier-travelers, it hardly need be stated that many Northerners wrote with a feeling of hostility to almost everything Southern except natural scenery, and some of these even permitted their hatred of slavery to deny beauty in landscapes or to allow that a Southern sunset could be alluring. Yet some Northern soldiers were genuine travelers and wrote with a surprising detachment from characteristic prejudices and from their chief business of making war. Southern soldier-travelers, on the other hand, could be counted on to exaggerate the good qualities in the people they visited and to overpraise their patriotic zeal for the Confederacy. Also, much that they would not think to comment on at all or would eschew mentioning, the Northerner would see and record. Closely allied to either the Northern or the Southern side in the struggle were various nonmilitary travelers, such as occasional civilians, army nurses, spies, and prisoners of war on their way to or escaping from prison. Those from the North in the first two groups necessarily confined their travels to that part of the Confederacy occupied by the Federal army. The narratives of prisoners differed little from those of soldiers except for their extreme bitterness.

Naturally the class to which the traveler belonged was of first importance. His account was of the very essence of himself. His education and his background, and therefore his ability to observe and understand what he saw, perforce colored his narrative. Apart from his ability, truthfulness, and good intentions, much depended on the time when he wrote. This fact leads to a consideration of the various kinds of travel material included in this bibliography.

There are diaries, series of letters written from the scenes of action, reminiscences, autobiographies, regimental histories and accounts of larger units, and the narratives written primarily as travel accounts. Diaries, within themselves and without reference to the individuals who kept them, are of high reliability, for they were written at the moment nearest to the events recorded; of course, when the personal element is taken into consideration, they may be wholly unreliable—depending on the character of the writer and on whether or not he wrote for a simple annal or for propaganda purposes. But there is less likelihood of error in diaries than in other accounts. More reliable than diaries, but generally less usable as travel material, are letters written at frequent intervals on a journey. As there is less reason to suspect that letters were written with any thought of publication than may be the case with diaries, the former may be considered freer from guile. Time is of the very essence of reliability in reminiscences, but as few people feel in the reminiscent mood until many years have elapsed since the event, there is constant danger that a treacherous memory will produce distortion of past events. Yet where the writer checks his memory against established records, diaries, or other personal material, his narrative becomes much more reliable. Autobiographies are in these respects essentially the same as reminiscences and, therefore, have the same values and discounts.

Regimental histories are in a class by themselves, and do not exist for any other period of Southern life. In the strictest sense, they might not, as a class, be considered travel material, except as they depart from the significance of their name. But the fact is that most regimental histories are much more (or much less) than histories of units of fighting men. The authors of most of these works made them highly personal, detailing where they went, what they saw, and what they inferred from what they saw. All of them, of course, give some attention to the regiment—its organization, its personnel, its marches and battles—but many of them are more nearly travel journals of the writers. A considerable number were written from diaries kept by the authors or from other personal material (but some claim this additional advantage without much internal evidence.) After the style was set for these histories, and their number is legion, there was a tendency for one author to copy from another and apply to his own unit some amusing incident that may or may never have happened.

An important consideration in regimental histories, as, indeed, in all other material, is whether the author was Northern or Southern—or foreign. The Northerner often had the complex of a conqueror which would lead him to belittle, defame, and assume a superior attitude toward his present or former enemy. As Northerners had begun to write their accounts during and immediately after the war and had gradually lost momentum and interest by the end of the century, time had not had a chance to exercise fully its mellowing effects on their judgment. But in some instances, accounts written in the twentieth century are more bitter and caustic than many earlier ones. The greatest extremes were reached in narratives by prisoners of war, many of whom were psychologically incapable of writing true accounts. Many Northern works, especially the last-named kind, were written for propaganda purposes and are, therefore, to be sharply discounted. To promote Negro suffrage in Reconstruction times, veterans wrote volumes to prove the high intelligence encountered among the slaves during marches through the former Confederacy; to aid the move for bigger and more widely-scattered pensions and to help elect Republican candidates to office, authors narrated the terrors through which they went in fighting the enemy, described the barbarisms of the Confederates, and otherwise "waved the bloody shirt" through many of their pages.

Southerners wrote much less than did Northerners. While the latter were pouring forth their volumes, the former dared not write or could not command the means to commemorate their marches and battles. When finally the Southerners did begin to write their regimental histories and other works, they had grown mellow toward their former enemies. Few Southern works are bitter, but what they gain in freedom from bias and bitterness, they lose in accuracy from the lapse of time. Not until the twentieth century did the mass of Southern material make its appearance. Unless such belated works can prove the use of diaries or other personal material, they are almost worthless except for certain generalizations.

It is too much to expect that all works, Northern, Southern, and foreign, have been located and included in this bibliography; and it would be equally playing with perfectionism to hope that the exclusion of some works will meet with universal agreement. This bibliography, in fact, could have been almost indefinitely extended had an attempt been made to exhaust the list of authors who concern themselves with their Civil War services primarily and only incidentally touch on observations characteristic of travelers. Nevertheless some works of this nature have been included, more to serve as examples than to be classed as first-rate travel accounts. The compiler has, therefore, deliberately left out some narratives which seemed to be across the border line of minimum value; but he does not attempt to justify his inclusion of certain others that might appear to be as worthless. A line had to be drawn somewhere in this twilight zone. But he believes that the following test for inclusion will meet with the approval of all. No work has been considered travel material and included whose author was not present on the trip he describes (except for a few instances in which the author made most of the trip and finished his narrative from other sources). This test eliminates a considerable number of regimental histories which were written by authors not members of the respective regiments.

The omission of birth or death dates for many authors hardly needs explanation to those who are familiar with the problem of securing data on obscure authors, for whom public records are few or unavailable. The dates, when known, are given as they appear on the Library of Congress catalog cards.

In connection with each narrative included in this bibliography, the compiler, as far as space would allow, has given some estimate of the nature of its content, its reliability, and the itinerary of the author. There is no major area in the South through which some traveler included in this bibliography did not pass and offer some comment on the countryside, cities, people, or institutions. The compiler has, in all instances of extended journeys, constructed maps giving the routes taken as far as the author detailed them, but cost requirements have made their reproduction here impossible. It is believed, however, that this volume will be made sufficiently practical, through use of the index, to lead investigators into the wealth of descriptive details embraced in the books included in this bibliography.

In using travel accounts, a common-sense amount of caution will warn the reader and recall to him the fact that there are human frailties even in the most honest writers, and that all records must be used in the light of the limitations heretofore stated and others easily inferred.

E. M. C.

TRAVELS IN THE
CONFEDERATE STATES
A BIBLIOGRAPHY

Abbott, Allen O. 1

Prison life in the South: at Richmond, Macon, Savannah, Charleston, Columbia, Charlotte, Raleigh, Goldsborough, and Andersonville, during the years 1864 and 1865. By A. O. Abbott ... New York, Harper & brothers, 1865.

x p., 1 l., ₁13₁–374 p. incl. front., illus., plates. 18½ cm.

Illustrations: Frontispiece, "Digging Tunnels"; "Captured"; "Fresh Fish"; "Camp Ogle-thorpe, Macon, Georgia"; "Washing"; "Shoulder-straps on Police Duty"; " 'Bucked' "; "Filling up the Sinks at Savannah, Georgia"; "Washing—under Difficulties"; "Jail-yard, Charleston, South Carolina"; "Work-house, Charleston, South Carolina"; "Roper Hospital, Charleston, South Carolina"; "Burnt District at Charleston, South Carolina"; "Capture of the Fugitives"; "Hauling Wood, Camp Sorghum"; "Drawing Mean Ration"; "Shanties, Columbia, South Carolina"; "Asylum Prison, Columbia, South Carolina"; "Dividing Wood"; "Sutler's Estab-lishment"; "Delivering the Mail"; "Skirmishing"; "Passing the Line for Exchange, North Caro-lina"; "Pursuing Knowledge under Difficulties"; "Recaptured"; "Rebel Barbarities—John W. January, Corporal Co. B, 4th Illinois—Smith and Churchill—John H. Matthews, Corporal Co. F, 4th Pennsylvania—Calvin Bates, Corporal Co. E, 20th Maine—Calvin Bates—Benjamin T. Daugherty, Co. K, 31st Illinois—Benjamin T. Daugherty, Co. K, 31st Illinois (Fig. 2)—

Inclusive dates: May, 1864–February, 1865.

This is one of the early prison accounts from which both text and illustrations have often been copied without acknowledgement by later prisoner-of-war authors. Though not as extreme in treating the subject as some other accounts, it is liberally sprinkled with atrocities. It has the valid feature, not found in most similar narratives, of giving much attention to the railway travel from one prison to another. Abbott describes in considerable detail his trip from northern Virginia, where he was captured near Spottsylvania Courthouse, to Richmond and, after a short imprisonment in Libby, on through Danville to Greensboro on one of the first trains to run over the new link of road between those towns, on to Salisbury, Charlotte, Columbia, and Augusta to Macon, where he was imprisoned during most of the summer of 1864. He was then sent to Savannah, Charleston, and to each of the two prisons in Columbia, to be moved out of the latter just before Sherman arrived. After a few weeks of moving from Charlotte to Greensboro and to Goldsboro, he was turned over to the Federal forces near Wilmington. Abbott was a lieutenant in the First New York Dragoons. In addition to his own account he has included in this volume the short accounts of prison experiences, escapes, and atrocities of nine other authors, two of whom are not identified.

Adams, Francis Colburn 2

The story of a trooper. With much of interest concerning the campaign on the Peninsula, not before written. By F. Colburn Adams ... New York, Dick & Fitzgerald, 1865.

2 p. l., ₍3₎–616 p. 18¼ cm.
Inclusive dates: 1861–1862.
Other editions: Another edition with the same text was: A troopers adventures in the war for the union. A thrilling history of the campaigns, battles, exploits, marches, victories and defeats of the Army of the Potomac. Being a complete and graphic narrative of the Peninsula campaign under McClellan. By a cavalryman. New York, Hurst & co. ₍18—₎

This author was critical of the pillaging done in northern Virginia by occupation troops after the first Battle of Manassas, and also of the treatment meted out to inhabitants of the Peninsula during General McClellan's invasion in 1862. His work is therefore notable. Adams is quite discursive in his narrative, bringing in many subjects apart from the immediate scene on which he wishes to express opinions. His war experience as narrated here relates only to northern Virginia and McClellan's Peninsula campaign. Adams was an Englishman who wrote several books before and after the outbreak of the Civil War. He served with a New York unit after having enlisted in New York City.

Adams, John Gregory Bishop, 1841–1900 3

... Reminiscences of the Nineteenth Massachusetts regiment. By Captain John G. B. Adams. Boston, Wright & Potter printing company, 1899.

viii, 186 p. incl. front. (port.), ports. 22 cm.
Illustrations: "Color-Sergeant Benj. F. Falls, With flags of the 19th Massachusetts carried at Battle of Gettysburg"; "Captain 'Jack' Adams. July, 1865."
Inclusive dates: 1861–1865.

Perhaps this volume is hardly worth notation, because it adds little to many other and better accounts of the events described and the country covered. Adams took part in some of the principal fighting north of Richmond, even as far as Gettysburg, until he was captured at Cold Harbor in the summer of 1864. This part of the book contains no comment on matters of importance in the Confederacy. From his capture to his final exchange, he followed the route to Libby at Richmond, to Lynchburg and across country to Danville, by rail to Greensboro, Charlotte, and Augusta to Macon, then to Charleston and on to Columbia, with an escape there that took him into Georgia, only to be recaptured and returned to Columbia and back to Charlotte, Salisbury, Raleigh, Goldsboro, and to the Union lines near Wilmington. His account of cruelties and starvation in prison is stereotyped.

Adamson, Augustus Pitt, 1844–[1]   4
Brief history of the Thirtieth Georgia regiment. Griffin, Ga., The Mills printing co., 1912.

157 p.   front. (ports.), illus.   23 cm.
Illustrations: Frontispiece, "A. P. Adamson," and seven illustrations of other members of the regiment.
Inclusive dates: 1861–1864.

This account, though brief, is a well-written, straightforward, and unvarnished narrative. Various incidents of camp life and travel are mentioned but none of them at length. Reliance can be placed on what Adamson writes, as he used a short personal diary as well as other sources to check statements of fact. He enlisted in the fall of 1861 and received his first training at Fairburg, Georgia. In January, 1862, his unit entrained for Savannah, where it was based until the middle of the following year, making various expeditions up and down the coast. First the Thirtieth Georgia Regiment went to the outskirts of Jacksonville, Florida, when the Federals were in possession of that place; then it made a sortie into South Carolina as far as Coosawhatchie; at another time it went to Charleston; and finally, before permanently leaving Savannah, it went to help protect Wilmington, North Carolina. In the early summer of 1863 the regiment was transferred to Jackson, Mississippi, to aid General Joseph E. Johnston. It operated out of Clinton as far as Vicksburg and, after the fall of that stronghold, returned to Georgia and took part in the Battle of Chickamauga in September. Adamson continued with Johnston's forces as they opposed Sherman's march on Atlanta, until his capture in May, 1864. Thereafter until February following, he was held prisoner of war at Rock Island, Illinois.

Ambrose, Daniel Leib   5
History of the Seventh regiment Illinois volunteer infantry, from its first muster into the U. S. service, April 25, 1861, to its final muster out, July 9, 1865. By D. Leib Ambrose. Springfield, Ill., Illinois journal co., 1868.

xiii, 391, [1] p.   18½ cm.
Inclusive dates: 1861–1865.

Daniel Leib Ambrose gives a day-by-day account of the marches and fighting of the regiment, during which he rose to the rank of first lieutenant. Though not indicating that he kept a diary, the narrative has that form. It gives the life and movements of the regiment without much comment on other than military matters except for occasional short statements. This regiment, formed in the summer of 1861, floated down the Mississippi from Alton to Cairo and went into camp for a short while before transferring to the Sulphur Springs and Cape Girardeau ports of Missouri. From these places it made raids into the hinterland

[1] Incomplete dates follow entries on the Library of Congress catalog cards, as explained in the preface.

as far as Ironton. It then operated in western Kentucky around Columbus before embarking on the Ohio to the mouth of the Tennessee and to Fort Henry. After the fall of this post it marched overland and participated in the reduction of Fort Donelson on the Cumberland, continued up the Cumberland to Clarksville, Tennessee, and soon proceeded to Nashville. In the spring of 1862 it went down the Cumberland and Ohio rivers and up the Tennessee to the zone of conflict at Shiloh. After that engagement it marched over to Corinth, made raids into Mississippi, western Tennessee, and into Alabama as far as Florence and Tuscumbia, and later moved into Middle Tennessee in the neighborhood of Pulaski and Columbia. Being granted a furlough, the regiment went by rail to Nashville, Louisville, and Springfield, Illinois; returning the same way, it reached Chattanooga and participated in the engagements around that city after Chickamauga. In the spring of 1864 it accompanied Sherman on his famous march to the sea and up through the Carolinas. After the surrender of Johnston it marched on to Washington for the "Grand Review," and then by train proceeded to Parkersburg, West Virginia, where it embarked on steamers down the Ohio to Louisville and was mustered out in the summer of 1865.

Amory, Charles Bean, 1841–   6

A brief record of the army life of Charles B. Amory; written for his children. ₁Boston?₁ Privately printed, 1902.

2 p. l., ₁3₁–43 p.   front. (port.)   22 cm.
Illustrations: Frontispiece, "Chas. B. Amory" ₁Signature₁.
Inclusive dates: 1861–1865.

The author of this brochure joined the 24th Massachusetts Volunteers in September, 1861, and was immediately commissioned a first lieutenant. After a few months training near Boston, Amory went to Annapolis, where he joined General A. E. Burnside's flotilla bound for the Roanoke Island venture. After the reduction of that place he went on to Newbern and inland as far as Goldsboro. In the late summer of 1862 he went to Beaufort, South Carolina, to engage in operations in the Department of the South, which took him to the environs of Charleston and southward to St. Augustine, Florida. He returned northward and in the summer of 1864 took part in Grant's onset against Petersburg, was captured at the Battle of the Crater, taken to Columbia, South Carolina, and imprisoned there until Sherman's advance on that place early in 1865, when he was removed to Charlotte, North Carolina, where he escaped. After wandering eastward for a few days in the hopes of meeting Sherman's forces he turned westward, made his way across the North Carolina mountains into East Tennessee, and came upon Federal troops at Greeneville. This sketch of his wartime travels is brief and of little value, except for the diary which he kept while he was a fugitive from the Charlotte prison. Apart from the diary, the booklet was evidently written just prior to its publication.

Anderson, Ephraim McD.

Memoirs: historical and personal; including the campaigns of the First Missouri Confederate brigade. By Ephraim McD. Anderson. Saint Louis, Times printing co., 1868.

2 p. l., vi p., 1 l., ₍9₎–436, ₍2₎ p.   front. (port.) plates   22 cm.
Illustrations: Frontispiece, "Gen. Sterling Price"; "Gen. Little"; "Death of Gen. Little"; "Gen. Bowen"; "Bombardment of Grand Gulf"; "Explosion of the Mine at Vicksburg"; "Negotiating for the Surrender of Vicksburg"; "Gen. Cockrell."

This is a well-written, even-tempered, observant account of four years' service. Anderson, a resident of Missouri, was closely related to the famous McDowell and Shelby families of Kentucky and, characteristic of the upper class in the South, found relatives in almost every state he visited. He therefore noted not only the social conditions among the planter class, who seemed never to let the war interfere with social activities of the feminine set, but he also observed with much interest the natural scenery, the character of the towns, and, of course, the ravages of war and the corpse-strewn battlefields. Anderson's military activities were confined to the Mississippi Valley, first in Missouri, then from Boonville to Springfield, back to Lexington, and on the Kansas border. After the Battle of Pea Ridge, his forces went on through Arkansas by way of Fayetteville, Van Buren, and Des Arc to Memphis, reaching the latter place over the White and Mississippi rivers. After this period most of his experiences were in Mississippi. He participated in the battles of Corinth and Iuka, was in Vicksburg at its fall, was paroled and sent to Demopolis, Alabama, and later exchanged. On various furloughs, which seemed to have been easy for him to obtain, he visited at Port Gibson, Demopolis, Selma, and at the plantation of an uncle down the Alabama River from the latter place, where he was when the war ended. He describes the sacking of this plantation and its mansion by Negro troops. This is among the best of all accounts relating to the South during the war, being more a genuine travel narrative than a war record.

₍Anderson, James S.₎

Nineteen months a prisoner of war in the hands of the Rebels: experiences at Belle Isle, Richmond, Danville, and Andersonville: some items with reference to Capt. Wirz, with a map of Andersonville prison camp, called Camp Sumter. Milwaukee, Starr & son, printers, 1865.

67 p.   front. (fold. plan)   21½ cm.
Maps: "Map of Camp Sumter, Andersonville, Ga., drawn and Brought through the Lines by Wm. O. Pitt, a Prisoner of War 19 months at Belle Isle, Richmond, Danville and Andersonville." (Folding map, 54 cm by 40 cm.)

In a badly organized and episodical brief account, Anderson does little more than describe the route of his travels to various Confederate prisons and the people he saw along the way. The general tone is extremely bitter, and frequently the author is mistaken in names of places through which he passed. He was a Wisconsin soldier who was captured at the Battle of Chickamauga and taken to Richmond by way of Atlanta, Augusta, Columbia, Chester, Charlotte, Salisbury, Greensboro, Raleigh, Weldon, and Petersburg. After spending some time in Richmond prisons, he was taken back over the same route to Augusta, then through Millen and Macon to Andersonville. In March, 1865, he was taken west to the Mississippi River at Vicksburg. In this latter move, the Wisconsin soldier was somewhat confused about the route, but evidently he went through Montgomery and Selma, down the Alabama river to its confluence with the Tombigbee and up that river to Demopolis, and from there by rail through Jackson to Vicksburg where he went aboard a boat for St. Louis and thence to Milwaukee.

Andrew, Abram Piatt, 1843–   9

Some civil war letters of A. Piatt Andrew, III. Gloucester, Mass., Privately printed, 1925.

x p., 2 l., 3–146 p., 1 l.   front., plates, ports., facsims.   20 cm.

Illustrations: Frontispiece, "A. Piatt Andrew, III ... 1863"; "Recruiting Poster Issued when Battery was being Organized"; "Recruiting Poster Urging Enlistments"; "War-Time Letterheads and Envelopes"; "Chickamauga, September 19, 1863"; "Helen Merrell (Mrs. Andrew)"; "A. Piatt Andrew, III, as Captain"; "Monument at Chickamauga."

Inclusive dates: 1862–1865.

The author, born in northern Indiana, was a student in Wabash College when the Civil War began and did not join the Federal Army until the autumn of 1862; soon thereafter he was commissioned a second lieutenant, and rose to the rank of captain before the end of the war. He served first in central Kentucky, beginning around Covington and continuing southward to Paris, Lexington, Nicholasville, and Danville. In early 1863 he went down the Ohio River and up the Cumberland to Nashville and thence up river to Carthage. Thereafter to the end of the war he served in central and East Tennessee, around Decherd, Jasper, Chattanooga, Nashville, and Columbia. The most prominent engagement in which Andrew participated was Chickamauga. In letters the author wrote home he gives interesting glimpses and observations relative to the country and its people. He believed Kentuckians were incurably secessionists, and he was much interested in his encampment on the grounds of Henry Clay's old home in the outskirts of Lexington; he thought Columbia, Tennessee, the most beautiful and aristocratic town he had ever seen; and he referred more than once to the fact that he was boarding with the wife of a "rebel major," but that she had been born in the North and was "a perfect lady and fine woman."

Andrews, Eliza Frances, 1840–   10

The war-time journal of a Georgia girl, 1864–1865. By Eliza Frances Andrews; illustrated from contemporary photographs. New York, D. Appleton and company, 1908.

4 p. l., 387 p.   front., plates, ports.   20½ cm.

Illustrations: Frontispiece, "Eliza Frances Andrews"; "Photograph of the Original Manuscript of the Diary"; "Metta Andrews"; "A Group of Confederate Children"; "A Belle of the Confederacy in Evening Dress"; "From beyond the Blockade"; "Julia, Daughter of Mrs. Troup Butler"; "War-Time Fashions"; "Judge Garnett Andrews, 1827"; "Mrs. Garnett Andrews, nee Annulet Ball, 1827"; "The Old Bank Building in Washington, Ga., 1865"; "Mrs. Sarah Ann (Hoxey) Brown"; "A Group of Confederate Officers"; "A Group of Confederate Belles"; "Survivors of Judge Andres's Household Servants, Photographed, 1903"; "Haywood, the Old Home of Judge Garnett Andrews, Erected in 1794 or 1795."

Inclusive dates: December, 1864–August, 1865.

Miss Andrews, a Georgia girl in her early twenties during the war, has written an excellent account of social life in Georgia near the end of the war. She was a daughter of Judge Garnett Andrews, a staunch Unionist, with whom she was violently though lovingly and respectfully in opposition. In December, 1864, after Sherman had passed on his famous march, she made a trip from her home in Washington, Georgia, to a southern Georgia plantation between Albany and Thomasville. She recounts the widespread destruction wrought by the Federal troops as she saw it on her way south. She visited widely among kindred and acquaintances in southwest Georgia, and gives an excellent picture of social activities among a people who were still unable to renounce gaiety, and vivid descriptions of dirty hotels and ramshackle trains. Near the end of the war she returned to her home just in time to see the breakup of the Confederacy in this little Georgia town, along with the scattering of Davis, the remnants of his cabinet, and some of his generals. The book ends with occupation of the town by Federal troops and the growing problem of dealing with Negroes. Miss Andrews was highly cultured and well educated, having attended school at La Grange (Georgia) College where she became much interested in botany. She later wrote two books on this subject, and at least three works of fiction. As a clear insight into the minds and sentiments of many southern women during wartime and early Reconstruction this work is unexcelled. In later life the author mellowed her attitude toward the former enemy, but at the time, despite the feelings of her father, she had a keen dislike for all Yankees and for all they represented. Wisely she left her diary as it was originally written, with a few exceptions, though much of it was omitted because she felt that it was not of sufficient general interest.

Aten, Henry J., 1841– *comp.* 11

History of the Eighty-fifth regiment, Illinois volunteer infantry. Comp. and pub. under the auspices of the Regimental association. By Henry J. Aten ... Hiawatha, Kan., 1901.

xi, ₍1₎, ₍13₎–506 p. incl. front., ports. 19 cm.
Illustrations: Twenty-three portraits of members of the regiment.
Inclusive dates: 1862–1865.

As a commentary on the conditions prevailing in the Confederacy the writings of Henry J. Aten have little value. Being written thirty-five years after the war, and based on memory, a few contemporary documents, and various secondary accounts, it adds little if anything to the other regimental histories. The Eighty-fifth Illinois Volunteer Infantry, in which Aten was a corporal, was organized in the fall of 1862, went immediately to Louisville and was engaged in the movement to expel Bragg from Kentucky, fought at Perryville and marched on to Nashville and later to Chattanooga to engage in the various conflicts around that stronghold in the fall of 1863. In the spring of 1864 it followed Sherman through Georgia and the Carolinas and on to Washington for the "Grand Review." It returned to Illinois by way of the Baltimore and Ohio Railroad to Parkersburg, West Virginia, thence by boat to Lawrenceburg, Indiana, and by rail to Springfield.

Austin, J. P. 12

The blue and the gray: sketches of a portion of the unwritten history of the great American civil war, a truthful narrative of adventure, with thrilling reminiscences of the great struggle on land and sea. By J. P. Austin ... Atlanta, Ga., The Franklin printing and publishing co., 1899.

xi, ₍1₎, 246 p.   col. front.   20 cm.
Illustrations: Artist's symbol of Union with the hand-clasp across a grave, with representation of United States and Confederate flags.
Inclusive dates: 1861–1865.

Running through this narrative are personal reminiscences, but often the routes are not clear. The work also contains many details of the Civil War which had no relationship to the author. Yet there are interesting comments on the country through which Austin marched and on the people he met. As he used no diary or personal notes, and as he evidently did not check his narrative against ascertainable facts, there are some inaccuracies. Austin, a resident of Galveston, Texas, when war began, immediately joined a force which went by sea to the mouth of the Rio Grande to deal with the Federal troops stationed in the lower valley. He returned to Galveston on horseback, and then rode to the mouth of the Red River and traveled by steamer to Memphis and on to Corinth by rail. From this point to the end of the war he operated in Middle and East Tennessee, Kentucky, Georgia, and later through the Carolinas in opposition to Sherman's march. He was captured in the early part of the war and taken first to Camp Chase in Columbus, Ohio, and then to Johnson's Island. He was exchanged later at Vicksburg.

Bacon, Alvin Q., d. 1863. 13

Thrilling adventures of a pioneer boy (of the John M. Palmer, 14th Ill., regiment.) while a prisoner of war. Alvan ₍!₎ Q. Bacon, his capture at the Battle of Shiloh, and escape from Macon, Ga. ... Written by himself ... ₍n.p., n. pub., 18—?₎

32 p.   21 cm.
Illustrations: Cut of Bacon, presumably, on title page.
Inclusive dates: 1861–1863.

The first and last portions of this pamphlet are the work of an unknown author but the major part was written by Alvin Q. Bacon. It was published probably a decade or more after the war. Bacon was born in the state of New York about 1842 and as a youth migrated to Illinois, where he was living when the Civil War began. He joined an Illinois regiment in the summer of 1861 and saw extensive service in Missouri, to which he alludes without giving details. He then went to Shiloh, traveling up the Tennessee River, where he was captured. This pamphlet is largely an account of his movements through the Confederacy either as a prisoner or as a refugee attempting to make his way back to the Federal lines. It parallels similar accounts of Federal prisoners in describing the jeers of the southern population, the barbarities of Confederate prison life, the friendly services performed by the Negroes for fleeing Federal prisoners, and the brutal attacks by pursuing bloodhounds. Some details of Bacon's story appear improbable, but the main story seems to be authentic. From Shiloh he was taken to Memphis, soon conveyed by rail to Mobile, and then by steamer up the Alabama River to Montgomery, where he was imprisoned for some months. Later he was taken to Bellfonte, Alabama, to be exchanged, going by rail to Atlanta and north to Chattanooga, and thence down the river. The negotiations for exchange ended in failure and Bacon was being returned to Montgomery when he leaped from the train in Alabama and made his way northward. He was recaptured, imprisoned in Rome, Georgia, and then removed to Macon. Here he again escaped and floated down the Ogeechee and Altamaha rivers to Darien on the coast where he was captured a third time, only to escape immediately and paddle out to a Federal gunboat in nearby Doboy Sound. He then returned north to New York City, and proceeded to Vicksburg where he rejoined his regiment and was killed eleven days before the fall of the city.

Bacon, Edward, 1830—1901. 14

Among the cotton thieves. By Edward Bacon ... Detroit, The Free press steam book and job printing house, 1867.

299, ₁1₁ p. 21½ cm.
Inclusive dates: 1862–1863.

The activities narrated in this account were confined to the regions of Louisiana lying around Port Hudson, Baton Rouge, New Orleans, and Lake Maurepas. As the title indicates, the "cotton fever" was widespread among the soldiers and traders. Bacon was a colonel of the Sixth Michigan Volunteers.

Barber, Lucius W., 1839–1872. 15

Army memoirs of Lucius W. Barber, Company "D", 15th Illinois volunteer infantry. May 24, 1861, to Sept. 30, 1865. Chicago, The J. M. W. Jones stationery and printing co., 1894.

v p., 1 l, ₁9₁–233 p. front. (port.) 23 cm.
Illustrations: Frontispiece, "Lucius W. Barber" ₁Signature₁.
Inclusive dates: 1861–1865.

Barber was one of the most widely traveled soldiers of the war. Although he indicates the use of neither diary nor letters, the narrative is in diary form. Enlisting in Illinois, he trained first at Freeport and then at Alton. Proceeding to the war zone Barber went down the Mississippi and up the Missouri rivers and operated in the north central part of the state around Mexico and Sedalia. In early 1862 he proceeded by river to the Fort Henry–Fort Donelson region and continued up the Tennessee to Shiloh. After the engagement there he participated in the operations around Corinth and in northern Mississippi, then went by way of Memphis and the Mississippi to take part in the Vicksburg campaign. At the end of this campaign, which extended as far eastward as Jackson, the author returned up the Mississippi to Memphis and proceeded eastward through western Tennessee and northern Alabama into the neighborhood of Chattanooga. Joining Sherman's command in the spring of 1864 he fought in the Atlanta campaign as far as Acworth, where he was captured. The Confederates took him to Andersonville, passing through Columbus, Georgia, on the way. Later he was moved to the Millen prison and was soon paroled and turned over to the Federals at the mouth of the Savannah River, taken by sea to the parole camp in Annapolis, and later exchanged. After a trip home he went to New York City and joined an expedition going by sea to Hilton Head on the coast of South Carolina. Almost immediately Barber proceeded by boat to Wilmington, North Carolina, and marched inland through Goldsboro to join Sherman's forces again. After Johnston's surrender at Durham Station, he marched northward through Virginia to Washington for the "Grand Review." He then proceeded to Cairo, Illinois, passing over the Baltimore and Ohio Railroad to Parkersburg and down the Ohio River. He saw a short term of service in the Leavenworth, Kansas, region before being mustered out. Barber was travel-minded to a considerable extent. In his narrative he describes much of what he saw and makes frequent comments on the towns and landscapes. As an example, he gives an interesting account of the sacking of Jefferson Davis' plantation in Mississippi, describing how his letters and household effects were scattered. This work may be regarded as a faithful contemporary account.

Barney, C.   16

Recollections of field service with the Twentieth Iowa infantry volunteers; or, what I saw in the army, embracing accounts of marches, battles, sieges, and skirmishes, in Missouri, Arkansas, Mississippi, Louisiana, Alabama, Florida, Texas, and along the northern border of Mexico. By Captain C. Barney. Davenport, Iowa, "Printed for the author at the Gazette job rooms," 1865.

viii, 9–323 p.   19½ cm.
Inclusive dates: 1862–1865.

Like many soldiers, Captain Barney wrote his narrative from memory, but not so long after the events as to make it unreliable. He was much interested in the new scenes that met his eye as he marched through the Confederacy—the country, the inhabitants, and army life. He notes carefully the route as well as the mode of travel, whether by boat or train or marching. The regiment embarked at Davenport, Iowa, in the autumn of 1862 and floated down the Mississippi to St. Louis, where it went ashore to march into southwestern Missouri. It proceeded through Springfield and on into Arkansas through Fayetteville and to Van Buren on the Arkansas River, retraced its steps to St. Louis, and then marched southward to Pilot Knob and St. Genevieve on the Mississippi where it embarked for the Vicksburg region. In Mississippi the regiment moved up the Yazoo River to Yazoo City and eastward to raid Canton. After the fall of Vicksburg it continued down the Mississippi to Port Hudson and New Orleans, raided across Lake Pontchartrain to Madisonville, and went across the Gulf of Mexico to Brownsville, Texas, returning to New Orleans and up the Mississippi and White rivers to Duvall's Bluff in Arkansas. Barney was absent from later movements of the regiment to Mobile and Pensacola.

Barron, Samuel Benton, 1834–1912.   17

The Lone Star defenders; a chronicle of the Third Texas cavalry, Ross' brigade. By S. B. Barron ... New York and Washington, The Neale publishing company, 1908.

> 3 p. l., 3–276 p. front., 10 ports. 20 cm.
> *Illustrations:* Frontispiece, "Battle-Flag of the Third Texas Cavalry Regiment"; "Peter F. Ross"; "Lieutenant-Colonel Jiles S. Boggess"; "Captain D. R. Gurley"; "Frank M. Taylor"; "John Germany"; "Jesse W. Wynne"; "Captain H. L. Taylor"; "Leonidas Cartwright"; "G. A. McKee"; "Lieutenant S. B. Barron."
> *Inclusive dates:* 1861–1865.

This work parallels the narrative of the Ross Brigade by Victor M. Rose (*q.v.*) entitled *Ross' Texas Brigade*. This narrative is a more detailed account of army life, of the country traversed, and of conditions in the Confederacy, but it has the disadvantage of having been written more than forty years after the war. Barron does not mention a diary or other personal manuscripts; he seems to have depended upon recollections alone. Lacking such data, the account can not be accepted at face value, yet it makes a contribution in general atmosphere.

₁Bartlett, Napier₁ 1836–1877.   18

A soldier's story of the war; including the marches and battles of the Washington artillery, and of other Louisiana troops ... New Orleans, Clark & Hofeline, 1874.

> 1 p. l., 252 (i.e. 262) p. front., port. 22½ cm.
> *Inclusive dates:* 1861–1865.

Somewhat episodical in organization, this book leads the reader from New Orleans, where the Washington Artillery originated, by railway through Corinth, Chattanooga, Knoxville, and Lynchburg to Richmond and on to Manassas Junction. The Washington Artillery took part in all the principal engagements from Richmond northward to Gettysburg and southeastward to Appomattox. Bartlett gives interesting glimpses into the life of the Confederate soldier in camp, on the march, and on furlough in Richmond and elsewhere. He also notes the extreme enthusiasm with which his unit was met wherever it went, especially in the early part of the war. This book is written without the slightest rancor toward the enemy.

Barton, Thomas H., 1828– 19

Autobiography of Dr. Thomas H. Barton, the self-made physician of Syracuse, Ohio, including a history of the Fourth regt. West Va. vol. inf'y, with an account of Col. Lightburn's retreat down the Kanawha Valley, Gen. Grant's Vicksburg and Chattanooga campaigns, together with the several battles in which the Fourth regiment was engaged, and its losses by disease, desertion and in battle. By Dr. T. H. Barton. Charleston, West Virginia printing co., 1890.

viii, 340 p. front. (port.) 20½ cm.
Illustrations: Frontispiece, "Dr. Thos. H. Barton." ₍Signature₎
Inclusive dates: 1861–1863.

This Ohio physician first saw active service with Federal troops in the Great Kanawha River country of West Virginia between Point Pleasant and Charleston. Thereafter, until the fall of 1863 when he returned north on account of bad health, he operated in the Mississippi River region around Vicksburg. In his autobiography Dr. Barton confines himself mostly to military affairs with special emphasis on the medical service; but incidentally he records his observations on the slaves he met, and on the landscapes of the Mississippi River country. This volume adds little, except by way of personal experience, to what has appeared in many other works written by Federal soldiers.

Battle-fields of the South, 20

from Bull Run to Fredericksburg; with sketches of Confederate commanders, and gossip of the camps. By an English combatant, (lieutenant of artillery on the field staff.) ... London, Smith, Elder and co., 1863.

Vol. I, xxxvi, 339 p; Vol. II, viii, 399 p. 19¾ cm.
Maps: "Sketch Map illustrative of the Battles of Seven Pines, Fair Oaks and the 'Week's Campaign' Before Richmond &c." (7¼ by 9 inches); "Sketch Map of the Battle Field of Fredericksburg, Burnside's Defeat, Decr. 13th. 1862" (5 by 8 inches).
Inclusive dates: 1861–1862.
Other editions: Edition with same title: New York, J. Bradburn, 1864.

This account was written by an Englishman who, because of long residence in the South, was "southernized" to the extent of being a defender of slavery. He is vague as to where he lived and where he joined the Confederate army, but by inference it seems to have been Alabama. He was sent first to Corinth, Mississippi, thence by railway through Chattanooga and Lynchburg to the concentrations in northern Virginia around Manassas, and he seems to have taken part in all the principal battles from Bull Run to Fredericksburg. The writer's exaggerated statements, especially his hostility to the medical service and chaplains and his tendency towards "tall talk," militate against the reliability of his work. He was a great admirer of Jefferson Davis and a thorough sympathizer with the Confederate cause.

Beale, George William, 1842– 21

A lieutenant of cavalry in Lee's army, By G. W. Beale. Boston, The Gorham press, 1918.

231 p.   19 cm.
Inclusive dates: 1861–1865.

Writing many years after the war, Beale remembered mostly the duties which took him away from home to join the Confederate Army. His main concern was to march and fight, to march and fight again until the last soldiers should lay down their arms. Beale's military activities were confined to the territory from Gettysburg to Appomattox. Between these two points he participated in most of the major campaigns of the war, excepting the two battles of Manassas. He accompanied Stuart in his remarkable ride around McClellan's army on the Peninsula in 1862. He also spent some time in Confederate hospitals. As travel literature this book is of minor importance.

Beale, Richard Lee Tuberville, 1819–1893. 22

History of the Ninth Virginia cavalry, in the war between the states. By the late Brig. General R. L. T. Beale. Richmond, Va., B. F. Johnson publishing company, 1899.

192 p.   front. (port.)   22 cm.
Illustrations: Frontispiece, "Most affectionately R. L. T. Beale" [Signature].
Inclusive dates: 1861–1865.

Beale's cavalry was part of Stuart's unit. Its commander entered the Confederate service at the outbreak of war, was first stationed near Fredericksburg, and arrived at the battle of First Manassas in time to see the results of the engagement. Thereafter he was active in cavalry operations as far north as Carlisle, Pennsylvania, having followed Stuart there before the Battle of Gettysburg. He was also in the Confederate forces which rounded up and killed Dahlgren on his famous raid against Richmond, and fought with Lee against Grant to the final surrender. Beale wrote this account in 1865, a fact which gives it freshness and authenticity not only as a military narrative but as a travelogue. Naturally the author was not as ready to note conditions in Virginia as was a person less well acquainted with that region, but observations and comments are not entirely lacking.

Beatty, John, 1828–1914.

The citizen-soldier; or, Memoirs of a volunteer. By John Beatty. Cincinnati, Wilstach, Baldwin & co., 1879.

vii, 9–401 p. 18 cm.
Inclusive dates: June, 1861–January, 1864.

This diary relates to General McClellan's campaign in West Virginia in 1861, to General Buell's invasion of Kentucky and Tennessee in 1862 and his subsequent retrogression on General Bragg's movement into Kentucky in the fall of that year, to service with Federal forces in Middle Tennessee and northern Alabama, to activities around Chattanooga resulting in the Battle of Chickamauga, and to a trip into East Tennessee as far as Knoxville. The author spent a great deal of time in Murfreesboro, Tennessee, and in Huntsville, Alabama. He wrote with rare good feeling and common sense, and thereby produced a dependable account of conditions in the regions he visited. He was much interested in the native population, white and Negro, and found a great deal of Union feeling among both elements. He was much interested in the old slave characters, especially the preachers, as well as in the native whites in whose homes he made frequent visits. He deplored both the vandalism and drunkenness of the Federal troops. Yet Beatty believed in a rigorous national policy directed toward the freeing of the slaves and, therefore, disliked Buell's gentleness toward the "peculiar institution." In 1861 he joined the Third Ohio Volunteer Infantry and was immediately made its lieutenant colonel. After the war Beatty wrote various military and political books and entered politics in his native state of Ohio, where he attained considerable prominence. He served in Congress and later sought the governorship unsuccessfully.

Beers, Mrs. Fannie A.

Memories. A record of personal experience and adventure during four years of war. By Mrs. Fannie A. Beers. Philadelphia, Press of J. B. Lippincott company, 1888.

336 p. front. 19¼ cm.
Illustrations: Frontispiece, "Mnemosyne (The Goddess of Memory)."
Inclusive dates: 1861–1865.

This is a realistic account of hospital conditions in the Confederacy. Mrs. Beers at the outbreak of the war went to her home in an undesignated Northern city, but soon decided to return South. Securing a pass in Baltimore she went to Fortress Monroe on a Federal transport and made her way from there through the Confederate lines to Richmond, where she spent a year administering to the sick and wounded. For the rest of the war she was in Alabama, Mississippi, and Georgia, serving in hospitals at Gainesville, Alabama, and at Ringgold and Newnan, Georgia. Most of these "Memories" were written about twenty years after the war, though a few were composed slightly earlier and appeared first in the *Southern Bivouac*. There is no reason to doubt that this is a true picture of hospital life in the Confederacy.

Bell, John Thomas, 1842– 25

Tramps and triumphs of the Second Iowa infantry, briefly sketched by John T. Bell, lieut. Co. "C". Omaha, Gibson, Miller & Richardson, printers, 1886.

32 p. 21½ cm.
Inclusive dates: 1861–1865.

Because it is short and sketchy this pamphlet is of little value as a travel record. Its author makes no mention of a diary or other contemporary material. The text was originally published in the *Omaha Bee*. Leaving Omaha in 1861, John T. Bell went down the Missouri River to St. Joseph, where he enlisted in the Federal Army, proceeded to St. Louis, and embarked on a river boat for Fort Donelson, arriving there after the battle. Going west across country to the Tennessee River he moved upstream to Shiloh and Corinth and operated in northern Mississippi a short time before moving on to Middle and East Tennessee. He was stationed at Pulaski before joining Sherman's command, and then followed Sherman throughout his campaign to Atlanta, Savannah, and the Carolinas, ending with the "Grand Review" in Washington. He was mustered out at Louisville, Kentucky, proceeding there over the usual route; by railway to Parkersburg and down the Ohio by boat.

Bennett, Andrew J., 1841/2– 26

The story of the First Massachusetts light battery, attached to the Sixth army corps. A glance at events in the armies of the Potomac and Shenandoah, from the summer of 1861 to the autumn of 1864. By A. J. Bennett ... Boston, Press of Deland and Barta, 1886.

200 p. pl., port., maps, facsim. 22½ cm.
Illustrations: Ten illustrations: Portraits of soldiers, battle scenes, and one facsimile of a manuscript letter.
Maps: Three rough sketches by the author: "The Virginia Peninsula"; "The Vicinity of Gettysburg"; "From Brandy Station to Petersburg."
Inclusive dates: 1862–1865.

The journeyings of Private Bennett and his battery were confined to the eastern area of the war. He fought as far north as Gettysburg, as far south as Yorktown, and in the summer of 1864 he was among the re-enforcements which Grant sent up the Chesapeake to Washington to ward off the threatened invasion of Jubal Early. Bennett's term of enlistment having expired in October, 1864, he was mustered out and did not return to the war. This is an even-tempered account emphasizing military happenings with some consideration of the Confederate population and special interest in the slaves. On one occasion Bennett's unit met up with the old Virginia Unionist John Minor Botts, who, on being asked for information about the Confederate forces, refused to divulge anything of advantage to the Federals.

Bentley, William H. 27

History of the 77th Illinois volunteer infantry, Sept. 2, 1862–July 10, 1865. By Lieut. W. H. Bentley, with an introduction by General D. P. Grier. Peoria, Ill., E. Hine, printer, 1883.

396 p.   18½ cm.
Inclusive dates: 1862–1865.

Bentley's travels were limited to the Ohio and Mississippi valleys and to Texas. He left Peoria, Illinois, in 1862 for Central Kentucky, passing through Cincinnati and down the railway to Lexington. After operating as far eastward as Richmond, Kentucky, he proceeded to Louisville and went by river boat to Vicksburg, stopping for a short while in Memphis. From Vicksburg he traveled north to Arkansas Post and east to Jackson. After the fall of Vicksburg, he went down the Mississippi to Carrollton and New Orleans, proceeded westward by rail to Berwick Bay and New Iberia, returned to New Orleans, and crossed the gulf to Matagorda Bay on the Texas coast. After a short stay there, he returned to New Orleans and operated in the Teche country, going as far northward as Alexandria on the Red River. After participating in the Mansfield campaign he returned down the Red and Mississippi rivers to Baton Rouge. His last service was in the Mobile Bay area. Bentley wrote the narrative from notes taken on his travels and from information secured from his comrades. His interest was not entirely absorbed by military service; he also recorded his impressions of the country traversed as well as many incidents of army life.

Berry, Thomas Franklin, 1832– 28

Four years with Morgan and Forrest. By Col. Thomas F. Berry ... Oklahoma City, Okla., The Harlow-Ratliff company, 1914.

1 p. l., ₍vii₎–xv, 476 p.   front., plates, ports.   19½ cm.
Illustrations: Frontispiece, "Captain Thomas F. Berry," and twelve badly-executed cuts of men and scenes.
Inclusive dates: 1861–1865.

At the outset the author admits that readers may doubt some of the facts, but facts they are. Although he asserts that he used a diary in composing this narrative, it still is peppered with elements of the well-known American "tall tale." Berry claims to have made "thirteen thrilling escapes," seven from prison and six times from captors on the way to prison. The book has little to recommend it as a travelogue, despite the author's having followed Morgan and Forrest throughout Kentucky and Tennessee and the former in his raid through Indiana. He seldom makes clear the route he took, and only infrequently departs from his personal experiences and adventures to describe the country or the people. He grew up in Kentucky, starting his eventful life in the Mexican War, and after the Civil War, before settling down in Oklahoma, he again took a fling in Mexico in connection with the Maximilian episode. His apparent carelessness with what should seem to be the truth is heightened by his carelessness in the spelling of well-known names, especially his references to the Confederate Secretary of War Seddon as "Sheldon."

Betts, Alexander Davis, 1832–   29

Experience of a Confederate chaplain, 1861–1864 [i.e. 1865] By Rev. A. D. Betts ... chaplain 30th N. C. troops. Edited by W. A. Betts. [Greenville? S. C., 19—?]

103, [1] p. illus., ports. 18 cm.
Illustrations: Group of seven Confederate chaplains, "Rev. A. D. Betts, D. D., North Carolina Conference, Methodist Episcopal Church, South." Frontispiece; "Rev. W. A. Betts, Ph. B. (Univ. of N. C.) Methodist Episcopal Church, South. South Carolina Conference."
Inclusive dates: 1861–1865 (Diary continues to the end of the war.)

This minister's diary is choppy and annalistic. Rarely it continues a subject through more than a single sentence; yet, taken as a whole, it gives a clear picture of the work of a Confederate army chaplain, his administration to the spiritual wants of the soldiers as well as assisting the wounded and running errands for soldiers. He entered the service at Smithville, now Southport, North Carolina, and soon joined the Confederate armies in Virginia. He was at Sharpsburg and Gettysburg, but had returned to North Carolina before Lee's surrender. He was paroled at the end of the war, having attached himself to General Johnston's forces. This diary is for the most part reproduced just as it was written originally, though it appears that the author, about 1896, reworked it somewhat and added some easily detected comments.

Bevens, W. E.   30

Reminiscences of a private. Company "G" First Arkansas regiment infantry. May, 1861 to April, 1865. n. p., n. pub., 1912?

58 p. 23¼ cm.
Illustrations: Frontispiece, "W. E. Bevens—1861", "W. E. Bevens—1912", "Three Veterans of Company 'G'."
Inclusive dates: 1861–1865.

Bevens joined the regiment in Jacksonport, Arkansas, and was immediately sent to Virginia to participate in the First Battle of Manassas. The area was reached by passing down the White and up the Mississippi rivers to Memphis and thence by railway through Corinth, Chattanooga, Knoxville, Lynchburg, Richmond, and Fredericksburg. The unit was soon ordered back to aid in the West, going first to Corinth, thence to Mobile, Montgomery, Atlanta, Chattanooga and on into Middle Tennessee where it joined Bragg's invasion of Kentucky in the late summer of 1862. After the Battle of Perryville it went from Kentucky by way of Cumberland Gap into East Tennessee, soon swinging around through Knoxville and Chattanooga into Middle Tennessee again for the Battle of Murfreesboro and the operations around Chattanooga. It was with General Johnston's retreat to the Chattahoochee in 1864, and after the fall of Atlanta it followed Hood in his excursion to the edge of Nashville where the army was scattered in defeat. After this, Bevens operated in Mississippi for a short time before going to Mobile and on through Montgomery to Milledgeville and Augusta, Georgia. With the war approaching its end, he returned westward through Selma, Alabama, and Jackson, Mississippi, to his home in Jacksonport. This account lacks nothing in distance covered, but its observations and comments are too brief to be of any particular value.

Bickham, William Denison, 1827–1894. 31

Rosecrans' campaign with the fourteenth army corps, or the Army of the Cumberland: a narrative of personal observations with an appendix, consisting of official reports of the battle of Stone River. By "W. D. B." ... Cincinnati, Moore, Wilstach, Keys & co., 1863.

viii, 9–476 p.   front. (map)   18½ cm.
Maps: Frontispiece, "Topographical Sketch of the Battle Field of Stone's River."
Inclusive dates: 1862–1863.

Bickham, a correspondent of the *Cincinnati Commercial,* joined General Rosecrans' army at Bowling Green, Kentucky, in October, 1862, and remained with it until the conclusion of the Battle of Stone's River, or Murfreesboro. As the distance traveled was so short, he could scarcely make his book much of a travel account; but, true to his newspaper instinct, he saw much to write about besides military matters—though everything he wrote was carefully correlated with army activities. He was particularly interested in the women of Secessia, their extreme loyalty to the Confederacy, and social conditions in Nashville. A great deal of the book is devoted to the Battle of Stone's River.

Bicknell, George W. 32

History of the Fifth regiment Maine volunteers, comprising brief descriptions of its marches, engagements, and general services from the date of its muster in, June 24, 1861, to the time of its muster out, July 27, 1864. By Rev. Geo. W. Bicknell ... Portland, H. L. Davis, 1871.

xii, [3]–404 p.   front. (port.), pl.   18 cm.
Illustrations: Frontispiece, "John R. Adams" [Signature]; "The Charge at Rappahannock Station"; "Grand Charge, May 10th 1864 near Spottsylvania Court House."
Inclusive dates: 1861–1864.

Joining the Federal Army in 1861, Bicknell left Portland, Maine, for Washington, traveling the customary route: railway to Fall River by way of Boston, the Fall River steamship line to New York, and by rail through Baltimore. He was soon across the Potomac River and on his way to what turned out to be the First Battle of Manassas. After further operations in northern Virginia,

Bicknell joined McClellan's forces down the Chesapeake Bay on York Peninsula. After this campaign he returned to northern Virginia, but was not in the Second Battle of Manassas. He marched into Maryland and fought at Sharpsburg. With the exception of Chancellorsville, he took part in all the major campaigns until his service expired in March, 1864. From sources other than his own observations, he continues the narrative to Lee's surrender. It is an excellent travelogue, well-written and even-tempered. Bicknell tells of souvenir hunters whittling away the stairs in the Marshall House in Alexandria where Ellsworth lost his life, and he describes the church where Washington worshiped. In the earlier part of the war he was convinced that there were no Union people in Virginia.

Billings, John Davis, 1842– 33

History of the Tenth Massachusetts battery of light artillery in the war of the rebellion. Formerly of the Third corps, and afterwards of Hancock's Second corps, Army of the Potomac. 1862–1865. By John D. Billings ... Boston, Hall & Whiting, 1881.

xii p., 2 l., 400 p. incl. front., plates (1 col.) ports., 2 plans   23¼ cm.
Illustrations: Eight portraits including one of Billings and four illustrations of military scenes.
Maps: "Map of Ream's Station Battlefield, August 25, 1864"; "Map of Boydton Plànk Road, or Hatcher's Run Battlefield, October 27, 1864."
Inclusive dates: 1862–1865.
Other editions: Boston, The Arakelyan press, 1909.

As a travel account, this work is better than the majority of regimental histories. Billings used a diary which he kept through part of the war, and almost three hundred letters which he wrote during the struggle. He also had at his disposal a manuscript written immediately after the war by a member of the company. The author gives considerable attention to the country through which he marched, including in his descriptions the state of agriculture, the condition in which he found the old Virginia mansions, the attitude of the people toward Federal soldiers, and the treatment Union soldiers meted out to the property of Confederates. He gives an extensive description of the Sulphur Springs resort near Warrenton. His military service and hence his travels lay entirely in Virginia and Maryland.

₁Bixby, O. H.₁ 34

Incidents in Dixie; being ten months' experience of a Union soldier in the military prisons of Richmond, N. Orleans and Salisbury. Published for the benefit of Maryland state fair for the Christian and Sanitary commissions. Baltimore, Printed by James Young, 1864.

89 p.   14½ cm.
Inclusive dates: 1861–1862.

The author was captured at the First Battle of Manassas and taken by train to Richmond, where he was held for a short time before being transferred to a jail in New Orleans. He went by railway through Petersburg, Wilmington, Kingsville, South Carolina, Augusta, and Atlanta to Montgomery. Here he was placed aboard a river steamer on the Alabama River and transported to Mobile, where he entrained for New Orleans, going by way of Meridian to Jackson, Mississippi, and southward to New Orleans. He returned over the same route a few months later, early in 1862, to Kingsville and thence northward through Columbia and Charlotte to Salisbury. Here he was imprisoned a few months and then paroled, leaving the Confederacy by rail through Raleigh and Goldsboro, and thence by boat down the Tar River to Washington, North Carolina, where he was turned over to the Federals who gave him ocean passage to New York City. This account reveals conditions in the Confederacy to some extent but the author seemed to be more interested in the landscape than in the people.

Blackburn, James Knox Polk, 1837–1923.   35

Reminiscences of the Terry rangers. By J. K. P. Blackburn. ₁Austin₁ Published by the Littlefield fund for southern history, the University of Texas, 1919.

vii, 79 p.   25½ cm.
Inclusive dates: 1861–1865.

From an old man's memory, fifty years after the events described, Blackburn wrote a narrative that has little value as contemporary description. For the route taken by Terry's Rangers see the entry on Leonidas Banton Giles, *Terry's Texas Rangers,* in this bibliography.

Blackford, Mrs. Susan Leigh (Colston), 1833–1903, *comp.*   36

Memoirs of life in and out of the army in Virginia during the war between the states. Comp. by Susan Leigh Blackford from original and contemporaneous correspondence and diaries. Annotated and edited exclusively for the private use of their family by her husband, Charles Minor Blackford ... Lynchburg, Va., J. P. Bell company, printers, 1894–96.

Vol. I, vi, 292 p.; Vol. II, 279, viii p.   23½ cm.
Inclusive dates: 1861–1865.

Here is a composite of letters by Charles M. Blackford and his wife, and of liberal excerpts from a diary of his father, William M. Blackford, until his death in April, 1864. The continuity of the narrative follows the career of Charles M. Blackford, who for the first two years of the war was an officer in the Second Virginia Cavalry, and during the latter years was judge advocate in General Longstreet's corps. Most of his activities were centered in northern Virginia around the Rappahannock and the Rapidan, in the Shenandoah Valley, and in the Gettysburg campaign. In 1864 Blackford followed Longstreet to Chattanooga, going by Weldon, Wilmington, Augusta, and Atlanta. He returned the same way and later rejoined Longstreet in East Tennessee, making his way back by Bristol and Lynchburg. The book, written by a Virginia aristocrat, gives an unusually interesting and important glimpse into the social conditions among the aristocratic classes in Virginia during wartime, and characterizations of high Confederate officers with whom Blackford was thrown. There are good descriptions of some of the old Virginia mansions, especially those on the Rappahannock, some of which were in their original splendor while others were in ruins. On his trip southward to Chattanooga the author saw little that made him ashamed of his own Virginia, whether it was natural scenery and agriculture or patriotism of the people.

Blackford, William Willis, 1831–1905. 37
War years with Jeb Stuart. New York, Charles Scribner's sons, 1945.

xvi, 322 p.   20 cm.
Illustrations: Frontispiece, "William Willis Blackford (1831–1905)."
Inclusive dates: 1861–1865.

The author's travels as a Confederate soldier were entirely in the eastern theater of war, where he took part in all the main campaigns. As a member of an important Virginia family, Blackford was related to or acquainted with many other prominent families and did considerable visiting among them during his war travels. The narrative, being highly personalized and written in the first person, gives interesting glimpses into wartime Virginia social conditions, but, as should be expected, its emphasis is on military activities. The author wrote his account sometime before 1889, using his memory to supply atmosphere and many family letters and other records for more specific facts. It is written in an engaging style and may be taken as a faithful account in practically every detail. For another item in this bibliography relating to the same family and same field of travel, see Susan Leigh Blackford.

Blake, Henry Nichols, 1838–1933. 38
Three years in the Army of the Potomac. By Henry N. Blake, late captain in the Eleventh regiment Massachusetts volunteers ... Boston, Lee and Shepard, 1865.

vi, 7–319 p.   18 cm.
Inclusive dates: July, 1861–June, 1864.

Henry N. Blake is unusual among Union soldier authors because of his highly critical attitude toward Federal military management in the field. He found fault with officers from the lowest to the highest, reserving his special detestation for McDowell and Meade. Likewise he had a disdain for all foreign private soldiers, intensified to the fullest for Germans. Being so filled with consuming dislikes, Blake naturally expressed his contempt for the Southern people in the invaded regions and at every opportunity he applied the hard rigors of war against them. He was unable to discover any Unionism in the South. Blake fought first in the Battle of Bull Run in 1861, and thereafter participated in the

Peninsula campaign, Second Bull Run, Fredericksburg, Chancellorsville, Gettysburg, and was with Grant in the drive against Richmond in 1864. In June of that year he was mustered out. The Captain's keen hatreds led him to comment on almost everything that he saw, from Federal soldiers acquiring souvenirs of Ellsworth from the stairways and doors of the Marshall House in Alexandria, to the Rebel girl who told the Yankees that nobody but "niggers and trash" watched the Federal soldiers march along the roads.

Blakeslee, Bernard F. 39

History of the Sixteenth Connecticut volunteers. By B. F. Blakeslee. Hartford, The Case, Lockwood & Brainard co. printers, 1875.

116 p.   18 cm.
Inclusive dates: 1862–1865.

The regiment was organized in Hartford, Connecticut, in 1862 and was soon sent to Washington, going by boat to New York City and by train to the national capital. After some slight service in northern Virginia, it marched into Maryland and participated in the Battle of Sharpsburg. Returning to Virginia, it fought at Fredericksburg and then went by boat to Norfolk, operating on the Peninsula for a short time and then in the Suffolk region. It passed through the Dismal Swamp to Plymouth, North Carolina, and in the battle at this place Blakeslee was captured. As a prisoner of war, he was sent to Andersonville, passing by railway through Wilmington, Florence, Charleston, Savannah, and Macon. He was soon returned to the Macon prison, but on the approach of Sherman he was moved successively to Savannah, Charleston, and Columbia. When Sherman approached Columbia, he was moved out to Charlotte and on through Raleigh to Wilmington, where he was turned over to the Federal authorities. From Wilmington Blakeslee went by boat to Annapolis. This account was written from a diary which the author kept, but the narrative is sketchy and of little value.

Blanding, Stephen F. 40

Recollections of a sailor boy; or, The cruise of the gunboat Louisiana. By Stephen F. Blanding ... Providence, E. A. Johnson & co., 1886.

vi, [7]–330 p.   18¾ cm.
Inclusive dates: June, 1862—Latter half of 1865.

What little value this book has lies in the author's description of his activities on the coast of North Carolina, Washington, Newbern, and along the Tar River. Blanding enlisted in the Federal Navy at Boston in June, 1862, and went to Brooklyn to be assigned to a ship. He proceeded to Fortress Monroe and was attached to a squadron operating in Pamlico Sound inside the sand-spit fringe of North Carolina. Blanding had a few shore leaves which took him into the town of Washington, and on one occasion he proceeded on a minor expedition up the Tar to Greenville. He found much Union sentiment among the North Carolinians along the coast, a circumstance which led some of them to enlist in the Federal forces. For some reason unknown to the author, these troops were called "Buffaloes." The account was written many years after the war and is composed in a style adapted to young readers. Consequently it is embellished with many imaginary conversations and other details probably not true, but as a general picture it has some value.

[Blessington, Joseph P.]   41

The campaigns of Walker's Texas division. By a private soldier. Containing a complete record of the campaigns in Texas, Louisiana, and Arkansas; the skirmish at Perkins' Landing and the battles of Milliken's Bend, Bayou Bourbeux, Mansfield, Pleasant Hill, Jenkins' Ferry, &c., &c., including the federal's report of the battles, names of the officers of the division, diary of marches, camp scenery, anecdotes, description of the country through which the division marched, &c., &c. New York, Published for the author by Lange, Little & co., 1875.

314 p. 22 cm.
Inclusive dates: 1861–1865.

Written ten years after the war from various notes and documents and from memory, this work is explicit about the journeying of the military unit to which the author belonged and is also peppered with brief comments on the country through which he marched. Blessington was more travel-minded than the usual writer of regimental histories. He entered the Confederate service early in 1861 and was stationed at Camp Groce near Hempstead, Texas. He then went through Houston to Virginia Point near Galveston, and soon returned to Camp Groce, from which he marched overland through east Texas to Little Rock, Arkansas. After various marches and countermarches in that state he proceeded southward into Louisiana, where he spent the rest of the war, except for two journeys into Arkansas. This unit seems to have had little rest, for there was not much of the northern half of Louisiana over which it did not march. Its chief centers of activity were around Alexandria and Monroe. At the end of the war it marched out of Louisiana by way of Shreveport to Camp Groce where it disbanded.

Boggs, Samuel S.   42

Eighteen months a prisoner under the Rebel flag, a condensed pen-picture of Belle Isle, Danville, Andersonville, Charleston, Florence and Libby prisons from actual experience. Lovington, Ill., S. S. Boggs, 1887.

73 p. front. 19¼ cm.
Illustrations: Twelve crudely drawn illustrations designed to depict prison horrors, the last being the previously published drawing showing the capture of President Davis in women's clothing. The Davis drawing appeared in 1865 in R. H. Kellogg, Life and death in Rebel prisons ... treated elsewhere in this bibliography.
Inclusive dates: September, 1863–February, 1865.

This is a highly unreliable account of prison life concocted by the author from previously published books, from his imagination, and from experiences long past. He evidently desired not only to capitalize on any remaining bitterness over the prison question, but also to influence votes in the approaching presidential election of 1888. Though the booklet is filled with almost unmeasured horrors, he naively says that he is leaving out the worst part "lest we destroy the credit of the whole story" (p. 3). Boggs, born about 1840, enlisted in 1861 in the Twenty-first Illinois Infantry and participated in various battles until he was captured in September, 1863, at Chickamauga. He was held at Atlanta, Belle Isle at Richmond, Danville, and Andersonville. As Sherman approached Atlanta, Boggs and many of the Andersonville prisoners were sent to Charleston and on to Florence. He reported a few escapes in order to introduce the fierce pack of bloodhounds which habitually tore fugitive prisoners to pieces. Boggs escaped this fate, finally to be freed and sent into Sherman's lines in northeastern South Carolina. Though the author traveled over the Confederacy considerably in passing from one prison to another, he has little to say about either the country or its people. In fact, the whole account may be considered valueless except as a comment on the prisoner-of-war question in American politics.

Boggs, William Robertson, 1829–1911.   43
... Military reminiscences of Gen. Wm. R. Boggs, C. S. A.; introduction and notes by William K. Boyd. Durham, N. C., The Seeman printer, 1913.

xxiii, 115 p. front. (port.)   19 cm.   (The John Lawson monographs of the Trinity college historical society. vol. III)
Illustrations: Frontispiece, "General William R. Boggs."
Inclusive dates: 1861–1865.

These memoirs, written in 1891, are little concerned with the author's travels during his Civil War career and contain only occasional comments on places visited and civilians met. Boggs, born in Georgia, was graduated at the United States Military Academy at West Point. He remained in the service of the United States until his native state seceded, but from that time to the end of the war he was either in the service of Georgia or of the Confederate States. In his military career he saw action at Pensacola, Savannah, in Bragg's invasion of Kentucky in 1862, and with Kirby Smith in the Trans-Mississippi Department. Boggs attained the rank of brigadier general.

Boies, Andrew J.   44
Record of the Thirty-third Massachusetts volunteer infantry, from Aug. 1862 to Aug. 1865. By Andrew J. Boies. Fitchburg, Sentinel printing company, 1880.

168 p. front. (port.) 22¾ cm.
Illustrations: Frontispiece, "Corp'l A. J. Boies" ₍Signature₎
Inclusive dates: 1862–1865.

Originally a diary kept during the war by Boies, the material was somewhat amended later for publication. It is more factual and annalistic than discursive, though the author sometimes sustains a connected account for a few paragraphs. There are numerous short entries on the aspects of the country traversed, and on the characteristics of its people. Boies was either bitter or supercilious in his references to the natives, repeating the stock charges that Southerners habitually used the expressions, "we'uns and you'uns." He served first in northern Virginia, including the Fredericksburg battle, passed through Chancellorsville, and marched to Gettysburg and back to Virginia. In the fall of 1863 he was transferred to the Army of the Cumberland, going to Chattanooga by railway, around and about through West Virginia, Ohio, and Indiana to Louisville, and southward by rail to Chattanooga. He campaigned then in East Tennessee as far as Knoxville, was with Sherman in his march, and finally went by boat from Richmond to Washington for the "Grand Review."

Booth, Benjamin F., 1837?–   45

Dark days of the rebellion, or, Life in southern military prisons, giving a correct and thrilling history of unparalled ₍!₎ suffering, narrow escapes, heroic encounters, bold achievements, cold blooded murders, severe tests of loyalty, and patriotism. Written from a diary kept while in Libby and Salisbury prisons in 1864–5, and now in possession of the author. Indianola, Ia., Booth publishing company, 1897.

375 p. front., illus. (incl. ports.) 19 cm.
Illustrations: First frontispiece, "Attempted Escape of Salisbury Prisoners, Nov. 25, 1864"; Second frontispiece, "Yours Truly B. F. Booth" ₍Signature₎; "Sheridan at Cedar Creek"; "Appearance when Captured, Weight 181 Pounds"; "My Chum, D. W. Connely"; "Large Brick Hospital Building"; Repetition of First frontispiece; "Interior of Brick Hospital"; "Winter Costume in Salisbury"; "A Case of Scurvy"; "Southern Rail Road Bridge"; "Weight 81½ Pounds"; Repetition on inside of back cover of the "Interior of Brick Hospital, Salisbury Prison." All these illustrations, excepting the photograph of Booth, are pen and ink sketches.
Inclusive dates: 1862–1865.

Although thirty-two years had elapsed between the experiences and the date of publication, Booth lost none of his extreme bitterness towards the Confederate prison regime. His military career from 1862 to his capture in the Shenandoah Valley in October, 1864, is so briefly sketched as to be of no value. He describes his movement from Iowa City, where he enlisted, to St. Louis with some excursions through Missouri, down the Mississippi to Vicksburg and New Orleans, into the interior of Louisiana in connection with Banks' Red River expedition, a trip across the Gulf of Mexico to Matagorda Bay, Texas, and thence to Harpers Ferry. After his capture he was taken through Staunton to Richmond and imprisoned briefly before being removed to Salisbury, North Carolina. As the end of the war approached he was marched to Greensboro, placed on a train, taken to the Federal lines near Wilmington, and released. Thence he went by boat to Annapolis. Booth kept a diary while in prison, and that document, undoubtedly much worked over and embellished, makes up the main part of the narrative. He was so consumed with bitterness toward his captors and jailers and the inconveniences of prison life and the horrors of travel in the "cattle cars" from one prison to another that he had little energy left to comment on other features of the Southern scene. This book, of course, should be accepted only at great discount, for it is as much a comment on the enduring war psychosis of Booth as it is on the scene he describes.

[Booth, George Wilson] 1844–1914.   46

Personal reminiscences of a Maryland soldier in the war between the states, 1861–1865. For private circulation only. Baltimore [Press of Fleet, McGinley & co.] 1898.

177 p.   23 cm.
Inclusive dates: 1861–1865.

Because Booth does not record innumerable details that could never have been remembered, his book may be considered more reliable than many other long narratives. He was in Baltimore when the Massachusetts regiment marched through on April 19, 1861, and participated briefly in the so-called massacre. Thereafter, finding it dangerous to remain in Maryland, he joined the First Maryland Regiment of Confederate troops and marched off to Harpers Ferry to become a part of General Johnston's army. With this force he participated in the First Battle of Manassas, returning afterwards to the Shenandoah Valley, which became somewhat the center of his later activities even though he followed Stonewall Jackson to the aid of Lee on the Peninsula. He was in the Gettysburg campaign, marched with Jubal Early's forces to the gates of Washington in 1864, and later went to Chambersburg with the expedition which burned that city. In early 1865 he was sent to guard the Salisbury, North Carolina, prison, where he remained until the prisoners were sent away to be set free within the Federal lines near Wilmington. Booth held no malice but had much to say about the life of a soldier, fearing above all the prisons and hospitals.

Borcke, Heros von, 1835–1895.   47

Memoirs of the Confederate war for independence. By Heros von Borcke ... Philadelphia, J. B. Lippincott & co., 1867.

4 p. l., [vii]–x, 438 p.   map.   18½ cm.
Maps: Folding map in back, 14 x 16½ inches. "Map of the Seat of War in Virginia."
Inclusive dates: May, 1862–December 25, 1864.
Other editions: Same title: Edinburgh and London, W. Blackwood and sons, 1866; New York, P. Smith, 1938, 2 vols. German edition: Swei jahre im sattel und am feinde; erinnerungen aus dem unabhangigkeitskriege der Konföderirten. Berlin, E. S. Mittler und sohn, 1898, 2 vols.

Heros von Borcke was a Prussian officer who ran the blockade near Charleston to reach the Confederacy. From Charleston he went to Richmond, where he received a commission as captain in the Confederate Army. He was attached to J. E. B. Stuart as chief of staff, and fought through the war in Virginia from the Battle of Seven Pines until he was badly wounded at Middleburg on June 19, 1863, in an engagement incident to Lee's march into Pennsylvania, and was unable to take part in further military operations for the rest of the war. In the latter part of 1864 he ran the blockade out of Wilmington on a trip to England to carry out a mission to which he was appointed by the Confederate Government. With the downfall of the Confederacy he re-entered the military service of Prussia and took part in the Austro-Prussian War of 1866. He then settled on a farm in Germany, leaving it for a visit to the Southern states in 1884. By admission he knew practically no English when he came to the Confederacy, but undoubtedly he either learned the language with great speed, or had someone translate his account into good English. It is written in a lively style without any trace of foreign ineptitudes. The author shows throughout his work the same intense loyalty as that exhibited by native-born Confederates, among whom he became a favorite. He was especially loved by J. E. B. Stuart, a kindred rollicking character. The Confederate Congress voted the Prussian officer a special resolution of thanks for his services, and he received promotion to a colonelcy, but not to the major-generalship requested for him by Stuart. His account is largely military in aspect and is intensely personal. Bordering on the heroic most of the time, it is made up of narrow escapes and remarkable personal experiences. This book is particularly valuable for the light it throws on army life, and if due weight is given the limitations suggested above, it is a valuable commentary on the military phase of the Confederacy in so far as Von Borcke was able to note it. The narrative first appeared in *Blackwood's Magazine*.

Bosbyshell, Oliver Christian, 1839–   48

The 48th in the war. Being a narrative of the campaigns of the 48th regiment, infantry, Pennsylvania veteran volunteers, during the war of the rebellion. By Oliver Christian Bosbyshell ... Philadelphia, Avil printing company, 1895.

4 p. I., 17–205 p.   front., pl., port.   22½ cm.
Illustrations: Frontispiece, "Fraternally Yours C. C. Bosbyshell" ₍Signature₎; and fourteen other illustrations, mostly of soldiers.
Maps: "Petersburg, June 17, 1864."
Inclusive dates: 1861–1864.

Despite the fact that no diary is mentioned, one must have been used for this account has a freshness which could hardly have been imparted so many years after the events described. The author joined the Federal Army in 1861 and remained in its service until October, 1864, when he was mustered out, after attaining the rank of major. His narrative, however, encompasses the entire war. He was a keen observer and seems to have been more interested in recording his impressions of the country he traversed than in recounting purely military events. For this reason, the book is an excellent travel work. Bosbyshell writes without rancor or bias or extreme statements. His travels were extensive. He reached Baltimore by rail from Harrisburg, Pennsylvania, and then went by boat to Fortress Monroe, where he was stationed long enough to develop much interest in the surrounding country. Thence he was sent by boat to Roanoke Island and later to the mainland at Newbern, North Carolina. In 1862 he was returned to the scene of the war in Virginia, landing at Aquia Creek and marching to the battlefield of Second Manassas. After this engagement he participated in the Sharpsburg campaign and moved back into Virginia to fight at Fredericksburg in December, 1862. In early 1863 he was sent to the area of the war in the West, passing through Pittsburgh, Columbus, and Cincinnati, where he crossed the Ohio River and went by train to Lexington, Kentucky. He remained there for some months before going eastward through Cumberland Gap to Knoxville and the general area of conflict in East Tennessee. In early 1864 he returned over the same route to the eastern theater and joined Grant's forces in their march on Richmond. He was mustered out in the Petersburg area in October, 1864, after he had reached the rank of major.

Bradley, George S. 49

The star corps; or, Notes of an army chaplain, during Sherman's famous "march to the sea." By Rev. G. S. Bradley. Milwaukee, Jermain & Brightman, printers, 1865.

xi, ₁13₁–304 p. front. (port.) 19¼ cm.
Illustrations: Frontispiece, "Yours truly, G. S. Bradley" ₁Signature₁.
Inclusive dates: March, 1864–May, 1865.

Letters from the front, portions of a diary, poetry, official reports, and newspaper excerpts make this a conglomerate mass of material, but continuity is maintained by liberal use of the letters and diary. Chaplain of the Twenty-second Wisconsin Regiment, which was a part of Sherman's forces, Bradley begins the narrative with his departure from Nashville for Chattanooga preparatory to the march on Atlanta. After the capture and destruction of that city, he followed the left wing of Sherman's army through Social Circle, Rutledge, Madison, Milledgeville, and Sandersville to Savannah. He then continued northward through South Carolina to Columbia, Camden, Cheraw, and on into North Carolina, passing through Fayetteville, Goldsboro, and to Raleigh. After Johnston's surrender the Federal army marched northward into Virginia, passing through Petersburg, Richmond, Fredericksburg, and Alexandria. This account is a simple narrative of the widespread pillaging and burning that continued to the North Carolina line, and is generally free from bitterness. Bradley found the slaves jubilant and the white people downcast and ready to quit the war.

Briant, Charles C. 50

History of the Sixth regiment Indiana volunteer infantry. Of both the three months' and three years' services ... By C. C. Briant ... Indianapolis, W. B. Burford, printer and binder, 1891.

iv p., 1 l, 423 p. front., ports. 19 cm.
Illustrations: Frontispiece, "C. C. Briant"; "Thomas T. Crittenden"; "Philemon P. Baldwin"; "Hagerman Tripp."
Inclusive dates: 1861–1864.

Briant's war services and travels were divided into two parts. First, as a "three months, volunteer," he went from Indianapolis by way of Cincinnati to Parkersburg in western Virginia, where he remained until the brief term expired. Second, he re-enlisted and went to Louisville, then southward through Kentucky into Tennessee, passing through Nashville on his way to Shiloh. After that battle he went on to fight in the Corinth campaign and saw service in northern Mississippi before hurrying back to Kentucky to intercept Bragg's march on Louisville. He returned to Nashville and Middle Tennessee and in 1863 participated in the Chattanooga-Chickamauga campaign. He then made an excursion into East Tennessee to Knoxville and the regions beyond to help defend the country against Longstreet's attacks. In 1864 he marched with Sherman to Atlanta and in September left the service as his term of enlistment had expired. Briant includes in his narrative some comments on conditions in the Confederacy, but his account is not as rich in atmosphere, comment, and incident, as he would lead the reader to believe. He saw little good in the Confederacy, passing some derogatory comments on Southern women especially.

Brinton, John Hill, 1832–1907. 51

Personal memoirs of John H. Brinton, major and surgeon U. S. V., 1861–1865 ... New York, The Neale publishing company, 1914.

361 p. front. (port.) 20 cm.
Illustrations: Frontispiece, "The Author, from a Wartime Photograph."
Inclusive dates: September, 1861–March, 1865.

Concerned primarily with hospital activities and life in the Federal army, this volume nevertheless gives interesting insights into conditions in the occupied parts of the Confederacy, with special emphasis on visits to Nashville and St. Louis. Brinton, a cousin of General McClellan, was a graduate of the University of Pennsylvania and of Jefferson College. He offered his services soon after the outbreak of the war and was prominently associated with the army's hospital service. His first work was in St. Louis and Cairo, and with Grant on his invasion of Kentucky and Tennessee from Forts Henry and Donelson to Shiloh. He visited most of the battlefields of the Peninsula campaign, as well as Fredericksburg, Chancellorsville, Sharpsburg, and Gettysburg. Stationed in Washington during part of his army career, Brinton was sent on tours of inspection to Louisville, Nashville, and St. Louis. The book was written many years after the war, but by an eminent surgeon and able scholar.

Britton, Wiley. 52

Memoirs of the rebellion on the border, 1863. By Wiley Britton ... Chicago, Cushing, Thomas & co., 1882.

> 458 p.   19¼ cm.
> *Inclusive dates:* 1863.
> *Other editions:* No other edition found. Including this story and other material is another work by Britton: The civil war on the border ... New York, G. P. Putnam's sons, 1890–1904, 2 vols.

Britton's writing is unusual because it deals with a region that was little known by those who fought there and later wrote about it. The author, a member of the Sixth Kansas Cavalry, confined this account of his activities to the area comprising the southwestern part of Missouri, northwestern Arkansas, and eastern Oklahoma and Kansas, bringing into the narrative Springfield, Missouri, Fayetteville and Van Buren, Arkansas, Fort Gibson, Oklahoma, and Fort Scott, Kansas. He not only writes of army movements and military activities involving the Indians and guerilla warfare, but also gives considerable space to both the country and the inhabitants.

Brown, Augustus Cleveland, 1839– 53

The diary of a line officer. By Captain Augustus C. Brown ... ₁New York, 1906?₁

> 1 p. l, 117 p.   front. (port.)   18 cm.
> *Illustrations:* Frontispiece portrait of a soldier unnamed—presumably of Brown.
> *Inclusive dates:* 1864.

The diary relates only to Grant's campaign against Richmond from the Wilderness to Petersburg. In December, 1864, Brown entered a hospital and ended his travels as well as his writing. Few comments go beyond observations on military affairs. The author was not at all favorably impressed with the gentility of Virginia women.

₁Brown, Edmund Randolph₁ 1845– 54

The Twenty-seventh Indiana volunteer infantry in the war of the rebellion, 1861 to 1865. First division, 12th and 20th corps. A history of its recruiting, organization, camp life, marches and battles, together with a roster of the men composing it ... By a member of Company C ₁Monticello, Ind., 1899₁

> 640, ₁2₁ p. incl. front., illus,, (incl. ports.)   22 cm.
> *Illustrations:* One hundred and twenty-four portraits of soldiers, battle scenes, and pen-and-ink sketches.
> *Maps:* Crudely drawn maps or plans of the battles of Winchester, Cedar Mountain, Antietam, Chancellorsville, Gettysburg, Resaca, and Peach Tree Creek.
> *Inclusive dates:* 1862–1864.

Composed from various soldiers' diaries, letters, and the author's own memory, this account details the travels of a Federal soldier to both eastern and western theaters of war. Brown left Indianapolis for Washington in 1861, going by way of Pittsburgh, Harrisburg, and Baltimore. He was with Banks at the Battle of Winchester, and participated in the major campaigns in Virginia, Maryland, and Pennsylvania. Immediately after Gettysburg he was sent by way of Chesapeake Bay and the Atlantic to New York to help quell the draft riots. Soon after his return to Virginia, Brown was sent to the Chattanooga area over the usual route by way of Bellaire, Columbus, Indianapolis, Louisville, and Nashville. In the spring of 1864 he followed Sherman from Chattanooga to Atlanta. His term of enlistment having expired before Sherman set out for Savannah, Brown returned home. This narrative has a moderate amount of description and comment on other matters than military affairs.

Brown, Philip Francis, 1842–   55

Reminiscences of the war of 1861–1865. Richmond, Va., Whittet & Shepperson, 1917.

62 p. 22¼ cm.
Illustrations: Frontispiece, Philip F. Brown, unlabeled.
Inclusive dates: 1861–1865.
Other editions: First edition: ₍Roanoke, Va., Printed by the Union printing co., c.1912.₎

In 1860, Philip F. Brown left the small Virginia trading center of Columbia and ascended the James River to seek a larger fortune in Richmond. On the outbreak of war he joined the Confederate Army and was sent to Norfolk where he remained until the fall of the city in 1862. He then took some part in the fighting around Richmond incident to McClellan's Peninsula campaign, and continued with the main Confederate forces, fighting in the Second Battle of Manassas and in that of Sharpsburg, where he was wounded. Being permanently incapacitated for further military service, he secured a clerkship in a Richmond hotel, and it is mostly of his experiences there that he writes. This short sketch of army life and civilian experiences in Richmond during the war is of little value.

Browne, Junius Henri, 1833–1902.   56

Four years in Secessia: adventures within and beyond the Union lines: embracing a great variety of facts, incidents, and romance of the war. Including the author's capture at Vicksburg, May 3, 1863, while running the rebel batteries; his imprisonment at Vicksburg, Jackson, Atlanta, Richmond, and Salisbury; his escape and perilous journey of four hundred miles to the Union lines at Knoxville. By Junius Henri Browne ... Hartford, O. D. Case and company; ₍etc., etc.₎1865.

vi, 450 p. 8 pl. (incl. front.) 20½ cm.
Illustrations: Frontispiece, "Our Capture before Vicksburg"; "The Bohemians as Housekeepers"; "Bohemia as a Belligerent"; "Gunboat Fight at Fort Pillow"; "Union Bushwhackers Attacking Rebel Cavalry"; "The Escaped Correspondents Enjoying the Negro's Hospitality";

"Conference of the Correspondents with Bushwhackers"; "The Bohemians Climbing the Mountains."

Inclusive dates: September, 1861–January, 1865.

Other editions: Same title, Hartford, O. D. Case and company; Chicago, G. and C. W. Sherwood, 1865.

Here a *New York Tribune* correspondent reports his experiences in the first two years of the war. He writes of military activities in Missouri, the fall of Forts Henry and Donelson, and the Battle of Shiloh. In May, 1863, he was taken prisoner while trying to run the batteries at Vicksburg by means of a small flotilla of barges on the Mississippi. From this point Browne is concerned with his prison life, which was spent principally at Libby and Castle Thunder in Richmond, and in Salisbury Prison in North Carolina. He escaped from the latter and was able finally to enter the Union lines near Knoxville, Tennessee. Browne's account is largely episodical and disjointed, giving a hazy picture of his travels, except for his escape journey. He was fiercely hostile to all things Confederate, and was certain slavery had made Southerners less than normal human beings. He bitterly condemned the Confederacy for treatment meted out to prisoners of war, and was little less reserved in his loathing of Secretary of War Stanton for his refusal to exchange prisoners. From his capture throughout the rest of the account Browne was accompanied by Albert D. Richardson, another *Tribune* correspondent, and from internal evidence it appears that he borrowed somewhat from Richardson's account (*Vide* No. 392). As between the two accounts Browne's is the less valuable. Born in Seneca Falls, New York, he grew up in Cincinnati and began work as a journalist there before joining the *New York Tribune* at the outbreak of the Civil War. After the war he wrote a volume on New York City and a book on his travels in Europe.

Brownlow, William Gannaway, 1805–1877. 57

Sketches of the rise, progress, and decline of secession; with a narrative of personal adventures among the rebels. By W. G. Brownlow ... Philadelphia, George W. Childs; Cincinnati, Applegate & co., 1862.

458 p. front. (port.), plates, facsims. 18½ cm.

Illustrations: Frontispiece, "Very Respectfully, &c, W. G. Brownlow" [Signature]; "Brutal treatment of Rev. Wm. H. H. Duggan by the Rebels"; "Rebels whipping a man for expressing Union sentiments"; "Charles S. Douglas shot by the Rebels while sitting at his window in Gay Street, Knoxville"; "Robert B. Reynolds the drunken Commissioner who committed Parson Brownlow to prison"; "District Attorney J. C. Ramsey (the man who swore out the warrant for the arrest of Parson Brownlow) drummed out of Zollicoffer's camp"; "Parson Brownlow entering the Knoxville Jail"; "Removing Prisoners from Knoxville Jail to Tuscaloosa, Alabama"; "Hanging of Fry and Hensie near the railroad, by Colonel Leadbetter"; "C. A. Haun, parting from his Family before his Execution"; Facsimile of a letter by Parson Brownlow; "Execution of Jacob Harmon and his son Henry"; "Interview of W. H. H. Self with his daughter in Knoxville Jail"; "Interview of Madison Cate with his Family."

Inclusive dates: 1861–1862.

Other editions: Many printings. No other editions found.

During the latter part of 1861 this fiery Knoxville newspaper editor became so obnoxious to the Confederates that he sought safety in the Great Smoky Mountains of East Tennessee. Being induced to come back to Knoxville he was arrested and imprisoned in the local jail until it seemed advisable to allow him to retire to his home in the city because of poor health. In March, 1862, the Confederates decided to let him go North and Brownlow was escorted by a guard to the Federal lines near Nashville. Leaving Knoxville he traveled by rail to Chattanooga, thence to Wartrace and Shelbyville. After a short time in Nashville, Brownlow went by boat down the Cumberland and up the Ohio rivers to Cincinnati. Thereafter he made extensive tours in the North. This is an extremely virulent account of Brownlow's experiences with the Confederates in East Tennessee and it had an important effect on Northern enthusiasm for the war. A Virginian by birth, he became the postwar Radical governor of Tennessee and later sat in the United States Senate. This well-known book is made up mostly of matters other than Brownlow's travels.

Bryner, Byron Cloyd, 1849–   58

Bugle echoes; the story of Illinois 47th ... By Cloyd Bryner ... ₁Springfield, Ill., Phillips bros., printers, 1905₁

ix p., 1 l, 11–262 p.   front., plates, ports.   22½ cm.
Illustrations: Frontispiece "Yours in F. C. & L. B. C. Bryner" ₁Signature₁; and thirty-five other illustrations, mostly of soldiers.
Inclusive dates: 1861–1865.

The 47th Illinois Regiment, of which Bryner was a member, confined its operations almost entirely to the widespread Mississippi Valley. In 1861 Bryner left Peoria by railroad for Alton, took a steamer to St. Louis, and continued into north central Missouri as far as Jefferson City and Boonville. Returning to St. Louis he went down the Mississippi to Fort Pillow and by the Mississippi, Ohio, and Tennessee rivers to Hamburg near Shiloh. He operated around Corinth and over northern Mississippi to Memphis, went by steamer to Vicksburg and the Red River country, joined the Mobile Bay expedition across the Gulf, and was at Montgomery when the war ended. He then proceeded westward, passing through Selma. This narrative is strictly factual without much imagination or incidental comment. The larger picture of the war crowds out much that an observant traveler would have included.

Burdette, Robert Jones, 1849–1914.   59

The drums of the 47th. By Robert J. Burdette ... Indianapolis, The Bobbs-Merrill company ₁c.1914₁

5 p. l., 211, ₁1₁ p.   18½ cm.
Inclusive dates: 1862–1865.
Other editions: Another and fuller account of the marches of this regiment is by Byron Cloyd Bryner, Bugle echoes: The story of Illinois 47th ... (*q. v.*).

Burdette came to be much better known for other activities than the writing of this narrative. After the war he was engaged briefly in gun running to Cuba and later attained some standing as a newspaperman, humorist, and Baptist clergyman. It was as a member of the Forty-seventh Regiment of Illinois Volunteers, however, that Burdette made his travels through the Confederacy. The routes are not clearly defined, but this much is evident: he joined the regiment at Corinth and was later in the Vicksburg and Red River campaigns. He was also in the expedition to Mobile and at one time or another reached Tupelo, Mississippi, and Selma, Alabama. It is an unusual narrative by an unusual man; something like a philosophical essay interspersed with reconstructed conversations. As a travelogue it is of little value. It first appeared in the *Sunday School Times*.

Burson, William, 1833–   60

A race for liberty; or, My capture, imprisonment, and escape. By William Burson, of Company A, 32d reg't O.V.I. With an introduction by W. B. Derrick ... Wellsville, O., W. G. Foster, printer, 1867.

xii, [5]–135 p.   15½ cm.
Inclusive dates: 1864.

Burton, a native of Ohio, joined the Federal Army in 1861 and did some soldiering in Kentucky and Tennessee before being mustered out on account of his health. In 1864 he again joined the army and was sent to Cairo by way of Cincinnati, thence by boat up the Ohio and Tennessee rivers to Clifton, Tennessee, where he disembarked and marched across country to Rome, Georgia, to join Sherman's army on its march against Atlanta. On the outskirts of that city he was captured, marched to Griffin, and put on a train for Macon and Andersonville. Later he was transferred to Florence, South Carolina, going by rail through Augusta and Branchville. As the prison camp was being organized at Florence he was able to escape. He wandered across North Carolina in a northwesterly direction through Randolph, Wilkes, and other counties until he reached Ashe County, continued through Boone, in Watauga County, and crossed over into East Tennessee to Carter County where he met Federal patrols and made his way to Greeneville and Knoxville. This narrative, written soon after the events, is a valuable document on the wanderings of an escaped prisoner. Burson describes the country through which he passed; the Union sentiment he found constantly among the North Carolinians as evidenced in the secret society known as the H. O. A., or Heroes of America, which he joined; the consistent attention and aid he received from Confederate deserters; and the ease with which he escaped lukewarm Confederates who twice captured him on his journeyings. It is conspicuous neither for bitterness nor for improbable details.

Burton, Elijah P.   61

Diary of E. P. Burton, surgeon, 7th reg. Ill., 3rd brig., 2nd div. 16 A. C. Prepared by the Historical records survey, Division of professional and service projects, Works projects administration. Des Moines, Iowa, The Historical records survey, 1939.

3 p. l., 92 numb. l.   24¼ cm.
Inclusive dates: March, 1864–June, 1865.

Although written by a surgeon in the hospital service of the Federal Army, this diary concerns itself little with hospitals. On the contrary it is a valuable comment on life among the Federal soldiers in camp and in battle, and also on the people and the country through which they marched. Burton remarks frequently on drunkenness among soldiers, especially during the burning of Columbia, South Carolina; he was much interested in the slaves who streamed into the Federal camps, and he saw many Southerners who were tired of war. Though never condemning pillaging, he remarked on how indiscriminately and constantly it occurred. Burton began his diary at Nashville and continued it throughout the whole journey over a route by Pulaski, Athens, Alabama, Chattanooga, Rome, Atlanta, Fort McAllister, and to Hilton Head by water; back to Savannah, Columbia, Camden, Cheraw, Fayetteville, Morehead City, Goldsboro, Raleigh, Petersburg, Richmond, Fredericksburg, and Washington. He arrived in the capital in time to participate in the "Grand Review" on Pennsylvania Avenue, and went on to Louisville, Kentucky, to be mustered out. Burton's material is presented in a matter-of-fact style into which little opinion or bitterness is injected.

Butler, Jay Caldwell, 1844–1885.   62

Letters home ₍by₎ Jay Caldwell Butler, captain, 101st. Ohio volunteer infantry, arranged by his son Watson Hubbard Butler ... ₍Binghamton, N. Y.₎ Privately printed, 1930.

x, 153 p.   20½ cm.
Inclusive dates: 1862–1865.

Butler's travels as a soldier were not widespread. He started somewhat late, having left Monroeville, Ohio, in 1862, just in time to reach Louisville by way of Cincinnati for the push against Bragg's invasion of Kentucky in the late summer. Butler marched to Perryville and on to Nashville and Murfreesboro. In the fall of 1863 he participated in the Chattanooga-Chickamauga campaign, and the next year followed Sherman to Atlanta. After the fall of that city he returned to Tennessee to help foil Hood's attempts to take Nashville and was there when the war ended. Butler's letters, written from the battlefields and line of march, are short but they indicate a moderate interest in the country and his new situations. He noted the Kentucky girls waving at Union soldiers as they marched by, and was attracted by the many towns and villages which lay in ruins or were almost entirely deserted by their inhabitants.

Buzhardt, Beaufort Simpson.   63

Beaufort Simpson Buzhardt, 1838–1862, Newberry, S. C. Prepared by

Carrie Buzhardt Traywick. Newberry, S. C. (?) Printed for private distribution. 1916(?)

73 p.   front. (port.), port.   19½ cm.
Illustrations: Frontispiece, "Beaufort Simpson Buzhardt. Aged 20 years"; "Beaufort Simpson Buzhardt. Aged 23 years."
Inclusive dates: 1861–1862.

Immediately after the firing on Fort Sumter Buzhardt joined a unit of the South Carolina army in Newberry, South Carolina. Soon mustered into the Confederate service at Columbia, he went by railway to Manassas, Virginia, by way of Wilmington, Weldon, Petersburg, and Richmond. He took part in the First Battle of Manassas and then wintered in northern Virginia. When McClellan's Peninsula campaign was begun, he was sent to Yorktown and on up the Peninsula, to fight until he was killed in a skirmish before Richmond in the latter part of June. This diary gives interesting glimpses into the life and feelings of both Confederate civilians and soldiers. As Buzhardt traveled northward from his South Carolina home to Virginia he was pleased with the reception soldiers were given all along the line. When terms of enlistment expired, many soldiers wanted to return home, and it took much explaining of the Confederate Conscription Act to induce some of them to remain.

Byers, Samuel Hawkins Marshall, 1838–1933.   64

What I saw in Dixie; or, Sixteen months in Rebel prisons. By Adjutant S. H. M. Byers. Dansville, N. Y., Robbins & Poore, printers, 1868.

3 p. l., 126 p.   17¼ cm.
Inclusive dates: November, 1863–March, 1865.

Other editions: No other edition found. In 1911 another account of Byers' prison experiences, appeared supplemented by his army service from his first fighting in Missouri through Tennessee and the capture of Vicksburg to his own capture at Missionary Ridge. Aided by a fading and treacherous memory and doubtless by the desire to make a good story, Byers adds in this work many details and embellishments which never occurred to him when he wrote the original account which he claimed was largely a diary. Major S. H. M. Byers, With fire and sword. New York, The Neale publishing company, 1911.

This author paints conditions in the prisons about as bad as the usual account has them, claiming that many prisoners were shot by the guards without provocation. His work, however, is unusual among prison books in that it gives considerable attention to conditions in the Confederacy and to experiences in traveling between various prisons. Though disclaiming any desire to arouse further bitterness over the prisoner-of-war question, Byers' pages undoubtedly had that effect and were evidently intended to serve as a powerful document in support of Radical Reconstruction of the South, and especially to promote Negro suffrage. The booklet is dedicated to a slave who had befriended him. Byers belonged to the Fifth Iowa Regiment, Infantry, took part in the Vicksburg campaign, was transferred with Sherman's army to Chattanooga, and was taken prisoner in November, 1863, at the Battle of Missionary Ridge. He was sent to

Atlanta, Belle Isle, and Libby in Richmond, transferred to Macon, and escaped to reach Atlanta when Sherman was besieging that city. Recaptured and sent back to Macon and Columbia, he escaped again just before Sherman arrived and was present when the city was burned. Afterwards Byers went northward with the Federal Army to Fayetteville where he was dispatched as a special messenger to Grant at Petersburg. He traveled down the Cape Fear River and around the coast from Wilmington. After the war the author attained some prominence as a writer of fiction, poetry, drama, religious works, other Civil War books, and an account of his observations in Europe where he served as a consul general.

Cable, George W., *ed.* 65

"War Diary of a Union Woman in the South," *in* Famous adventures and prison escapes of the civil war. New York, The Century co., 1893.

x p., 1 l., 338 p. incl. front., illus. 21 cm.
Inclusive dates: December 1, 1860–August 20, 1863.
Other editions: Text originally appeared in The Century magazine.

This is one of the few diaries kept by Union women who remained in the Confederacy. The author's name is not revealed, though she was known to George W. Cable. The full text of the diary was not published and all names of people and most of the locations were concealed with fictitious names or initials. The text produced here was originally published in *The Century Magazine.* The author began her diary in New Orleans and apparently resided in that city until about the beginning of 1862, when she married and moved to an unnamed village in Arkansas, apparently located on an oxbow lake near the Mississippi. Later the family removed to Mississippi, floating down the river in a small boat. For a time the diarist lived at a small station on the railway between Jackson and New Orleans, but by the beginning of 1863 she had joined her husband in Vicksburg and was present during the famous siege, the hardships of which she describes with some realism. Being a Union woman from the beginning she looked with great disdain on the warlike women of her acquaintance, like the one "who talks nothing but blood and thunder, yet faints at the sight of a worm." She also gives interesting details of the privations of the people and describes some of the substitutes for common household necessities.

Cadwell, Charles K. 66

The old Sixth regiment, its war record, 1861–5. By Charles K. Cadwell ... New Haven, Tuttle, Morehouse & Taylor, printers, 1875.

227, [1] p. 20 cm.
Inclusive dates: 1861–1865.

Military operations on the coast of South Carolina from Beaufort up to James Island near Charleston, the reduction of Fort Pulaski at the mouth of the Savannah River, and the capture and burning of Jacksonville, Florida, are the principal events covered in this account. In 1864 the Sixth Connecticut Regiment was transferred to Bermuda Hundred and there assigned to Butler. In September, 1864, the author's term of enlistment expired and he was mustered out. From that time to the end of the war, the regiment's history lacks a personal touch. From his personal diary Cadwell wrote an even-tempered account of considerable value in estimating conditions along the coast of the South Atlantic States. He held that the wanton burning of Jacksonville was a disgrace to the Federal troops.

Caldwell, James Fitz James. 67

The history of a brigade of South Carolinians, known first as "Gregg's" and subsequently as "McGowan's brigade." By J. F. J. Caldwell ... Philadelphia, King & Baird, printers, 1866.

247 p. 19 cm.
Inclusive dates: 1861–1865.

The fact that this work was written and published immediately after the war gives it a freshness and reliability lacking in accounts long deferred. It is less concerned with incidents, observations, and atmosphere than are most such books, yet there are enough of these characteristics, incidental though they are, to give it a place in travel literature. Caldwell indicates routes of travel and frequently records the life and reactions of the soldiers. He gives a touching description of at least one soldier's utter desolation on learning that Lee had surrendered. The unit with which Caldwell served moved early in the war from Charleston to northern Virginia, arriving there in time to take part in the First Battle of Manassas. Thereafter it fought throughout the war in all the major campaigns in Virginia, and in Maryland and Pennsylvania.

Calvert, Henry Murray. 68

Reminiscences of a boy in blue, 1862–1865. By Henry Murray Calvert. New York and London, G. P. Putnam's sons, 1920.

vii, 347 p. 20 cm.
Inclusive dates: 1862–1865.

Although not published until 1920, the author says in his preface that the narrative was "written long ago, while the events were fresh in my memory." Even so, it appears to have been written later, when age had mellowed recollection, for it is more interpretative than factual, with some reconstructed or imaginary conversations. As travel material it is of mediocre value.

Calvert served in two widely separated areas. Leaving New York in 1862, he reached Washington and northern Virginia to be present at the Second Battle of Manassas and remained for some time in the Maryland regions near Washington. After a trip to Harpers Ferry in June, 1863, he went by ocean steamer to New Orleans and operated in the Mississippi Valley for the remainder of the war, making raids into the Louisiana plantation country west of the river and eastward around Baton Rouge. He was in two long raids, to Brookhaven, Mississippi, and into the Pascagoula River country. He then went up the Mississippi River to Memphis, headed southward through Arkansas into Louisiana through Bastrop, back to the Mississippi River, and was in Memphis when the war ended.

₁Campbell, John Francis₁ 1822–1885.   69

A short American tramp in the fall of 1864, by the editor of "Life in Normandy." Edinburgh, Edmonston and Douglas, 1865.

2 p. l., vii, 427 p. incl. front., illus., map. 20½ cm.
Illustrations: Frontispiece, "Harbour of St. John's." Caricature of author in center of title-page.
Inclusive dates: Fall of 1864.

The author dipped into the slave states at only two points. He made a short sojourn in St. Louis, crossed southern Illinois and Indiana by railroad to Louisville, Kentucky, and visited the interior as far as Mammoth Cave. From Louisville he went by steamer to Cincinnati, and then made his way out of the country through Boston. Campbell wrote in a humorous and half flippant style which indicates none of the reforming zeal that characterized most Britons who visited America. As for the war, he thought both sides were "darned fools for fighting." He frequently noted his impressions of the slaves but never lost his good humor over their lot. He was primarily interested in geology and watched for scratches on the rocks which would indicate the area of glaciation. Campbell was a Scotsman, educated at Eton and the University of Edinburgh. He was greatly interested in Highland folklore as well as in geology and meteorology, and published several works relating to these subjects.

Cannon, J. P.   70

Inside of rebeldom: the daily life of a private in the Confederate army ... By J. P. Cannon ... Washington, D. C., The National tribune, 1900.

xx, 21–288 p. incl. front. (port.), illus. 21¼ cm.
Illustrations: Frontispiece, "J. P. Cannon, M.D. (From a recent photograph and from a war-time portrait.)" and seven crude drawings.
Inclusive dates: 1862–1865,

Most of this cheaply printed, paper-back book covering the years from December, 1862, through December, 1864, is a diary which the author kept during the war; but the general tenor of it indicates that it was revised as a volume in the "Old Glory Library." There is no reason to doubt its reliability as the experience record of a Confederate soldier in the war but it contains no observations or considered judgments on the people and the times. As for traveling, Private Cannon covered in frequent marchings and retreats the states of Alabama, Tennessee, Kentucky, Mississippi, and Georgia; all his routes are clearly indicated in the diary. He enlisted in northern Alabama in the latter days of

1861 and went down the Tennessee River to Fort Henry just in time to escape from that place. He also participated in Bragg's expedition into Kentucky in the late summer of 1862, passing through Cumberland Gap and southward through East Tennessee. In early 1863 he was fighting Banks at Port Hudson and participated later in the activities around Vicksburg, after which he was in General Johnston's retreat on Atlanta and after its fall in General Hood's disastrous campaign against Nashville. He finally was paroled at the end of the war at Eastport, Mississippi. As a book of personal experiences it is entertaining; as a serious comment on the South it has little value.

Carter, Howell.   71

A cavalryman's reminiscences of the civil war. By Howell Carter. New Orleans, The American printing co., ltd. [19—]

2 p. l., [9]–212 p. incl. ports.   17 cm.
Illustrations: Frontispiece, "The Author in 1900"; and thirty portraits of inconspicuous Confederate officers and privates.
Inclusive dates: 1861–1865.

This is an episodical, anecdotal, sketchy account of a soldier's life with Colonel John S. Scott's First Louisiana Cavalry. Written more than a third of a century after the war, the book has little contemporary atmosphere. The extensive travels of these troops began when they embarked at Baton Rouge on a Mississippi River steamer for Memphis and proceeded by train for Nashville and Bowling Green, Kentucky. They retreated southward with General Albert Sidney Johnston in the spring of 1862 and fought in the Battle of Corinth in northern Mississippi. Thence northward into East Tennessee around Kingston, they were soon marching into Kentucky as a part of Bragg's invasion in the early fall of 1862. They traveled as far north as Versailles and westward through Frankfort toward Louisville, reaching a point within twenty miles of that place before they retreated to take part in the Battle of Perryville and afterward marched back to Tennessee. They fought in the Battle of Murfreesboro, raided into East Tennessee and back into Kentucky, were transferred to Mississippi and Louisiana, and were operating farther eastward into Alabama when the surrender came. They signed paroles at Gainesville, Alabama.

Casler, John Overton, 1838–   72

Four years in the Stonewall brigade. By John O. Casler. Private, Company A, 33d regiment Virginia infantry, Stonewall brigade, 1st division, 2d corps, Army of Northern Virginia, Gen. Robert E. Lee, commanding ... Guthrie, Okla., State capital printing company, 1893.

495 p. incl., illus., plates, ports., facsims., fold. facsim.   19¾ cm.
Illustrations: Frontispiece, "John O. Casler, 1893"; and twenty-eight pen-and-ink sketches, portraits, and facsimiles of documents.
Inclusive dates: 1861–1865.
Other editions: Second edition: Girard Kan., Appeal publishing co., 1906.

Casler's contribution is a first-rate human-interest story of a Confederate soldier's experiences in the war. He wrote without a trace of bitterness, and designed his book for both young and mature readers. It is almost entirely concerned with life in the army and only incidentally do the face of the country and the character of the civilians enter the picture. Its locale is the eastern theater of war. Casler was in Sedalia, Missouri, when the secession movement began, but being a Virginian he hastened to his old home in the northwestern part of the state to join a local regiment which was to become a part of Stonewall Jackson's Brigade. He operated with this unit until January, 1865, when he joined the Eleventh Virginia Cavalry. The next month he was taken prisoner and sent to Fort McHenry in Baltimore harbor. He participated, up to the time of his capture, in most of the principal engagements in Virginia, as well as those of Sharpsburg and Gettysburg. Though Casler waited more than a quarter of a century to write his narrative, he based it partially upon a fragmentary personal diary which was checked against other documents. It may, therefore, be considered trustworthy.

Cate, Wirt Armistead, 1900–   *ed.*   73

Two soldiers; the campaign diaries of Thomas J. Key, C.S.A., December 7, 1863–May 17, 1865, and Robert J. Campbell, U.S.A., January 1, 1864–July 21, 1864; edited, with an introduction, notes and maps, by Wirt Armistead Cate. Chapel Hill, The University of North Carolina press, 1938.

xiii, 277 p.   front., illus. (maps), 2 ports. on 1 pl., facsims.   21½ cm.

Illustrations: Frontispiece, "Facsimile Fly-Leaf from Captured Union Diary"; "Reproduction of Daguerreotype Miniatures of Thomas J. Key and his Wife"; "Facsimile of Part of a Page from Diary of Thomas J. Key"; "Facsimile Page Showing Part of Last Entry of R. J. Campbell and a Notation by Thomas J. Key."

Maps: "Railroads in 1864"; "The Atlanta Campaign 1864"; "Siege of Atlanta, July 19–Sept. 2, 1864"; "Battle of Nashville, Dec. 15 and 16, 1864"; "Sherman's Meridian Expedition, 1864."

Inclusive dates: 1863–1865; January–July, 1864.

Key, a native of Tennessee and a newspaper editor by profession, joined the Confederate Army in 1862 in an Arkansas unit and before the war ended reached the rank of first lieutenant. His diary begins in winter quarters at Dalton, Georgia, in the winter of 1863. He participated in the march southward to Atlanta and the surrounding region, and on the fall of that city accompanied Hood on his disastrous campaign to the outskirts of Nashville. Afterwards he returned to Georgia by way of Columbus, Mississippi, where he boarded a boat for Mobile, steamed up the Alabama River to Montgomery, and went by train to Columbus and Macon, Georgia. Here he remained until the end of the war. He then left by train to Atlanta, Chattanooga, and on to Nashville. Going across to the Tennessee River he went by boat on the Ohio and the Mississippi rivers to his home in Helena, Arkansas. In early 1864, while on furlough, he was able to visit his Arkansas home, going and returning across Alabama and Mississippi by railway and muleback. This diary gives interesting observations and comments on army life, the conditions of the country and the people, and on Confederate policy, with some biting comments on Governor Brown's near treason in Georgia. Campbell, born in New York but moving to Iowa sometime before the outbreak of war, joined a unit from the latter state. His diary begins when he was encamped near Vicksburg in January, 1864, and in a sketchy, brief fashion deals with Sherman's Meridian expedition early in that year. After this excursion, Campbell received a furlough to visit his Iowa home. He returned down the Mississippi River to Cairo and up the Ohio and Tennessee rivers to southern Tennessee, thence marching across northern Alabama to Rome and Atlanta, where he was captured. His diary is of little value in assessing conditions in those parts of the Confederacy through which he traveled.

Chamberlaine, William W., 1836?– 74

Memoirs of the civil war between the northern and southern sections of the United States of America, 1861–1865. By Captain William W. Chamberlaine ... Washington, D. C., Press of B. S. Adams, 1912.

138 p.   front. (port.)   20 cm.
Illustrations: Frontispiece, "Captain Wm. W. Chamberlaine in 1863."
Inclusive dates: 1861–1865.

These typical soldier's memoirs, published many years after the war, are based on memory without benefit of diary or letters. They are therefore of little value as a commentary on actual conditions in the South during the war. Chamberlain began his service in the Confederate Army around Norfolk, and after the fall of that city early in 1862 he became a part of the forces defending the Peninsula and Richmond. After being sent to Rockymount, in southwestern Virginia, to round up deserters, he returned in time to take part in the Sharpsburg campaign into Maryland. Back in Virginia he fought at Fredericksburg, Chancellorsville, Gettysburg, and against Grant's efforts to take Richmond in 1864–1865. This is little more than a résumé of military happenings and it is not always correct.

Chamberlayne, John Hampden, 1838–1882. 75

Ham Chamberlayne—Virginian; letters and papers of an artillery officer in the war for southern independence, 1861–1865; with introduction, notes, and index, by his son, C. G. Chamberlayne. Richmond, Va., Press of the Dietz printing co., 1932.

xxx p. 1 l., 440 p.   front., plates, ports., maps (2 fold.), facsims.   23 cm.
Illustrations: Frontispiece, "Capt. John Hampden Chamberlayne As Editor of the *State,* Richmond, Va., 1876–1882"; and sixty other illustrations, mostly of Confederate officers, but including photographs of buildings and of manuscripts.
Maps: "Sketch of the Entrenched Lines in the Immediate Front of Petersburg, N. Michler, Major of Engrs. Bvt. Col. U. S. A." (7½ by 9 inches); "Map of Eastern Virginia, with Parts of West Virginia, Maryland, and Pennsylvania, Showing Places Mentioned in the Letters." (12 by 16 inches).
Inclusive dates: 1861–1865.

Chamberlayne, of the minor aristocracy of Virginia, was educated at the University of Virginia. At the outbreak of war he enlisted as a private and by the end of the war had attained the rank of captain; a position which he felt was somewhat beneath his deserts and due to a lack of systematic promotion in the Confederate Army. As a soldier he was sent first to Acquia Creek and soon thereafter to the western Virginia area of fighting around Cheat Mountain. From the end of that campaign to the final days of war he participated in the various eastern campaigns of the Peninsula, Second Manassas, Sharpsburg, Fredericksburg, Chancellorsville, Gettysburg, and of Richmond and Petersburg in 1864–1865. Chamberlayne, in many letters to his mother and sister, gives a rather complete picture of what went on in the mind of an intelligent artillery officer, especially policies of the army and civil government, as well as social conditions among the people he visited on the march and while in camp. This work is unusually valuable in showing his thoughts and actions as the war was nearing its close. When surrender seemed inevitable at Appomattox, he slipped through the lines and made his way southward to General Johnston's army near Greensboro, North Carolina, but finding no hope of continuing the war there he continued on across North Carolina, South Carolina, Georgia, Alabama, and into Mississippi, hoping to find new forces to continue the war in Texas. By this time, however, all hope of further military activity had disappeared and he began to think of migrating to the southern hemisphere "where the Great Bear is no longer seen & men walk on their heads." He later returned to Virginia and engaged in newspaper work, first at Norfolk and then at Richmond.

Chapman, Robert D., 1839– 76

A Georgia soldier in the civil war, 1861–1865. By R. D. Chapman. Houston, Tex., 1923.

108 p. 1 l., illus. 19 cm.
Illustrations: Frontispiece, "Captain Robt. D. Chapman, Company E, 55th Georgia Regiment, C. S. A. at the Age of Twenty-One, Atlanta, Georgia"; "Capt. Robt. D. Chapman From a Recent Photograph, Houston, Texas."
Inclusive dates: 1861–1865.
Other editions: [Little Rock, General T. J. Churchill chapter, United daughters of the confederacy, 1932.]

This paper-bound narrative makes a good story about a Confederate soldier, who enlisted in 1861 and was stationed first near Savannah and then sent into East Tennessee where he was captured. He escaped and wandered among the bushwhackers and Union mountaineers of eastern Kentucky until he was recaptured and sent by way of Louisville to Johnson's Island Prison in Lake Erie. After a stay here he was sent to Point Lookout Prison in Maryland, but before reaching that destination he escaped near Frederick. Making his way across the Potomac at Harpers Ferry, Chapman continued up the Shenandoah Valley until he again entered the Confederate lines. Passing through Richmond he returned to Georgia and was stationed as a guard at Andersonville Prison. He later returned to Savannah, and was with the Confederates at their final surrender to Sherman in North Carolina. The account makes no pretensions to being based on a diary or any other personal wartime record. As it was written more than a half century after the war, it has little value beyond the general impressions that remained in the memory of an old man.

Cheek, Phillip (1841–?) and Mair Pointon. 77

History of the Sauk County riflemen, known as company "A" sixth Wisconsin veteran volunteer infantry. Madison, Wis., Democrat Printing Company, 1909.

220.1, illus. front. 21½ cm.
Inclusive dates: 1861–1866.

Written thirty-five years after the war, this narrative is a compilation from memory and contemporary records, with some personal travel flavor. He notes such incidents in his army career as the capture of a few trains, and his marches and countermarches. Baylor enlisted in Virginia at the beginning of the war and continued either as soldier or prisoner until its end. He operated almost wholly in northern Virginia and the Shenandoah Valley, with occasional raids into West Virginia. In 1863 he was captured and taken to Fort McHenry in Baltimore harbor, later removed by boat down Chesapeake Bay to Fort Delaware, on the Delaware River, and finally exchanged at City Point, to return and serve in the Confederate army to the war's end.

[Clare, Mrs. Josephine] 78

Narrative of the adventures and experiences of Mrs. Josephine Clare, a resident of the South at the breaking out of the rebellion, her final escape from Natichitoches, La., and safe arrival at home, in Marietta, Pa. Lancaster, Pa., Pearson & Geist, 1865.

36 p. 16¼ cm.
Inclusive dates: January–June, 1863.

When conscription went into effect in the Confederacy in 1862, Mr. Clare (husband of Josephine) with others banded together in and around Natchitoches, Louisiana, and secreted themselves. On learning that her husband was about to be apprehended, Mrs. Clare set out for Marietta, Pennsylvania, where she had lived before she and her husband had come South two years previously. She went by stage to Alexandria and thence down the Red River and up the Mississippi to Vicksburg by steamer. Being unable to continue northward she took the railway to Jackson and then southward (erroneously saying that she went by way of Meridian) to Ponchatoula, Louisiana. Unable to pass through the lines into New Orleans, she went to Clinton for a short stay before returning northward by train to Canton, Mississippi. Unable to go farther, she returned to Jackson and went eastward by rail to Meridian, southward to Mobile, thence to Montgomery and on to Augusta, Columbia, Weldon, and Richmond. She obtained a pass to leave the Confederacy through the lines in northern Virginia by way of Leesburg. From Leesburg she continued to Baltimore and on to Marietta. Mrs. Clare gives little more than her travelogue and the difficulties of the journey. Her husband made his way on horseback through Louisiana northward through Arkansas, passing around Little Rock, to Springfield, Missouri, where he entered the Federal lines. He then made his way to St. Louis where he boarded a steamer which took him to Quincy and later to Rock Island. Thence he went by rail to Freeport, Illinois. His account is brief, though he makes some comment on the Unionism of the people he met on his way to Missouri.

Clark, George, 1841– 79

A glance backward; or, Some events in the past history of my life. By George Clark. ₍Houston, Tex., Press of Rein & sons company, 1914?₎

93 p.   21½ cm.
Inclusive dates: 1861–1865 ₍1867 ff₎

Written from memory fifty years after the events described, George Clark's book has the limitations inherent in such delay. In its general atmosphere and the main events described the book has some value, but there is some confusion in details. The narrative is largely military, since Clark was a Confederate soldier throughout the war. He was born in Eutaw, Alabama, and was educated at the University of Alabama, leaving that institution to take part in the war in Virginia. He went by rail through Montgomery, Atlanta, Knoxville, and Lynchburg to Richmond. He was sent to Winchester, Virginia, whence he began his march to the First Battle of Manassas, arriving the day after that engagement took place. Thereafter he fought with the Army of Northern Virginia in the Peninsula campaign and at Fredericksburg, Chancellorsville, Gettysburg, the defense of Richmond against Grant in 1864–1865, and Appomattox. He returned to Alabama after the war, and in 1867 moved to Texas, making his home eventually in Waco. Later in life he attained some importance in state politics.

Clark, James H., 1842– 80

The iron hearted regiment: being an account of the battles, marches and gallant deeds performed by the 115th regiment N. Y. vols. Also a list of the dead and wounded; an account of hundreds of brave men shot on a score of hard fought fields of strife; a complete statement of Harpers Ferry surrender; sketches of the officers; a history of the flags and those who bore them, together with touching incidents, thrilling adventures, amusing scenes, etc., etc., etc. By James H. Clark ... Albany, J. Munsell, 1865.

xii, 337 p.   18¼ cm.
Inclusive dates: 1862–1865.

First Lieutenant Clark's extensive travels with his regiment began around

Charlestown, West Virginia, where he, like most other Federal soldiers who visited there, found much of interest in both the John Brown associations with that place and in the attitude of the inhabitants towards the invaders. From Charlestown, Lieutenant Clark was sent for a short time to Camp Douglas near Chicago to guard Confederate prisoners. He returned to Washington and sailed from Baltimore for Port Royal, South Carolina. In this Southern clime he was much annoyed by myriad insects and reptiles. Soon he went with an expedition to Jacksonville, Florida, and on to take part in the Battle of Olustee. From Jacksonville he sailed for City Point, Virginia, and for a time in the summer of 1864 took part in the investment of Petersburg. In early 1865 he participated in the reduction of Fort Fisher at the mouth of the Cape Fear River, and when Sherman reached North Carolina Clark became a part of "Uncle Billy's" (Sherman's) forces which were soon to receive Johnston's surrender near Durham Station, after which he proceeded to City Point and back to New York City. This book is not as elaborate as its title would indicate; nevertheless it contains many interesting glimpses of conditions in the Confederacy. He intimates that the narrative is based on a journal he kept in the field; certainly it is fresh, for it was composed immediately after the war.

Clark, James Samuel, 1841– 81

Life in the Middle West; reminiscences of J. S. Clark. Chicago, The Advance publishing company, [1916]

226 p. incl. front., ports. 19 cm.
Illustrations: Frontispiece "J. S. Clark" [Signature]; "J. S. Clark, Private in First Iowa"; "General Nathaniel Lyon"; "General G. W. Clark"; "Captain J. S. Clark, President Anchor Insurance Company"; "Mrs. J. S. Clark."
Inclusive dates: April, 1861–August, 1865.

The first seventy-five years of the author's life are covered in this book, but a considerable portion of the text is concerned with his career in the Federal army during the Civil War. Clark, born in Indiana, grew up in Iowa and in April, 1861, he joined the First Iowa Infantry Regiment as a three-months volunteer. He was sent down the Mississippi River to St. Louis and up the Missouri to participate in the expedition to Boonville and thence to Springfield. He returned to Iowa when his enlistment had expired, but soon joined the Thirty-fourth Iowa Regiment and attained the rank of captain. For the rest of the war he traveled widely over the South. He participated in both Vicksburg campaigns and after the fall of that city was sent to New Orleans for a short time before being ordered across the Gulf to Brownsville, Texas. From there he marched up the coast to Aransas Pass and spent the winter of 1863–1864. He was then ordered back to Louisiana where he participated in the Red River expedition to Alexandria. Later he was stationed in Baton Rouge for a while and then at Pensacola; early in 1865 he took part in the capture of Mobile. He then made a trip up the Alabama River to Selma, and on the cessation of hostilities was sent across the Gulf to Galveston and inland to Houston, to be mustered out in

August, 1865. This account, based on a diary written during the conflict, shows an excellent spirit of regard for the enemy and can be accepted as a truthful, straightforward narrative.

Clark, Walter Augustus 82

Under the stars and bars; or, Memories of four years service with the Oglethorpes, of Augusta, Georgia. By Walter A. Clark ... Augusta, Ga., Chronicle printing company, 1900.

234, ₍3₎ p. 20 cm.
Inclusive dates: 1861–1865.

This narrative, though written about a third of a century after the war, was re-enforced by a diary and various letters written by the author during the struggle. It is somewhat garrulous and discursive, yet it gives a good-natured, close-up picture of a Confederate soldier's life as well as intimate descriptions of the civilian population. Clark joined the Confederate Army in 1861, and with some interruption remained in the service until the end. He served first in northern and western Virginia, returned in 1862 to Augusta, Georgia, where he re-enlisted and moved to Chattanooga, to Knoxville in East Tennessee, and westward to Clinton and Jacksboro. Later he returned to Georgia and participated in General Johnston's holding operations against Sherman in his march on Atlanta. He spent some time in the hospital at Oxford, Georgia, but later joined Hood's march on Nashville, after which he returned to Augusta by way of Meridian, Mississippi, Montgomery, Alabama, and Columbus and Milledgeville, Georgia. From Augusta he went on through South Carolina and ended his service in eastern North Carolina at the battle of Bentonville.

Coffin, Charles Carleton, 1823–1896. 83

Four years of fighting: a volume of personal observation with the army and navy, from the first battle of Bull Run to the fall of Richmond. By Charles Carleton Coffin ... Boston, Ticknor and Fields, 1866.

xv, ₍1₎, 558 p. front. (port.), illus., plates, plans. 22 cm.
Illustrations: Frontispiece, "Yours truly Charles Carleton Coffin" ₍Signature₎; "Shiloh Church"; "Mississippi School-House"; "Antietam"; "Sherman's Bummers"; "John Brown in Charleston"; "President Lincoln in Richmond."
Maps: (Plans of Battles) "Fredericksburg"; "Franklin's Attack" (Fredericksburg); "Chancellorsville"; "Sedgwick's Attack" (Chancellorsville); "Salem Church"; "Advance to Gettysburg"; "Wilderness"; "Spottsylvania"; "North Anna"; "Cold Harbor"; "Petersburg, July 17, 1864"; "Petersburg, July 30, 1864"; "Gettysburg Battle-Field."
Music: "Roll Jordan"; "Freedman's Battle-Hymn."
Inclusive dates: 1861–1865.
Other editions: Adding this phrase to his title, The boys of '61: or, ... this work went through at least three editions, 1881, 1885, 1896, published by Estes and Lauriat, in Boston, Mass. Another work covering this same period was his My days and nights on the battle-field. Boston, Dana Estes and co., 1887.

This work is first-rate, vivid travel reporting, though the author does not always make clear how he proceeded from one place to another. He wrote with imagination and artistry and viewed the scene with the eye of a traveler and a newspaper correspondent. Towns, hotels, people, their opinions, the country-side, slavery, all of these and many other subjects engaged Coffin's attention and his pen. He made no effort to write objectively; he hated slavery and everything connected with it. The author was born in New Hampshire, published many works on the war and other subjects, and came to be a well-known figure in his generation. In the war he moved rapidly from one area of military operations to another, always trying to be on hand for some important operation. His earliest activities were in Maryland around Annapolis, in Washington, and in northern Virginia around Alexandria and the Bull Run battlefield. He then hurried West and saw much that was going on in Missouri, and especially in Kentucky around Louisville, Frankfort, and Lexington. He was present in the operations through Tennessee following the capture of Fort Henry and Fort Donelson which culminated around Shiloh and Memphis. He moved eastward to Sharps-burg, Fredericksburg, Chancellorsville, and Gettysburg, and followed Grant on his campaign against Richmond. In the meantime Coffin made two trips to the South Atlantic areas of operations which took him to Port Royal, Savannah, and the attacks on Fort McAllister and Charleston. Again he was back in Vir-ginia, this time to be present at the fall of Richmond.

Cogley, Thomas Sydenham, 1840–   84

History of the Seventh Indiana cavalry volunteers, and the expeditions, campaigns, raids, marches, and battles of the armies with which it was con-nected, with biographical sketches of Brevet Major General John P. C. Shanks, and of Brevet Brig. Gen. Thomas M. Browne, and other officers of the regiment; with an account of the burning of the steamer Sultana on the Mississippi river, and of the capture, trial, conviction and execution of Dick Davis, the guerrilla. By Thomas S. Cogley ... Laporte, Ind., Herald company, printers, 1876.

> 2 p. l., v, ₍5₎–267 p.   front., illus., port.   18 cm.
> *Illustrations:* Frontispiece (Steel Engraving) "Thomas M. Browne" ₍Signature₎; "The Sul-tana"; "Major James H. Carpenter"; "Thomas S. Cogley."
> *Inclusive dates:* 1863–1865 ₍1866₎

The regiment was formed at Indianapolis in December, 1863, and proceeded by train to Cairo, where it boarded steamers for Columbus, Kentucky. Its first service was in western Kentucky and western Tennessee, in connection with raids and campaigns incident to Forrest's activities. It also fought southward into Mississippi and back again to Memphis, where it boarded boats for Vicks-burg and from that vicinity raided through Mississippi and Louisiana. Cogley was absent when his regiment made an expedition into Arkansas and Missouri in the latter part of 1864. For a time he was a prisoner in Mississippi but soon made his escape and wandered through that state until he reached the Federal lines at Holly Springs. Subsequently an expedition was started down the Mississippi to Bastrop, Louisiana, and thence up into Arkansas. Near the end of the war (again Cogley apparently was absent) the regiment went down the Mississippi and up the Red River to Alexandria, later marching across country to Hempstead, Texas, and on to Austin, where the unit was mustered out in February, 1866, and immediately left for Galveston to embark for New Orleans. This work has some interesting descriptions of the country through which the regiment marched, especially of the trip across Louisiana and into Texas; but most of that account was taken from a diary not written by Cogley.

Cole, Jacob Henry, 1847–   85

Under five commanders; or, A boy's experience with the Army of the Potomac. By Jacob H. Cole ... Paterson, N. J., News printing company, 1906.

ix p., 1 l., 253 p. incl., illus., plates, ports. 20 cm.
Illustrations: Frontispiece, "Jacob H. Cole"; and twenty-one other portraits and drawings.
Inclusive dates: 1861–1864.

As Cole was a mere boy of fourteen when he joined the Federal Army, as he kept no diary, and as he wrote this narrative forty years after the events described, it is mostly an old man's superficial story of dim recollections, written in a matter-of-fact style unembellished with thrilling deeds and heroic dialogues. The young New Yorker first joined Ellsworth's New York Fire Zouaves and marched into Alexandria with that unit, which gained its greatest distinction there through the death of Ellsworth in the Marshall House. When Cole's short term of enlistment expired, he returned to New York, joined the Fifty-seventh New York Volunteers, and remained in the service until September, 1864. He participated in most of the marching and fighting north of the James.

Collins, Elizabeth.   86

Memories of the southern states. By Elizabeth Collins ... Taunton, ₁Eng.₁ J. Barnicott, printer, 1865.

3 p. l., 116 p. 17½ cm.
Inclusive dates: 1859–1863.
Parallel accounts: For another narrative dealing with this same region, written by the "Mr. M—" in Miss Collins' book, see Rev. William Wyndham Malet, *An errand to the south in the summer of 1862,* included in this bibliography.

Elizabeth Collins, an English woman, came to South Carolina in 1859 to visit on a plantation owned by a South Carolinian with an English wife. She landed in Boston and went by railway to New York City, where she boarded a steamer for Charleston and continued by a coastal boat to Georgetown and up the Waccamaw to the plantation. From there she journeyed to Columbia. In the late summer of 1863 she left for England, going to Wilmington where she ran the blockade. Miss Collins was much interested in the slaves and the methods of running a plantation, giving at the end of her narrative "Rules and Management for the Plantation." Though realistic in her descriptions of slaves as well as of the white population, she was thoroughly sympathetic with the Confederacy and the Southern type of civilization.

Collins, R. M. 87

Chapters from the unwritten history of the war between the states; or, The incidents in the life of a Confederate soldier in camp, on the march, in the great battles, and in prison. By Lieut. R. M. Collins ... St. Louis, Nixon-Jones printing co., 1893.

335 p. front., illus. (incl. facsims.), port. 19 cm.
Illustrations: Frontispiece, "Yours Truly R. M. Collins" ₁Signature₁; "A. Faulkner Capt Comdg Co G 15th Texas Cavalry C S A"; and four sketches of scenes described in the narrative.
Inclusive dates: 1862–1865.

This narrative is well written, in excellent temper, often bordering on the humorous, and carefully conforming to established facts. It lists numerous incidents in the life of a Confederate soldier, with many comments on the character of the people along the author's journey. This work follows closely the form of a travel account, stating clearly the route taken and the mode of conveyance, whether walking or riding on train or steamer. Lieutenant Collins was born in East Tennessee and moved to Texas at an unstated time, settling in Decatur in the northern part of the state. Early in 1862 he joined the Confederate army and rose to the rank of lieutenant in the Fifteenth Texas Cavalry. He marched from Texas into Arkansas and operated up and down the Arkansas River around Little Rock and Pine Bluff. He was captured in the engagement at Arkansas Post, taken up the Mississippi to Alton, sent by rail through Cincinnati to Camp Chase in Columbus, Ohio, later transferred by rail to Fort Delaware on the Delaware River below Philadelphia, taken to City Point, Virginia, and exchanged. After visiting Richmond, he went by rail through East Tennessee to Tullahoma where he joined Bragg's Army, to take part in the Battle of Chickamauga and in the subsequent fighting around Chattanooga. In the spring of 1864 he fought with Johnston and later with Hood in Sherman's campaign against Atlanta. After the fall of that city he followed Hood to the gates of Nashville; after the defeat there he retreated into northern Mississippi and thence to Mobile, Montgomery, Macon, Augusta, Chester, South Carolina, and Raleigh to fight again under Johnston just prior to the surrender. He returned to Texas by marching through western North Carolina, passing through Asheville and down the French Broad River, and on to Greeneville, Tennessee, by train to Chattanooga and Nashville, by steamer down the Cumberland, the Ohio, and the Mississippi to New Orleans and Galveston, thence by train to the end of the track and completed the journey to Decatur in a buggy.

Conner, James, 1829–1883. 88

Letters of General James Conner, C.S.A. ₁Columbia, S. C., The State co., 1933₁

226 p. 24 cm.
Inclusive dates: 1861–1865.

A South Carolinian born in Charleston, a lawyer and an attorney general of South Carolina after the war, has given in this series of letters an excellent view of conditions in the Confederacy. He had no sympathy for the critical position assumed by Alexander H. Stephens and other opponents of the Davis administration. Conner began his service around Charleston but soon proceeded to Columbia and continued to the battlefields of Virginia, going by rail through Charlotte, Raleigh, and Petersburg. In the spring of 1862 he moved down to the Peninsula from his station in northern Virginia, to stop McClellan's march on Richmond. He was wounded in this campaign and remained about a year in the hospitals of Richmond. There are gaps in his letters from June, 1862 to April, 1863, and from May, 1863, to February, 1864. He opposed Grant in his march from the Wilderness to Petersburg. In the fall of 1864 Conner went to the Shenandoah Valley and at the Battle of Cedar Creek received a wound which prevented further service.

Conyngham, David Power, 1840–1883.   89

Sherman's march through the South. With sketches and incidents of the campaign. By Capt. David P. Conyngham. New York, Sheldon and co., 1865.

431 p. 18¼ cm.
Inclusive dates: Spring, 1864–May 23, 1865.

David P. Conyngham became a war correspondent of the *New York Herald* at the outbreak of the Civil War and served in the Virginia area before joining General Sherman's army in March, 1864, at Chattanooga. In addition to being a war correspondent, he served as volunteer aide-de-camp until the end of the war. He followed Sherman on his campaign through Georgia and the Carolinas and appeared in Washington at the "Grand Review." Though Sherman had no love or respect for the newspaper men, Conyngham admired "Uncle Billy" and found little to criticize throughout this account. Conyngham was not only interested in army movements and military affairs, which he describes fully, but was also concerned with the conditions of the people and the country through which he passed. He described the attitude of the civilians towards the war, and the reaction of the slaves toward their deliverers. He devoted considerable attention to the pillaging and devastation wrought by Sherman's army and described most realistically the horrors of war. In these respects, the work is notable among the many accounts of Sherman's march. Many long conversations are recorded that could hardly have been verbatim, and some hearsay is included.

Cook, Benjamin F., 1835–6?   90

History of the Twelfth Massachusetts volunteers (Webster regiment)

By Lieutenant-Colonel Benjamin F. Cook. Boston, Twelfth (Webster) regiment association, 1882.

167 p.   pl., 2 port. (incl. front.), fold. map (in pocket)   23 cm.
Illustrations: Two portraits of officers (unnamed) and a pen-and-ink sketch of the regimental camp.
Inclusive dates: 1861–1864.

This regiment, organized in Boston, traveled by the customary route—railway to Fall River, boat to New York City, and railway through Baltimore—and saw service first around Harpers Ferry. It participated in the principal campaigns of northern Virginia—Second Manassas, Fredericksburg, Chancellorsville—as well as in the Sharpsburg and Gettysburg battles. It also operated with Grant against Richmond until July, 1864, when its term of service expired. It was commanded by Fletcher Webster, son of Daniel, until his death at Second Manassas. Cook reached the rank of lieutenant colonel. He wrote the account from various diaries of his comrades, but apparently kept no records himself. His narrative is annalistic and choppy, being concerned mostly with the marches day by day. Yet he succeeds here and there in adding some color, with a tinge of travel consciousness, especially when he describes the sacking of a medical school and the theft of a skeleton.

Cook, Joel, 1842–1910.   91
The siege of Richmond: a narrative of the military operations of Major-General George B. McClellan during the months of May and June, 1862. By Joel Cook ... Philadelphia, G. W. Childs, 1862.

viii, 7–358 p.   18½ cm.
Inclusive dates: 1862.

As special correspondent of the *Philadelphia Press,* Joel Cook accompanied McClellan on his Peninsula expedition in 1862. He went by boat from Baltimore down the Chesapeake Bay to Fortress Monroe and thence up the Peninsula to the environs of Richmond. With unusual ability and keenness of observation, he describes the landscape, the rivers, the old mansions, the log cabins, the historic towns, and both white and black people. This work is highly valuable as a travel account in this restricted part of Virginia. Subsequently Cook wrote many books of travel.

Cooper, Alonzo, 1830–   92
In and out of rebel prisons. By Lieut. A. Cooper ... Oswego, N. Y., R. J. Oliphant, printer, 1888.

vii, [8]–335 p. incl. 10 pl., front. (port.)   22½ cm.
Illustrations: Frontispiece, "A Cooper" [Signature]; "The Cavalry Sent to Capture a Boat's Crew"; "Skirmishing at Macon, Ga."; "Capt. Irsh Bucked and Gagged"; "Capt. Alban on Police Duty"; "Fresh Fish"; "Tunnelling at Macon, Ga."; "Mr Cashmeyer's Sutler Wagon"; "Washing Clothes at Savannah, Ga."; "Escaped Prisoners Searching for the Road at Night";

"Pencil Sketch of Author." Some of these are crude redrawings (without credit being given) of illustrations which appeared in A. O. Abbott, Prison Life in the South ... (New York, 1865), which work is criticized in this bibliography.
Inclusive dates: April, 1864–February, 1865.

Writing twenty-five years after the Civil War, this author claims use of a diary kept during his prison days. Describing his disposition as happy and inclined to look always on the bright side of his experiences, he has omitted details of starvation and other horrors. Yet, with an eye to the politicians and larger pensions, he has included some choice atrocities. The feature distinguishing this from most travel books by prisoners of war is the long trip he took from the Columbia prison, through northwestern South Carolina, northeastern Georgia, and western North Carolina by way of Asheville eastward to the end of the railroad at Morganton, North Carolina, and by train to the Danville, Virginia, prison. He was a fugitive for the first part of the trip, where he found many Union people throughout that "deserter country," but was recaptured by Confederate authorities before he got out of Georgia. Born in Cayuga County, New York, and a merchant's clerk and trader before enlistment, he soon became a lieutenant in the Twelfth New York Cavalry. Taken prisoner at the fall of Plymouth, North Carolina, in April, 1864, he was sent by railway to the Macon, Georgia, prison and later transferred to the prisons at Savannah, Charleston, Columbia, and Danville. Near the end of the war he was removed to Richmond, sent down the James River to be exchanged, taken to Annapolis, and after a short furlough sent to Sherman's army, then about to receive the surrender of Johnston.

Copley, John M. 93

A sketch of the battle of Franklin, Tenn.; with reminiscences of Camp Douglas. By John M. Copley ... Austin, Tex., E. Von Boeckmann, printer, 1893.

206 p. plates. 17 cm.
Illustrations: Four highly imaginative sketches of scenes described in the narrative.
Inclusive dates: 1861–1865.

John Copley, born in Nashville, Tennessee, joined the Confederate Army as a fifteen-year-old boy. Thirty years after the events described he wrote this book. When Nashville was captured by the Federals in 1862 he was sick in a hospital there and was left behind by the Confederates. A short time later he escaped, rejoined his unit, and served until 1864. Until the fall of that year and Hood's invasion of Middle Tennessee he merely alludes to his activities in the war. In the Battle of Franklin, Copley was captured by the Federals and taken to Camp Douglas in Chicago by way of Nashville and Louisville. Most of this narrative relates to his experiences in prison, where he remained until the end of the war. Generally the book is of little value.

Copp, Elbridge J., 1844– 94

Reminiscences of the war of the rebellion, 1861–1865. By Col. Elbridge

J. Copp, the youngest commissioned officer in the Union army who rose from the ranks. Published by the author. Nashua, N. H., Printed by the Telegraph publishing company, 1911.

536, iv p. incl., illus., plates, ports.   front.   22½ cm.
Illustrations: About 169 illustrations, consisting of portraits of Union officers, battle scenes, drawings of torpedoes, army insignia, etc. Some of them are contemporary photographs and pen sketches. Most of them are clearly reproduced.
Maps: Various maps relating to the Beaufort region of South Carolina, the Charleston harbor and vicinity, Petersburg and Richmond. Clearly reproduced.
Inclusive dates: October, 1861–May, 1864.

Written almost half a century after the events, without the aid of a diary or contemporary documents and confessedly from memory and the "subconscious storehouse," this account is marked by vehemence and rancor toward the enemy. Copp served with New Hampshire troops from the first year of the war until he was wounded in 1864. He first went from Annapolis with the expedition which landed at Port Royal, South Carolina, in the fall of 1861. Later Copp took part in the reduction of Fort Pulaski on the Savannah River, and was in the long siege of Charleston from Morris and James islands. After a short vacation trip to Fernandina and St. Augustine, Florida, he took part in the Butler expedition around Bermuda Hundred and Petersburg, Virginia, in the summer of 1864. With a discount for bitterness, Copp's account has some value as a commentary on the slaves and white natives whom he saw in his travels.

Corby, William, 1833–1897.   95
Memoirs of chaplain life. By Very Rev. W. Corby, C.S.C. of Notre Dame University, Indiana. Three years chaplain in the famous Irish brigade, "Army of the Potomac." Notre Dame, Ind., "Scholastic" press, 1894.

391 p.   front., plates, ports.   19½ cm.
Illustrations: Sixteen illustrations, mostly portraits of Catholic priests.
Inclusive dates: 1861–1865.

A professor in Notre Dame University, Corby went to Washington when the war began and became chaplain in the New York Irish Brigade. Stationed first at Alexandria, he marched south to the old battlefield of Manassas. Returning he shipped to the Peninsula in the spring of 1862, and became a part of McClellan's forces assaulting Richmond. From that time to the end of the war he took part in the principal campaigns in the East. Corby was especially observant of historic sites and old homesteads. The narrative is not a well-constructed travelogue; here and there the author adds a chapter to defend and glorify the Catholic Church.

Corcoran, Michael, 1827–1863.   96
The captivity of General Corcoran. The only authentic and reliable narrative of the trials and sufferings endured, during his twelve months im-

prisonment in Richmond and other southern cities. By Brig.-General Michael Corcoran ... Philadelphia, Barclay & co., 1862.

1 p. I., ₁21₁–100 (i.e. 54) p., 3 p.   illus.   23½ cm.
Illustrations: Frontispiece, General Corcoran; and three imaginary sketches illustrative of incidents mentioned in the narrative.
Inclusive dates: 1861–1862.
Other editions: Another edition was printed by the same publishers at the same place in 1864.

Michael Corcoran, born in Ireland, became a commander of the Sixty-ninth New York Regiment at the outbreak of the Civil War. Captured at the First Battle of Manassas, he was taken to Richmond and imprisoned a short time before being moved to Castle Pinckney in Charleston harbor. He went by rail, passing through Petersburg and Wilmington. From Charleston he was removed to Columbia and then taken on to the prison in Salisbury, North Carolina. In 1862 he was returned to Richmond and later was exchanged at City Point. This narrative is much like other accounts of prisoners of war in Confederate hands. He was humiliated by being searched and robbed of all articles which his captors wanted; he marveled at the extreme hatred and discourtesies shown by the populace along his journeys from prison to prison; yet he found some people of gentlemanly instincts who showed him respect.

₁Corsan, W. C.₁   97
Two months in the Confederate States, including a visit to New Orleans under the domination of General Butler. By an English merchant. London, R. Bentley, 1863.

2 p. l., 299 p.   20 cm.
Inclusive dates: October–December, 1862.

This English merchant visited the Confederate States primarily to investigate the status of debts owed by Southerners to English and foreign merchants. He found no evidence of intention or desire to repudiate or evade the debts. Even the Confederate sequestration acts merely postponed payment. Landing at New York, Corsan took ship again for New Orleans, where he spent a few days before making his way through the lines across Lake Pontchartrain and going by railroad to Jackson, Mississippi, and on to Meridian and Mobile. From there he traveled by train to Montgomery, Atlanta, Augusta, Charleston, Wilmington, Petersburg, and Richmond, staying only a few days in each city. He was interested in the attitude of the people toward their new government, and found amazing loyalty everywhere. No one complained against the generals or the government. He found that people looked upon secession as a cure for their actual and fancied personal ills, and that, except for two or three individuals, the people had no desire ever to return to the United States government. There was no chance that the slaves would rise in servile insurrection, and their owners never feared such an eventuality. Strangely for an Englishman, he had no complaints to make against the institution of slavery; in fact, he gave it little space in his account. He predicted that the Confederacy could never be conquered, for it had all that was necessary for fighting the war. The region was turning rapidly to manufacturing, and it had reorganized its agriculture to the point where it could never be starved into submission. This account is thoroughly sympathetic with the Confederacy, and though the author gives realistic descriptions of the hardships of travel, he surprisingly refrains from complaints. As a close-up view of economic and social conditions in the Confederacy it is a reliable account.

Craft, David, 1832–1908. 98

History of the One hundred forty-first regiment, Pennsylvania volunteers, 1862–1865. By David Craft, chaplain ... Published by the author. Towanda, Pa., Reporter-journal printing company, 1885.

ix, 270, ₍4₎ p.   front., pl., port.   22 cm.
Illustrations: Four portraits of soldiers and a representation of regimental colors.
Inclusive dates: 1862–1863 ₍–1865₎

Craft, a chaplain in his regiment, left Harrisburg, Pennsylvania, in the autumn of 1862 for Washington and the area of operation in northern Virginia. He was discharged in February, 1863, on account of illness after being present at the Battle of Fredericksburg. Craft used diaries of various soldiers of the regiment in constructing his narrative, and continued the account to the end of the war. The latter part would, therefore, not be admissible as travel data, and there is little apart from military details in the volume. It was originally published in the Bradford, Pennsylvania, *Reporter.*

Crawford, J. Marshall. 99

Mosby and his men: a record of the adventures of that renowned partisan ranger, John S. Mosby, ⟨Colonel C. S. A.⟩ including the exploits of Smith, Chapman, Richards, Montjoy, Turner, Russell, Glasscock, and the men under them. By J. Marshall Crawford, of Company B. New York, G. W. Carleton & co.; ₍etc., etc.₎ 1867.

375 p.   front., port.   18½ cm.
Illustrations: Frontispiece, "John S. Mosby"; "A. E. Richards"; "Walter Frankland"; "Sam Alexander"; "William R. Smith"; "Thomas W. S. Richards"; "George Baylor"; "Alfred Glasscock."
Inclusive dates: 1861–1865.

For the most part this narrative is not personal to the author but it describes in some detail a trip Crawford made from Washington to Montgomery in 1861, and conditions in Richmond when he returned to that city upon its selection as the capital of the Confederacy. Crawford joined Mosby's band in 1863, and from then to the end of the war he details the many incidents of Mosby's operations in northern Virginia.

[Cronin, David Edward, 1839–   ]   100

The evolution of a life, described in the memoirs of Major Seth Eyland [pseud.] ... New York, S. W. Green's sons, 1884.

336 p.   map   19½ cm.
Maps: Plan of the battle of Darbytown Road.
Inclusive dates: April, 1861–April, 1865.

Though this book covers the life of "Major Eyland" up to the time it was written, the main part of it relates to his experiences and observations during his service in the Civil War. Born in Greenwich, New York, Cronin became an artist and spent some time in Europe before he joined a New York unit in April, 1861. He crossed the Potomac with the first contingent to invade Virginia, and was assigned to the army around Harpers Ferry. The chief significance and value of this account lies in descriptions of regions in southeast Virginia and northeast North Carolina, especially the Dismal Swamp, and of the occupation of Williamsburg on the Peninsula. Notable is his description of the depredations in the Governor John Page mansion there, in which he mentions the scattering and theft of the Page library, including many Jefferson letters, Washington documents, early Revolutionary files of the *Virginia Gazette,* and manuscript minutes of the secret sessions of the Continental Congress. While in the military service Cronin served as an artist for *Harper's Weekly.* During his stay at Williamsburg he was provost marshal. After the war he made a trip to Texas. This work is far more valuable than the average war memoir.

Croom, Wendell D.   101

The war-history of Company "C", (Beauregard volunteers) Sixth Georgia regiment, (infantry) with a graphic account of each member. Written by Wendell D. Croom ... and published by the survivors of the company. Fort Valley, Ga., Printed at the "Advertiser" office, 1879.

2 p. l., 37 p.   22½ cm.
Inclusive dates: 1861–1865.

This little pamphlet, by an untrained writer, is badly organized and the route he followed is not clearly designated. The narrative is chiefly valuable in showing the war enthusiasm in the Confederacy in the early days. Croom's unit, organized at Fort Valley, Georgia, went by rail to Atlanta and thence by an undesignated route to Yorktown, Virginia. He took part in the fighting up the Peninsula, at Second Manassas, and at Sharpsburg. He then went to Charleston, South Carolina, and on to Florida where he fought at Ocean Pond (Olustee), and in Virginia to the end of the war.

Crossley, William J.   102

Extracts from my diary, and from my experiences while boarding with Jefferson Davis, in three of his notorious hotels, in Richmond, Va., Tuscaloosa, Ala., and Salisbury, N. C., from July, 1861, to June, 1862. Being Sixth series, No. 4 of Personal narratives of events in the war of the rebellion, being papers read before the Rhode Island soldiers and sailors historical society. Providence, R. I., Published by the society, 1903.

49 p. 20 cm.
Inclusive dates: July, 1861–June, 1862.

Written many years after the Civil War, the narrative was based on and includes much of a diary kept by the author. Crossley, sergeant of Company C, Second Rhode Island Infantry, Volunteers, enlisted at the beginning of the war and was taken prisoner at the First Battle of Manassas. He was imprisoned in Libby for a few months, then sent to Tuscaloosa Prison in Alabama, by train through Petersburg, Wilmington, and Montgomery, and by steamboat down the Alabama to its confluence with the Tombigbee, ascending that river and into its tributary, the Black Warrior. After about three months he was returned as far as South Carolina by the same route, and was diverted to the railway leading through Columbia, Charlotte, and Raleigh. At Charlotte he was turned back to Salisbury Prison for two months before he was paroled and returned by rail through Raleigh and Goldsboro to the Federals in Washington, N. C. After reaching the Union lines Crossley was placed aboard a steamer for New York City. He was later exchanged in the Annapolis parole camp and upon parole, re-entered the army and fought to the war's end. This slight account is a valuable comment on Confederate railroads and travel, and a temperate account of prison life.

Cudworth, Warren Handel, d. 1883. 103

History of the First regiment (Massachusetts infantry), from the 25th of May, 1861, to the 25th of May, 1864; including brief references to the operations of the Army of the Potomac. By Warren H. Cudworth, chaplain of the regiment ... Boston, Walker, Fuller and co., 1866.

528 p. plates. 19 cm.
Illustrations: "The Sixth Massachusetts Regiment in Baltimore, April 19, 1861"; "The First Blunder at Bull Run"; "Assault on a Rebel Lunette"; "Battle of Williamsburg"; "Excitement in the Hospital at White Oak Swamp"; "Destruction of the Railroad Train"; "Care of the Wounded at Harrison's Landing"; "In the Woods at the Second Bull Run"; "Fight for the Bridge over Antietam Creek"; "Charge on the Heights at Fredericksburg"; "Capture of Fredericksburg Heights, during the Battle"; "Charge of the Rebels upon Cemetery Hill"; "On the Lookout, Wapping Heights"; "The Dead Soldier in Locust Grove"; "Cavalry Charge near Spottsylvania Court-House"; "Surrender of the Rebel Army to Gen. Grant."
Inclusive dates: 1861–1864.

Cudworth, chaplain of the First Massachusetts Regiment, saw all the scenes and events which he describes. Reliability of the narrative is enhanced by diaries of other members of the regiment. With characteristic intense ministerial feeling Cudworth bitterly hated slavery and Confederates, and his reports of slavery conditions and conversations with slaves became propaganda. Having an interest in history, he describes many of the old plantation homes and a few of the historic Virginia towns, especially Williamsburg, Fredericksburg, Warrenton, and Alexandria. Cudworth's regiment fought in most of the main battles from First Bull Run to Spottsylvania Courthouse of the eastern area. His enlistment terminated in the summer of 1864 and he was mustered out in Boston.

Cumming, Kate, 1835– 104

A journal of hospital life in the Confederate army of Tennessee, from the battle of Shiloh to the end of the war: with sketches of life and character, and brief notices of current events during that period. By Kate Cumming. Louisville, J. P. Morton & co.; New Orleans, W. Evelyn, [c.1866]

199, 1 p.   23 cm.
Inclusive dates: April 7, 1862–July, 1865.
Other editions: No other editions found, but the following work, written by her years after the war, practically amounts to another edition. It contains long extracts from the journal and in other parts is largely a more connected narrative which follows that source closely. Gleanings from Southland. Sketches of life and manners of the people of the South before, during and after the war of secession, with extracts from the author's Journal and an epitome of the new South. Birmingham, Roberts & son, 1895.

Kate Cumming was born in Scotland, but in infancy her family came to Mobile, Alabama, where she grew up. Though an intensely loyal Southerner, she never forgot her Scottish birth, and often referred to her native country though she could not remember it. At the outbreak of the Civil War a Mobile clergyman appealed for volunteers for Confederate hospitals, and Miss Cumming offered her services. She began her work in Corinth, Mississippi, following the battle of Shiloh and was almost constantly in hospital service to the end of the war. During this time she nursed the wounded in hospitals in Corinth, Okolona, Chattanooga, Dalton, Ringgold, Newnan, Griffin, and Americus. She describes with unusual realism hospital life and scenes, the horrors of amputations with consequent tubs of blood and heaps of arms and legs, pathetic cases of gangrene, the difficulties of securing proper food for patients, and frequent moving of hospitals to keep out of reach of the enemy. Although most of the journal refers to hospital experiences, she also describes her journeys back and forth between Mobile and the various hospitals. She found some prejudice among both doctors and many women of the Confederacy against women entering the hospital service. She felt that women generally were not doing their part to win the war, but mentions many instances in which women performed valiant services in both hospitals and other activities. As a realistic description of the Confederate hospital service, this journal is of first-rate importance.

Cunningham, John Lovell, 1840– 105

Three years with the Adirondack regiment, 118th New York volunteers infantry, from the diaries and other memoranda of John L. Cunningham, major 118th New York volunteers infantry, brevet lieutenant colonel United States volunteers. ₁Norwood, Mass., The Plimpton press₁, 1920.

v p., 1 l., 286 p.   front., plates, ports.   20½ cm.
Illustrations: Thirty portraits of soldiers.
Inclusive dates: 1862–1864.

This Federal soldier's travels were confined to Virginia and Maryland, principally around Harpers Ferry, the Norfolk-Suffolk region, and in the area of Petersburg and eastward. The regiment was organized at Plattsburg, New York, in 1862. Cunningham was mustered out of service in September, 1864, but he continues his narrative to the end of the war. Written when the author was eighty years old, the account is all in one piece, without chapter heads or other divisions. The use of a diary kept during the war greatly aided the old man's memory and gives validity to his account. Naturally it has little value as a travel narrative.

Curtis, Newton Martin, 1835–1910.   106

From Bull Run to Chancellorsville; the story of the Sixteenth New York infantry together with personal reminiscences by Newton Martin Curtis ... New York and London, G. P. Putnam's sons, 1906.

xix, 384 p.   4 port. (incl. front.)   22½ cm.
Illustrations: Frontispiece, "Newton Martin Curtis" ₁Signature₁ and three portraits of other soldiers.
Inclusive dates: 1861–1863.

As the title indicates, Curtis's area of military travel lay in Virginia with a dip into Maryland for the Sharpsburg campaign. He joined the Federal Army in Albany, New York, and reached northern Virginia by boat down the Hudson to New York City and thence by train. He was greatly impressed by the old, historic parts of Virginia, became acquainted with George Mason, descendant of the Revolutionary George, and was attracted equally by the old gentleman and his historic home. Curtis's interest in historic scenes led him to locate the spot on the Chickahominy where Pocahontas saved John Smith's life. The narrative is based on personal records and public documents, and indicates respect for the former enemy. Curtis was the author of other works and after the war became a member of the New York Assembly; he also served three terms in Congress.

Curtis, Orson Blair, 1841?–1901.   107

History of the Twenty-fourth Michigan of the Iron brigade, known as the Detroit and Wayne county regiment ... By O. B. Curtis ... Detroit, Mich., Winn & Hammond, 1891.

483 p. incl., illus. (incl. maps, plans) pl., ports.   front., col. pl.   24¼ om.
Illustrations: One hundred and fifty-four illustrations, consisting of maps, sketches of

battlefields, scenes in the South, and portraits of members of the regiment and of other Federal soldiers.

Inclusive dates: 1862–1865.

Curtis intermixed personal reminiscences, official documents, and personal letters in his story, which contains much material of a general historical nature and therefore is not strictly a travel account. Yet there are occasional notes on the journeys made by this brigade during the war. It was organized in Detroit in late summer, 1862, and moved by boat to Cleveland and by rail to Pittsburgh and Harrisburg. Apart from the Gettysburg and Sharpsburg campaigns and the return northward, the travels of this unit were entirely in Virginia at Fredericksburg, Chancellorsville, and in the principal battles of Grant's campaign against Richmond and Petersburg. Instead of returning to Detroit to be mustered out, it was detailed to Springfield, Illinois, where it was disbanded in 1865. There are some worthwhile comments on the country traversed and on the Confederate population.

Daly, Mrs. Louise Porter (Haskell), 1839–1910.   108

Alexander Cheves Haskell; the portrait of a man. By Louise Haskell Daly. Norwood, Mass., Privately printed at the Plimpton press, 1934.

viii p., 2 l., 224 p.   front., ports.   24 cm.

Illustrations: Frontispiece, Alexander Cheves Haskell "[1908]"; Alexander Cheves Haskell "[1861]"

Inclusive dates: 1861–1865.

This narrative is composed from letters Haskell wrote home during the war, and of half-century-old recollections. It deals mainly with family interests, but there are comments on his war experiences and on the attitude of the civilian population toward the war. He found that soldiers were led to desertion by letters from their relatives, as well as by what they learned on furloughs home. Haskell enlisted in a South Carolina company immediately after that state seceded, was present at the bombardment of Fort Sumter, and thereafter served through the main campaigns and engagements of the Army of Northern Virginia. Haskell was a grandson of Langdon Cheves.

Dame, William Meade, 1844 or–5   109

From the Rapidan to Richmond and the Spottsylvania campaign; a sketch in personal narration of the scenes a soldier saw. By William Meade Dame ... Baltimore, Green-Lucas company, 1920.

4 p. l., xi–xvi, 213 p.   3 ports. (incl. front.)   22¾ cm.

Illustrations: Frontispieces, "William Meade Dame. Private First Company of Richmond Howitzers, 1864" and "William Meade Dame, D. D., Rector Memorial Protestant Episcopal Church, Baltimore, Md., 1920."

Inclusive dates: 1864–1865.

This soldier's memoirs, written many years before publication, deal almost entirely with soldiers' life in the Army of Northern Virginia from the time it went into winter quarters on the Rapidan through the campaigns of the Wilderness, Spottsylvania, and Cold Harbor, to the final one at Appomattox. It includes only the most meager account of fighting south of the James, and occasional references to the countryside. Among incidents of army life are the capture of a pig in a farmyard, how the soldiers built their huts for winter quarters, how they instinctively embraced religion, the blood-curdling rebel yell, and how they fought and died in battle. After the war Dame studied theology and was for many years rector of an Episcopal church in Baltimore.

Dana, Charles Anderson, 1819–1897. 110

Recollections of the civil war, with the leaders at Washington and in the field in the sixties. By Charles A. Dana ... New York, D. Appleton and company, 1898.

xiii, 296 p. front. (port.) 21 cm.
Illustrations: Frontispiece, "C. A. Dana" ₍Signature₎
Inclusive dates: 1863–1865
Other editions: This work was reprinted in 1902 by the same publishers.

Charles A. Dana, well-known in history as newspaper editor and publicist, and as Assistant Secretary of War during Lincoln's administration, made various trips to the areas of military operations to report on Federal commanders. He said little about the routes he took, but made many comments on conditions, military and otherwise. As a result, his narrative is valuable as travel literature. While at Vicksburg he observed the gigantic dishonesty in the cotton trade being allowed by Federal authority. He also made trips to Chattanooga to report on Rosecrans in 1863, and later to the Shenandoah Valley and to Grant's field of operations against Richmond. Although Dana wrote this account some years after the war, he did not depend on memory alone but used much personal data recorded at the time, such as letters and reports, and thereby made the account dependable. Much of what went into this book was originally published in *McClure's Magazine,* in the *North American Review,* and elsewhere.

₍Daniel, Frederick S.₎ 111

Richmond howitzers in the war. Four years campaigning with the Army of northern Virginia. By a member of the company. Richmond, 1891.

155 p. 19 cm.
Inclusive dates: 1861–1865.

Daniel fought with his Confederate comrades throughout the war, his activities extending as far north as Gettysburg and as far south as Appomattox. Between these two points he engaged in most of the campaigns in Virginia and Maryland, outside of the Shenandoah Valley. The account is almost entirely of military affairs, with little comment on matters of travel.

Darby, George W.

Incidents and adventures in rebeldom; Libby, Belle-Isle, Salisbury. By Geo. W. Darby. Pittsburg ₍h₎, Pa., Press of Rawsthorne engraving & printing company, 1899.

1 p. l., ₍7₎–228 p.   front. (port.) illus. pl.   22½ cm.

Illustrations: Frontispiece, "Geo. W. Darby"; " 'The Specter of the Rebel Prison Hell' "; "Gaskell and the Ice Cream"; "Squawk"; "Manassas-Gap"; "Snakes"; "Sojer Fotch Back Dat Goose"; "Death of Sisler"; "Libby Prison—(After Photo.)"; "Belle Isle—(After Photo.)"; " 'Maddern Hell' "; "I'll Have You Hung For a Spy"; "Dead House of Hospital No. 21"; "Salisbury—(After Photo.)." Drawings by J. W. Rawsthorne.

Inclusive dates: April, 1861–March, 1865.

Distilled thirty-five years afterwards "from the vivid recollections of the events as they occured" (p. 8), this book was professedly written to show how barbarous the Confederates were in their treatment of prisoners, and to prove that General McClellan (consistently spelled McClelland) was a traitor to the North. Darby somewhat forgets his twin purposes as he proceeds, for he includes much good humor intermixed with profanity. Unlike many prisoner-of-war accounts, he does not make slaves into paragons of virtue and loyalty; instead he treats them with levity. Darby fought up and down through northern Virginia and at Sharpsburg and Gettysburg with a Pennsylvania unit called the Fayette Guard. In the summer of 1864 he was captured near Petersburg and was confined in Libby, Castle Thunder, and one of the Richmond hospitals, except during three escape journeys which always ended in recapture.

Davenport, Alfred.

Camp and field life of the Fifth New York volunteer infantry. (Duryee zouaves.) By Alfred Davenport. New York, Dick and Fitzgerald, 1879.

485 p.   front. (port.) pl.   18½ cm.

Illustrations: Frontispiece, "Francis Spelman" ₍Signature₎

Inclusive dates: 1861–1863.

Davenport's writing is unusual in that it gives details of travel and military operations on the eastern shore of Virginia, an area infrequently visited by Federal troops. Apart from this feature the narrative describes army movements in the customary field of action in Virginia; along the Peninsula in the first invasion of 1861, as well as the invasion of McClellan, Second Manassas, Sharpsburg, Fredericksburg, and Chancellorsville. After Chancellorsville the Fifth New York Volunteers returned to New York, and with this event Davenport ends the narrative. Although the book was written more than a dozen years after the war, the fresh descriptions suggest the use of diaries and personal letters in its composition; there is no mention of such material, but some letters are included in the text. The author gives considerable attention to the country and the people, including slaves, poor whites, and Virginia gentlemen.

Davidson, Henry M., d. 1900.

Fourteen months in southern prisons; being a narrative of the treatment of federal prisoners of war in the rebel military prisons of Richmond, Danville, Andersonville, Savannah, and Millen; describing the author's escape with two comrades, from Andersonville and the blood hounds; his adventures during a fourteen nights' march in the swamps of western Georgia, and his subsequent re-capture; to which is added a large list of those who have died in various prisons in the confederacy. By H. M. Davidson ... Milwaukee, Daily Wisconsin printing house, 1865.

viii, [9]–393 p. front. (fold. plan) 19¼ cm.

Maps: Folding plan, 7¼ by 8½ inches, "Andersonville Stockade, Showing Plan of Fortifications soon after Gen. Stoneman's Cavalry Raid upon Macon, August, 1864."

Inclusive dates: September, 1863–November, 1864.

Other editions: The same text with some additional paragraphs and other changes appeared as "Experience in rebel prisons for United States soldiers at Richmond, Danville, Andersonville, Savannah, and Millen," p. 149–398 in Asa B. Isham, Henry M. Davidson, and Henry B. Furness, Prisoners of war and military prisons. Personal narratives of experiences in the prisons at Richmond, Danville, Macon, Andersonville, Savannah, Millen, Charleston, and Columbia. With a general account of prison life and prisons in the South during the war of the rebellion, including statistical information pertaining to prisoners of war; together with a list of officers who were prisoners of war from January 1, 1864. Cincinnati, Lyman & Cushing, 1890. This reprint contains a picture of Davidson, the plan of Andersonville in the previously cited work, and thirty-nine other illustrations, some without captions. One of them is a picture of the Elmira, New York, prison to contrast with the Confederate prisons.

Henry Davidson originally intended his book to induce the Federal Government to benefit prisoners of war by effecting exchanges, but it appeared too late for that purpose. It might be assumed, therefore, that the author would paint as dark a picture as he could, and the book is sprinkled with enough horrors to add zest for Northern readers; yet it is a surprisingly well-tempered and straightforward account of the author's experiences in Confederate prisons and of his attempt to escape from Andersonville. A member of Battery A, First Ohio Volunteer Light Infantry, he was taken prisoner at the Battle of Chickamauga and hurried away to Libby Prison in Richmond, traveling by rail through Atlanta, Augusta, Columbia, Charlotte, Raleigh, Weldon, and Petersburg. He was sent to Danville for a short stay, returned over the same route as far as Augusta, and switched southward through Millen and Macon to Andersonville. From there he escaped through the Flint River swamps and pine woods to the outskirts of Atlanta, then held by Sherman, before he was recaptured and returned to Andersonville. Davidson was soon transferred to Savannah Prison, and then to Millen, where he was exchanged in November, 1864. He was observant of both the country and the people. Much of the narrative is devoted to his wanderings while trying to escape. As a dependable account of conditions in the Confederacy, it is far superior to other books of this type, and is surprisingly free from hackneyed stories of heroic slaves assisting prisoners of war to escape.

Davis, Charles E. 1842/3?–1915.   115

Three years in the army. The story of the Thirteenth Massachusetts volunteers from July 16, 1861, to August 1, 1864. By Charles E. Davis, jr. Boston, Estes and Lauriat, 1894.

xxxv, 476 p.   23¾ cm.
Maps: Seventeen maps indicating movements of the regiment.
Inclusive dates: 1861–1864.

Five diaries re-enforced with data from official documents form the basis for this composite book. It is notably a travelogue because it gives unusual attention to the country, to the people, to visiting among them, to their conversations, and to their attitude towards the Union; much more of this type of material than appears in most regimental histories. The regiment served entirely north of the James River, except for a crossing to City Point in the summer of 1864, shortly before the unit was disbanded.

Davis, Nicholas A.   116

The campaign from Texas to Maryland. By Rev. Nicholas A. Davis ... Richmond, Printed at the office of the Presbyterian committee of publication of the Confederate States, 1863.

165, [1] p.   2 port. (incl. front.)

This is an excellent comment on army life and travels by a member of Hood's Texas Brigade. Davis took great pains to describe realistically the march of his regiment, from its rendezvous at Buffalo Bayou near Houston to its arrival in Richmond in the summer of 1861. It went by train to Beaumont, by steamer to Niblett's Bluff on the Sabine, on foot across Louisiana to New Iberia, by steamer to Brashear City, by train to New Orleans, and on to Richmond by way of Knoxville; the route from Meridian to Chattanooga (through Montgomery and Atlanta, or Corinth) is not indicated. After reaching Richmond the brigade was sent to the Potomac for the winter of 1861–1862, but when McClellan advanced up the Peninsula toward Richmond, the Texans returned to the neighborhood of Yorktown and retreated back to Richmond before the Federals. Following McClellan's drive the regiment marched northward to the old battlefield of Manassas and participated in the second battle there. Thence it proceeded to Sharpsburg in Maryland and back across the Potomac. Davis, besides describing many incidents relative to these campaigns, gave interesting insights into conditions in the Confederate capital, especially those in the hospitals. This brief work is a valuable travel commentary.

Dawes, Rufus R., 1838–1899.   117

Service with the Sixth Wisconsin volunteers. By Rufus R. Dawes ... Marietta, O., E. R. Alderman & Sons, 1890.

2 p. l., v, [5]–330 p.   front. illus., port.   22 cm.
Illustrations: Nineteen portraits and four other illustrations.
Inclusive dates: 1861–1864.

This book is almost entirely a collection of letters and a diary written during the Civil War. The routes Dawes took are not always described, but his movements indicate the main lines of travel. The account is highly dependable but there are few travel notes among comments on military and family affairs. In 1861 he left Madison, Wisconsin, proceeded to Washington, and soon crossed the Potomac to participate in the principal battles in the eastern theater of war until his enlistment expired in the autumn of 1864. His routes of travel are indicated by his presence at Second Manassas, Sharpsburg, Fredericksburg, Chancellorsville, Gettysburg, Wilderness, Spottsylvania, Cold Harbor, and Petersburg.

Dawson, Mrs. Sarah (Morgan). 118

A Confederate girl's diary. By Sarah Morgan Dawson; with an introduction by Warrington Dawson, and with illustrations. Boston and New York, Houghton Mifflin company, 1913.

xviii, [1]–439, [3] p.   front. plates, ports., double facsim.   20¼ cm.
Illustrations: Frontispiece, "Sarah Fowler Morgan"; "Miriam Morgan"; "James Morris Morgan"; "Facsimile of a Page of the Diary"; "Sarah Fowler"; "Linwood"; "The Ante-Bellum Home of Judge Thomas Gibbes Morgan"; "Judge Thomas Gibbes Morgan."
Inclusive dates: March, 1862–June, 1865.

Sarah Morgan was one of nine children of Judge Thomas Gibbes Morgan of Baton Rouge, who died in November, 1861. When the war came his family was divided in allegiance. Sarah, strongly partisan to the Confederacy, was not unreasoning or bitter until after the pillaging of the Morgan home. After the capture of Baton Rouge by the Federals in 1862, she and other members of her family sought refuge in various plantation homes in the vicinity, and at Clinton. In 1863 she went around the east side of Lake Pontchartrain and crossed over to New Orleans, the home of a Unionist brother. This diary is written with keen intelligence, and is well-balanced in its statements. Naturally most of it is concerned with family associations and social activities, but there is also much that relates to both the spirit of the time and its author's reactions. This is one of the best war diaries relating to the Confederacy.

Day, Lewis W., 1839/40– 119

Story of the One hundred and first Ohio infantry. A memorial volume. By L. W. Day. Cleveland, W. M. Bayne printing co., 1894.

xiv, [15]–463 p. incl. illus., port. front.   20 cm.
Illustrations: Fifty-two portraits and four scenes.
Inclusive dates: 1862–1865.

Day enlisted in the Federal Army in August, 1862, at Galion, Ohio, and rose from corporal to sergeant. He was later detailed as a topographical engineer, and was discharged for disability in December, 1863. He wrote this account of his regiment thirty years after the war, basing it upon his memory, a few diaries by others, and official war records, and continuing the narrative to the end of the war. The work is less a travel book than a repetition of well-known facts about army movements and the life of an average Federal soldier. Before entraining through Indiana to Louisville the regiment was first stationed on the Kentucky side of the Ohio River across from Cincinnati. It took part in the Battle of Perryville and then followed Bragg's retreat out of Kentucky, going by way of Bowling Green to Nashville. At the end of 1862 the regiment participated in the Battle of Murfreesboro and in raids thereabouts before being involved at Chickamauga. In 1864 it engaged in the march on Atlanta, whence it headed northward to Chattanooga and Middle Tennessee to intercept Hood's attack on Nashville. After Hood's army was scattered the Ohioans moved through Huntsville, Alabama, and then through Chattanooga and Knoxville into western North Carolina, bent on heading off Confederate armies in North Carolina and Virginia. On the defeat of Lee and the surrender of Johnston, it returned by way of Chattanooga and Nashville to Ohio, where it was mustered out in the summer of 1865.

Day, Samuel Phillips. 120

Down South: or, An Englishman's experience at the seat of the American war. By Samuel Phillips Day, special correspondent of the Morning herald ... London, Hurst and Blackett, publishers, 1862.

Vol. I, x, 328 p.; Vol. II, vii, 327 p.   front. (port.)   19½ cm.

Illustrations: Vol. I, Frontispiece, Jefferson Davis (steel engraving); p. 314, flag of Culpepper Minute Men. Vol. II, Frontispiece, G. T. Beauregard (steel engraving).

Inclusive dates: June, 1861–September 21, 1861 (sailing from New York, October 12, 1861).

S. Phillips Day, an Englishman, came to the United States as correspondent for the London *Morning Herald* to report conditions North and South. He landed at New York and, being unable to go directly by railroad through Philadelphia, Baltimore, and Washington because of the interruption caused by the "Baltimore Massacre," he reached the South by way of Niagara Falls, across Canada to Detroit, and to Cincinnati. He went to Lexington, Kentucky, and thence to Nashville, presumably by Louisville, and on through Chattanooga, Knoxville, and Lynchburg to Richmond, where he spent most of his time. From this place he made trips to the seat of war in western Virginia, to the battlefield of Manassas, and down the James to Jamestown, Williamsburg, and Yorktown. He left by railroad from Richmond to Norfolk, embarked on a flag-of-truce boat to Fortress Monroe, went by steamer to Baltimore and by railway to Washington and direct to New York. His account is concerned almost wholly with the South, partly because he ran into trouble in Washington in his effort to secure a pass to visit the Federal armies. Day's sympathies were with the Confederates; he even defended slavery and registered no objections to the custom of chewing tobacco. He was thoroughly convinced that the Confederacy would win its independence and he hoped for immediate recognition by England and France. There are many digressions into historical details of the South, and much attention is given to Confederate armament and fortifications. Confederate civil authorities were generous, passes to scenes of conflict were easily obtained, and he was entertained by such commanders as Beauregard, Longstreet, and Magruder. Though not greatly concerned with social customs, the author gives fascinating insights into the life of the people during wartime. Except for some erroneous details and an intense Southern partisanship, Day gives a faithful account of what he saw. Besides being a newspaper reporter he was an author of some note, having written several books.

Day, William W. 121

Fifteen months in Dixie; or, My personal experience in rebel prisons. A story of the hardships, privations and sufferings of the "Boys in blue" during the late war of the rebellion. Owatonna, Minn., The People's press, 1889.

2 p. l., 80 p. 21 cm.
Inclusive dates: 1861–1864.
Other editions: The text of this work originally appeared serially in the *People's Press*, a newspaper published in Owatonna, Minnesota.

The author, a private in the Tenth Regiment Wisconsin Volunteer Infantry, joined the army in the fall of 1861. He left Milwaukee by rail for Evansville, Indiana, and went on to Louisville, to operate in Kentucky and Tennessee until September, 1863, when he was captured at the Battle of Chickamauga. As a prisoner of war he was held briefly at Atlanta and Richmond, and longer at Danville but, in keeping with the policy of the Confederacy to transfer as many prisoners as possible to Andersonville, Georgia, Day was sent by rail through Burkeville Junction, Petersburg, Weldon, Raleigh, Columbia, Branchville, South Carolina, and Macon. In 1864 he was moved to Charleston where he was paroled and turned over to the Federals at the outer rim of the harbor. He proceeded by steamer to Annapolis and Camp Parole and was given a furlough. This narrative was written about a quarter of a century later and apparently from memory, with no mention of a diary or contemporary letters. Day was still bitter toward his captors and jailors, yet he recorded numerous interesting observations on the country and the people of the Confederacy. He detested Georgia Crackers, but had a wholesome respect for South Carolinians, even though they had led the secession movement. Day's description of the battlefield of Chickamauga as it appeared a few weeks after the engagement is vivid. With an allowance for prisoner-of-war psychosis, this narrative may be accepted as a valuable commentary.

De Forest, Bartholomew S. 122

Random sketches and wandering thoughts; or, What I saw in camp, on the march, the bivouac, the battle field and hospital, while with the army in

Virginia, North and South Carolina, during the late rebellion. With a historical sketch of the second Oswego regiment, Eighty-first New York state V. I.; a record of all its officers, and a roster of its enlisted men; also an appendix. By B. S. De Forest ... Albany, Avery Herrick, 1866.

324 p.   pl.   19 cm.
Illustrations: "Ruins of the Old Episcopal Church, at Hampton, Va."; "Woodbine Cottage"; both signed "Ferguson."
Inclusive dates: September, 1862–September, 1864.

On August 26, 1862, De Forest became first lieutenant of the regiment, was promoted to regimental quartermaster on February 17, 1863, and was discharged on September 19, 1864, for physical disability incurred in service. In September, 1862, in charge of 118 men, he joined the regiment at Yorktown, Virginia, as part of the Army of the Potomac. After seeing service on the Yorktown Peninsula and around Norfolk the regiment was sent to Beaufort, North Carolina, later to Beaufort, South Carolina, and back to Beaufort, North Carolina, visiting Newbern, Wilmington, and Winton. It was then returned to the Norfolk region where it made further raids into the hinterland. The account is concerned mostly with descriptions of the places visited, with little comment on the people of the South. Holding that the slaves were inferior beings who seemed to be pretty well satisfied with their servitude, he had little respect for them. De Forest indicated becoming patriotism toward the cause for which he was fighting without portraying bitterness toward the foe. This account is more valuable for its descriptions of places than of people or conditions.

De Leon, Thomas Cooper, 1839–1914. 123

Four years in Rebel capitals: an inside view of life in the southern confederacy, from birth to death. From original notes, collated in the years 1861 to 1865, by T. C. De Leon ... Mobile, Ala., The Gossip printing company, 1890.

6, viii, 11–376 p.   21¾ cm.
Inclusive dates: 1861–1865.
Other editions: The same publishers issued an edition in 1892.

De Leon spent most of the war years in Richmond, but his travels and comments warrant consideration. When the secession movement began De Leon was in Washington, but when delegates met in Montgomery to organize a central Confederate government he went to that city and also visited New Orleans and Pensacola. When the Southern capital was moved to Richmond he followed the government there. Writing years after the war, but from notes kept during the struggle, the author gave his account maturity of judgment, comprehensiveness, and perspective. De Leon was much interested in people and personalities and has much to say on such subjects and on the life in general of which he was a part. Though not hypercritical, this work shows the seams that developed early in the Confederacy and eventually led to its downfall. De Leon wrote various other books, of both fact and fiction, dealing mostly with the Civil War. Born in Columbia, South Carolina, he was educated at Georgetown University in Washington. After the war he was engaged, among other activities, in editing the *Mobile Register*.

Derby, William P. 124

Bearing arms in the Twenty-seventh Massachusetts regiment of volunteer infantry during the civil war, 1861–1865. By W. P. Derby. Boston, Wright & Potter printing company, 1883.

xvi, 607 p. front., port., maps. 23 cm.
Illustrations: Frontispiece, "A. E. Burnside" [Signature]; "J. G. Foster" [Signature]; "H. C. Lee" [Signature]. All are steel engravings.
Maps: "Plan of the Battle of Newbern, N. C."; "Dept. of North Carolina"; "Topographical Map of Newbern, N. C."; "Washington, N. C., during the seige of 1863"; "Map of Bermuda Hundred and Vicinity"; "Battle-field of Drewry's Bluff, May 16, 1864"; "Gum Swamp N. C. and Vicinity."
Inclusive dates: 1861–[1864] 1865.

William Derby's carefully written account may be considered dependable despite the facts that it was produced fifteen years after the war and describes some events subsequent to his mustering out in September, 1864. He was a private in Company A of the Twenty-seventh Regiment, which was organized at Springfield, Massachusetts, in 1861 and proceeded by railroad to Hudson, New York, by steamer to New York City, and by rail to Annapolis, where it joined Burnside's expedition for Roanoke Island. It operated in eastern North Carolina until 1864 and among the towns captured or visited were Newbern, Washington, Tarboro, Plymouth, and Edenton. In 1864 the regiment was transferred to Newport News and thereafter took part in activities around Richmond and Petersburg. The account gives interesting glimpses of landscapes in the regions traversed as well as of characteristics of the people, and is frank in descriptions of pillaging.

Dicey, Edward James Stephen, 1832–1911. 125

Six months in the federal states. By Edward Dicey ... London and Cambridge, Macmillan and co., 1863.

Vol. I, x, 310 p.; Vol. II, vi, 326 p. 18¾ cm.
Inclusive dates: January–June, 1862.

Edward Dicey was an English author and journalist, born in Leicestershire in 1832, and educated at Trinity College, Cambridge. He was associated with the *Daily Telegraph* in 1861, but on his trip to America he was the special correspondent of *Macmillan's Magazine* and the *Spectator*. Portions of his American account appeared in the pages of these periodicals before being published with additions in book form. He was a good observer, but his characteristic English dislike of slavery colored his observations. He spent most of his time in the North, making direct acquaintanceship with slave states through visits along the border. He made a trip to the battlefield of Manassas soon after the Confederates evacuated it in early 1862, journeyed over the Baltimore and Ohio Railroad from Washington to Wheeling and Cincinnati, and by steamer on the Ohio to Louisville, continuing as far south as Nashville and dipping into Missouri to see St. Louis. The account is valuable for his comments on that part of the South which lay within the Federal lines. Wherever he saw slavery he saw dirt and decay, and only in St. Louis, where there was less slavery, did he see much to commend.

Dickert, D. Augustus. 126

History of Kershaw's brigade, with complete roll of companies, biographical sketches, incidents, anecdotes, etc. By D. Augustus Dickert. Introduction by Associate Justice Y. J. Pope. Newberry, S. C., Elbert H. Aull company, 1899.

583, 5, 2 p. front., ports. 22½ cm.
Inclusive dates: 1861–1865.

It is a well-written narrative, notably concerned with the atmosphere of army life, visits with the civilian population, and descriptions of interesting points on the line of march. Kershaw's Brigade was organized in South Carolina at the outbreak of the war and fought to the end. After its first service around Charleston, it entrained for northern Virginia and arrived in time to participate in the First Battle of Manassas. Thereafter this brigade went the full rounds of service in Virginia, including the two invasions across the Potomac which resulted in Sharpsburg and Gettysburg. In the fall of 1863 it was transferred to Georgia, reached the Chattanooga region about the time of the Battle of Chickamauga, and went on into East Tennessee where it wintered. In the spring it joined Lee in his campaign against Grant. Near the end of the war this brigade was sent back to South Carolina where it met Sherman below Columbia, retreated into North Carolina, and surrendered to Sherman near Durham Station. Writing about a third of a century after the war, Dickert was somewhat garrulous, but there is no reason to believe that he embellished the story beyond the general outlines of established truth.

Dodge, William Sumner. 127

A waif of the war; or, The history of the Seventy-fifth Illinois infantry, embracing the entire campaigns of the Army of the Cumberland. By Wm. Sumner Dodge ... Chicago, Church & Goodman, 1866.

vii, [17]–241, [1] p. 21 cm.
Inclusive dates: 1862–1865.

In 1862 Dodge left Chicago for Louisville to help stop Bragg's invasion of Kentucky. As the Confederates retreated, he followed them to Murfreesboro, later engaged in the Chattanooga-Chickamauga campaign, and still later in

1864 fought with Sherman's army as far as Atlanta. He returned northward after the fall of that city to engage in the campaign against Hood, which resulted in the battles of Franklin and Nashville. Dodge was not a member of the regiment whose history he writes, but he was in the same army, and his rather meager observations and comments on conditions in the Confederacy are valid travel material.

Dornblaser, Thomas Franklin, 1841–   128

Sabre strokes of the Pennsylvania dragoons, in the war of 1861–1865. Interspersed with personal reminiscences. By T. F. Dornblaser ... Published for the author. Philadelphia, Lutheran publication society, 1884.

viii, 9–264 p.   fold. map.   18½ cm.
Maps: Southeastern United States (not contemporary with the Civil War) 6½ by 8½ inches.
Inclusive dates: 1861–1865.

The scene of operations in which Dornblaser participated lay in the western area of the war, with service in Kentucky, Tennessee, Georgia, and Alabama. The author boarded a steamer in Pittsburgh, went down the Ohio River to Louisville, and soon was marching south to Bardstown, continuing to Nashville early in 1862 when the Confederates were being driven southward. He operated in central Tennessee for a time in fruitless efforts to trap Morgan and his men. In the fall of 1863 he fought in the Battle of Chickamauga, in the following spring participated in Sherman's march on Atlanta, and retreated into Tennessee after the fall of Atlanta to fight Hood's army on the outskirts of Nashville. In the spring of 1865 he went to Eastport, Mississippi, and joined in Wilson's raid through Alabama to Columbus and Macon, Georgia. He was part of the forces scouring the country south of Macon in search of President Davis and was present at his capture. In August he returned by rail through Atlanta, Chattanooga, Nashville, and Louisville to Harrisburg, Pennsylvania. Dornblaser wrote this narrative almost twenty years after the war, "principally from memory" but somewhat from diaries and letters of the war period. He indicated no bitterness against the Confederates, and showed no relish for freeing the slaves. All Confederate prisoners whom he interviewed informed him they were fighting for the independence of the South, not for slavery. Strangely differing from so many other Union soldiers who wrote war narratives, Dornblaser found slaves who preferred to remain with their masters because they had been kindly treated. He did not relish foraging and pillaging, but sometimes was forced by circumstances to engage in them.

Dougherty, Michael   129

Prison diary, of Michael Dougherty, late Co. B, 13th., Pa., cavalry. While confined in Pemberton, Barrett's, Libby, Andersonville and other southern prisons. Sole survivor of 127 of his regiment captured the same time, 122 dying in Andersonville. Bristol, Pa., C. A. Dougherty, printer, 1908.

2 p. l., 75, [1] p.   front. (port.)   19½ cm.
Illustrations: Frontispiece, "Michael Dougherty."
Inclusive dates: 1863–1865.

Though Dougherty moved around extensively in the Confederacy, most of his narrative is devoted to conditions in the prisons where he was held. This work, therefore, is of little value as a travel account. Dougherty shows the customary bitterness towards the prison authorities and holds them directly responsible for the many deaths which took place. Written as a diary, though evidently amended later, this work has the freshness of a contemporary account. Dougherty was captured near Winchester, Virginia, in the fall of 1863 and spent the rest of the war in prison. He was first taken to Richmond and held at one time or another in most of the prisons there. He was later removed to Andersonville Prison, in Georgia, going by way of Raleigh, Branchville, South Carolina, and Macon. At the end of the war he was turned over to Federal authorities and was moved across Alabama and Mississippi where he took passage on the ill-fated *Sultana*. He was miraculously saved in this disaster on the Mississippi north of Memphis, and was taken first to Annapolis and then to Philadelphia.

Dowling, Morgan E. 130

Southern prisons; or, Josie the heroine of Florence. Four years of battle and imprisonment. Richmond, Atlanta, Belle Isle, Andersonville and Florence, a complete history of all southern prisons, embracing a thrilling episode of romance and love. Detroit, William Graham, 1870.

xii, [13]–506 p.   16 pl., 2 port. (inc. front.)   21¼ cm.
Illustrations: Frontispiece, "Morgan E. Dowling (Lith. of P. Heppenheimer & Co., 22 & 24 N. Wm. St., N. Y.)"; "Charge of the Seventeenth Michigan at South Mountain (By Earl, Detroit)"; "My Capture (By Earl)"; "Belle Isle (By Earl, Detroit)"; "The Old Flag in Sight (By Earl, Detroit)"; "Interior View of Andersonville (By Earl, Detroit)"; "Our Conflict with the Guard (By Earl, Detroit)"; "The Graveyard at Andersonville (By Earl, Detroit)"; "The Dead Line (By Earl)"; "Photographs of Horror (By Earl)"; "The Spread-Eagle Stocks (By Earl)"; "Our Meeting (By Earl, Detroit)"; "Miss Josie Seymour (Lith. of P. Heppenheimer & Co., 22 & 24 N. Wm. St., N. Y.)"; "Horseback Excursion (By Earl, Detroit)"; "Josie's Intercession (By Earl, Detroit)"; "My Re-Capture (By Earl)"; "My Parole Withdrawn (By Earl)"; "Josie's Death (By Earl, Detroit)."
Inclusive dates: August, 1862–December, 1864.

In addition to being another "true story" of prison life in the Confederacy, this account has an unusual element of romance. As incongruous as romance and barbarism are, this book plays on each to its fullest limits, claims to be the first "full and correct account of the sufferings of the private Union soldiers in the rebel prisons" (p. 14), and expresses the hope that it will become "a standard authority upon the dark, but all-absorbing subject" (p. 16). Dowling enlisted at Detroit in 1862 in the Seventeenth Michigan Volunteers and saw service in Kentucky. He was present in Grant's Vicksburg campaign, and in November, 1863, was taken prisoner in the vicinity of Knoxville, having previously become a member of Burnside's forces which had marched from Cincinnati into East

Tennessee. Most of the account relates to happenings between this point and the author's ultimate exchange at Florence, South Carolina, in December, 1864. Dowling was first imprisoned in Atlanta, where he met Josie Seymour, the daughter of a South Carolinian who lived near Florence. This Union-loving offspring of a bitter rebel followed Dowling to Andersonville where he spent the major part of his prison life, and thence to Florence. Dowling made six escapes in all, but was recaptured in every attempt. The volume cannot be wholly ignored as a comment on wartime travel in the Confederacy, though it is peppered with many improbabilities and is marred by extreme bitterness and bias. Dowling claims to have run into a secret Union society in South Carolina known as the Union League, with a membership scattered all over the Confederacy.

Downs, Edward C., *ed.* 131

Four years a scout and spy. "General Bunker," one of Lieut. General Grant's most daring and successful scouts. Being a narrative of the thrilling adventures, narrow escapes, noble daring, and amusing incidents in the experience of Corporal Ruggles during four years' service as a scout and spy for the federal army; embracing his services for twelve of the most distinguished generals in the U. S. army. By E. C. Downs ... Zanesville, O., Hugh Dunne, 1866.

xii, 5–404 p. incl. plates, front. (port.) 22 cm.
Illustrations: Frontispiece, "General Bunker" and four other crude line drawings.
Inclusive dates: 1861–1865.
Other editions: Third revised edition: The great American scout and spy, "General Bunker." A truthful and thrilling narrative of adventures and narrow escapes in the enemy's country. New York, Olmsted & Welwood, 1868. Another printing in 1870, by the same publishers: Perils of scout-life; or, exploits and adventures of a government scout and spy in our great rebellion. New York, M. L. Byrn, 1873. This edition is by "C. L. Ruggles."

Although it has all the earmarks of a tall tale, there is sufficient proof that the narrative is not fabricated "out of whole cloth," for Ruggles undoubtedly belonged to the Federal Army and acted as a scout and spy. In a short introduction about his earlier life this Ohio-born rover reviews his activities as a shingle and lumber cutter in Arkansas. Across the river in Mississippi he hunted bears and wild hogs. He joined an Ohio unit in the latter part of 1861, met many generals on both sides of the struggle, and once talked with Jefferson Davis in Jackson, Mississippi, and with high Federal officials in Washington. He posed as a spy for both sides, assuming a guise to fit prevailing circumstances, and lived through many hairbreadth escapes, arrests, and trials, including a sentence or two which called for his execution. He operated in Mississippi and west Tennessee for the most part, but before the war was over he had made a trip to Washington and City Point, participated in Sherman's march to the sea, and taken a horseback ride from Savannah to Mobile. Before he was mustered out near the end of 1865, he had been to New Orleans, made a landing at Galveston, Texas, and ridden hundreds of miles into the interior to see whether all the

Confederates had surrendered. Grains of truth may be garnered from this grandiloquent narrative, such as glimpses of the country through which the author passed, of the people he met, of trading in cotton with the enemy, and of the devastations of war.

Drake, James Madison, 1837–1913. 132

Fast and loose in Dixie. An unprejudiced narrative of personal experience as a prisoner of war at Libby, Macon, Savannah, and Charleston, with an account of a desperate leap from a moving train of cars, a weary tramp of forty-five days through swamps and mountains, places and people visited, etc., etc. By J. Madison Drake ... New York, The Authors' publishing company, 1880.

x, ₍11₎–310 p. incl. front., plates, ports. 19 cm.

Illustrations: Frontispiece, "Your ob't serv't, J. Madison Drake" ₍Signature₎; "Prison Yard at Savannah"; "Yours Truly J. E. Lewis" ₍Signature₎; "A Leap for Liberty"; "Yours truly S. B. Ryder" ₍Signature₎; "Fed by Darkies"; "Meeting with a Confederate General"; "Meeting with Deserters"; "Crossing the Blue Ridge Mountains"; "Crossing the Chuckey River"; "Entering the Lines at Knoxville"; "William Estes" ₍Signature₎.

Inclusive dates: May–December, 1864.

Other editions: This book is an extension of an account of 93 pages which he published in 1868 (place not given) under the title: Narrative of the capture, imprisonment and escape of J. Madison Drake, captain Ninth New Jersey veteran volunteers ... Parts of his 1880 edition were previously published in Harper's weekly, Philadelphia times, Newark advertiser, and Albany press.

This author was mostly concerned with his escapes from a moving train out of Charleston and his subsequent wanderings northward through South Carolina and into North Carolina near Charlotte. From Charlotte he moved northwestward along the Western North Carolina Railroad to a point near Morganton and across the Catawba River into Caldwell County, thence through the Appalachians by way of Grandfather Mountain into East Tennessee to enter the Union lines at Knoxville. Drake continued southward to Chattanooga and to Nashville, Louisville and Washington. During this long trip he was constantly befriended by deserters and Union-loving Southerners. The book is almost free from bitterness and contempt for the enemy, but its reliability is greatly marred by embellished details of marches, alarms, and hairbreadth escapes. Besides the tall tales, he makes such mistakes as having General Sherman marching into Augusta, Georgia. Aside from these faults, the account is valuable as depicting the viewpoint of people in the "deserter country" of western North Carolina and East Tennessee. Drake, born in New Jersey, worked on various newspapers before the war. He joined the Federal forces and became Captain of the Ninth New Jersey Veteran Volunteers, was taken prisoner near Richmond in May, 1864, was incarcerated in Macon and Charleston after a short stay in Libby Prison, and was being transferred to Columbia when he escaped.

Opening of the Mississippi; or Two year's campaigning in the Southwest. A record of the campaigns, sieges, actions and marches in which the
8th Wisconsin volunteers have participated. Together with correspondence,
by a non-commissioned officer. Madison, Wis., Wm. J. Park & co., printers,
1864.

> 149, [1] p.   20 cm.
> *Inclusive dates:* 1861–1863.

This short travelogue, by a member of the Eighth Wisconsin Volunteers, is
based on numerous letters, presumably written to some newspaper, which sup-
plement the narrative sketch to make a remarkably interesting and valuable
commentary on the country and its people. The writing is somewhat humorous and "smart," but there is little bias or bitterness. He left Camp Randall at
Madison in 1861 for St. Louis, going by rail. Soon he was deep in southeastern
Missouri, skirmishing with the Confederates at Pilot Knob, Sulphur Springs,
Greenville, and other places. Returning to St. Louis he went to Cairo, Illinois,
and operated down the Mississippi as far as Island No. 10, but soon after the
fall of Forts Henry and Donelson he went up the Tennessee to Shiloh and was
active for some time in northern Mississippi, going southward to Oxford, in
northern Alabama to Tuscumbia, and in western Tennessee. Driggs then went
down the Mississippi and finally arrived in the vicinity of Vicksburg, around
which place he operated in both Louisiana and Mississippi until the fall of the
city.

Dufur, Simon Miltimore, 1843–   134

Over the dead line; or, Tracked by blood-hounds; giving the author's
personal experience during eleven months that he was confined in Pemberton, Libby, Belle Island, Andersonville, Ga., and Florence, S. C., as a prisoner of war. Describing plans of escape and recapture; with numerous and
varied incidents and anecdotes of his prison life. By S. M. Dufur ... [Burling-
ton, Vt., Printed by Free press association, 1902]

> viii, 283 p.   front. (port.)   21 cm.
> *Illustrations:* Frontispieces, "S. M. Dufur at 19" and "S. M. Dufur at 59."
> *Inclusive dates:* 1864–1865.

There is little travel value or reliability in this account. Dufur, a member of
the First Vermont Cavalry, was taken prisoner near Richmond while on the
famous Dahlgren raid in early 1864, and was held in three different prisons
(Pemberton, Libby, and Belle Isle) before being taken to Andersonville, Georgia.
The route he outlines was evidently constructed from memory or imagination,
for he could not have gone by railway through Danville and Atlanta in March,
1864, as he says he did. Though he claims to have used a diary, there is no evi
dence except a few easily improvised entries at the beginning of his captivity.

His experiences in Andersonville read like many others, and his route after leaving there in the fall of 1864 is the familiar one through Savannah and Charleston to Florence. There he made the usual escape and was chased by the inevitable bloodhounds, but not before he had been tenderly cared for by the slaves. In early 1865 he was sent to Charleston and turned over to the Federals, who took him aboard a ship waiting outside the harbor and sent him to Annapolis.

Dugan, James, *corporal 14th Ill. infantry*. 135

History of Hurlbut's fighting Fourth division: and especially the marches, toils, privations, adventures, skirmishes and battles of the Fourteenth Illinois infantry; together with camp-scenes, ancedotes, battle-incidents; also a description of the towns, cities, and countries, through which their marches have extended since the commencement of the war; to which is added official reports of the battles in which they were engaged; with portraits of many distinguished officers. By James Dugan ... Cincinnati, E. Morgan & co., 1863.

viii, 9–265 p.   front. port.   19 cm.
Illustrations: Three portraits of soldiers.
Inclusive dates: 1861–1863.

Traveling as a Federal soldier James Dugan remained entirely inside the Mississippi Valley. He joined the army in 1861 and soon left Jacksonville, Illinois, for the field of operations in Missouri. Reaching Hannibal by rail, he moved around the state, touching Canton, Macon, St. Charles, St. Louis, Rolla, Jefferson City, and Springfield. He left Missouri by boat for fighting in northern Mississippi, passing through Cairo and up the Ohio and Cumberland rivers to Fort Donelson, across country to Fort Henry on the Tennessee, and up this river to Shiloh. In Mississippi and western Tennessee he passed through many places, among which were Corinth, Holly Springs, Oxford, Memphis, and Bolivar. Dugan produced a first-rate travel account, as by one looking for interesting things to record rather than for a shot at the enemy. He appears to have been more a wide-awake traveler on a lark than a fighting soldier. He describes people, places, and interesting characters; and he found no Unionism in the Confederacy. He wrote in a light-hearted and frank fashion, admitting that his book was not only intended to amuse but also to make some money if possible. He claimed to have composed most of the narrative while in camp.

Duganne, Augustine Joseph Hickey, 1823–1884. 136

Camps and prisons. Twenty months in the department of the Gulf. By A. J. H. Duganne ... New York, J. F. Robens, publisher, 1865.

424 p.   front., pl.   18¼ cm.
Illustrations: Frontispiece, "Camp Groce"; "Quartermasters Grave"; "My Real Estate";

"Washington, His Tomb"; "Lt. Collins and the Bloodhounds"; "Punishment of Capt. Reed"; "Camp Ford."

Inclusive dates: June, 1863–July, 1864.

It is a well written, observant account of conditions in the Federal Army, in Confederate prisons, and in the countryside of Louisiana and Texas. Duganne was an author of some reputation before he became a lieutenant colonel of the 176th New York Volunteers. He entered Louisiana by way of the Mississippi River after Butler's departure and was active west of New Orleans in the Teche country. In June, 1863, he was captured at the fall of Brashear City, and marched across southern Louisiana to the Sabine River, sent by steamer to Beaumont, and by rail to Houston and Camp Groce near Hempstead. After some months he was transferred to Camp Ford, near Tyler, Texas, and in July, 1864, was exchanged at the mouth of the Red River, after traveling by horseback from Marshall, by rail to the end of the line twenty miles away, on foot to Shreveport, and thence by steamer. Duganne wrote with reserve and discernment, describing the sugar country of Louisiana and the system of labor contracts developed there by the Federal agents, the beauties of the country, the peculiarities of Cajuns and the splendor of rich sugar planters, the plains and characteristics of Texas and Texans, a stagecoach trip with a talkative Texan driver, and prison life in the two camps where he was incarcerated. The book is a first-rate travel account by a Boston-born author who also wrote histories, novels (including some Beadle numbers), poems, satires, and studies of governments.

Duke, John K. 1844–   137

History of the Fifty-third regiment Ohio volunteer infantry, during the war of the rebellion, 1861 to 1865. Together with more than thirty personal sketches of officers and men. By John K. Duke, company F, Fifty-third O. V. V. I. Portsmouth, O., The Blade printing company, 1900.

4 p. l., 303, ₁l₁ p.   front., plates, ports.   21 cm.

Illustrations: Forty-one illustrations, principally portraits of officers and men of the regiment.
Inclusive dates: 1861–1865.

A work of little value, written thirty-five years after the events described, and containing a few excerpts from an unidentified diary. A sketch of the author, written by another person, states that Duke joined the Fifty-third Regiment early in 1864, though he frequently used "we" and "I" in the narrative prior to 1864. Additional evidence indicates that Duke joined the regiment at its formation in 1861, for there is a picture of him as a soldier boy of seventeen, and he was born in 1844. This regiment was formed at Jackson, Ohio, but it did not leave camp until early in 1862, embarking on a river steamer at Portsmouth, and proceeding down the Ohio and up the Tennessee to the battle area of Shiloh. It then marched on to Corinth and Memphis and thence across Mississippi to Vicksburg. After the fall of that city, it moved by steamer to Memphis, marched through Tennessee to Chattanooga, and after the Battle of Chickamauga to Knoxville for defense against Longstreet. The next spring (1864) it took part in Sherman's march on Atlanta, moved on to Savannah and up through the Carolinas to force the surrender of Johnston in April, 1865, and then marched to Washington to participate in the "Grand Review." Afterwards the regiment entrained for Parkersburg, transferred to a river steamer, and proceeded by the Ohio, Mississippi, and Arkansas rivers to Little Rock to be mustered out in August.

Dunaway, Wayland Fuller. 138

Reminiscences of a Rebel. By the Rev. Wayland Fuller Dunaway, formerly captain of Co. I, 40th Va. regt., Army of northern Virginia ... New York, The Neale publishing company, 1913.

133 p. 18¾ cm.
Inclusive dates: 1861–1865.

These even-tempered reminiscences of a Confederate soldier are so brief that they avoid the unreliability of more detailed narratives, but add nothing to a general understanding of conditions in the Confederacy. Dunaway was a student at the University of Virginia when the war began, immediately enlisted, and ultimately became a captain in the Fortieth Virginia Regiment. He spent the first winter of the war guarding the Potomac but with the coming of spring moved down to the Peninsula to oppose McClellan's advance on Richmond. Thereafter he fought at Second Manassas, Sharpsburg, Fredericksburg, Chancellorsville, and Gettysburg, being taken prisoner in Maryland in the retreat from Pennsylvania. He was first sent to the Old Capitol Prison in Washington and then to Johnson's Island in Lake Erie. Here he remained until March, 1865, when he was paroled preparatory to being exchanged. The war ended before he could get back into service.

Duncan, Thomas D. 139

Recollections of Thomas D. Duncan, a Confederate soldier. Nashville, Tenn., McQuiddy printing company, 1922.

213 p. ports. 19 cm.
Illustrations: "Lieut. Gen. Nathan Bedford Forrest"; "Thomas D. Duncan. Fifty-seven years after his last ride with Forrest"; "Mrs. Juliette Elgin Duncan"; "Thomas D. Duncan. At the age of fourteen ... "
Inclusive dates: 1861–1865

At the age of seventy-six Duncan recorded his memories of the Civil War in which he fought with Forrest's cavalry. His narrative is a straightforward account without prejudice or rancor, yet of practically no value as a commentary, except for infrequent notes about the effect of war on landscapes and people. He crisscrossed middle and western Tennessee, participating in the battles of Fort Donelson, Shiloh, Murfreesboro, Fort Pillow, and many smaller skirmishes; fought through northern Mississippi, Alabama, and into Georgia, and took part in the Battle of Chickamauga and in Forrest's capture of Streight's army at Rome, Georgia. He invaded Kentucky with Bragg's army in 1862. Duncan was a native of Mississippi, joining the Confederate Army at Corinth soon after the firing on Fort Sumter.

Du Pont, Henry Algernon, 1838–1926.   140

The campaign of 1864 in the valley of Virginia and the expedition to Lynchburg. By H. A. Du Pont ... New York, National American society, 1925.

5 p. l., 3–188 p.   front. (port.) maps.   23 cm.
Illustrations: Frontispiece, "H. A. DuPont" [Signature].
Maps: Battle of New Market, the Shenandoah Valley, Battle of Lynchburg, Battlefield of Winchester (2 maps for different periods of the battle), Battle of Fisher's Hill, Battlefield of Cedar Creek.
Inclusive dates: 1864.

This narrative, by a prominent member of the Delaware Du Pont family, is notable as one of the few which deals with the campaign in the Shenandoah Valley in 1864. Du Pont begins with his service under Sigel at Martinsburg, West Virginia, and the march southward up the Valley which brought on the battle of New Market. He continued with Hunter through Lexington to Lynchburg, thence westward through West Virginia to Parkersburg on the Ohio River, and back to the Shenandoah Valley to serve under Sheridan. The narrative ends with the Battle of Cedar Creek. Although this account is predominantly military, it contains enough description, comment, and condemnation of the ruthless destructions by Hunter in Lexington and elsewhere to make it worthwhile as travel literature. Although continuing in the army for some years after the war he ultimately joined the powder works firm, and in 1906 became a United States Senator. Also he was the author of other books.

Dyer, John Will   141

Reminiscences; or Four years in the Confederate army. A history of the experiences of the private soldier in camp, hospital, prison, on the march, and on the battlefield. 1861 to 1865. By Jno. Will Dyer. Evansville, Ind., Keller printing and publishing co., 1898.

323 p., front., illus.   19½ cm.
Illustrations: Frontispieces: "The Author (1898)", "The Author (1861)"; "Stars and Stripes"; "Stars and Bars"; "Gen. Ben Hardin Helm"; "Gen. Albert Sidney Johnston"; "Gen. S. B. Buckner"; "Capt. R. W. Crabb"; "Theo. B. Clore"; "Capt. Frank M. Kuykendall"; "Col. Bennett H. Young"; "Interrupted by a Shell"; "Capt. Ed Porter Thompson"; "Sam Davis"; "Maj. Robert Cobb"; "Jefferson Davis"; "Hon. Polk Laffoon"; "Capt. L. D. Hockersmith"; "Capt. John L. Howell"; "Jas. H. Bozarth"; "A. R. Yeizer (Bruz) and Wife"; "John H. Shaw"; "John C. Latham"; "Gen. W. B. Bate"; "Gen. Pat Cleburne"; "Major Thomas J. Johnson"; "Maj. Rice E. Graves"; "Feeling for a Furlough"; "C. Lewis Curry"; "Judge A. M. (Dolph) Hearin"; "Lieut. J. P. Pierce"; "Confederate Steam Cruiser Alabama (or '290')."
Inclusive dates: 1861–1865.

These recollections of an old man, unaided by a diary or contemporary data, make an entertaining but somewhat garrulous tale, embellished with improbable details and marred by errors in names and dates. Within those limitations it gives many glimpses into wartime conditions in the South. Dyer enlisted in the Confederate Army in 1861 at Sulphur Springs, Union County, Kentucky, and was in the retreat early in 1862 until he was sent to a hospital in northern Alabama. Near Athens he was captured and sent to Camp Chase in Columbus, Ohio. In July he was paroled and returned to Cincinnati, thence by railway to Cairo and down the Mississippi River by steamer to Vicksburg. Here he was turned over to the Confederate authorities, who sent him by way of Mobile, Montgomery, Atlanta, and Chattanooga to a parole camp in Knoxville. Awaiting exchange at Knoxville he was able to get a furlough permitting him to visit Kentucky, where he combined experiences of visiting with the young ladies and eluding Federal soldiers. He joined the Confederate forces again on the Cumberland and was soon engaged in East Tennessee. He took part in the Chickamauga campaign and then went into winter quarters in north Georgia with General Johnston's forces. In the late spring and summer he retreated before General Sherman to Atlanta, and here he was detailed to purchase supplies for Confederate hospitals. He went as far south as Americus and took a look at Andersonville Prison as he passed by. When Sherman marched toward the sea, Dyer was part of the Confederate forces attempting to impede his progress, retreating to Milledgeville, Savannah, and through South Carolina into North Carolina. He became part of the force detailed to accompany President Davis in his attempt to escape beyond the Mississippi River. Dyer was paroled at Washington, Georgia, and immediately afterwards made his way back to Kentucky, going by railway to Atlanta, Chattanooga, Nashville, and thence by steamer.

Early, Jubal Anderson, 1816–1894. 142

Lieutenant General Jubal Anderson Early, C. S. A. Autobiographical sketch and narrative of the war between the states, with notes by R. H. Early. Philadelphia, J. B. Lippincott company, 1912.

xxv, ₁1₁, 496 p. front., plates, ports. 22½ cm.

Illustrations: Frontispiece, "General Jubal Anderson Early"; "General Jubal Anderson Early" ₁Profile₁; "General Robert E. Lee on his Horse 'Traveller', 1867"; "Major Andrew L. Pitzer"; "Major Samuel Hale"; "Captain Samuel H. Early"; "Major John Warwick Daniel. From a photograph taken late in life. The Cross of Honor was bestowed by U. D. C."; "Wall (on the Left of Road) at Marye's Heights. Chancellorsville and Fredericksburg Battlefields"; "Lee's Headquarters—The Wilderness"; "Cedar Creek Battlefield"; "General Early Disguised as a Farmer while Escaping to Mexico, 1865"; "Major Thomas P. Turner. Commandant of Libby Prison, and General Early in Havana, 1865"; "Jefferson Davis, President C. S. A., and Mrs. Davis."

Inclusive dates: 1861–1865.

Other Editions: A Memoir of the Last Year of the War for Independence, in the Confederate States of American, Containing an Account of the Operations of his Commands in the Years 1864 and 1865.

General Early's memoir is almost entirely concerned with military movements and army affairs, but as he moved for four years throughout the eastern theater of war, and made his famous raid to the city limits of Washington, he may be called a traveler. He resented the Federal devastations and retaliated by demanding $100,000 in gold from Chambersburg, Pennsylvania, threatening its destruction if payment were refused. The city was burned and he never regretted the action. Since General Early was relieved of his command a few weeks before the end of the war he was not included in any army paroles. In escaping the clutches of the Federal troops he traveled over an undesignated route through North Carolina, South Carolina, Georgia, Alabama, Mississippi, Arkansas, and Texas. Early began preparation of his memoirs, beginning with his last war year and his march on Washington, immediately after the war and worked on them for several years thereafter.

Eby, Henry Harrison, 1841– 143

Observations of an Illinois boy in battle, camp and prisons—1861 to 1865. By Henry H. Eby. Mendota, Ill., Published by the Author, 1910.

284 p. incl., front., illus., ports. map.   19½ cm.
Illustrations: Forty-one illustrations, consisting of portraits and sketches of scenes described in the narrative.
Maps: "Map of Island No. 10, and Vicinity": "Chickamauga Map."
Inclusive dates: 1861–1864 ₍1865₎

Eby joined an Illinois regiment in 1861, first as a three-months volunteer when he was nineteen years old, and soon thereafter extended his service to three years. He went from Springfield to East St. Louis and by steamer to Cairo, Illinois. He was later stationed on the Missouri side of the Mississippi at Bird's Point, and afterward went to Corinth by way of the Mississippi, Ohio, and Tennessee rivers. He marched eastward across country from Hamburg Landing on the Tennessee into northern Alabama and on to Nashville where he remained while Buell raced to Louisville to head off Bragg. In the winter of 1862–1863 he fought at Murfreesboro and in September he was captured at Chickamauga, conveyed by rail to Atlanta, and thence through Augusta, Columbia, Charlotte, Weldon, and Petersburg to Richmond, where he was imprisoned at three different places, including Libby and Belle Isle. He was later taken to Danville, where he escaped and made his way to Rockymount, Virginia, before being recaptured. He was returned to Virginia and in 1864 was exchanged at City Point. He then proceeded by steamer to Annapolis and Baltimore, by rail through Parkersburg and Cincinnati to St. Louis, and down the Mississippi to Memphis to rejoin his regiment. Eby completed this narrative forty-five years after the war, using twenty-nine letters which he had written during the conflict, memoranda written immediately afterwards, and his memory. He was mildly interested in other than military matters as he traveled and his prison experiences were not painted as luridly as many others, but he still felt that the Confederacy had not done all that it could to lighten the life of its prisoners.

Eddy, Richard, 1828–1906.   144

History of the Sixtieth regiment New York state volunteers, from the commencement of its organization in July, 1861, to its public reception at Ogdensburgh as a veteran command, January 7th, 1864. By Richard Eddy, chaplain. Philadelphia, Published by the Author, Crissy & Markley, printers, 1864.

xii, 360 p.   18½ cm.
Inclusive dates: 1861–1864.

Eddy writes with the bitterness born of a highly-wrought emotionalism which often characterizes men of strong religious convictions. He repeats the discovery, so often made by Northern writers, of the slave who was so nearly white, because his Negro blood was diluted with that of his master, that the Northerner, unsuspecting the extent of amalgamation in the South, could not believe that the person was a Negro slave. Eddy's religious principles did not prevent him from noting with approval the raids on lawyers' offices in northern Virginia and the sending to New York of many law books. In fact, he himself raided the postoffice at the Fauquier White Sulphur Springs and appropriated the letter scales as a memento of his prowess. This narrative is confined almost entirely to the area around Harpers Ferry, Charlestown, Warrenton, and the village of Washington in northern Virginia. The author's only activities elsewhere were in Maryland where he was stationed at the Relay House for a time in 1861, and in 1862, when he was present at Sharpsburg. He resigned in 1863, but continued the history of the regiment through the campaigns of Gettysburg and Chattanooga, in the fall of 1864. After the war Eddy became a prominent Universalist minister and wrote many books and pamphlets of a religious nature.

Eden, Robert C., d. 1907.   145

The sword and gun, a history of the 37th Wis. volunteer infantry. From its first organization to its final muster out. By Major R. C. Eden. Madison, Atwood & Rublee, printers, 1865.

120 p.   16 cm.
Inclusive dates: 1864–1865.

This regiment was organized in Madison, Wisconsin, in the spring of 1864, and was transferred to Washington the latter part of April. It moved over to Alexandria, Virginia, and embarked on the Potomac for the White House landing on the Pamunkey, whence it marched across the peninsula through Cold Harbor to Harrison's Landing and crossed the James for action around Petersburg. After the fall of Petersburg in 1865 it returned by water to Washington, proceeded by rail through Baltimore and Pittsburgh to Cleveland, embarked on Lake Erie for Detroit, and went by rail to Madison. This little volume was written immediately after the war by a member of the regiment who reached the rank of lieutenant colonel. Eden was especially interested in the towns and countryside of Virginia. Though he wrote from memory, supplemented by a few military records and reminiscences of others, he has left a trustworthy travel narrative.

Edmonds, S. Emma E.   146

Nurse and spy in the Union army: comprising the adventures and experiences of a woman in hospitals, camps, and battle-fields. By S. Emma E. Edmonds ... Hartford, W. S. Williams & co.; Philadelphia, [etc.] Jones bros. & co., 1865.

384 p. front. (port.) pl. 20½ cm.

Illustrations: Frontispiece (steel engraving by Geo. E. Perine, New York) "S.E.E. Edmonds" [signature]; "Hospital Tree at Fair Oaks"; "Catering for Hospitals"; "Disguised as a Contraband"; "Making Hoe-Cake for a Sick Rebel"; "Acting Orderly on the Battle-Field"; "Riding for Life"; "Disguised as Female Contraband"; "Playing Possum." (All these "Drawn and Engraved on Wood by R. O'Brien, New York.")

Inclusive dates: July, 1861–July, 1863.

Other editions: The female spy of the Union army. The thrilling adventures, experiences, and escapes of a woman, as nurse, spy and scout, in hospitals, camps, and battle-fields. Boston, De Wolfe, Fiske & co., 1864.

Kranken- und spionemdienst für die unions-armee. Abenteur und erfahrungen eines frauenzimmers in hospitalern, lagern und auf dem schlachtfelde. Hartford, W. S. Williams & co., Philadelphia and Cincinnati, Jones bros. & co. [etc., etc] 1865.

Unsexed: or, The female soldier. The thrilling adventures, experiences and escapes of a woman, as nurse, spy and scout, in hospitals, camps and battlefields. Philadelphia, Philadelphia publishing co., [186?]

Nurse and spy. Thrilling story of the adventures of a woman who served as a Union soldier. Washington, The national tribune, 1900.

Miss Edmonds, a native of New Brunswick, was engaged in missionary activities in the Far West of the United States when the war began. She enlisted as a nurse and soon turned spy, with surprising versatility disguising herself first as a Negro boy, then as an Irish woman selling cakes and pies, and finally as a Confederate soldier. She began in Virginia with McClellan on his Peninsula campaign, but was transferred to the war in the West and saw some action in Kentucky south of Louisville. Later she was sent to Vicksburg, arriving there in time for the fall of the city. The account is highly personal and is filled with thrills. Little attention is given to the actual work of a nurse and there is no picture of hospital life. Her book gives little information on the Confederacy in wartime, being a personal narrative with a tinge of tall tales.

Egan, Michael, 1826?–1888.   147

The flying gray-haired Yank; or, The adventures of a volunteer. A personal narrative of thrilling experiences as an army courier, a volunteer captain, a prisoner of war, a fugitive from southern dungeons, a guest among the contrabands and unionists, and finally, a skirmisher at the very front at Appomattox. A true narrative of the civil war. Philadelphia, Hubbard brothers, 1888.

414 p. incl. front., plates, ports, plates. 18½ cm.
Illustrations: Sixteen rather crude drawings of battle scenes, prison and escape incidents, and portraits of officers.
Inclusive dates: July, 1861–June, 1865.

The outstanding significance of this book is its detailed description of the author's journey after escaping from the Columbia, South Carolina prison. He traveled northward through Greenville and Walhalla, South Carolina, Clayton, Georgia, Franklin, North Carolina, and across the Great Smoky Mountains into Tennessee where he reached the Union lines at Knoxville by way of Cade's Cove. He continued on to Chattanooga by rail and back to Knoxville, then to Cincinnati through Cumberland Gap and Kentucky. Egan, a native Irishman, was living in the western part of Virginia when the Civil War broke out. He volunteered in a West Virginia unit and was made military express courier in Rosecrans' campaign in that state in 1861. He later became captain, Company B, Fifteenth Regiment, West Virginia Infantry, Volunteers, and continued his military activities in that region until he was captured in May, 1864. He was taken to Macon, Georgia, and imprisoned there until Sherman's campaigning made that prison camp unsafe. Thereupon he was transferred to Charleston and later to Columbia, where he made his escape. Like other refugees who wandered through the upper South and the Southern Appalachian Mountains, he was befriended by slaves in the plantation country, and in the hills by the mountaineers, most of whom were either bushwhackers or deserters. A few months before the end of the war he returned to active service and was present at Lee's surrender at Appomatox.

Ellis, Daniel, 1827–   148
Thrilling adventures of Daniel Ellis, the great Union guide of east Tennessee, for a period of nearly four years during the great southern rebellion. Written by himself. Containing a short biography of the author. ... New York, Harper & brothers, 1867.

1 p. l., ₅₋430 p. incl. illus., ports., map, front. 18 cm.
Illustrations: Frontispiece, "Portrait of Daniel Ellis"; "Escape of Ellis"; "Captain R. Brown's Cruelties"; "Ellis Viewing the Skeletons"; "Ellis Piloting a Party over the Mountains"; "Ellis Delivering Letters to his Regiment"; "Ellis Relating his Adventures"; " 'Brave Bill Parker' "; "John Morgan's Raiders"; "Fight with Vaughn's Rebels"; "Duvall Murdering Union Men"; "Massacre of Union Men"; "Bozen's Atrocities"; "Portrait of ₍Albert D.₎ Richardson"; "Portrait of Miss Stephens"; "Ellis Attacking"; "Thomas's Rebel Indians Murdering Union Men"; "Horrible Scenes during the Rebellion."
Maps: "Map of the Trail over the Mountains."
Inclusive dates: 1861–1865.

Ellis was an East Tennessean from Carter County who remained loyal to the Union, with most other people of that region. He soon began to pilot Unionists through the mountains to Kentucky to join the Federal armies there. According to his account he made many trips from the Elizabethton vicinity to Cumberland Gap, occasionally going northward as far as Lexington and Louisville. He accompanied Burnside's forces across the mountains from eastern Kentucky to Knoxville, following its fall made many trips by railway to Nashville, and near the end of the war made a scouting journey to Asheville, Waynesville, and Franklin, North Carolina. He writes of the miniature civil war which was going on in East Tennessee between the Unionists and Confederates. The account is highly personal and at times appears to be exaggerated.

Ellis, Thomas T. 149

Leaves from the diary of an army surgeon; or, Incidents of field, camp, and hospital life. By Thomas T. Ellis ... New York, John Bradburn, 1863.

312 p. 18 cm.
Inclusive dates: October, 1861–October, 1862.

The book contains some descriptions of the dead and wounded on battlefields, and of the forces from both sides gathering up fallen comrades after the fighting, but practically no account of the inside of army hospitals. Most of the work is devoted to campaign and battle details, and in these respects adds little to the formal military histories. Dr. Ellis, an Englishman, had fought in the Kaffir wars of South Africa where he was wounded and mustered out of the British service on a pension. He came to America and was in the vicinity of New York City when the Civil War broke out. He offered his services to the Federal Government as post surgeon and inspector of army camps on Staten Island. When General McClellan began his Peninsula campaign Dr. Ellis became part of his forces as medical director at White House on the Pamunkey River. He was also present in the Second Manassas and Sharpsburg campaigns. He was an admirer of General McClellan, to whom he dedicated his book, and, strangely for an Englishman, he believed that nowhere in the world was the Negro as well off as on the Southern plantations. As might be expected, this account is free from the bitterness which characterized contemporary accounts by Northerners and Southerners.

Ely, Alfred, 1815–1892. 150

Journal of Alfred Ely, a prisoner of war in Richmond. Edited by Charles Lanman. New York, D. Appleton and company, 1862.

359 p. front. (port.) pl. 19½ cm.
Illustrations: Frontispiece, "Alfred Ely [Signature] Engd. by J. C. Butture, New York." (Steel engraving).
Inclusive dates: July–December, 1861.

Alfred Ely was a member of the United States House of Representatives from the state of New York who with other members of Congress appeared at Bull Run the day before the first battle there. He was captured, taken to Manassas Junction, sent by train to Richmond and imprisoned for the next five months in a tobacco warehouse. In late December he was freed and sent out of the Confederacy by rail to Petersburg and Norfolk where he boarded a steamer for

Fortress Monroe before re-embarking for Baltimore and going by rail to Washington. Ely's account is of considerable importance in assessing the spirit of the people of the Confederacy during the first year of war. He makes observations on his trip to Richmond, on prison conditions there, and on his passage out of the Confederacy. He writes with candor and conviction which make a convincing, straightforward story. He found a great many cultured and friendly people in Richmond and was visited almost daily by Confederate congressmen, military officers, and a wide variety of people, all of whom treated him with respect. This book stands out in marked contrast to most prisoner of war accounts.

Emmerton, James Arthur, 1834–1888.   151

A record of the Twenty-third regiment Mass. vol. infantry in the war of the rebellion 1861–1865 with alphabetical roster; company rolls; portraits, maps; etc. Boston, William Ware & co., 1886.

xx, 352 p.   front., pl., port., maps (partly fold.)   22¾ cm.
Illustrations: Frontispiece, "Asst. Surg. J. A. Emmerton" and twenty-eight other plates of illustrations, many of them containing more than one portrait or building.
Maps: Nine maps, mostly of the North Carolina coast.
Inclusive dates: 1861–1865.

A composite of diaries and letters supplemented by official documents, this book is significant as a travel account largely for its descriptions of towns and slavery in eastern North Carolina, with particular attention to Newbern. Emmerton and his unit spent most of their time on the North Carolina coast, though they were also sent to Beaufort, South Carolina, and to the lower James River in Virginia.

Ennis, John W.   152

Adventures in rebeldom; or, Ten months experience of prison life ... New York, "Business Mirror" print, 1863.

60 p.   19 cm.
Inclusive dates: 1861–1862.

Ennis was a member of the 79th Highland Regiment, New York State Militia, who enlisted in New York City at the beginning of the war and went by rail through Philadelphia and Baltimore to Washington. He crossed the Potomac and reached Manassas in time to be captured in the first battle there. His movements from that point were many and rapid: a short imprisonment in a tobacco warehouse at Richmond; by rail through Petersburg, Weldon, and Wilmington to Charleston, South Carolina; to Castle Pinckney in the harbor; to Columbia, where he escaped and wandered northward through Spartanburg and into the mountains of North Carolina; to the French Broad River some forty miles west of Asheville before being recaptured and taken to Asheville; through Hendersonville to Greenville and by train to the Columbia prison; to Richmond by rail through Charlotte, Salisbury, Raleigh, Weldon, and Petersburg; finally to be exchanged and sent down the Potomac to Fortress Monroe and by boat to Washington. The narrative is principally about travels. He objected strongly to the treatment in various prisons but mentions special consideration in Asheville, where a group of ladies presented him with a large cake. He found more Union sympathy in North than in South Carolina. Discounting remarkable and improbable privations, and highly colored details of physical prowess, the account is a valuable commentary on conditions in out-of-the-way parts of the Confederacy in the early months of the war.

[Estabrooks, Henry L.]   153
    Adrift in Dixie; or, A Yankee officer among the Rebels. With an introduction by Edmund Kirke [pseud]. New York, Carleton, 1866.

   224 p.   18¼ cm.
   Inclusive dates: September–November (?), 1864.

This was one of the many propaganda books of the Civil War period, designed to bolster the program of the Radicals in their reconstruction of the South. It must, therefore, be so evaluated as a picture of the Negroes. Estabrooks, of Dorchester, Massachusetts, was a lieutenant in the Twenty-sixth Regiment of Massachusetts Infantry who was taken prisoner at the Battle of Berryville in northwestern Virginia in September, 1864, sent temporarily to Libby Prison and later to a prison in the lower South. Near Danville, Virginia, he escaped and floated down the Dan River in a small boat to the Roanoke. Near Clarksville, Virginia, he left the river and made his way across country to the Federal lines near City Point. The narrative is largely an account of his perilous adventures and of assistance by Negroes, most of whom he describes as highly intelligent and ready for suffrage.

Estvàn, Bela, b. 1827.   154
    War pictures from the South. By B. Estvàn ... New York, D. Appleton and company, 1863.

   viii, 352 p.   20 cm.
   Inclusive dates: 1861–1862.
   Other editions: London, Routledge, Warne and Routledge, 1863. 2 vols., frontispiece, portraits, 2 folding plans. Same title as American edition. Kriegsbilder aus Amerika. Leipzig, F. A. Brockhaus, 1864. 2 vols.

Estvàn was a Hungarian soldier of fortune who previously had seen service in the Russian Army at the siege of Sevastapol in the Crimean War. Being in Virginia when the Civil War broke out he was made a colonel of cavalry by the Confederate Government. He went to Charleston shortly before its bombardment, soon went on to Montgomery and Pensacola, returned to Virginia, took part in the First Battle of Manassas, and participated in the engagements around Richmond when McClellan attempted to seize the city. He had also been sent to the coast of North Carolina after the fall of Roanoke Island, and his last service to the Confederacy was in Savannah where he contracted yellow fever, received a discharge, and was allowed by the Federal Army to cross the lines and return to the North, whence he sailed for Europe. There is some reason to believe that Estvàn was a fraud, and was never in the Confederate army. His account is of little value since most of it is not about personal experiences but is an attempted history of the Confederate military campaigns during his service.

Favill, Josiah Marshall   155
The diary of a young officer serving with the armies of the United States during the war of the rebellion. By Josiah Marshall Favill, adjutant, captain, and brevet major 57th New York infantry, brevet lieutenant-colonel, and colonel U. S. volunteers. Chicago, R. R. Donnelley & sons company, 1909.

298 p. fronts., plates, ports. 20 cm.
Illustrations: Frontispiece, "Lieut. J. M. Favill", and sixteen other individual portraits or groups of soldiers.
Inclusive dates: 1861–1864.

This diary begins in April, 1861, and ends with the Battle of Spottsylvania Courthouse in May, 1864. Favill left New York City by boat for Annapolis, went to Washington by railway, and soon was in the field of operations in northern Virginia. He fought at First Manassas and in the spring of 1862 went on McClellan's Peninsula expedition. Thereafter he fought in all the principal campaigns in Virginia, Maryland, and Pennsylvania, until his retirement. Favill was much interested in the new scenes which met his eye and especially attracted by Southern women, old homesteads, and historical spots. It is a worthwhile travel record, unmarred by prejudice.

Fearn, Mrs. Frances (Hewitt) *ed.*   156
Diary of a refugee, ed. by Frances Fearn; illustrated by Rosalie Urquhart. New York, Moffat, Yard and company, 1910.

ix, 149 p. front., plates. 19 cm.
Illustrations: Frontispiece, "Old Creole House"; "The Old Plantation House"; "Evangeline Oak"; "The Dark Forest"; "Gen. U. S. Grant"; "The Camp on the Plains"; "Mexican Water Jars"; "Havana Harbor"; "Clarice"; "A Review Day under the Empire"; "Napoleon III"; "Christine Nilsson"; "The Empress Eugenie"; "The Tuileries in 1880"; "The Writer of the Diary"; "The Clarice of To-day."
Inclusive dates: 1862–1867.

The author was an anonymous Louisiana lady who lived on Bayou Lafourche, near Donaldsonville. After the fall of New Orleans her family became refugees. Loading such belongings as they could on a river steamer they traveled up the Mississippi and Red rivers to Alexandria where they spent several months. Later they moved on to Shreveport and into Texas, staying for a time at Fairfield and, after some months in Texas, departed for Europe by way of San Antonio and Laredo and over the Rio Grande to Matamoras in Mexico, and by steamer for

Havana, Liverpool, and Paris. After the war they returned to New Orleans. This is a rather brief surface account of the hardships of a war-torn family, with a few glimpses into the removal of their slaves from the Louisiana plantation to Texas and of their travel across that state.

Feemster, Zenas E., 1813—   157

The travelling refugee; or, The cause and cure of the rebellion in the United States; embracing a sketch of the state of society in the South, before, and at the commencement of the rebellion. Illustrated by facts and incidents. By Rev. Zenas E. Feemster, refugee from Mississippi, in 1862. Springfield, Ill., Steam press of Baker & Phillips, 1865.

iv p., 2 l., [9]–195, [1] p.   17½ cm.
Inclusive dates: 1861–1863.

Feemster was a South Carolinian who accompanied his parents to Mississippi in 1820. He became a minister and traveled extensively in northern Mississippi and eastern Alabama, making Columbus, Mississippi, his home. With the coming of secession, he was suspected because of his Unionism and in 1862 he decided to leave the Confederacy. He wandered into northern Alabama and back through Mississippi to Pittsburg Landing, in Tennessee, where he boarded a steamer for St. Louis and continued to Decatur, Illinois. In the summer of 1863 he went by steamer from Cairo to Memphis for a visit in northern Mississippi and then by rail to Corinth, returning north to remain for the duration of the war. This highly personal account is written in the contentious vein of a martyr, yet it gives an interesting glimpse into social conditions in northern Mississippi where Unionism was characteristic of the inhabitants.

Ferguson, Joseph.   158

Life-struggles in Rebel prisons: a record of the sufferings, escapes, adventures and starvation of the Union prisoners. By Joseph Ferguson ... Containing an appendix with the names, regiments, and date of death of Pennsylvania soldiers who died at Andersonville. With an introduction by Rev. Joseph T. Cooper, D. D. ... Philadelphia, James M. Ferguson, 1865.

206, xxiv p. incl. front. (port.) pl.   17 cm.
Illustrations: Frontispiece, "Yours Truly, Joseph Ferguson" [Signature]; "Libby Prison, Richmond, Va.,"; "Recaptured"; "Wash-Day"; "Murder of Lieutenant Turbayne."
Inclusive dates: 1864–1865.

Extreme bitterness and bias make Joseph Ferguson's narrative practically valueless. A captain in the First New Jersey Volunteers, he was captured in the Battle of the Wilderness in early May, 1864, was taken by way of Lynchburg to Danville, and through Greensboro, Salisbury, Charlotte, Columbia, and Augusta (where he made a brief escape) to Macon. Afterwards he was held at Savannah, Charleston, and Columbia; when Sherman neared that point he was moved northward through Charlotte, Raleigh, and Goldsboro to be released on parole near Wilmington, whence he went by steamer to Annapolis.

Field, Charles D.   159

Three years in the saddle from 1861 to 1865; memoirs of Charles D. Field; thrilling stories of the war in camp and on the field of battle. The cavalry soldier—scout and dispatch bearer—private, non-commissioned officer—commander of skirmish lines. In over thirty engagements—hospital life etc. By Charles D. Field ... [Goldfield? Ia., c.1898]

74 p.   front. (port.)   21 cm.
Illustrations: Frontispiece, "Charles D. Field."
Inclusive dates: 1861–1864 [1865].

Field belonged to the Thirteenth Illinois Cavalry, organized in Joliet, Illinois. He went first to St. Louis and then to Camp Douglas near Chicago. Returning to St. Louis he operated for the remainder of his war service in Missouri around Ironton and Pilot Knob, southward in Arkansas around Helena, Pine Bluff, and Little Rock, and in northwestern Arkansas in pursuit of the Confederate commander Shelby. This narrative is of little value as a travel account, containing only a few useful comments.

[Figg, Royal W.]   160

"Where men only dare to go!" or, The story of a boy company (C. S. A.) By an ex-boy ... Richmond, Whittet & Shepperson, 1885.

viii, [17]–263 p.   front., port.   20½ cm.
Illustrations: Frontispiece, "Brig. Gen. Del. Kemper, Lieut. Gen. S. D. Lee, Brig. Gen. E. P. Alexander. Col. Frank Euger. Maj. Wm. W. Parker. Capt. J. Thomas Brown. Lieut. Ed. S. Wooldridge. Lieut. J. C. Parkinson. Lieut. Geo. E. Saville."
Inclusive dates: 1862–1865.

Although written twenty years after the war and embellished with many supposed conversations, this narrative has considerable value as a commentary on the wartime South. The author was a member of the Parker Battery which fought throughout the war in most of the engagements in the East, including the Peninsula campaign, Sharpsburg, and Gettysburg. After Gettysburg Figg's company was sent with General Longstreet to Chattanooga, going by way of Wilmington, Augusta, and Atlanta. It wintered in East Tennessee and in the spring of 1864 moved back into Virginia where it fought from Spottsylvania Courthouse to Appomattox. Just before Lee's surrender, Figg was captured, taken to City Point, and sent by boat to the Federal prison camp at Point Lookout. He writes of visiting among civilians during slave times, and gives intimate accounts of foraging in East Tennessee among the Union element. Though less bitter than Northern accounts of Southern prisons, this Confederate describes the hard life in the marshy, windswept prison at Point Lookout.

The Yankee conscript; or, Eighteen months in Dixie. By George Adams Fisher. With an introduction by Rev. William Dickson. Philadelphia, J. W. Daughaday, 1864.

251 p.   front. (port.) plates.   17½ cm.
Illustrations: Frontispiece, " Geo. A. Fisher" ₍Signature₎ and three sketches of incidents.
Inclusive dates: 1857–1862.

This book, written in support of prosecuting the war, was evidently composed as a campaign document in the presidential election of 1864. The author attributes to himself much heroism as well as trickery and deceit in making his escape from Texas, where he had gone in 1857 to engage in sheep raising. The narrative, despite its exaggerations, is valuable as a picture of Texas society and politics at the outbreak of the Civil War. He also describes the livestock business and plantation activities in Texas. Fisher left St. Louis and went by steamer to Hannibal where he set out for Texas, crossing Missouri and the Indian Territory and settling in Denton. Drafted into the Confederate Army in early 1862, he got himself out of the service by trickery, was arrested and forced into the Army again, and later made his escape. He left through the southeast corner of Indian Territory and crossed through Arkansas into Missouri, passing through Springfield and Rolla on his way to St. Louis.

₍Fiske, Samuel Wheelock₎ 1828–1864.   162

Mr. Dunn Browne's experiences in the army ... Boston, Nichols and Noyes; New York, O. S. Felt, 1866.

2 p. l., iii–xii, 11–390 p.   front. (port.)   18 cm.
Illustrations: Frontispiece, (Steel engraving by H. W. Smith) "Yours Dunn Brown ₍Samuel Wheeler Fiske₎" ₍Signature₎
Inclusive dates: September, 1862–May, 1864.

Letters originally published in the *Springfield Republican* comprise the text of this book. Fiske was a native of Massachusetts, was educated at Amherst College, and entered the ministry. With the coming of war he enlisted in the Fourteenth Regiment of Connecticut Volunteers, and was later made captain of Company G. He began the letters shortly before his participation in the Battle of Sharpsburg and continued them as he moved from one northern Virginia campaign to another. Fiske was at Gettysburg, fought at Fredericksburg and Chancellorsville, and was taken prisoner in the latter engagement. He spent two weeks in Libby Prison, where he found conditions comfortable and the food good but not plentiful. His only complaint was that he was robbed of all his personal belongings by the Confederate authorities. When he was exchanged, he was taken to City Point and turned over to the Federal Army. The next year he was mortally wounded in the Battle of the Wilderness and died soon thereafter. Fiske was mostly interested in army life among his fellow-soldiers and in political developments in the North, and had little to say about that part of the Confederacy which he invaded. While stationed at Harpers Ferry he was thrilled to be quartered for a short time in the firehouse which John Brown and his men had occupied.

Fleharty, Stephen F. 163

Our regiment. A history of the 102d Illinois infantry volunteers, with sketches of the Atlanta campaign, the Georgia raid, and the campaign of the Carolinas. By S. F. Fleharty. Chicago, Brewster & Hanscom, 1865.

192, xxiv p.   19 cm.
Inclusive dates: 1862–1865.

Based on a diary and written immediately after the war, it is an excellent commentary on methods of warfare practiced in Georgia and the Carolinas. It deals also with natural features of the country, the state of civilization, and the sentiments of the people. Fleharty, a resident of Galesburg, Illinois, was sergeant major in the 102nd Regiment Illinois Infantry Volunteers, which was organized in September of 1862. It went by rail from Peoria to Louisville, marched eastward to Frankfort, Kentucky, turned southward through Bowling Green into Middle Tennessee, and spent the next year around La Vergne, Gallatin, and Lebanon. In early 1864, it moved on to Chattanooga to join in Sherman's campaign through Georgia and the Carolinas. This regiment fought in various engagements on the way to Atlanta and during the march to the sea it passed through Madison, Rutledge, Eatonton, Milledgeville, Sandersville and various other Georgia towns before reaching Savannah. It marched through South Carolina and North Carolina, and after Johnston's surrender continued northward through Virginia, to participate in the "Grand Review" in Washington and to go by rail through Baltimore, Harrisburg, and Pittsburgh to Chicago.

Fletcher, William Andrew, 1839– 164

Rebel private, front and rear; experiences and observations from the early fifties and through the civil war. By W. A. Fletcher. Beaumont, Texas, Press of the Greer print, 1908.

193 p. incl. port.   23 cm.
Illustrations: "The author, W. A. Fletcher."
Inclusive dates: 1861–1865.

Fletcher, a private in Hood's Brigade, produced this unreliable account from memory more than forty years after the war. He was so uncertain about dates, names, and routes traveled that he confessedly ignored many such details. This garrulous stream of army experiences, checked against established facts, is valuable only for atmosphere of Civil War times in the South. The author was transferred in the summer of 1864 to the Terry Texas Rangers. For the routes followed as a member of Hood's Brigade and after becoming a Terry Ranger, see Leonidas Banton Giles, *Terry's Texas Rangers,* in this bibliography.

Floyd, David Bittle. 165

History of the Seventy-fifth regiment of Indiana infantry volunteers, its organization, campaigns, and battles (1862–65). By Rev. David Bittle Floyd ... with an introduction by Major-General J. J. Reynolds ... Published for the author. Philadelphia, Lutheran publication society, 1893.

457 p. front., illus., port., maps. 21½ cm.

Illustrations: Twenty-one illustrations of battlefields and other objects, and portraits of soldiers.

Maps: "Battlefield of Chattanooga"; "Map of the Atlanta Campaign"; "Marches of the 75th Indiana Regiment from Atlanta, Ga., to Raleigh, N. C."

Inclusive dates: 1862–1865.

Like many other Union soldiers from the Middle West, Floyd made the great swing around the circle. In the autumn of 1862 he left Indianapolis for Louisville to head off Bragg's march on that city, was soon chasing John Morgan south of Louisville, and went as far east as Frankfort. He then operated in Middle Tennessee and in 1863 was engaged in the occupation of Chattanooga and the Battle of Chickamauga. In 1864 he followed Sherman to the sea and up through the Carolinas to Johnston's surrender at Durham Station, and thence across Virginia to Washington for the "Grand Review." He returned home over the Baltimore and Ohio Railroad to Parkersburg on the Ohio, by boat to Lawrenceburg, and by railway to Indianapolis. The work is more nearly a regimental history than a travel narrative. Floyd based his account on the diaries of various comrades and on their combined recollections.

Fonerden, Clarence A. 166

A brief history of the military career of Carpenter's battery, from its organization as a rifle company under the name of the Alleghany Roughs to the ending of the war between the states. By C. A. Fonerden. New Market, Va., Henkel & company, printers, 1911.

78 p. 3 pl. 19 cm.

Illustrations: Three war scenes.

Inclusive dates: 1861–1865.

In following his Confederate Army unit, Fonerden engaged in all the principal eastern campaigns of the war, including Jackson's Romney and Valley campaigns and Early's march on Washington in 1864. This work was written fifty years after the events described, apparently without personal or contemporary records, and is too brief to have value as a travel commentary.

Forbes, Eugene, d. 1865. 167

Diary of a soldier, and prisoner of war in the Rebel prisons. Written by Eugene Forbes ... Trenton, [N. J.] Murphy & Bechtel, printers, 1865.

iv, 68 p. 22½ cm.

Inclusive dates: 1864–1865.

The author was a sergeant in Company B, Fourth Regiment New Jersey Volunteers, but the account does not cover his full war career. He began the diary May 1, 1864, and ended it February 5, 1865, two days before his death. He was captured in May, 1864, early in Grant's campaign against Richmond, and was taken to Andersonville, Georgia, by way of Lynchburg, Danville, and over the new railway to Greensboro, Charlotte, Augusta, and Macon. In the fall he was transferred to Florence, South Carolina, where he died. Forbes gives a straightforward and trustworthy account of his travels and of his experiences in prisons, with little of the bitterness so common in most similar accounts.

Fosdick, Charles. 168

Five hundred days in Rebel prisons. By Charles Fosdick, formerly of Co. K, 5th Iowa vols. ... Chicago, Chicago electrotype & stereotype co., 1887.

118, [1] p. illus. 19¼ cm.
Illustrations: "Portrait of Author before Capture"; "Portrait of Author at Time of Release"; "Andersonville Prison (Camp Sumter), As It Appeared August 1st, 1864 When It Contained 35,000 Prisoners of War, Drawn from Memory by Thomas O'Dea"; "Nero and Spot"; "Different Modes of Punishment." These are all crude drawings.
Inclusive dates: November, 1863–March, 1865.
Other editions: Another edition of this book (containing 132 pages): Bethany, Mo., Clipper book and job office, 1887.

Many of Fosdick's statements are extremely bitter or wholly irresponsible and may be ignored as comments on conditions in the Confederacy. The book seems to have been designed to promote more and bigger pensions for Federal veterans and to serve as Republican campaign literature in the presidential election of 1888. It is a cheap paper-bound volume, written a quarter of a century after the war. In November, 1863, Fosdick was taken prisoner in the battles around Chattanooga and was sent to Belle Isle Prison in Richmond over the rail route leading through Atlanta, Augusta, Columbia, Charlotte, Raleigh, Weldon, and Petersburg. From Petersburg he was transferred to Andersonville, retracing his route to Augusta, where he branched off by way of Millen and Macon. On Sherman's invasion of Georgia Fosdick was transferred to Savannah and Charleston, and later taken to Florence. When Sherman entered South Carolina Fosdick was taken through Wilmington as far north as Goldsboro, but when that point was threatened he was turned loose through the Federal lines near Wilmington.

[Fowler, William] 1839– 169

Memorials of William Fowler. New York, Anson D. F. Randolph & company, 1875.

172 p. front. (port.) 18¼ cm.
Illustrations: Frontispiece, "William Fowler" [Signature].
Inclusive dates: 1863–1865.

The book covers Banks' military activities in Louisiana, including the fall of Port Hudson, the war in Virginia, especially around Richmond in 1864, and the fighting of the next year leading to the final engagement at Appomattox. The account consists mainly of letters written by Fowler, who rose to the rank of major, and deals almost exclusively with military matters. Yet he was not insensitive to the country invaded and noted with sorrow the devastation of old mansion homes in Louisiana.

Fox, James D. 170

A true history of the reign of terror in southern Illinois, a part of the campaign in western Virginia, and fourteen months of prison life at Richmond, Virginia; Macon, Georgia; Charleston, South Carolina, and Columbia, South Carolina. Aurora, Ill., J. D. Fox, 1884.

> vi, 1 l., [7]–60 p. incl. front., pl.   20½ cm.
> *Illustrations:* Frontispiece, "View of Libby Prison"; "Among the Mountains."
> *Inclusive dates:* 1863–1865.

Containing none of the familiar lurid pictures of prison experiences, this little book is restrained and fair but too short to have much value. Fox became a second lieutenant in Company H, Sixteenth Illinois Cavalry Volunteers. Apart from some activities in southern Illinois, he saw brief service in southwestern Virginia, where at Jonesville he was made prisoner in January, 1864. He had crossed the Ohio River at Cincinnati and marched across Kentucky to Cumberland Gap late in 1863, and had passed on into southwestern Virginia where he was captured. He was taken to Bristol and then by train to Richmond and Libby Prison. After a few months he was transferred to the officers' prison in Macon, Georgia, going by rail through Salisbury, Columbia, and Augusta; later he was held briefly in Savannah, Charleston, and Columbia. When Sherman approached that point Fox was transferred by way of Charlotte to Goldsboro where he signed a parole and was handed over to the Federal authorities at Wilmington, whence he went by steamer to Annapolis. Written twenty years after the war, apparently without the aid of a diary or other personal material, the narrative suffers from the infirmities of memory, but indicates an interest in the countryside of Kentucky and in all classes of people.

[Fox, Simeon M.] 1842– 171
Story of the Seventh Kansas. [Topeka? 1902?]

> 36, [1] p.   22½ cm.
> *Inclusive dates:* 1861–1865.
> *Other editions:* 1908, 59 pages, Topeka, State printing office. 1910, 16 pages, Topeka, State printing office.

Traveling with this unit of the United States Army through eastern Kansas, Leavenworth, Topeka, Lawrence, across Missouri to St. Louis and down the Mississippi to Memphis, Fox proved to be only slightly travel-minded. He proceeded to Corinth and operated until 1864 in central and northern Mississippi and western Tennessee. His last service was in Missouri, helping to beat off the invasion of Price. This brief narrative was given as an address before the Kansas State Historical Society in 1902.

Francis, Charles Lewis. 172

Narrative of a private soldier in the volunteer army of the United States, during a portion of the period covered by the great war of the rebellion of 1861. By Charles Lewis Francis ... Brooklyn, William Jenkins and company, 1879.

viii, (7)–185 p. 18 cm.
Inclusive dates: 1861–1863.

An unusual tale, written with spicy frankness, a touch of humor, and somewhat in the spirit of a gentleman of fortune looking for excitement. Francis was a lad of only eighteen when the Civil War began. Although he lived in Washington, his family's business was conducted in Baltimore. There is some reason to suspect that Francis was born in England. If his story is to be believed, he moved around as a free lance with whatever unit of the Federal Army seemed to suit his fancy. He went to Harpers Ferry, to various points in Maryland, and to the Peninsula with McClellan. Finally Francis determined to go West and settle in Illinois. He appeared in Chicago in 1862 but was overcome by military ardor and enlisted in the Eighty-eighth Illinois Regiment Volunteers, set out for Jeffersonville, Indiana, and went on to Cincinnati to be ready to help drive Bragg out of Kentucky. He participated in the Perryville and Murfreesboro engagements and lived the life of a soldier until he was taken prisoner by the Confederates. He was sent by way of Chattanooga and Atlanta to Montgomery but soon returned over the same route to Richmond by way of Knoxville and Lynchburg. After a short stay in Libby Prison he was paroled, passing down the James River to City Point and on to Annapolis. In December, 1863, he was sent to St. Louis and mustered out. This is an interesting and somewhat improbable story, highly personalized, with many descriptions of scenes, places, and people.

Frederick, Gilbert, b. 1841 *or* 1842. 173

The story of a regiment: being a record of the military services of the Fifty-seventh New York state volunteer infantry in the war of the rebellion, 1861–1865. By Gilbert Frederick ... [Chicago] Pub. by the Fifty-seventh veteran association, 1895.

xii, 349 p. front., illus., pl., port. 20½ cm.
Illustrations: Frontispiece, "The Battle-Flag of the Regiment"; "Samuel K. Zook, Brevet Major-General U. S. Volunteers"; "On Pennsylvania Avenue, Washington, D. C."; "Camp California. Fifty-Seventh Regiment on Dress Parade"; "Major-General William H. French"; "Field Hospital at Savage Station"; "Sunken Road and Cornfield"; "Sunken Road and Rebel Dead"; "Major-General Israel B. Richardson"; "Heights at Harpers Ferry"; "Street in Harpers Ferry"; "Clearing the Streets of Fredericksburg, December 11th, 1862"; "Crossing the Rappahannock, December 12th, 1862"; "Battle of Fredericksburg, Va., December 13th, 1862"; "Confederates behind the Stone Wall"; "Chancellor House"; "Commanders of the Army of the Potomac: George B. McClellan, Ambrose E. Burnside, Joseph Hooker, George G. Meade";

"Good-Bye to Falmouth"; "Where Zook Fell"; "Apex of Pickett's Charge"; "View of Battlefield [Gettysburg] from Round Top"; "The Fifty-Seventh Monument at Gettysburg"; "Standing Guard"; "Commanders of the Second Corps: Edwin V. Sumner, Darius N. Couch, Winfield S. Hancock, Gouverneur K. Warren"; "Colonel Alford B. Chapman"; "The Fire in the Woods"; "Battle of Ream's Station"; "Lieutenant-General U. S. Grant."

Maps: "Manassas and Vicinity"; "Fair Oaks, Position of the Fifty-Seventh Regiment"; "The Seven Days Retreat"; "Fifty-Seventh Regiment at Antietam"; "Gettysburg. Positions of the Fifty-Seventh at Gettysburg"; "The Wilderness, May 5 & 6, 1864. Position of the Fifty-Seventh"; "Map of Petersburg"; "Map of Ream's Station"; "Map of the Last Retreat."
Inclusive dates: 1861–1865.

Gilbert Frederick, nineteen years old when the Civil War began, enlisted immediately and rose to the rank of captain. His unit participated in the war in the East from its beginning to its end and was engaged in the main battles from Gettysburg to Appomattox. The author therefore marched and countermarched through the three states of Pennsylvania, Maryland, and Virginia. Although this account was written more than a quarter of a century later, the author claimed to have had access to many letters which he wrote home during the conflict. It is a rather personal narrative, in which foraging, camp life, and some descriptions of the country traversed have a place, but it adds little to the other regimental histories dealing with this region.

[Freeman, Warren Hapgood] 1844?   174

Letters from two brothers serving in the war for the union to their family at home in West Cambridge, Mass. Cambridge, Printed for private circulation [by H. O. Houghton and company] 1871.

2 p. l., 164 p. 2 l.   front. (port)   17 cm.
Illustrations: Unlabeled photograph as frontispiece, probably Warren Hapgood Freeman.
Inclusive dates: December, 1861–March, 1865.

This set of letters is unusually valuable as it gives the intelligent and remarkably unbiased observations of two brothers from Massachusetts, Warren H. Freeman, who served first in the Thirteenth and later in the Thirty-ninth Massachusetts Regiment, and his brother, Eugene H., who was in the transport branch. The former served in the campaigns of northern Virginia as well as around Richmond in the final stages of the war. He also fought at Sharpsburg and at Gettysburg, where he was taken prisoner but paroled a day or two later and soon exchanged. Eugene's services were confined to the shores of Chesapeake Bay and the eastern coast of North Carolina. These brothers were mostly interested in their army life and the military movements, but they were alert and observant of all that was to be seen in the invaded country. They wrote about such subjects as the Chesapeake and Ohio Canal, ducks on the waters of eastern Virginia, and the old Virginia mansions, including Westover.

Fremantle, Sir Arthur James Lyon, 1835–1901.   175

Three months in the southern states: April–June, 1863. By Lieut.-Col. Fremantle ... New York, John Bradburn, 1864.

309 p. front. (port.) 18½ cm.

Illustrations: Frontispiece, Jefferson Davis (Steel engraving with his signature).

Inclusive dates: Left England March 2, 1863 and sailed from New York on his return July 15, 1863.

Other editions: Edinburgh and London, W. Blackwood and sons, 1863. Mobile, S. H. Goetzel, 1864. This edition is bound in wallpaper covers.

The author entered the British Army at the age of 17 and the following year joined the Coldstream Guards. He had a long army career in which he was steadily advanced in rank. He took part in the Soudan campaign and from 1894 to 1899 was governor of Malta; at the time of his death in 1901 he was near the top in rank among the generals of the British army. Coming to America in 1863 to observe the Civil War, he landed at Brownsville, Texas, and leisurely crossed the state, passing through San Antonio, Houston, Galveston, Houston again and into Louisiana by way of Shreveport. He crossed Louisiana to Monroe and thence southwestward to Natchez, Mississippi, continuing eastward through Jackson to Mobile. Traveling by rail wherever possible, he crossed Alabama and reached Atlanta, with a side trip into Tennessee to visit the Confederate Army there; on his return to Atlanta he went on to Augusta and Charleston. He then visited Wilmington, North Carolina, and moved on to Richmond by way of Weldon and Petersburg. He overtook Lee's army in northern Virginia on its second invasion of the North and was present at the Battle of Gettysburg. Immediately after Gettysburg, Fremantle left for New York City, so that he might not overstay his leave. The account is readable and incisive. This Englishman was in sympathy with the Confederacy but did not fail to record some uncomplimentary observations. He was much impressed by what he saw in Texas as shown by the large amount of attention he gave the Texans in his book. He had great admiration for the Confederate soldiers and spoke with respect of the Confederate leaders whom he met, such as Lee, Joseph E. Johnston, Bragg, Beauregard, Ewell, Longstreet, and others. He observed not only the military situation, but was also impressed by the patriotism of the masses, especially of the women. He also commented upon the bad roads, dilapidation of the railroads, the stagecoaches, the hotels, and the loyalty of the slaves. He met the chief civil officials of the Confederacy in Richmond and had great respect for all of them. This is a well-considered, reliable account of what an observant and intelligent Englishman saw during a three-months journey from one end of the Confederacy to the other.

French, Samuel Gibbs, 1818–1910. 176

Two wars: an autobiography of General Samuel G. French ... Mexican war; war between the states, a diary; reconstruction period, his experience; incidents, reminiscences, etc. Nashville, Tenn., Confederate veteran, 1901.

xv, [1], 404 p. incl., illus., port. front. (port.) 23 cm.

Illustrations: Frontispiece, "Samuel G. French," and twenty-one portraits and battle scenes.

Maps: Ten maps and plans of battle in the Mexican and Confederate wars.

Inclusive dates: 1843–[1861–1865]–1870.

A native of New Jersey and a graduate of the United States Military Academy, Samuel G. French took part in the Mexican War, settled in Greenville, Mississippi, and on the outbreak of the Civil War became an officer in the Confederate Army. He first operated in eastern North Carolina and Virginia, and in the summer of 1863 joined General Joseph E. Johnston's forces in Mississippi. He fought against Sherman in the Atlanta campaign and after the fall of Atlanta followed Hood to the outskirts of Nashville. He returned after the war to his home in Mississippi. Though this narrative is largely military, it has considerable comment on matters of travel interest, especially in that part of the account which contains the author's diary. Except where the diary is used, the exact route which he took is never very clearly indicated.

Gage, Moses D. 177

From Vicksburg to Raleigh; or, A complete history of the Twelfth regiment Indiana volunteer infantry, and the campaigns of Grant and Sherman, with an outline of the great rebellion. By M. D. Gage, chaplain. Chicago, Clarke & co., 1865.

xiv, ₁15₁–356 p. 18½ cm.
Inclusive dates: June, 1861–May, 1865.

Writing of the activities of the Twelfth Indiana Regiment the author made a prologue of its experiences before the Vicksburg campaign. He thus introduced what happened on the march from Memphis (which the army reached by boat up the Mississippi) to Chattanooga and thence through Georgia and the Carolinas to the "Grand Review" in Washington at the end of the war. There is little to distinguish it from the many other books dealing with this march. Gage was chaplain of the regiment, but had no compunction of conscience about describing the unbridled pillage and destruction not only in Georgia and the Carolinas but also in northern Mississippi, Alabama, and Tennessee. He dismissed it as necessary to the winning of the war, and furthermore as tolerated though unauthorized by General Sherman.

Gammage, W. L. 178

The camp, the bivouac, and the battle field. Being a history of the Fourth Arkansas regiment, from its first organization down to the present date; "its campaigns and battles." With an occasional reference to the current events of the times, including biographical sketches of its field officers and others of the "Old brigade." The whole intersperced ₁sic₁ here and there with descriptions of scenery, incidents of camp life, etc. Selma, Ala., Cooper & Kimball, Mississippian ₁sic₁ book and job office, 1864.

164 p. 20½ cm.
Inclusive dates: 1861–1863.

around Cincinnati. At the time Fort Sumter was fired upon Geer held the pastorate of the George Street Methodist Protestant Church. He immediately volunteered in the Federal Army, and on March 4, 1862, moved up the Tennessee River as a member of the 48th Regiment of Ohio Volunteers. He was taken prisoner at Shiloh and was first lodged in Corinth, then at Columbus, Mississippi, and for short intervals at Mobile, Selma, Tuscaloosa, Montgomery, Columbus, Georgia, and Macon. He escaped from that prison, wandered a few weeks in the swamps of the Ogeechee River, and was attempting to reach Darien before he was apprehended and returned to Macon. From there he was held at Atlanta and Madison, Georgia, until arrangements for exchange were made, when he traveled by way of Augusta, Columbia, Salisbury, Raleigh, and Petersburg to Richmond and was exchanged at Aiken's Landing, fourteen miles down the James from the Confederate capital. This account is highly wrought propaganda, designed to arouse love and sympathy and deep appreciation for the slaves of the South, detestation for the Confederates and their inhuman cruelties toward prisoners of war, a horror in the minds of Federal soldiers against being taken prisoner because of the harsh treatment they would receive, and a loathing among patriotic Northerners for the Copperheads. The work, therefore, has little value as an unbiased account of what the author saw or experienced. He uniformly found the slaves loyal and intelligent and the native whites brutal, dirt-eating trash, haughty aristocrats, or, to a slight degree, suppressed Unionists.

Gerrish, Theodore, 1846–   182

Army life; a private's reminiscences of the civil war. By Rev. Theodore Gerrish ... With an introduction by Hon. Josiah H. Drummond. Portland, [Me.] Hoyt, Fogg & Donham [1882.]

372 p.   18¾ cm.
Inclusive dates: 1862–1865.

The author's good-tempered reminiscences of life in the Federal Army are inaccurate in details and indicate little curiosity about the enemy. There are some observations, such as the ancient appearance of Fredericksburg, foraging in search of honey, and the swapping of trinkets and mementos at Lee's surrender. He mentions the Barbara Frietschie affair at Frederick but makes no statement that he saw the old lady wave the flag. These reminiscences in a simpler form first appeared in the *Republican Journal* of Belfast, Maine. Gerrish was a member of the Twentieth Maine Volunteers, who got into the fighting first at the Battle of Antietam. Thereafter he was at Gettysburg and in the Virginia campaigns of Fredericksburg, Chancellorsville, and in Grant's drive against Richmond in the summer of 1864.

Gibbon, John, 1827–1896.   183

Personal recollections of the civil war. By John Gibbon, brigadier-general, U. S. A. New York, London, G. P. Putnam's sons, 1928.

vii, 426 p. front. (port.) maps. 23 cm.
Illustrations: Frontispiece, "Brig-General John Gibbon, U. S. A."
Maps: "Battle of Gettysburg, July 3rd. 1863. Third Day."
Inclusive dates: 1861–1865.

John Gibbon's reminiscences are concerned very little with travel; mainly with military matters. He mentions particularly the difficulty, early in the war, of enforcing rules against pillaging and destruction of fences. When the war broke out, the author was stationed in Utah Territory, whence he marched his forces across the country to Fort Leavenworth and made his way to Washington to join the fighting in the East. Gibbon was present in the main engagements, including Gettysburg, which is given much attention in this book. At Appomattox he was the senior officer to receive the surrender of the Army of Northern Virginia, and after the war he had an important military career.

Giles, Leonidas Blanton, 1841–   184

Terry's Texas rangers. By L. B. Giles. ₁Austin, Tex., Von Boeckmann-Jones co., printers, c1911.₁

105 p. 18½ cm.
Inclusive dates: 1861–1865.
Other editions: No other edition found. For an account of the experiences of a Terry Texas Ranger, who joined the Rangers in the summer of 1864, see in this bibliography William Andrew Fletcher, Rebel private, front and rear. The reminiscences of another Terry Ranger is James Knox Polk Blackburn, Reminiscences of the Terry Rangers. Austin, Texas: The University of Texas, 1919. This account was written fifty years after the war, from memory, and though it was edited for publication by Professor Charles W. Ramsdell and therefore checked on the main facts, it is of little value as a travel book. It was originally published in The Southwestern Historical Quarterly, XXII, 38-77, 143-179. Blackburn was born in 1837 in Tennessee and died in 1923.

The author waited almost a half century after the war to write this book, and then he depended upon an admittedly defective memory. The result therefore has little value because of faulty sources and limited local color. Terry's Rangers were organized in the summer of 1861, in a rendezvous at Bastrop, Texas. They proceeded, mostly by rail, to Houston and Beaumont, thence by boat to Niblett's Bluff on the Sabine River, and to Nashville by way of New Iberia, Brashear City, and again by rail to New Orleans. They finally reached Bowling Green, Kentucky, only to retreat southward before the Federal forces through Nashville to Corinth. The Rangers fought at Shiloh and then marched eastward into Alabama and back into Middle Tennessee. In the autumn of 1862 they moved northward with Bragg in his invasion of Kentucky. After the Battle of Perryville the Texans withdrew eastward through the Appalachian Mountains to Knoxville and returned to Middle Tennessee, where they maneuvered, took part in the Battle of Murfreesboro, and after much activity in the region marched to Chattanooga. In September, 1863, they were in the famous engagement at Chickamauga, after which they invaded East Tennessee, this time going with Longstreet to Mossy Creek. As a part of Wheeler's cavalry this command harassed Sherman throughout his march to the sea and into the Carolinas.

[Gill, John] 1841–   185

Reminiscences of four years as a private soldier in the Confederate army, 1861–1865. Baltimore, Sun printing office, 1904.

xii, [13]–136 p.   1 l., front. (port.)   21¼ cm.
Illustrations: Frontispiece, "John Gill."
Inclusive dates: 1861–1865.

Concerned principally with military movements, this brief narrative adds little to an understanding of wartime conditions in the South. John Gill was a Marylander, born in Annapolis, who enlisted in the Confederate cavalry at the outbreak of the Civil War and occasionally was detailed to scout duty. Apart from the battles of Spottsylvania Courthouse and Yellow Tavern, his activities were confined to northern Virginia, especially in the Valley, and to the major Maryland and Pennsylvania campaigns. On occasions when Gill was prostrated with fever he was cared for in the homes of Virginia aristocrats.

Gilmor, Harry, 1838–1883.   186

Four years in the saddle. By Colonel Harry Gilmor ... New York, Harper & brothers, 1866.

xii, [13]–291 p. incl. front.   18¾ cm.
Illustrations: Frontispiece, unlabeled pen and ink sketch of a cavalryman, presumably Gilmor.
Inclusive dates: 1861–1865.

Gilmor's highly embellished account of a Confederate cavalryman's experiences throughout the war is filled with hard riding, narrow escapes, and gallantry toward many young lady acquaintances. In detail it cannot be taken at face value but, with liberal allowances for the author's desire to produce good reading, it has some value as a general account. A Marylander, Gilmor crossed the Potomac soon after the outbreak of the Civil War and enlisted in the Confederate Army. Except for participation in the Gettysburg campaign, in McCausland's raid into Pennsylvania which burned Chambersburg, and his outriding to the environs of Baltimore on the occasion of Early's expedition against Washington in the summer of 1864, his activities were limited almost entirely to the Shenandoah Valley. He was twice captured by the Federals, the first time in September, 1862, when he was held six months in Baltimore, and again in February, 1865, when he was taken to Fort Warren in Boston harbor and held until July of that year.

[Gilmore, James Roberts] 1822–1903.   187

Among the pines: or, South in secession-time. By Edmund Kirke [*pseud.*] New York, J. R. Gilmore [etc.] 1862.

310 p.   18 cm.
Inclusive dates: December, 1860–January, 1861.
Parallel accounts: Rev. William Wyndham Malet visited this same corner of South Carolina

in 1862 and left this account: An errand to the South in the summer of 1862. London, Richard Bentley, 1863.

Although the author affirms his book "is not a work of fiction" but "a record of facts," it is evidently highly colored and consists mainly of conversations which could not have been recorded verbatim. Indeed, Gilmore's purpose was to set the Radicals against Lincoln to induce him to free the slaves, and the book must be regarded as propaganda, with just enough truth to make a plausible story. In December, 1860, Gilmore, a New York trader profiting from Southern trade, decided to visit one of his Southern acquaintances. He landed at Charleston, South Carolina, boarded a coastal boat for Georgetown, and hired a Negro hack driver to take him into the northeastern tip of the state near present-day Conway. Within the story framework Gilmore strikes home his anti-slavery message to the war-torn North. He gives accounts of cruelty to slaves, of chasing runaways with bloodhounds, of whites made poor by slave owners, and of the general tyranny of the system; but the book is factually valueless.

[Gilmore, James Roberts] 1822–1903.   188
Down in Tennessee, and back by way of Richmond. By Edmund Kirke [pseud.] ... New York, Carleton, 1864.

282 p.   18¼ cm.
Inclusive dates: May–June, 1863; July, 1864.
Other editions: London, S. Low, son, & Marston, 1864.

Despite the title, this work is hardly a travel book, nor did the author go "back by Way of Richmond"; that was a separate venture, from Washington and back by boat. The trip described here was by rail from Louisville to Nashville and beyond to Murfreesboro. Using a conversational style, he gave the North his views on slavery and on the degradation it brought to the region's "poor whites." In this respect the book adds little to his previous work, *Among the Pines: or, South in Secession-Time*. The chief value is an account of the interview Gilmore and Col. James F. Jacquess had with Jefferson Davis in their efforts to find a peace formula. Gilmore here takes special pains to inform his readers that the conversations with Davis may be taken as absolutely correct.

[Girard, Charles Frédéric] 1822–1895.   189
Les États Confédérés d'Amérique visités en 1863. Mémoire adressé à S. M. Napoléon III. Paris, E. Dentu, 1864.

viii, [9]–160 p.   fold. map.   22½ cm.
Maps: "Carte Politique de l'Amèrique du Nord." A folding map, 29½ cm. by 32 cm.
Inclusive dates: 1863.

M. Girard entered the Confederacy at Charleston and, after a short stay, journeyed northward by rail through Florence, Wilmington, Goldsboro, Weldon, and Petersburg to Richmond, where he remained except for visits to Fredericksburg and Lee's Army of Northern Virginia. He was interested in all aspects of this new nation, its president, cabinet members, armies, munitions factories, citizens, and slave population; the account is highly laudatory.

Glazier, Willard Worcester, 1841–1905.   190

The capture, the prison pen, and the escape; giving a complete history of prison life in the South, principally at Richmond, Danville, Macon, Savannah, Charleston, Columbia, Belle Isle, Millen, Salisbury, and Andersonville: describing the arrival of prisoners, and plans of escape, together with numerous and varied incidents and anecdotes of prison life, embracing, also, the adventures of the author's escape from Columbia, South Carolina, his recapture, subsequent escape, recapture, trial as spy, and his final and successful escape from Sylvania, Georgia ... By Captain Willard W. Glazier ... To which is added an appendix, containing the name, rank, regiment, and post-office address of prisoners ... New York, R. H. Ferguson & co., 1870.

xiv p., 2 l., ₁19₁–446 p. incl. plates front. (port.)   18½ cm.
Illustrations: Frontispiece, "W. W. Glazier ₁Signature₁ Bvt Captain U. S. V. Engraved by J. C. Buttre, N. Y."; "The Capture—Cavalry Fight at Buckland Mills" ₁By Hoey₁; "Libby Prison" ₁By J. Hoey₁; "Interior View of Libby Prison"; "The Hole in the Floor"; "Tunnelling—The Narrow Path to Freedom"; "Jail Yard—Charleston, South Carolina" ₁By Hoey₁; "Rebel Mode of Capturing Escaped Prisoners" ₁By Hoey₁; "The Escape from Columbia, S. C.—Crossing the Dead Line" ₁By J. Hoey₁; "The Escape—Crossing the Savannah at Midnight" ₁By J. Hoey₁; "The Escape—Fed by Negroes in a Swamp"; "Recaptured"; "The Escape and Pursuit"; "The Escape from Sylvania, Georgia"; "Approaching the Federal Lines"; "Came too Near the Dead Line"; "Interior View of Andersonville."
Inclusive dates: October, 1863–January, 1865.
Other editions: Albany, N. Y., Joel Munsell, 1866 (which appears to be the first edition, although the work was copyrighted in 1865); New York, United States publishing company, 1868; Hartford, Conn., H. E. Goodwin, 1868.

Captain Glazier's book is a highly emotional account of prison life in the Confederacy and attempts to escape with comments on the country and the people as seen in traveling from one prison to another. Based on a diary, the narrative was dressed up for propaganda purposes after the war, and the author claimed that 400,000 copies were sold. Glazier, born at Fowler, New York, enlisted in the Second Regiment of New York Harris Light Cavalry in the first year of war. Late in 1863 he was taken prisoner in northern Virginia, sent to Libby Prison, and moved after some months to Macon, Georgia, with short stops at Danville, Greensboro, Charlotte, and Columbia. From Macon he was transferred to Savannah Prison and back to Columbia where he made his escape. He wandered westward through South Carolina, with the inevitable slaves befriending and guiding him, crossed the Savannah River below Augusta, was recaptured near Savannah, and escaped again to join Sherman's Federal forces in Savannah and to go by ship to New York. Glazier wrote several other books dealing with the Civil War, and some travel books about his later journeys. Among these was a horseback trip to the Pacific Coast, and his more famous canoe trip to the headwaters of the Mississippi River where he claimed to have discovered for the first time the true springs of the Father of Waters.

Glazier, Willard Worcester, 1841–1905.   191

Three years in the federal cavalry. By Captain Willard Glazier ... New York, R. H. Ferguson & company, 1870.

xviii, 19–339 p. incl. front. plates, ports. 19 cm.

Illustrations: Frontispiece, "Willard Glazier ₍Signature₎ Bvt Captain, U. S. V." (Engraved by J. C. Butture, N. Y.); "Our Cavalry Leaders, Sheridan, Davies, Gregg, Pleasonton, Custer, Kilpatrick, Buford, Stoneman, Bayard" (engraved by J. A. O'Neill, N. Y.); "Cavalry Column on the March" (by D. R. Fay and J. Hoey); "Night Attack on Falmouth Heights" (by D. R. Fay and J. Hoey); "Burial of Captain Walters at Midnight, During Pope's Retreat" (by D. R. Fay and J. Hoey); "Cavalry Pickets Meeting in the Rappahannock" (by Hoey); "Cavalry Scouting Party Halting for the Night"; "Cavalry Fight at Brandy Station, June 9th, 1863" (by D. R. Fay); "The Cavalry Bivouac" (by D. R. Fay and J. Hoey); "The Capture—Cavalry Fight at Buckland Mills" (by D. R. Fay and J. Hoey).

Inclusive dates: August, 1861–October, 1863.

Other editions: No other edition found. Two other printings, by the same company, were in 1872 and 1874.

Dealing mostly with the author's military experiences, this book also contains some interesting comments on the destruction of forests in northern Virginia by the armies in winter quarters, where the trees were cut down for firewood and for constructing rude log huts, with notes on the loyalty of slaves and, in the earlier part of the war, the strict restrictions of Federal commanders against appropriation of private property. The tone of this account, based on a diary, is temperate and apparently a fair record of conditions, since it was finished within a few years after the close of the war. He saw service in most of the battles of northern Virginia and at Gettysburg and Sharpsburg until he was captured in October, 1863. The story of his captivity is told in his *The Capture, the Prison Pen, and the Escape.*

Goldsborough, William Worthington, 1831–1901.   192

The Maryland line in the Confederate States army. By W. W. Goldsborough ... Baltimore, Kelly, Piet & co., 1869.

357 p. front., port. 18¾ cm.

Illustrations: Frontispiece, "Maj. Gen. Arnold Elzey"; "Brig. Gen. Geo. H. Steuart"; "Brig. Gen. Bradley T. Johnson"; "Lt. Col. James R. Herbert"; "Maj. W. W. Goldsborough"; "Capt. Wm. H. Murray"; "Capt. Jno. W. Torsch"; "Lt. Col. Ridgley Brown."

Inclusive dates: 1861–1865.

Other editions: No other edition found. Another work by the same author bearing almost the identical title (The Maryland line in the Confederate Army. 1861–1865), but rewritten with a few exceptions: Baltimore; Gugenheimer, Weil & co., 1900 (?).

Goldsborough's Maryland unit of Confederate troops operated principally in the Shenandoah Valley and northern Virginia, but also participated in the Gettysburg campaign and, near the end of the war, in some activities south of the James.

Goldsborough confined his narrative largely to military affairs and related subjects, such as robbing the dead Yankees of their boots, the reception of Confederate troops by the cheering populace, and a burning ammunition train plunging into the Chickahominy River.

Goodhart, Briscoe, 1845–1927.   193

History of the Independent Loudoun Virginia rangers. U. S. vol. cav. (scouts) 1862–65. By Briscoe Goodhart, co. A. Washington, D. C., Press of McGill & Wallace, 1896.

vi, 234 p.   front., illus., plates, ports., maps.   22 cm.
Illustrations: Thirty-seven illustrations of soldiers and landscapes, and one diagram.
Maps: "Rebel Movements on Harper's Ferry and Antietam"; "Harper's Ferry and Surrounding Country"; "Map of Gettysburg and Vicinity"; "Map of Monocacy"; "Map of the Shenandoah Valley."
Inclusive dates: 1862–1865.

The Loudoun Volunteers was one of the units of Federal troops raised within the Confederacy. Their movements were confined to northern Virginia and the Shenandoah Valley, except for the Gettysburg campaign and General Early's invasion of Maryland in 1864. The author deals almost entirely with military matters, and only occasionally mentions details pertinent to peacetime travels.

Goodloe, Albert Theodore.   194

Some Rebel relics from the seat of war. By Albert Theodore Goodloe ... Nashville, Tenn., Publishing house of the Methodist Episcopal church, South, 1893.

315 p.   front. (port.)   18¼ cm.
Illustrations: Frontispiece, "Albert Theodore Goodloe."
Inclusive dates: 1862–1865.
Other editions: An enlargement of this work by Goodloe is: Confederate echoes: a voice from the South in the days of secession and of the southern confederacy. Nashville, Tenn., Printed for the author, Publishing house of the Methodist Episcopal church south, Smith & Lamar, 1907.

Early in 1862 Goodloe joined the Confederate army in La Grange, Alabama, ultimately becoming first lieutenant of the Thirty-fifth Regiment Alabama Volunteer Infantry. During his first two years of service he participated in the campaigns around Corinth, Holly Springs, Jackson, Meridian, and Vicksburg, and across the Mississippi line to Baton Rouge and Port Hudson in Louisiana. In early 1864 he joined General Johnston's forces in attempting to stop Sherman's invasion of Georgia. After the fall of Atlanta Goodloe followed Hood to the outskirts of Nashville and after the Confederate defeat there returned to Mississippi and soon went to Mobile and eastward by Montgomery to Milledgeville and Augusta, Georgia, thence across upper South Carolina to Charlotte, Greensboro, and to Kingston in eastern North Carolina. Just before Johnston's surrender near Durham Station, he started westward to join the Trans-Mississippi Department, reaching Meridian before he became convinced that the war was finished. He then went to Eastport, Mississippi, where he was paroled. The account, based partly on a diary, contains many diversions into other matters but gives a remarkably penetrating account of a soldier's daily life on the march and in camp, as well as comments on the countryside and means of travel.

Gordon, George Henry, 1825(?)–1886.   195

A war diary of events in the war of the great rebellion. 1863–1865. By George H. Gordon ... Boston, James R. Osgood and company, 1882.

vi p., 1 l., 437 p.   illus., maps.   20¼ cm.
Illustrations: "The Old Episcopal Church at Hampton, Va."; "Fort Sumter"; "Gunboat on the Mississippi."
Maps: "Map of West Point, Va., and its Fortifications"; "Charleston Harbor and its Approaches, Showing the Positions of the Rebel Batteries"; "Map of Eastern Virginia. South of James River" (each double-page size).
Inclusive dates: 1863–1865.

Written in a discursive style quite unlike most similar accounts, this diary is a valuable commentary on the South during the war. The author was concerned less with actual military affairs than with personal observations on the general scene. He was greatly interested in the attitude of the Southern people toward the war and in their mode of life; in the slaves and their activities, both work for their masters and enticement into the Federal lines; in the devastation of war and gruesome work of gathering up and identifying bodies weeks after they had fallen; and in the natural scenery of the country. The comments relate to the Frederick-Sharpsburg region of Maryland, northern Virginia from the Valley to Fredericksburg, the York Peninsula with special reference to Yorktown and Williamsburg, Charleston and the Sea Islands including Hilton Head, Jacksonville and St. Augustine, the Mississippi Valley from New Orleans to Memphis, the Mobile Bay country, and the Richmond-Appomattox area at the end of the war. Gordon's war observations prior to 1863 are found in his work: *Brook Farm to Cedar Mountain; in the War of the Great Rebellion, 1861–1862: A Revision and Enlargement (from the Latest and Most Authentic Sources) of Papers Numbered I, II, and III. Entitled "History of the Second Massachusetts Regiment," and the Second Massachusetts Regiment and Stonewall Jackson"* (Boston, James R. Osgood and Company, 1883.) Gordon was colonel of the Second Massachusetts Regiment Infantry and later brigadier general and brevet major general of United States Volunteers.

Gordon, Marquis Lafayette, 1843–1900.   196

M. L. Gordon's experiences in the civil war from his narrative, letters and diary; edited by Donald Gordon ... Boston, Privately printed, 1922.

7 p. l., [3]–72 p.   front., illus., plates, ports., facsims. (part fold.)   27½ cm.
Illustrations: Fourteen illustrations, mostly photographs of people mentioned in the book.
Maps: Charleston Harbour; James River.
Inclusive dates: 1861–1864.

Composed of three parts, this work presents: a narrative written in 1889–90, a series of letters, and a short diary. There is some semblance of a travelogue but little descriptive information. Gordon enlisted in the Federal Army at Waynesburg, Pennsylvania, in November, 1861, and soon left for Washington. Later he went down the Chesapeake to join McClellan's forces attempting to take Richmond and stopped briefly in the Suffolk region before going by sea to the North Carolina coast. He passed through Beaufort and Newbern, into the interior as far as Goldsboro, and returned by boat to Folly and Morris, the sea islands around Charleston, and the Hilton Head region. He later returned to the James River country in Virginia and was mustered out in 1864.

Goss, Warren Lee, 1835–1925. 197

The soldier's story of his captivity at Andersonville, Belle Isle, and other Rebel prisons. By Warren Lee Goss. With an appendix, containing the names of the Union soldiers who died at Andersonville ... Boston, I. N. Richardson & co., 1875.

2 p. l., 3–357 p.   front. (port.), plates, map, 3 plans (1 fold.)   21 cm.
Illustrations: Frontispiece, portrait of author, signed, steel engraving by H. W. Smith; eighteen illustrations, four of them being by Thomas Nast, all relating to prison life.
Maps: "Plan of prison bakery, Andersonville, Ga."; "Plan of prison grounds, Andersonville, measured by Dr. Hamlin"; "Map of part of Georgia"; "Plan of prison grounds, Andersonville, measured by Dr. Hamlin" (larger scale).
Inclusive dates: 1862–1864.
Other editions: This book was copyrighted in 1866, but no copy with that date has been located; also Boston, Lee and Shepard, 1867 and 1869. Doubtless the 1867 edition was the first.

Prison life at Libby, Belle Isle, Andersonville, Charleston, and Florence constitutes the principal portion of this book with considerable attention given to journeying from one prison to another and some details of escapes. Goss enlisted in the Second Massachusetts Regiment of Heavy Artillery early in the war. He was captured in the Peninsula campaign in 1862, first imprisoned in Libby and then on Belle Isle, soon exchanged, and sent down the James River aboard a flag-of-truce boat. He later appeared on the coast of North Carolina, and was again taken prisoner near Plymouth in 1864. Goss and his fellow prisoners were marched to Tarboro and sent by train to Andersonville, Georgia, where he spent most of his imprisonment. When Sherman invaded Georgia many of the Andersonville prisoners were taken first to Charleston and then to Florence, where Goss was paroled. He left the Confederacy on a flag-of-truce boat sailing from Charleston. His story of prison life, planned for sales appeal and propaganda, is among the most harrowing accounts written after the war. Allowing for a prisoner's bitterness and Goss's loathing for all Confederate people and affairs, the book has some value. After the war, Goss became a successful author, writing many books, most of them young peoples' accounts of the conflict.

Gould, John Mead, 1839– 198

History of the First-Tenth-Twenty-ninth Maine regiment. In service of the United States from May 3, 1861, to June 21, 1866. By Maj. John M. Gould. With the History of the Tenth Me. battalion. By Rev. Leonard G. Jordan. Portland, Maine, S. Berry, 1871.

709, ₁1₁ p.   front., illus., ports., maps.   22½ cm.
Illustrations: Twenty-four portraits of soldiers and two battle scenes.
Maps: "Battle of Cedar Mountain"; "Antietam from a Map of the U. S. Engineer Office"; "Battle of Opequan (Sheridan's Winchester)"; "Plan of Fisher's Hill"; "Plan of Battle of Cedar Creek."
Inclusive dates: 1861–1866.

Gould, a close observer of military affairs and general conditions, kept a diary throughout his service and used it in this book, which is valuable travel material. His Maine Regiment was a part of the various organizations and reorganizations mentioned in the title. Jordan accompanied those Maine troops who, after the Battle of Gettysburg, followed the usual route through West Virginia, Ohio, Indiana, and across the Ohio to Louisville, then southward over the Louisville and Nashville Railroad to Nashville, where it was soon engaged around Shelbyville, Tennessee. Ordered back to Louisville, the regiment went by rail to Cairo, boarded a Mississippi steamer for New Orleans, and joined other Maine troops among whom was Gould, who had come by coastal steamer from Portland, Maine. By this time the Maine troops had seen considerable service, including the hot battles of Bull Run, Sharpsburg, Chancellorsville, and Gettysburg, and the Red River expedition in Louisiana. In 1864 the Maine troops returned by boat to Washington, by way of the Gulf and Atlantic, arriving on the Potomac just in time to help beat off Early's attack. After that they operated principally in the Shenandoah Valley until, instead of being mustered out, they were sent by boat to Savannah and detailed for garrison duty at Georgetown, Florence, Darlington, and Cheraw, South Carolina.

Grant, Ulysses Simpson, *pres. U. S.,* 1822–1885.   199
Personal memoirs of U. S. Grant ... New York, Charles L. Webster & company, 1885–86.

Vol. I, 584 p.; Vol. II, 647, ₁1₁ p.   front. (ports.) plates, maps, facsims.   22½ cm.
Illustrations: Frontispiece, Vol. I, "U. S. Grant, Bvt. 2d Lt. 4th Infy." ₁Signature₁; "Birth-Place of General U. S. Grant, Point Pleasant Ohio. Etched by W. E. Marshall"; Frontispiece, Vol. II, "U. S. Grant, Lt. Gen." ₁Signature₁; "McLean House at Appomattox in which General Lee Signed the Terms of Surrender. Eng. by A. Dresher." Also three facsimiles of letters.
Maps: Forty-three, all relating to Civil War battles, excepting the first two.
Inclusive dates: 1861–1865.
Other editions: London, Low, 1885–86. 2 vol.; New York, Charles L. Webster & company, 1895. 2 vols. in one; "Second Edition," New York, The Century company, 1895. 2 vols.; also other printings by Century in 1909 and 1917.

Among Civil War memoirs, Grant's are generally considered classic because of their simple, direct style. They are not travel accounts, however, for Grant was concerned almost wholly with military movements and army affairs and he makes few comments on anything else. These memoirs begin with Grant's childhood, and attain breadth with the Mexican War and some rambles in Texas, but are most important for the Civil War period. The scenes of Grant's Civil War activities are well known: St. Louis, Paducah, Fort Henry, Fort Donelson, Nashville, Shiloh, Corinth, Memphis, and Vicksburg; and the Virginia area including his various battles ending with Appomattox. This book departs now and then from a narrative of reminiscences by interjecting chapters on other theaters of war, such as Sherman's March to the Sea. Direct and simple as his story is, it is ingenuous at times. Just who did burn Columbia and in what sort of garb was Jefferson Davis captured? Grant's evasions are clever.

Grayson, Andrew J. 200

"The spirit of 1861." History of the Sixth Indiana regiment in the three months' campaign in western Virginia—full of humor and originality, depicting battles, skirmishes, forced marches, incidents in camp life, etc., with the names of every officer and private in the Sixth regiment. By A. J. Grayson, Madison, Ind., Courier print, 1875?

52 p.   23 cm.
Inclusive dates: 1861.

Leaving Indianapolis by rail for the battle front in western Virginia, Sergeant Grayson went through Cincinnati, Marietta, Parkersburg, and over the Baltimore and Ohio Railroad to Grafton. He operated as far south as Philippi and Rich Mountain, and returned by way of Bellaire and Columbus. Grayson writes in a light vein, apparently without contemporary memoranda, but carefully notes the routes taken and mentions various incidents and impressions on the way.

Greene, John W. 201

Camp Ford prison; and how I escaped. An incident of the civil war. Toledo, Ohio, Barkdull printing house, 1893.

140 p.   front., illus.   20½ cm.
Illustrations: Frontispiece, John W. Greene; "The Tables Turned"; "Jno. W. Greene" [Signature]; "John A. Whitset" [Signature]; "At the Negro Cabin"; "At the Gray Plantation."
Inclusive dates: September, 1863–January, 1864.

From a memory dimmed by more than a quarter century, John Greene prepared this insignificant paper-back booklet. It is a superficial account of the capture, imprisonment, and escape of a Federal soldier who saw service in Louisiana. There are imaginary conversations with slaves, rich planters, and poor whites. Green was captured near Morganza and marched overland through Natchitoches, Mansfield, Shreveport, and on to Tyler, near which he was imprisoned for a few months in Camp Ford. Late in December, 1863, Green escaped, returned across northern Louisiana by way of Shreveport, and finally reached the Federal lines at Vidalia, across the Mississippi River from Natchez.

Grigsby, Melvin, 1845–
The smoked Yank. By Melvin Grigsby. No place, publisher, 1888.

244 p. illus., port. 22 cm.
Illustrations: Eighteen crude sketches, mostly related to prison life, including portrait of author on title-page.
Inclusive dates: 1862–1865.
Other editions: The book here used is the "revised Edition." The original edition: Sioux Falls, Dakota bell publishing co., 1888. Second edition: Chicago, Regan publishing company, 1891.

This book appears to be reasonably correct in all matters except minor details and conversations. Grigsby was living in Wisconsin in 1862 when he volunteered in a unit organized at Milwaukee. He was sent to St. Louis, marched across Missouri to Springfield, and southward through Arkansas to Helena on the Mississippi River. After some months he was shipped up river to Memphis but was soon attached to the army investing Vicksburg. After its fall he followed Sherman to Jackson and back to the vicinity of Vicksburg, later joining a small detachment in the Port Gibson region, engaged in rounding up cotton. On one of these forays he was taken prisoner, sent to Cahaba Prison a few miles below Selma, Alabama, and transferred to Andersonville for the major part of his confinement. In early fall, 1864, he was removed to Florence, where he escaped into North Carolina. Recaptured, he was returned to Florence only to escape a few weeks later, this time moving southwestward across South Carolina in the hope of meeting Sherman's advancing army. He reached it south of Columbia and was present at the burning of that city. He moved northward with Sherman's forces to Fayetteville, on to Goldsboro, entrained for Newbern, and took a boat for Washington. This book adds little if anything to the average prisoner-of-war accounts, except to relate conditions at Cahaba where a kind-hearted Southern lady circulated books from her library among the prisoners.

Grimes, Absalom Carlisle, 1834–1911.
Absalom Grimes, Confederate mail runner, edited from Captain Grimes' own story by M. M. Quaife ... New Haven, Yale university press; London, H. Milford, Oxford university press, 1926.

xii, 216 p. front. (port.) plates, facsim. 22¾ cm.
Illustrations: Frontispiece, "Absalom Carlisle Grimes (About 1863)"; "Bombardment and Capture of Fort Henry, Tenn."; "Gratiot Military Prison"; "Charge, Finding, and Sentence of the Military Commission" [Facsimile of manuscript].
Inclusive dates: 1861–1865.
Other editions: No other edition found. A book on the same subject is: James Bradley, The Confederate mail carrier or from Missouri to Arkansas, through Mississippi, Alabama, Georgia and Tennessee. An unwritten leaf of the "Civil War." Being an account of the battles, marches and hardships of the First and Second brigades, Mo., C. S. A. Together with the thrilling adventures and narrow escapes of Captain Grimes and his fair accomplice, who carried the mail by "the underground route" from the brigade to Missouri. Mexico, Mo., James Bradley, 1894.

Although these are reminiscences of an old man, their reliability is buttressed by the author's war diary and the editing of a careful scholar. The chief importance of the account is the light it throws on conditions in the Mississippi Valley between the battle lines and hinterlands of the two sections of the country. Grimes, having grown up as a riverman, knew many of the crews operating on the Mississippi and its tributaries, and had their help in making his way as a mail carrier between expatriated Missourians and Kentuckians and their relatives back home. He operated southward to Vicksburg, eastward to Chattanooga, and northward to the distributing and collecting centers of Louisville and St. Louis. Women in Kentucky and Missouri in sympathy with the Confederate cause acted as agents in collecting and distributing the mail he carried.

Grimes, Bryan, 1828–1880.   204

Extracts of letters of Major-Gen'l Bryan Grimes to his wife, written while in active service in the Army of northern Virginia. Together with some personal recollections of the war, written by him after its close, etc. Compiled from original manuscripts by Pulaski Cooper ... of Raleigh, N. C. Raleigh, N. C., Edwards, Broughton & co., printers, 1883.

137, ₍1₎ p.   22 cm.
Inclusive dates: 1861–1865.
Other editions: Another edition: Raleigh, N. C., A. Williams & co., 1884.

Grimes, a graduate of the University of North Carolina and a planter in the eastern part of the state, was greatly interested in the prospects of war in early 1861. He went to Charleston to see the firing on the fort, but arrived too late. He then went to Montgomery, Pensacola, and New Orleans, and up the river to Memphis. Here he boarded a train for Richmond, going by way of Chattanooga, Knoxville, and Lynchburg, and returned to his home in time to attend the state secession convention as a delegate. With North Carolina out of the Union he accepted a lieutenant-colonelcy in the Fourth North Carolina Regiment, and later rose to the rank of major general. Arriving too late for the First Manassas battle, he participated thereafter in most of the major engagements of the Army of Northern Virginia to the end at Appomattox. This account by General Grimes is almost entirely of a military nature, and offers little enlightenment on conditions in the Confederacy.

Grose, William, 1812–1900.   205

The story of the marches, battles and incidents of the 36th regiment Indiana volunteer infantry. By a member of the regiment. New Castle, Ind., The Courier company press, 1891.

256 p.   front., ports.   23 cm.
Illustrations: Frontispiece, "Wm. Grose, Brig. & Brev't Maj Gen" ₍Signature₎, and three other portraits of soldiers.
Inclusive dates: 1861–1864.

The 36th Regiment, formed at Richmond, Indiana, in 1861, was soon moved to Louisville and made a short dip into Kentucky before proceeding over the Ohio and Cumberland rivers to Nashville. It continued eastward into northern Alabama through Florence and Athens and back northward through Tennessee into Kentucky to intercept Bragg's invasion in the autumn of 1862. Grose was at Perryville, Murfreesboro, and later in the Chattanooga-Chickamauga campaign. He followed Sherman to Atlanta and was mustered out after the fall of that city. The narrative is almost entirely a military account, with little travel value.

Hadley, John Vestal, 1840–1915. 206

Seven months a prisoner. By J. V. Hadley. New York, Charles Scribner's sons, 1898.

3 p. l., 258 p.   16 cm.   ₍The ivory series₎
Inclusive dates: 1864.

Hadley's story is an unusually well-written narrative of a soldier's experiences in prison and of his escape journeys. It was written from memory alone after a third of a century, but it is not distorted by intentional bitterness. Hadley, from Plainview, Indiana, and an officer in the Union Army, was captured in May, 1864, in the Battle of the Wilderness. He was taken by rail to Lynchburg and Danville, with short stops at each place. Over the recently completed railroad to Greensboro, North Carolina, he went directly through Salisbury, Charlotte, Columbia, and Augusta to Macon, where he spent the first extended part of his imprisonment. In succession he was transferred to Savannah, Charleston, and Columbia, where, from "Camp Sorghum," he made his escape. Most of the narrative relates to Hadley's journey northward through South Carolina, North Carolina, and to Knoxville, Tennessee, where he made his way into the Union lines. He gives a vivid description of the "deserter country" of western North Carolina and of the people, especially Negroes in South Carolina, who aided him.

₍Haines, Zenas T.₎ 207

Letters from the Forty-fourth regiment M. V. M.: a record of the experience of a nine months' regiment in the Department of North Carolina in 1862–3. By "Corporal" ₍*pseud.*₎ Boston, Printed at the Herald job office, 1863.

121 p.   22½ cm.
Inclusive dates: October, 1862–June, 1863.

The anonymous writer of these letters, which originally appeared in the *Boston Herald*, was a close observer of the scene of operations in eastern North Carolina. He was almost as much concerned with towns, plantations, and people as with military matters. His descriptions are apt, though naturally colored by a leering New England conscience. He has much to say about Newbern, Kingston, Goldsboro, Hamilton and its destruction, Williamston, Plymouth, and Washington; he describes the swamps, pine woods, and homes of all types of people. He does not neglect to describe pillaging among the country folk, mentioning such touches as the old lady who defended her potato bank with a wooden rake, and the rifling of valuable papers from Judge Biggs' office. The book is of first-rate importance and reliability in evaluating wartime conditions in eastern North Carolina. The unit to which the "Corporal" was attached left Boston for Newbern in the fall of 1862, carried out raids in the hinterland for about eight months, and then returned to Boston to be mustered out at the termination of its nine-months enlistment.

Hall, Winchester, 1819–   208
The story of the 26th Louisiana infantry, in the service of the Confederate States. By Winchester Hall. No place, publisher, 1890?

> 4 p. l., 228, [2] p.   plan.   23 cm.
> *Maps:* "Sketch of Battle field of Chickasaw Bayou, December 28 and 29, 1862."
> *Inclusive dates:* 1862–1865.

This narrative merits consideration for both reliability and travel comments. Written twenty years after the war without benefit of a diary or other material, it contains few improbable personal details and most observations appear to be accurate. Hall lived in Lafourche Parish in Louisiana where, in 1862, after the fall of Fort Donelson, he organized a company and became its captain. The travels described here were not extensive, being entirely in Mississippi and Louisiana, except for one or two trips to Richmond. The captain first led his unit to Berwick Bay but was soon on his way to help defend New Orleans. After the fall of that city, he proceeded by rail to Vicksburg by way of Jackson. He was in Vicksburg at its fall and was paroled. Later he appeared at the parole camp in Alexandria, Louisiana, and was exchanged within a year. When the Confederacy fell he was moving toward Shreveport. Hall describes a Confederate soldier's life, including his diet of rat and mule in besieged Vicksburg.

Hancock, Cornelia, 1840–1926.   209
South after Gettysburg; letters of Cornelia Hancock from the Army of the Potomac, 1863–1865; Edited by Henrietta Stratton Jaquette. Philadelphia, University of Pennsylvania press, 1937.

> xiii, 173 p.   2 illus. (plans) plates   20¼ cm.
> *Illustrations:* "Second Corps Hospital, Gettysburg"; "Third Division Hospital, Brandy Station"; "Wharf at Belle Plain"; "Army Wagon Train in Virginia"; "White House Landing"; "Hospital at City Point."
> *Maps:* Chesapeake Bay region imprinted on title page, giving route taken by Cornelia Hancock.
> *Inclusive dates:* 1863–1865.

Cornelia Hancock served in the Federal hospitals, and her book is largely concerned with details of hospital life. She makes very few comments on the country or the people of the Confederacy. She was certain that Virginia could not compare with her native New Jersey, and few people she saw were Union in sentiment; not even the slaves appeared willing to follow the Federal Army, even when they were coaxed to do so. Though a Quaker, the author had no love for the "rebels," and she felt that the army was entirely too respectful of rebel property.

Hancock, Richard R., 1841?–1906. 210

Hancock's diary: or, A history of the Second Tennessee Confederate cavalry, with sketches of First and Seventh battalions; also, portraits and biographical sketches. Two volumes in one. Nashville, Tenn., Brandon printing company, 1887.

644 p. front., port. 22½ cm.

Illustrations: Frontispiece, "N. B. Forrest" [Signature]; "Sergeant R. R. Hancock, Co. C"; "Lieutenant-Colonel F. N. McNairy, Commander First Battalion"; "Private Monroe Knight, Co. E, First Battalion"; "Captain M. W. McKnight, Co. C."; "Sergeant J. C. McAdoo"; "Colonel J. D. Bennett"; "Lieutenant B. A. High, Co. G."; "Lieutenant-Colonel Geo. H. Morton"; "Captain T. B. Underwood"; "General James R. Chalmers"; "Lieutenant George Love, Co. D."; "Lieutenant A. H. French, Co. A."; "Private W. C. Hancock, Co. C (Killed July 14th, 1864.)"; "Lieutenant Geo. E. Seay"; "Lieutenant H. L. W. Turney, Co. C."; "Lieutenant F. M. McRee, Co. K"; "Lieutenant Geo. F. Hager, Co. G."; "Sergeant A. B. McKnight"; "Yr old Commander and Friend J. D. McLin" [Signature].

Inclusive dates: 1861–1864.

Twenty years after this diary was written it was revised and supplemented with information gained from the writer's comrades and from official documents. It is therefore somewhat impersonal but no less reliable. Its chief value as a travel book lies in the author's clearly indicated routes, with incidental observations on the country and occasional references to people visited. Hancock's wartime travels were confined entirely to northern Alabama and Mississippi, Tennessee, and southeastern Kentucky. Much of the time he was following General Forrest and, notably, he was present at the so-called Fort Pillow massacre. In October, 1864, he was wounded and thereafter took no part in the war.

Hannaford, Ebenezer, 1840– 211

The story of a regiment: a history of the campaigns, and associations in the field, of the Sixth regiment Ohio volunteer infantry. By E. Hannaford ... Cincinnati, Published by the author, Stereotyped at the Franklin type foundry, 1868.

xvi, 17–622 p. 21 cm.

Hannaford was a member of the Sixth Ohio Infantry, organized in 1861 at Cincinnati, and remained with it throughout its three-year enlistment. The organization left Cincinnati by train in the summer of 1861 for the Cheat Mountain front in western Virginia (West Virginia), going by way of Columbus, across the Ohio River at Bellaire, and thence to Grafton. After taking part in this campaign, Hannaford continued to Parkersburg over the Baltimore and Ohio Railroad and by steamer to Louisville. He went into camp near Hodgenville, south of Louisville, and after some weeks left to take part in Buell's drive against Nashville. On his journey southward he went down the Ohio and up the Cumberland to the Tennessee capital, continued southward to Shiloh and Corinth, and after the latter campaign marched eastward into Alabama and northward into Tennessee through Nashville and back into Kentucky to prevent Bragg's capture of Louisville. He participated in the Battle of Perryville in October, 1862, and returned to Nashville, taking part at the end of the year in the Battle of Murfreesboro. After various operations in Middle Tennessee he fought in the Battle of Chickamauga in September, 1863. After fighting around Chattanooga he went as far as Knoxville in East Tennessee. In the spring of 1864 he started with Sherman's march into Atlanta, getting as far as Kingston before his enlistment expired. He returned by railway to Nashville, where he boarded a Cumberland River steamer for Cincinnati. This rather extensive narrative deals little with other aspects of travel than military movements. Hannaford made few comments on the Southern country, its people, or even life within Federal lines.

Hanson, John Wesley, 1823–1901.   212

Historical sketch of the old Sixth regiment of Massachusetts volunteers, during its three campaigns in 1861, 1862, 1863, and 1864. Containing the history of the several companies previous to 1861, and the name and military record of each man connected with the regiment during the war. By John W. Hanson, chaplain ... Boston, Lee and Shepard, 1866.

352 p. front., port. 19 cm.
Illustrations: Two plates made up of various portraits of soldiers and of pictures of two monuments.
Inclusive dates: 1861–1864.

The Sixth Massachusetts Regiment is best known for the riot it precipitated when passing through Baltimore on April 19, 1861. After arriving in Washington, it was stationed for the rest of its ninety-day enlistment at Relay House and in Baltimore. The next year it enlisted for nine months and operated in the Dismal Swamp region and around Suffolk, Virginia. In its third term of service, one hundred days, it guarded prisoners at Fort Delaware in the Delaware River. The author was chaplain of the regiment, and he seemed to be more interested in "contrabands" than in military movements. He engaged in many conversations with the slaves and attended some of their religious meetings. He naturally devotes considerable space to the Baltimore riot and to the people of that city. Also the Dismal Swamp intrigued him so much that he made a short trip into it. The glimpses into these subjects are of some value in assessing both social conditions and natural scenes in the South.

Hard, Abner. 213

History of the Eighth cavalry regiment, Illinois volunteers, during the great rebellion. By Abner Hard ... Auro, Ill., 1868.

4 p. l., ₍33₎–368 p.   22 cm.
Illustrations: Eight portraits of soldiers.
Inclusive dates: 1861–1865.

A surgeon in his regiment, and later promoted to brevet lieutenant colonel, Abner Hard left St. Charles, Illinois, in 1861 for the area of fighting in the East, going through Chicago, Pittsburgh, Baltimore and Washington. He participated in the main campaigns in this region as well as in the attempt to stop Early's raid against Washington, and in the subsequent fighting in the Shenandoah Valley. Hard produced a first-class travel narrative, filled with descriptions, observations, and discussions of local incidents, including some humor as in his description of the capture of a mule (pp. 221–22).

Harris, James S. 214

Historical sketches. Seventh regiment North Carolina troops. By J. S. Harris. No place, publisher or date ₍1893?₎

70 p.   23 cm.
Inclusive dates: 1861–1865.

This booklet is composed almost entirely of the diary and notes kept by the author during the Civil War. He enlisted at Concord and was soon on his way to defend Newbern and Morehead City. As Harris had never before seen the ocean, he was much attracted by the tides, marine life, and coastal scenery. In the spring of 1862 he was transferred to Richmond and was soon in the midst of the Peninsula battles. He marched northward to take part in Second Manassas, and was in the Maryland invasion which resulted in the Battle of Sharpsburg. Back in Virginia he fought at Fredericksburg, Chancellorsville, and Gettysburg, after which he spent the winter of 1863–1864 in Virginia, and in the spring fought southward to protect Richmond. In the spring of 1865 he was transferred to Greensboro, North Carolina, and in April surrendered with General Johnston's forces. The narrative is a first-hand account of Harris' army career and includes a few comments on other matters.

Harris, Nathaniel Edwin, 1846– 215

Autobiography: the story of an old man's life, with reminiscenses of seventy-five years. By Nathaniel E. Harris ... Macon, Ga., The J. W. Burke company, 1925.

550 p.   front. illus. (incl. ports.)   19½ cm.
Illustrations: Frontispiece, "Nathaniel E. Harris"; and twenty-one other illustrations, which do not relate to the period 1861–1865.
Inclusive dates: 1862–1865.

Slightly more than a seventh of this work relates to the Civil War period. Harris was born in East Tennessee, and enlisted in the Confederate Army in 1862 when he was sixteen years old. For the first year and more he served in that part of the state, principally around Knoxville with trips to Chattanooga and smaller places. In 1864 he marched into southwestern Virginia and took part in repelling General Davis Hunter's march on Lynchburg. He then joined Early's march down the Valley through Lexington and across the Potomac to the outskirts of Washington, D. C. After participating in McCausland's raid on Chambersburg, Pa., he fought thereafter in the Valley and in southwestern Virginia. Near the end of the war he went to Charlotte, North Carolina, on his way to join General Joseph E. Johnston's army. On Johnston's surrender he went back to his East Tennessee home. He later migrated to Georgia and was elected governor in 1914. The narrative, written many years after the war, is subject to all the discounts of an old man's memory; but it is a lively account of a young Confederate soldier's experiences, with few observations of a traveler.

Harris, William Charles, 1830–1905. 216

Prison-life in the tobacco warehouse at Richmond. By a Ball's Bluff prisoner, Lieut. Wm. C. Harris ... Philadelphia, George W. Childs, 1862.

2 p. l., 9–175 p. incl. front.   18½ cm.
Illustrations: Frontispiece, "Our Last Day in the Richmond Tobacco Warehouse Prison."
Inclusive dates: October, 1861–February, 1862.

While most of this book tells about prison life in Richmond, a small but significant portion deals with Harris's trip after being captured on the battlefield of Ball's Bluff. The author gives details of his reception along the way and by the Richmond population. He also describes his trip down the James River for parole and delivery to Federal ships near Newport News. He was indignant at the treatment he received in captivity, but omits most of the atrocity stories common to many later accounts. Harris, a resident of Philadelphia before the war, joined "Col. Baker's California Regiment."

Harrold, John. 217

Libby, Andersonville, Florence. The capture, imprisonment, escape and rescue of John Harrold, a Union soldier in the war of the rebellion, with a description of prison life among the rebels—the treatment of Union prisoners—their privations and sufferings. Atlantic City, N. J., Daily union book and job printing office, 1892.

117 p.   17½ cm.
Inclusive dates: June, 1864–March, 1865.
Other editions: Philadelphia, W. B. Selheimer, 1870. 132 p.

Peppered with atrocities and ill-tempered in tone, this slim volume adds little to knowledge of conditions in the Confederacy. Harrold, a resident of Atlantic

City, New Jersey, joined the 138th Pennsylvania Regiment in 1862 and soon saw service on northern Virginia battlefields. In June, 1864, he was captured on the Peninsula below Richmond and imprisoned in Libby for a short time before being transferred by way of Danville, Charleston, Savannah, and Macon to Andersonville. Later, while imprisoned in Florence, he escaped and wandered northward through the swamps and pine woods, hoping to reach North Carolina where he believed the people were staunch Unionists. This book differs from most accounts of fleeing prisoners in that Harrold found friends among the well-to-do white residents rather than among the slaves, though he was aided by the latter. He was being peaceably harbored by a South Carolina family when Sherman's outriders came upon him and took him on their march to Fayetteville. Here Harrold boarded a steamer on the Cape Fear River for Wilmington and went by ocean vessel to Baltimore.

Hart, Ephraim J. 218

History of the Fortieth Illinois inf., (volunteers). By Sergeant E. J. Hart ... Cincinnati, H. S. Bosworth, 1864.

198 p.   18½ cm.
Inclusive dates: 1861–1863.

As a Federal soldier Hart traveled entirely within the Mississippi Valley. Leaving Camp Butler at Springfield, Illinois, he went by rail to St. Louis, by river through Paducah to Shiloh, continued to Corinth, and operated for some time in northern Mississippi and western Tennessee. Instead of taking a river boat as most soldiers did on the way to Vicksburg, he marched overland from Memphis through Mississippi. After the fall of Vicksburg, he returned to Memphis by river, marched eastward to Chattanooga, and made an excursion into East Tennessee. When his term of enlistment expired he was at Huntsville, Alabama. Hart organized the narrative in diary form, but there is reason to believe he did not write it originally as a diary in camp and field. Since this account was written before the end of the war, it is surprising that the author did not add more local color, comments, and descriptions relative to his travels.

Hartpence, William Ross. 219

History of the Fifty-first Indiana veteran volunteer infantry, A narrative of its organization, marches, battles and other experiences in camp and prison; from 1861 to 1866. With revised roster. By Wm. R. Hartpence ... Harrison, O., Pub. by the author; Cincinnati, The Robert Clarke company, printers, 1894.

viii, 405 p.   pl., 7 port. (incl. front.)   23 cm.
Illustrations: Eight, mostly of soldiers.
Inclusive dates: 1861–1866.

The travels of this Federal soldier were entirely incidental to the war in the

West and in Texas. His regiment formed in Indianapolis, went by rail to Madison, and took boat for Louisville. Passing southward overland through Nashville, it fought at Shiloh and Corinth and continued eastward into northern Alabama. In the autumn of 1862 it hurried northward to Louisville to intercept Bragg in his attempt to seize that place, and while pursuing him fought at Perryville and at Murfreesboro. The Fifty-first took part in Streight's attempt to cut the Western and Atlantic Railway in Georgia, and later fought around Chattanooga and marched as far into East Tennessee as Mossy Creek. Being detailed for an expedition to Matagorda Bay, it marched through Nashville to the Tennessee River, went by boat to New Orleans, and embarked for Texas, where it marched inland to San Antonio by way of Victoria. This work is one of the better regimental histories, but has little value as a travel book.

Hasson, Benjamin F. 220

Escape from the confederacy; overpowering the guards—midnight leap from a moving train—through swamps and forest—blood hounds—thrilling events. ₁By₁ B. F. Hasson ... Washington, D. C., Herbert A. Eby, printer, 1908?

57, 3 p. illus. 19 cm.
Illustrations: Pen and ink sketch, without title, depicting scenes of escape.
Inclusive dates: 1864.
Other editions: Internal evidence leads to the belief that an earlier edition of this pamphlet appeared in 1900, probably published at Bryan, Ohio.

As a straightforward account, unembellished with improbable details and free from bitterness, it may be accepted as additional evidence of the experiences of Federal prisoners escaping from the Confederacy; otherwise it has little value. There are the usual accounts of slaves befriending a fleeing prisoner, of bloodhounds following him, and of meeting an occasional white Unionist. Hasson, a lieutenant in the Twenty-second Pennsylvania Volunteer Cavalry, was taken prisoner in Virginia and lodged in both Libby and Belle Isle. In early 1864, while being transferred by train southward, he escaped from the moving cars near Franklinton, North Carolina, and wandered eastward toward the Federal lines at Washington, on the Pamlico River, passing through or near Louisburg, Wilson, and Greenville. From Washington he went by boat through Newbern, on to Fortress Monroe, and back to his regiment near Harpers Ferry. After the war Hasson retraced the route of his escape.

Hawes, Jesse, 1843–1901. 221

Cahaba. A story of captive boys in blue. By Jesse Hawes ... New York, Burr printing house, c. 1888.

xviii, 480 p. incl. front., pl., ports., plans. 23 cm.
Illustrations: Frontispiece, "Jesse Hawes, M. D."; "Castle Morgan, Cahaba, Ala., 1863–65."

Drawn from Memory by the Author"; "Hon. Ira F. Collins"; "Our 'Dormitory' at Meridian"; "G. J. Trenaman"; "Capt. H. S. Hanchette"; "Jacob W. Rush."
Maps: "Diagram of Cahaba Prison."
Inclusive dates: 1864–1865.

The account is devoted almost entirely to life in the little-known Confederate prison at Cahaba, Alabama, named Castle Morgan for General John Hunt Morgan, the Kentucky raider. Hawes, a member of the Ninth Illinois Cavalry, was captured in 1864 near Tupelo, Mississippi, taken by railway to Meridian and Selma, and by river steamer down stream to the prison. Except for one escape and quick recapture, he remained until near the end of the war, when he was taken to the Federal lines near Vicksburg and released. The author's experiences were similar to those described by many other writers. As for life in Castle Morgan, he claimed it was equally as bad as in Andersonville, and that prisoners were more crowded. One bright ray was the kind administrations of Mrs. Amanda Gardner, who lived nearby; she often sent the prisoners food and loaned them many books from her private library.

Haynes, Edwin Mortimer, 1836–   222

A history of the Tenth regiment, Vermont volunteers, with biographical sketches of the officers who fell in battle. And a complete roster of all the officers and men connected with it—showing all changes by promotion, death or resignation, during the military existence of the regiment. By Chaplain E. M. Haynes. ₁Lewiston, Me.,₁ Published by the Tenth Vermont regimental association, 1870.

viii, ₁9₁–249 p.   22½ cm.
Inclusive dates: 1862–1865.
Other editions: A much enlarged edition with a slightly changed title: Rutland, The Tuttle co., 1894.

This author wrote of little besides marching and fighting and camp life, with occasional descriptions of villages and towns through which he marched. Among these were Warrenton, Winchester, and especially Charlestown, where John Brown was executed. Here the army song "John Brown's Body" and the bands added to the noise as they marched through. The Tenth Regiment entered the war in 1862 and fought through to Appomattox. In the summer of 1864 it was sent from the James to Baltimore to aid in repelling Early's attack on Washington.

Haynes, Martin A., 1845–   223

History of the Second regiment New Hampshire volunteers: its camps, marches and battles. By Martin A. Haynes ... Manchester, N. H., Charles F. Livingston, printer, 1865.

viii. ₁9₁–223, ₁1₁ p.   18 cm.
Inclusive dates: 1861–1864.
Other editions: Reprinted under this title: A history of the Second regiment, New Hampshire volunteer infantry, in the war of the rebellion. Lakeport, N. H., 1896.

Among accounts of military movements are comments on the country and conditions; a description of Westover, the Byrd mansion, and other estates on the lower James River; and interesting details of fraternization between Confederate and Federal soldiers after the Battle of Fredericksburg. Haynes was a private in the regiment through the two battles of Manassas, Gettysburg, and McClellan's and Grant's campaigns in Virginia. When his enlistment expired in June, 1864, most of the regiment was mustered out and thereafter neither he nor his state of New Hampshire was interested in following the motley group of substitutes, foreigners, and bounty jumpers that replaced them. The book is well written and, as it appeared soon after the author's retirement from the army, it may be accepted as reliable.

Heartsill, William Williston, 1839–   224

Fourteen hundred and 91 days in the Confederate army. A journal kept by W. W. Heartsill, for four years, one month, and one day: or, Camp life; day-by-day, of the W. P. Lane rangers, from April 19th 1861, to May 20th 1865. [Marshall, Tex., W. W. Heartsill, 1876]

4 p. l., 264 p. 1 l.   61 phot. on 19 pl.   21½ cm.
Illustrations: Fifty-nine portraits of members of the regiment.
Inclusive dates: 1861–1865.
Other editions: No other edition found. A work of apparently similar nature by the same author, not seen nor listed in the Library of Congress Catalogue but included in Cadwell Walton Raines, A bibliography of Texas ... (Austin, 1896) is: History of Gen. W. P. Lane's regiment (Marshall, Texas, 1868). Another work dealing briefly with the same marches is: The adventures and recollections of General Walter P. Lane, a San Jacinto veteran. Containing sketches of the Texian, Mexican, and late wars, with several Indian fights thrown in (Marshall, Texas, 1887).

This unusual diary gives a minute account of the author, of his compatriots in the Confederate Army, of many details in the experiences of a soldier, and of the country through which he marched. Born in East Tennessee, he was living in Marshall, Texas, when the war broke out and enlisted in the Texas state forces, but was soon transferred to a Confederate unit where he served from 1861 throughout the war. He first marched to Austin and then to San Antonio to disarm the United States troops there, traveled westward as far as the Pecos River to take part in protecting the frontier from Indian depredations, returned to Austin and Marshall, and operated in Arkansas and Louisiana before being captured. He was conveyed to Alton, Illinois, and Springfield, imprisoned for some months at Camp Butler, and exchanged at City Point, Virginia, which he reached by rail through Toledo, Cleveland, Erie, Pennsylvania, Elmira, New York, and Harrisburg, Pennsylvania, to Baltimore, where he was placed aboard ship for City Point. After some time in Richmond, he went to Bragg's army in Tennessee near Tullahoma, and later participated in the Battle of Chickamauga. The next year, 1864, he traveled across Alabama and Mississippi, moved around in Arkansas and Louisiana, and returned to Marshall through Shreveport. He spent some time at Tyler, Texas, guarding Federal prisoners at Camp Ford. On May 20, 1865, he and his comrades were disbanded near Navasota, Texas.

Hedley, Fenwick Y. 225

Marching through Georgia. Pen-pictures of every-day life in General Sherman's army, from the beginning of the Atlanta campaign until the close of the war. By F. Y. Hedley ... Illustrated by F. L. Stoddard. Chicago, Donohue, Henneberry & co., 1890.

490 p. incl., illus., plates, facsims, front., pl. 19½ cm.

Illustrations: "Marching through Georgia"; "The First Dead"; "The Peach Orchard at Shiloh"; "On the Skirmish Line"; "Restoring Communication"; "Gen. Gresham Wounded"; "Gen. Belknap Capturing Rebel Colonel"; "A Struggle for a Flag"; "Portraits of Commanding Officers" ₍Sherman, McPherson, Grant, Howard, Logan₎; "A Demand for Surrender"; "The Defiance"; "Gen. Corse at Allatoona"; "Union Troops Destroying Railroad"; "On the March"; "The Bummer"; "Making Corduroy Road"; "A Real Camp Fire"; "Autograph Cipher Dispatch" ₍Gen. J. E. Johnston to Gen. Pemberton, May 24, 1863₎; "A Hungry Party"; "Laying Pontoons"; "Wading the Salkehatchie"; "Before Columbia"; "Refugee Train"; "Portrait and Autograph of Gen. Anderson"; "Action at Bentonville"; "Halt on the March"; "Portraits of Division Commanders." Facsimile of autograph letter by General Sherman, p. 15. Illustrations by F. L. Stoddard.

Maps: "Map of Battlefield, July 22, 1864" ₍on which Gen. McPherson was killed₎, Drawn by Engineer Officer, July 23, 1864.

Inclusive dates: 1861–1865.

Other editions: No other edition found, though the copyright date of 1884 indicates that it was first published at that time.

Although this volume purports to be written partly from notes it shows little evidence of such sources. It is largely concerned with life within the Federal Army, and only occasionally includes travel notes. The author claims to have been closely connected with the burning of Columbia and he gives considerable attention to that incident. Hedley was adjutant of the Thirty-second Illinois Infantry.

Heg, Hans Christian, 1829–1863. 226

The civil war letters of Colonel Hans Christian Heg; edited by Theodore C. Blegen. Northfield, Minn., Norwegian-American historical association, 1936.

ix p., 1 l., 260 p. front., plates, ports., facsims (1 fold.) 22¾ cm.

Illustrations: Frontispiece, "Hans C. Heg" ₍Signature₎; "An Extra Number of Emigranten, Issued to Promote Recruiting for the Fifteenth Wisconsin"; "Gunild and Hans Heg"; "The Heg Homestead at Muskego"; "Mrs. Hans C. Heg"; "The Heg Monument at Madison, Wisconsin"; "Colonel Hans Christian Heg"; "Ladies' Union League: A Broadside"; "Colonel Heg in the Spring of 1863"; "The Heg Monument at Chickamauga"; "Colonel Heg's Last Letter."

Maps: "Island No. 10: A Sketch by Dr. Himoe"; "A Sketch of Camp Erickson."

Inclusive dates: 1862–1863.

These letters describe Colonel Heg's army service and comment on the Confederate population and their slaves in western Tennessee, northern Alabama,

Mississippi, and the region around Chattanooga. The author disliked slavery but made use of a Negro servant whom he acquired. He describes foraging, tells of many repentant rebels coming in to take the oath of allegiance, and believed all the atrocity stories told by the poor mountain whites. Heg was born in Norway, came to America and settled in Wisconsin, and in 1861 helped to organize the Fifteenth Wisconsin Volunteer Infantry, whose colonel he became. His first service was down the Mississippi River at Island No. 10, followed by an expedition from Union City in northwest Tennessee southward to Corinth and Iuka. In 1862 he took part in the Buell-Bragg contest across Kentucky, and was present at the Battle of Perryville. Thereafter he marched southward to Nashville and fought at Murfreesboro. Through 1863 he operated between Nashville and Chattanooga until he was killed in the Battle of Chickamauga.

Hermann, Isaac, 1838–   227

Memoirs of a veteran who served as a private in the 60's in the war between the states; personal incidents, experiences and observations, written by Capt. I. Hermann ... Atlanta, Ga., Byrd printing company, 1911.

285 p. incl. front. (port.) plates.   20 cm.
Illustrations: Frontispiece, "Yours truly, I. Hermann", and six imaginary scenes.
Inclusive dates: 1861–1865.

Isaac Hermann was a French-born Jew who enlisted in the Confederate Army in 1861 at Davisboro, Washington County, Georgia, and served his first year's enlistment in the western Virginia campaign. He traveled as far as Cheat Mountain in northern Virginia, returned to Georgia, re-enlisted and went to Savannah for further training, and was sent to help defend Fort McAllister at the mouth of the Ogeechee River. Thereafter he was for a time in the hospital service, took part in the fighting around Jackson, Mississippi, in the summer of 1863, and in Hood's foray into Tennessee the next year. This account, written long after the war, is of little value apart from the picture it gives of a Confederate soldier's service.

Higginson, Thomas Wentworth, 1823–1911.   228

Army life in a black regiment. Boston, Fields, Osgood & co., 1870.

iv, 296 p.   17¾ cm.
Inclusive dates: 1862–1864.
Other editions: Another edition: Cambridge, Mass., The Riverside press, 1900. A new edition with notes and a supplementary chapter: Boston, Houghton, Mifflin and company, 1900.

In addition to giving an excellent description of the first regiment of Negro soldiers to be organized in the Federal Army during the Civil War, Colonel Higginson includes many interesting descriptions of Southern landscapes, old plantation homes in ruins, and such towns as Beaufort, South Carolina, St. Marys, Georgia, and Jacksonville. Higginson took charge of his colored regiment, the First South Carolina, at Beaufort in November, 1862, where he trained them for active fighting. In early 1863 he set out with them in a small flotilla to penetrate the St. Marys River country in Georgia in search of lumber and brick. He later raided up the St. Johns and occupied Jacksonville for a time. Before moving his regiment to the vicinity of Charleston, he made a raid up the Edisto River. In 1864 Higginson returned to the North on account of his health.

High, Edwin W., 1841–   229

History of the Sixty-eighth regiment, Indiana volunteer infantry, 1862–1865, with a sketch of E. A. King's brigade, Reynold's division, Thomas' corps, in the Battle of Chickamauga: By Edwin W. High ... Published by request of the Sixty-eighth Indiana infantry association, 1902. (Metamora? Ind.) 1902.

> xii p., 1 l., 416 p. front. pl., port. 23 cm.
> *Illustrations:* Forty-eight illustrations, mostly portraits of soldiers.
> *Maps:* Map of Chickamauga.
> *Inclusive dates:* 1862–1865.

Formed in Indianapolis in 1862, this regiment went to Louisville and marched southward through Kentucky almost to Tennessee, then doubled back to board an Ohio and Cumberland river boat for Nashville. Operating in Middle Tennessee for a period, it later took part in the Chattanooga-Chickamauga campaign, and subsequently marched on to Knoxville and Maryville, returning home through Chattanooga and Nashville. High writes almost entirely from the impersonal viewpoint and thus makes his work more truly a regimental history and less a travel account. Using a great many diaries and other personal material of his comrades he has produced a somewhat composite picture of the upper South.

Hight, John J., 1834–1886.   230

History of the Fifty-eighth regiment of Indiana volunteer infantry. Its organization, campaigns and battles from 1861 to 1865. From the manuscript prepared by the late chaplain John J. Hight, during his service with the regiment in the field. Comp. by his friend and comrade, Gilbert R. Stormont ... Illustrated with maps of campaigns, and marches, and portraits of a number of officers and enlisted men of the regiment. Princeton, Press of the Clarion, 1895.

> 577 p.   front., illus. (incl. maps) ports.   22½ cm.
> *Illustrations:* Frontispiece, "John J. Hight" [Signature] and forty-four other illustrations, principally portraits of members of the regiment.
> *Maps:* "Map of the Atlanta Campaign"; "Map of the Marches through Georgia and the Carolinas."
> *Inclusive dates:* 1861–1865.

The chaplain kept a diary but never got around to writing a history of his regiment. In 1894, Gilbert R. Stormont undertook to fill the gaps and to edit the material for publication, but it is still a contemporary narrative. Hight was uncompromising in his feeling toward the "rebels" and slavery, and was mostly concerned with soldiers and military matters, but he was observant of historical spots, monuments, and towns. He was especially interested in Savannah, which he described at considerable length. In following his regiment Hight went to Nashville from Indiana and was soon on the road to Shiloh and Corinth. Marching eastward into Alabama in the summer of 1862, he headed northward through Nashville to Louisville to intercept Bragg's attempt to conquer Kentucky, returned to the fighting at Perryville, and on to Nashville and Murfreesboro as the year ended. After operations in Middle Tennessee he proceeded to Chattanooga, Chickamauga, and as far into East Tennessee as Knoxville to protect that city against Longstreet. Returning southward he became a part of Sherman's march and after Johnston's surrender went to Washington for the "Grand Review." In the early summer he went by train to Parkersburg, West Virginia, and took steamer down to Louisville, where the regiment was mustered out.

Hill, Alonzo F. 231

Our boys. The personal experiences of a soldier in the Army of the Potomac. By A. F. Hill ... Philadelphia, John E. Potter, 1864.

1 p. l., vii–xii, 13–412 p.   17½ cm.
Illustrations: Frontispiece, an imaginary sentry scene.
Inclusive dates: 1861–1862.
Other editions: Reprinted in 1890 by the Keystone publishing company, Philadelphia, without change of title or text.

As indicated in this narrative Alonzo Hill's travels were restricted in both area and time. In 1861 he joined the Eighth Pennsylvania Reserves, trained at Pittsburgh, saw service in Maryland and northern Virginia, joined McClellan's Peninsula campaign, and returned to northern Virginia to participate at Second Manassas. He was wounded in the Sharpsburg campaign and there his narrative stops. Hill writes in the spirit of "wild adventure and careless glee." His book is sprinkled with reconstructed conversation and permeated with the atmosphere of the country. Although he claims the narrative is absolutely correct, there is reason to discount some of his statements. He visited George Washington's tomb at Mount Vernon and Mary Washington's grave at Fredericksburg; he talked with whites and with blacks both slave and free; and he wrote from fresh memory before the war ended.

Hill, Isaac J., 1826– 232

A sketch of the 29th regiment of Connecticut colored troops, by J. [sic] J. Hill, giving a full account of its formation, of all the battles through which it passed, and its final disbandment. Baltimore, Printed by Daugherty, Maguire & co., 1867.

42 p.   22½ cm.
Inclusive dates: 1864–1865.

This is one of the very few travel accounts by Negro Federal soldiers. Hill, a free Negro born in Pennsylvania, late in the war joined a colored regiment in Connecticut. He left New Haven by boat for Annapolis, continued to Beaufort, South Carolina, and soon was back in Virginia with forces around Petersburg. At the end of the war he went by boat to New Orleans and Brownsville, Texas, moved a short distance into the interior, and quickly returned by sea to Hartford, breaking the journey again at New Orleans.

Hinkley, Julian Wisner, 1838–1916. 233

... A narrative of service with the Third Wisconsin infantry. By Julian Wisner Hinkley ... ₁Madison₁ Wisconsin history commission, 1912.

xi, 197 p. front. (port.) 22½ cm. (Wisconsin history commission: Original papers, no. 7).
Illustrations: Frontispiece, "Julian Wisner Hinkley. From a photograph taken in July, 1864."
Inclusive dates: 1861–1865.

Hinkley, born in Connecticut and removed to Wisconsin in his eleventh year, joined the Third Wisconsin Infantry in 1861 and served in it to the end of the war. He reached the rank of captain and became acting major near the close of the struggle. Hinkley left Fond du Lac by rail for northern Virginia, passing through Toledo, Cleveland, and Buffalo to Frederick, Maryland. Until the Gettysburg campaign he was centered in Maryland and northern Virginia, including the battles of Sharpsburg and Chancellorsville. Immediately after Gettysburg he was sent by river and coasting vessels to New York City to quell the draft riots. Upon his return to Virginia he was sent west to engage in the campaigns around Chattanooga, moving by rail over the Baltimore and Ohio Railroad and through Columbus and Indianapolis, thence to Louisville and Nashville. He was in Sherman's march and after Johnston's surrender marched to Washington for the "Grand Review." He was mustered out in Louisville, Kentucky, reaching this point over the Baltimore and Ohio Railroad to Parkersburg and then southward by Ohio steamer. The narrative is constructed from the author's war diary, from letters written home and to newspapers, and from a manuscript he wrote soon after the war. Hinkley was mostly concerned with military experiences until he reached the war in the West; thereafter he became more interested in the people of the occupied regions, dealing specially with conditions in Middle Tennessee.

Hinman, Wilbur F. 234

The story of the Sherman brigade. The camp, the march, the bivouac, the battle; and how "the boys" lived and died during four years of active field service ... With 368 illustrations ... By Wilbur F. Hinman ... ₁Alliance, O.₁ By the author. Press of Daily review, 1897.

xxxii, 32–1104 p. illus., ports. (incl. front.) 22 cm.

Illustrations: Three hundred and sixty-eight illustrations, almost entirely portraits of officers and men of the Sherman Brigade.

Inclusive dates: 1861–1865.

One of the most extensive histories of the Federal Army, this volume is almost entirely about life and incidents among soldiers in the Sherman Brigade (a unit not officially so designated, but affectionately named for John Sherman, who was connected with it for a time). It deals not only with army life but also to a considerable extent with descriptions of the country, towns, and cities; with slaves, the proficiency of foraging, trading with Confederate soldiers; and with soldier life in the desert around Victoria, Texas. The story moves forward chronologically, designating the route followed and noting impressions along the way. Hinman, who rose to the rank of lieutenant colonel of the Sixty-fifth Ohio Volunteer Infantry, a unit in the Sherman Brigade, begins his account with its organization at Mansfield, Ohio, and follows it through Kentucky from Louisville through Bardstown, Bowling Green, Nashville, and Savannah, Tennessee, to the Battle of Shiloh and on to Corinth. Thence the unit went into Alabama, raced back to Louisville in the campaign to head off Bragg's invasion of Kentucky, marched through Bardstown to fight at Perryville in October, 1862, and back to Nashville and Murfreesboro in Rosecrans' campaign. The unit fought at Chickamauga in September, 1863, and from Chattanooga moved into East Tennessee to protect Knoxville against Longstreet's onset; thence back to Chattanooga and southward in the spring and summer of 1864 with Sherman against Atlanta. With the fall of that city the Sherman Brigade went again to Chattanooga and Nashville to beat off Hood's attack in December, 1864; thence back to Chattanooga, Knoxville, and eastward into the mountains to aid Sherman against Johnston for the finish in North Carolina. With Johnston's surrender this unit was again sent to Nashville, and instead of being mustered out Hinman was moved down the Tennessee, Ohio, and Mississippi rivers to New Orleans and then to Texas to Port Lavaca and on into the hinterland almost to Victoria; thence retracing the route to Cairo, Illinois, and on to Columbus to be mustered out near the end of 1865. This account was written about thirty years after the war and based on a diary, many other contemporary documents, and old soldiers' tales.

Hitchcock, Henry, 1829–1902. 235

Marching with Sherman; passages from the letters and campaign diaries of Henry Hitchcock, major and assistant adjutant general of volunteers, November 1864–May, 1865, edited with an introduction, by M. A. DeWolfe Howe. New Haven, Yale university press; London, H. Milford, Oxford university press, 1927.

6 p. l., 332 p.   plates, 2 ports. (incl. front.) fold. map, facsim.   22¾ cm.

Illustrations: Frontispiece, "Henry Hitchcock, in later Life"; "General Sherman"; "Facsimile Page of Major Hitchcock's Diary"; "Tarver's Mill, Georgia" (From Harper's Weekly, Jan. 7, 1865); "Destruction of Millen, Georgia, January 3, 1864" (From Harper's Weekly, Jan. 7,

1865); "Christmas Day in Savannah—General Sherman's Christmas Dinner at Mrs. Green's— (Sketches by Theodore R. Davis)" (From Harper's weekly, Jan. 28, 1865); "Theodore R. Davis's Sketch of Henry Hitchcock and his Tent"; "General Sherman's Entry into Columbia, South Carolina, February 17, 1865" (From Harper's Weekly, April 1, 1865).

Maps: "Combined Maps of the Marches 'From Atlanta to the Sea' and 'From Savannah to Goldsboro'." Prepared by Brvt. Brig. Gen. O. M. Poe, Chief Engineer. Engraved for Sherman and his Campaigns, written by Col. S. M. Bowman and Lt. Col. R. B. Irwin (New York, 1865).

Inclusive dates: November, 1864–May, 1865.

Henry Hitchcock was born near Mobile, Alabama, educated at the University of Nashville and Yale, graduating in 1848, studied law in Nashville, and settled in St. Louis in 1851. He was commissioned a major in October, 1864, and assigned to General Sherman's staff for the remainder of the war. *Marching with Sherman* is made up of letters from Hitchcock to his wife, and of campaign diaries which he sent home at intervals. Among the many accounts of Sherman's march this is one of the most valuable. Hitchcock, well educated and a close observer, wrote with discernment and good sense. He was most interested in the attitude of the people in the regions through which the Federal Army marched, and he recorded many conversations with them. He found most of them sorely tired of the war and inclined to be disgusted with the Southern leaders who precipitated secession. Hitchcock was much troubled by the pillaging and burning that went on everywhere and at times was inclined to blame Sherman for not putting a stop to it; but he always relieved his conscience by the firm conviction that the Southerners were solely responsible for the war, and that, therefore, they had no one but themselves to blame for their terrible suffering. He joined Sherman at Rome, Georgia, and continued with him to Raleigh. Just before Johnston's surrender near Durham Station, Hitchcock was sent to Washington on a highly confidential mission, and returned by boat from Washington to Morehead City, North Carolina, and thence by railroad to Raleigh.

Hobart-Hampden, Augustus Charles 1822–1886.   236

Sketches from my life. By the late Admiral Hobart Pasha. London, Longmans, Green, and co., 1886.

viii, 282 p.   front. (port.)   19 cm.
Illustrations: Frontispiece, "Hobart Pasha" ₍Signature₎.
Inclusive dates: 1863, 1864.
Other editions: New York, D. Appleton & co., 1887; and Leipzig, B. Tauchnitz, 1887.

This book touches travel in the Confederacy in only two minor particulars. As part of an exciting life, the author became a blockade runner during the Civil War, using Wilmington as his port of entrance. In 1863 he made a train trip from this port to Charleston and the following year to Richmond. Both experiences are recorded. Hobart Pasha was in reality Augustus Charles Hobart-Hampden, a son of the Earl of Buckinghamshire.

Hoffman, Wickham, 1821–1900.   237

Camp, court and siege; a narrative of personal adventure and observation during two wars: 1861–1865; 1870–1871. By Wickham Hoffman ... New York, Harper & brothers, 1877.

285 p.   18½ cm.
Inclusive dates: 1862–1865.

Less than half of this volume deals with the Civil War and the relevant part is so sketchy as to be of little value. Hoffman was first stationed at Hatteras on the North Carolina coast, but soon went to Fortress Monroe to join the fleet for Butler's expedition against New Orleans. He then went up the Mississippi in the attempt to take Vicksburg; that failing, he was engaged in operations around Port Hudson, on the Opelousas expedition, in the sea venture against Sabine Pass in Texas, and on Banks' Red River expedition. He comments briefly on conditions in New Orleans under Butler and on a few other matters not purely military.

Hood, John Bell, 1831–1879.   238

Advance and retreat. Personal experiences in the United States and Confederate States armies. By J. B. Hood ... New Orleans, Pub. for the Hood orphan memorial fund, G. T. Beauregard, 1880.

358 p.   front., port., plans.   21½ cm.
Illustrations: "Your friend J. B. Hood" ₍Signature₎; "Your friend J. B. Hood" ₍Signature₎, both frontispieces.
Maps: "Map Showing the Positions of the Confederate Armies of Mississippi & Tennessee May 19th 1864 under Command of General J. E. Johnston"; "Battles around Atlanta"; "Battle of Franklin, Tenn."; "Battle of Nashville."
Inclusive dates: 1863–1865.

Apart from some descriptive material relating to California and Texas and the ordinary military discussions dealing with Hood's Civil War career before he superceded General J. E. Johnston, his *Advance and Retreat* is almost entirely a reply to General Johnston. It therefore has little value as travel literature. Hood died before his manuscript was published.

₍Hopley, Catherine Cooper₎, (₍Sarah L. Jones₎), *circa* 1832–   239

Life in the South: from the commencement of the war. By a blockaded British subject. Being a social history of those who took part in the battles, from a personal acquaintance with them in their own homes. From the spring of 1860 to August 1862 ... London, Chapman and Hall, 1863.

Vol. I, xvi, 427 p.; Vol. II, 404 p.   19 cm.

Miss Catherine Cooper Hopley was an English school teacher who had been living with relatives in Indiana a few years before going South to teach in 1860. She was a cultured, middle-class woman, a close observer who also read newspapers and kept herself well informed on current events. Her statements of fact are almost invariably correct. Being interested in life and customs, she found many admirable qualities in the Southerners and, even with a preconceived dislike of slavery, learned to understand the system. She found none of the horrors of slavery she had expected to see, and even struggled hard to maintain the neutrality of a British subject. Until January, 1862, she taught children on plantations in the Northern neck of Virginia and south of Fredericksburg, and was an instructor in a Baptist Female Seminary at Warrenton. Early in 1862 she went to Florida to teach in the family of Governor Milton on his plantation west of the Appalachicola River. Between trips to these various places she spent much time in Richmond where she became acquainted with many high Confederate officials, including several congressmen, and formed high admiration for President Davis. On her way to Florida she met General Lee in the railway station at Savannah. She traveled by railway, steamboat, and stage and liberally recorded her observations. Miss Hopley was a facile writer and her work is a valuable commentary on Southern plantation life during the first part of the Civil War.

Horrall, Spillard F., 1829– 240

History of the Forty-second Indiana volunteer infantry. Comp. and written ... by S. F. Horall, late Captain of Company G, 42d Indiana regiment. Chicago, Donohue, Henneberry, printers, 1892.

x, 11–283 p. front., ports. 19 cm.
Illustrations: Twenty-eight illustrations, mostly portraits of soldiers.
Inclusive dates: 1861–1865.

Horrall, as a Federal soldier, took the same route as tens of thousands of soldiers from the Middle West. Reaching Henderson, Kentucky, from Evansville, Indiana, across the Ohio, where the regiment was formed, he marched southward through Nashville, Wartrace, and into Alabama as far as Huntsville, hurriedly returning northward into Kentucky to intercept Bragg on his march to the Ohio. Horrall was at the battles of Perryville and Murfreesboro, operated in Middle Tennessee during the first part of 1863, later in the Chattanooga-Chickamauga campaign, and in 1864 followed Sherman to the sea and up through the Carolinas, finally reaching Washington for the "Grand Review." The narrative is sketchy and choppy, with some atmosphere but journalistic in style.

Horton, Joshua H., and Solomon Teverbaugh 241

A history of the Eleventh regiment, (Ohio volunteer infantry,) containing the military record, so far as it is possible to obtain it, of each officer and enlisted man of the command—a list of deaths—an account of the veterans—incidents of the field and camp—names of the three months' volunteers, etc., etc. Compiled from the official records by Horton & Teverbaugh ... Dayton, W. J. Shuey, 1866.

xv, 17–287 p. 21 cm.
Inclusive dates: 1861–1864.

There is no indication of which author was responsible for which parts of the book. The regiment was organized at Columbus in the summer of 1861, marched to Gallipolis and boarded steamers for the Kanawha Valley where it operated as far as Charleston and the Gauley Bridge. Further movements were by the Baltimore and Ohio Railroad to Washington and into northern Virginia; Second Bull Run and Sharpsburg; through western Virginia and by steamer on the Kanawha, Ohio, and Cumberland rivers to a point near Nashville; and operations in Middle Tennessee and to Chattanooga and Chickamauga. In the spring of 1864 it marched with Sherman towards Atlanta but stopped at Resaca when the term of enlistment ended and returned to Ohio for mustering out. The chief travel interest in this book lies in descriptions of the people and countryside of western Virginia, now West Virginia.

Hosmer, James Kendall, 1834–1927. 242

The color-guard: being a corporal's notes of military service in the Nineteenth army corps. By James K. Hosmer ... Boston, Walker, Wise, and co., 1864.

xii, 9–244 p. 18 cm.
Inclusive dates: 1862–1863.

Here is a well-written and even-tempered account of army experiences and observations by a young Massachusetts parson who later became a prominent historian. Hosmer joined the Forty-second Regiment of Massachusetts Volunteers in the fall of 1862, went by ship from New York City to New Orleans, calling by Ship Island off the Mississippi coast, and visited a few days in New Orleans before going up the river to Baton Rouge. He saw his first fighting in the vicinity of Port Hudson and Clinton, but was soon off on an expedition southward into central and southern Louisiana, going by river to Donaldsonville and marching across country to Brashear City. His unit visited Opelousas and New Iberia before he took part in the final seizure of Port Hudson in early July, 1863. Hosmer noted with disapproval the wanton ravaging of the old Louisiana mansions and the intervening country, but was much impressed by the beauties of the Louisiana landscape.

Howard, McHenry. 243

Recollections of a Maryland Confederate soldier and staff officer under Johnston, Jackson and Lee. By McHenry Howard. Baltimore, Williams & Wilkins company, 1914.

1 p. l., 423 p. front., illus., pl., ports., fold. map, facsim. 22 cm.
Illustrations: Frontispiece, "Lieutenant McHenry Howard, C. S. A. From Ambrotype taken in Richmond, July, 1862"; and twenty-three other portraits, designs, facsimiles, and plans of battles and prison camps.
Maps: "War Map of Virginia 1864. By Branch B. Morgan, C. E. Based upon the Map of Northern Virginia 1864 in Battles and Leaders of the Civil War. By Permission of the Century Company." 7½ by 10½.
Inclusive dates: 1861–1865.

Howard was much interested in military and civilian personnel he met, and in the country he visited. His is among the most valuable of Confederate soldiers' reminiscences because he avoids improbable details and concocted conversations, depends on a diary and carefully checks his narrative with records of the times. A resident of Baltimore at the outbreak of the Civil War, Howard immediately made his way to Richmond to join a Virginia regiment, going by boat from headland to headland down the western Chesapeake shores of Maryland and Virginia. He was engaged in First Manassas, the Peninsula campaign of 1862, and Gettysburg, and spent much time in the Shenandoah Valley with Jackson. In 1864 he was captured at Spottsylvania and taken to Fort Delaware through the Potomac, Chesapeake Bay, and the Delaware River. While awaiting exchange after parole in the latter part of the year, he was transported by canal boat across Delaware to Chesapeake Bay and southward to Savannah, Georgia, where he was turned over to the Confederate authorities. During that wait he visited among acquaintances in Savannah and on the surrounding plantations, and spent some time around Charleston. Shortly before Sherman's arrival Howard was exchanged and sent to Richmond which he helped to defend until its evacuation. Just before Lee's surrender he was again captured and taken to the Old Capitol Prison in Washington and to Johnson's Island in Lake Erie. He was released in the latter part of May, 1865.

Howard, Richard L. 244

History of the 124th regiment Illinois infantry volunteers, otherwise known as the "Hundred and two dozen", from August, 1862, to August, 1865. By R. L. Howard ... Springfield, Ill., Printed and bound by H. W. Rokker, 1880.

ix, 519 p.   20 cm.
Inclusive dates: 1862–1865.

Traveling as a chaplain of his regiment, the author left Camp Butler, Illinois, in 1862, went by rail to Cairo, by boat to Columbus, Kentucky, and on foot southeastward through Kentucky and Jackson, Tennessee, into northern Mississippi around Holly Springs. Returning to western Tennessee he took a boat at Memphis for Vicksburg and spent the remainder of the war in the lower Mississippi Valley. He traveled widely through central Mississippi, passing through Brandon, Jackson, Meridian, Canton, and many other towns, and raided as far westward through Louisiana as Monroe. Returning to base he went down the Mississippi and through the Gulf of Mexico to Mobile, was present at the fall of that city, and marched to Montgomery, to remain for some time after the fall of the Confederacy; then down the Alabama River to Selma and by rail through Meridian and Jackson to Vicksburg, and up the Mississippi to his home in Illinois. Howard made a valuable record from his own diary and much personal material of comrades. He wrote with even temper of scenes and impressions, more as a traveler than as a soldier.

Adventures of an escaped Union prisoner from Andersonville. San Francisco, H. S. Crocker & co., printers, 1886.

48 p. port. 22½ cm.
Illustrations: Portrait of Thomas H. Howe on outside cover.
Inclusive dates: July, 1864–April, 1865.

Howe, a member of the 102d New York Volunteers, was captured in the Battle of Peachtree Creek on the outskirts of Atlanta, in July, 1864. He was imprisoned in Andersonville a few months; during removal to Millen he leaped from the train and made his way back along the Central of Georgia Railroad track to Macon and along the railway leading to Atlanta. Having found no Federal troops, Howe retraced his steps to a plantation between Barnesville and Macon and remained for about four months hidden in a slave cabin. After Lee's surrender he was rescued by Federal cavalry. The account is embellished with many improbable details but states plainly that he was taken care of and befriended by the slaves.

[Hubbard, Charles Eustis] 1842– 246
The campaign of the Forty-fifth regiment, Massachusetts volunteer militia. "The cadet regiment." Boston, Printed by James S. Adams, 1882.

xiv p., 1 l., 126 p. front., plates, 25¼ cm.
Illustrations: Frontispiece, "Camp Meigs at Readville, Mass."; "Fort Macon" [etc., dim drawings]; "Camp Amory" [etc., dim drawings]; "Battle of Kingston"; "Kingston Swamp" [etc., dim drawings]; "Battle of Goldsboro"; "Hardtack and Coffee" [etc., dim drawings]; "Quarters of Company A, at Newbern"; "Rear View of Quarters of Company A"; "The Field and Staff, 45th. M. V. M."; "Camp at Core Creek" [etc., dim drawings]; "Camp Massachusetts" [etc., dim drawings]; "Company A, at Readville." Some of these photographs also appear in Edward H. Rogers, Reminiscence of military service ... (q. v.)
Inclusive dates: 1862–1863.

This account, written soon after the events described, has an air of freshness and reliability. It covers practically the same ground as "Corporal," *Letters from the Forty-fourth Regiment MVM . . . (q.v.)* but is much less valuable. The author was with a "nine months" Massachusetts regiment on the coast of North Carolina and operated around Newbern and some inland towns such as Kingston, Goldsboro, and Trenton. He was interested in the landscape with its swamps and pine woods, and in the Negroes, of whom he had a low opinion.

Hubbard, John Milton. 247
Notes of a private. By John Milton Hubbard. St. Louis, Mo., Nixon-Jones printing co., 1913.

212 p. front. (port.) 19 cm.
Illustrations: Frontispiece, "J. M. Hubbard."
Inclusive dates: 1861–1865.
Other editions: First edition: Memphis, E. H. Clark & brother, 1909. Second edition, called

"Souvenir Edition": St. Louis, 1911. Third edition, called "Memorial Edition," is the one here used.

These personal reminiscences of a private soldier in General Forrest's cavalry, written almost half a century after the war, were evidently enjoyed by Southerners (principally Tennesseeans) of the early twentieth century, for they passed through three editions. The book is based on memory fifty years after the events and has little value beyond inferences from the many personal experiences recorded. Hubbard enlisted in southwestern Tennessee at the beginning of the Civil War, served briefly in southeastern Missouri, and was transferred to Columbus, Kentucky. Thereafter his activities were confined to western Tennessee and northern Mississippi and Alabama. He surrendered and signed the parole in Alabama immediately following Forrest's pursuit of Wilson which resulted in the destruction of Selma.

Huffman, James, 1840–1922. 248
Ups and downs of a Confederate soldier. By James Huffman ... New York, William E. Rudge's sons, 1940.

> 4 p. l., 175 p.   mounted illus. (incl. ports., facsim.)   20½ cm.
> *Illustrations* Twelve illustrations of people and objects.
> *Inclusive dates:* 1861–1865.

The author, a member of the Tenth Virginia Infantry, fought in all the principal engagements of the war in the East except Gettysburg. He was captured in 1864 at Spottsylvania Courthouse and was held a prisoner at Point Lookout and Elmira. Huffman was seventy-two years old when he wrote this narrative, but retraced his steps in order to familiarize himself with the regions over which he had traveled as a soldier. He mentions no diary or other personal records, but he used various public records and many personal interviews. As a result, this work partakes little of a travel account. The chapters dealing with Huffman's prison life were published originally in the *Atlantic Monthly*, April, 1939.

Humphreys, Charles Alfred, 1838– 249
Field, camp, hospital and prison in the civil war, 1863–1865: Charles A. Humphreys, chaplain, Second Massachusetts cavalry volunteers. Boston, Press of Geo. H. Ellis co., 1918.

> xi p., 1 l. 428 p. front., plates, ports. 20 cm.
> *Illustrations:* Frontispiece, "The latest photograph of the author"; and thirteen other illustrations of war scenes and soldiers.
> *Inclusive dates:* 1863–1865.

Written from memory more than half a century after the close of the Civil War, these reminiscences offer little as travel records because they include many things outside the author's experience. Humphreys enlisted in 1863, immediately went to northern Virginia, and saw service first in Grant's campaign against

Richmond in the spring of 1865. Shortly thereafter he was captured during an expedition bent on destroying Mosby's Rangers and was held briefly in Lynchburg and Danville before being sent to Macon, Georgia. He traveled from Danville over the usual route, opened after May, 1864, through Greensboro, Salisbury, Charlotte, Columbia, and Augusta. From Macon Humphreys was sent to Charleston, exchanged, and sent out of the Confederacy through Charleston harbor. He returned to Massachusetts and after recuperating joined the Federal Army again in northern Virginia, operated in the Shenandoah Valley with Sheridan, marched southward around Richmond to the Petersburg region, and took part in the military activities leading to Lee's surrender. Bitterness and extreme statements color the narrative.

Hunter, Alfred G. 250

History of the Eighty-second Indiana volunteer infantry, its organization, campaigns and battles. Written at the request of the members by Alf. G. Hunter ... Indianapolis, W. B. Burford, 1893.

255 p. incl. front., port. 18½ cm.
Illustrations: Frontispiece, "Alf. G. Hunter"; "Morton C. Hunter"; "Henry Davis"; "Gen. Slocum."
Inclusive dates: 1862–1865.

The passing years did not mellow Hunter's bitterness toward the "rebels." He wrote thirty years after the burning of Atlanta that "this fine sight filled my idea of soldiering" (p. 136). The regiment was organized in the late summer of 1862 and saw its first service in Buell's campaign against Bragg in his invasion of Kentucky. Entering Kentucky at Louisville, it fought at Perryville, marched on to Nashville, and was involved in the battles of Murfreesboro, Tullahoma, Chickamauga, those around Chattanooga, and in the march on Atlanta and Savannah. On the campaign up through South Carolina, Hunter was captured and taken to Augusta, Macon, and Andersonville. Near the end of the war he was moved southward to Albany and into Florida where he was finally deposited in Federal hands near Jacksonville. From there he went by boat to Hilton Head, South Carolina, with a side sight-seeing trip to Charleston and return, and to Annapolis by sea. Hunter was adjutant in the regiment. The book was prepared without reference to a diary and is of limited value.

Hurst, Samuel H. 251

Journal-history of the Seventy-third Ohio volunteer infantry. Chillicothe, O., 1866.

viii, ₍9₎–253, ₍1₎ p. 19 cm.
Inclusive dates: 1862–1865.

Hurst, who attained the rank of brevet brigadier general in March of 1865, writes principally of military activities but mentions aspects of the country. In Georgia he admired the beauty of some small towns; in East Tennessee he sensed much Unionism among the people. He wrote immediately after the war, expanding a sketchy diary with fresh memories. He found that the South, based on slavery, was beautiful enough at the top but degrading to the mass of the people. The regiment was formed in Chillicothe in the latter part of 1861 and early in the next year it moved by rail to Marietta and across into western Virginia (West Virginia), going from Parkersburg over the Baltimore and Ohio Railroad into the battle area and into northern Virginia to fight in the principal engagements and also at Gettysburg. Transferred to the fighting around Chattanooga in the fall of 1863, the unit followed the usual route through Columbus, Ohio, Indianapolis, Louisville, and Nashville. After the battles of Missionary Ridge and Lookout Mountain Hurst moved into East Tennessee and back to Chattanooga in time to go with Sherman in his campaign through Atlanta, Savannah, Columbia to Johnston's surrender in North Carolina, and on to Washington for the "Grand Review."

Hyde, Solon.   252

A captive of war. By Solon Hyde, hospital steward Seventeenth regiment Ohio volunteer infantry. New York, McClure, Phillips & co., 1900.

389 p.   19 cm.
Inclusive dates: 1863–1865.

Thirty-five years after the war the author was still bitter and charged the Confederacy with being a hell broth. Yet there is much temperate writing about the people, both masses and leaders, who made up this struggling new country. Hyde was captured at Chickamauga, taken to Richmond by way of Atlanta, Augusta, Columbia, Raleigh, and Petersburg, and confined there in various prisons. Later he was removed to Danville where he made an escape and wandered westward toward the mountains but was recaptured, returned to Danville, and sent to Andersonville by way of Greensboro, North Carolina, Columbia, Augusta, and Macon. Most of the book is devoted to his experiences in Andersonville. With Sherman's invasion of Georgia, he was removed to Macon and as far as Gordon on the road toward Savannah, where he turned northward through Milledgeville and across country to Washington, Georgia, which he especially noted as the home of Robert Toombs. He continued through Abbeville to Winnsboro, South Carolina, thence by rail to Charlotte, Salisbury, and Goldsboro, and was turned over to the Federal authorities in early 1865. He left the Confederacy by way of Wilmington.

Isham, Asa Brainerd, 1844–   253

Prisoners of war and military prisons; personal narratives of experience in the prisons of Richmond, Danville, Macon, Andersonville, Savannah, Millen, Charleston, and Columbia. With a general account of prison life and prisons in the south during the war of the rebellion, including statistical information pertaining to prisoners of war; together with a list of officers who were prisoners of war from January 1, 1864. By Asa B. Isham ... Henry M. Davidson ... and Henry B. Furness ... Cincinnati, Lyman & Cushing, 1890.

xii, 571 p. front., illus., pl., port., diagr. 23 cm.
Illustrations: "Asa B. Isham"; "Custer's Charge at Yellow Tavern, Va., May 11, 1864"; "Castle Thunder"; "Libby Prison—Front View"; "Libby Prison—Side View"; "Interior of Libby Prison"; "Camp Oglethorpe, Macon, Georgia"; "Tunneling at Macon"; "Jail and Work-House, Charleston, S. C."; "Camp Sorghum, Columbia, South Carolina"; "Of 'Fresh Fish' at Macon"; "Johnson's Island, Ohio"; and twenty-five other small pen sketches without titles but relating to prison life and experiences.
Inclusive dates: May–December, 1864.

Here was one Federal prisoner who was unable to escape, so he had no opportunity to observe the people of the Confederacy except in the prison surroundings and from railway tracks and stations. Isham was First Lieutenant, Company F, Seventieth Michigan Cavalry, First Brigade, First Division, Cavalry Corps, Army of the Potomac. He was captured in May, 1864, at the Battle of Yellow Tavern near Richmond and his prison life was spent in Libby Prison, a trip by way of Danville, Charlotte, Columbia, and Augusta to Macon and Camp Oglethorpe, Savannah, Charleston, and Columbia until in December, 1864, he was turned over to the Federal ships at Charleston and taken to Annapolis. The account has little value because it follows closely many other, more elaborate narratives.

Izlar, William Valmore. 254

A sketch of the war record of the Edisto rifles, 1861–1865, By William Valmore Izlar; Company "A," 1st regiment S. C. V. infantry ... Provisional army of the Confederate States 1861–1862; Company "G," 25th regiment S. C. V. infantry ... Confederate States army 1862–1865. Pub. by August Kohn. Columbia, S. C., The State company, printers, 1914.

168 p. 2 pl., 16 port. (incl. front.) 19 cm.
Illustrations: Frontispiece, "William V. Izlar, Esq., Sergeant Edisto Rifles." There are seventeen other illustrations, mostly of members of the regiment.
Inclusive dates: 1861–1865.

Izlar enlisted at Orangeburg, South Carolina, was first sent to Charleston, later participated in activities farther down the coast, and in 1864 was sent to Virginia to take part in the fighting around Richmond and Petersburg. Late in 1864 the Edisto Rifles were sent to Fort Fisher below Wilmington; on the fall of that fort the author was captured and sent by sea to Point Lookout Prison, where he remained a prisoner until June, 1865. His narrative is of slight incidental value as a travel account.

Jackson, Oscar Lawrence, 1840–1920. 255

The colonel's diary; journals kept before and during the civil war by the late Colonel Oscar L. Jackson of New Castle, Pennsylvania, sometime commander of the 63rd regiment O. V. I. [Sharon? Pa., 1922]

3 p. l., 232 p., 1 l., 233–262 p.   front., ports.,   21½ cm.
Illustrations: Eight portraits.
Inclusive dates: 1861–1865.

A Pennsylvanian by birth, Jackson was a school teacher in Ohio before the outbreak of the Civil War. Joining an Ohio regiment, he trained at Marietta, went down the Ohio and Mississippi rivers to New Madrid and Island No. 10, and returned up the Mississippi, Ohio, and Tennessee rivers to the battlefield of Shiloh. Afterwards he operated in northern Mississippi around Corinth, and in northern Alabama; from Memphis down the Mississippi to the Vicksburg region; back to northern Alabama and Middle Tennessee; home on a furlough and back to join Sherman's march and to Washington for the "Grand Review." Jackson's diary is a first-class travel account, with frequent comments on the country and people. Georgia seemed so neat that he dubbed it the Yankee state; and he "never met up with a slave who did not want to leave his master."

Johns, Henry T., 1827/8–   256
Life with the Forty-ninth Massachusetts volunteers. By Henry T. Johns ... Pittsfield, Mass., Published for the author, C. A. Alvord, printer, 1864.

391 p.   front., pl., port.   18½ cm.
Illustrations: Fourteen illustrations of which eleven are groups of portraits of soldiers, two are single portraits, and one a scene of the Battle of Port Hudson.
Inclusive dates: August, 1862–July, 1863.
Other editions: Another edition: Washington, D. C. [Ramsey & Bisbee, printers] 1890.

Devoted mainly to the services of his regiment, this book describes the encampments at Carrollton, Donaldsonville, and Baton Rouge, Louisiana, and the fighting at Port Hudson. The regiment sailed from New York in January, 1862, for Louisiana, passing up the Mississippi River to Carrollton above New Orleans. The author was much interested in the Negroes, studied them individually and in their religious meetings, and boldly advocated social equality. For a few weeks he operated with troops out of Donaldsonville in a highly successful search for provisions and, he admits, for any jewelry within reach. When the enlistment period ended the regiment sailed up the Mississippi to Cairo and returned to Massachusetts in cattle cars.

[Johnson, Adam Rankin] 1834–   257
The Partisan rangers of the Confederate States army; ed. by William J. Davis. Louisville, Ky., Geo. G. Fetter company, 1904.

xii p., 1 l., 476 p.   front., plates, ports.   22 cm.
Illustrations: Frontispiece, "Brigadier General Adam R. Johnson"; and sixty-four other portraits and scenes.
Inclusive dates: 1854 [1861–1865] 1871.

The heart of this narrative is an account of the wartime experiences and observations of its author, who was born in Kentucky but moved to Texas in 1854 and settled in Burnet County, where his work in surveying and scouting brought him into conflict with Indians on the frontier. On the outbreak of the war he went back to Kentucky and became attached at one time or another to both Forrest and John Hunt Morgan. He organized a force of Rangers, operated independently much of the time, and achieved the rank of brigadier general. He operated widely but for the most part ranged through western Kentucky and Middle Tennessee. He was with Morgan on the famous expedition north of the Ohio and occasionally made trips to Richmond and Texas. He was wounded, losing his sight, made prisoner by the Federals, and imprisoned at Fort Warren in Boston Harbor until exchanged. In many details the narrative must be accepted with caution, as it was written many years after the war, apparently from memory but from some official military documents.

Johnson, Charles Beneulyn, 1843–   258

Muskets and medicine; or, Army life in the sixties. By Charles Beneulyn Johnson ... Philadelphia, F. A. Davis company; [etc., etc.] 1917.

276 p.   front., plates, ports.   20½ cm.
Illustrations: Nineteen illustrations, most of them being half-tone reproductions of photographs of Federal officers, hospital appliances, a body louse ("grayback"), etc.
Inclusive dates: 1862–1865.

Using for the most part an old man's memory, Johnson has, nevertheless, produced a worthwhile narrative. Born in Illinois, he volunteered in 1862 and was assigned to the hospital service. His duties took him down the Mississippi River to Memphis, to Grant's forces besieging Vicksburg in 1863, and to New Orleans for an expedition in the fall to New Iberia in the Teche country. Returning to New Orleans, he sailed across the Gulf to Matagorda Bay and after some months went home on a long furlough to recover his health before resuming military activities in 1864. After a short stay in Baton Rouge he was in the Federal action against Mobile until the end of the war, when he was mustered out in New Orleans and returned home up the river.

Johnson, Charles F., 1843–   259

The long roll; being a journal of the civil war, as set down during the years 1861–1863 by Charles F. Johnson, sometime of Hawkins zouaves. Illustrated with many sketches & photographs. Duluth ed. East Aurora, N. Y., The Roycrofters, 1911.

5 p. l., 5–241, [1] p.   front., plates, ports.   19½ cm.
Illustrations: Forty-one plates of illustrations (some plates containing three or four scenes) relating mostly to the coast of North Carolina, especially Hatteras and Roanoke Islands. These are excellent crayon drawings.
Inclusive dates: 1861–1863.

This narrative's chief significance lies in Johnson's travels on the coast of North Carolina. Born in Sweden, he came to America as a small boy, settled in Minnesota, and was in New York on a visit when the war broke out. He joined a regiment from that state, went by boat from New York City to Newport News, operated up the Peninsula, and was transferred to the coast of North Carolina. He touched Hatteras Island, Roanoke Island, and the mainland, and operated around Albermarle Sound, northward to Currituck Courthouse, and on to Winton, where he observed the burning of that town. He then passed through the Dismal Swamp by canal into the Elizabeth River and up Chesapeake Bay to engage in the Sharpsburg campaign in Maryland, and returned to the Norfolk region, where his account ends. With his foreign background, Johnson was admirably conditioned both to observe and comment on the new scenes of his travels. He was much opposed to the burnings and plunderings around Hampton on the Peninsula, Winton, and other places in North Carolina. The work is outstanding in the field of travel in the Confederacy.

Johnson, Hannibal Augustus, 1841–   260

The sword of honor. From captivity to freedom. By Hannibal A. Johnson, lieutenant Third Maine infantry. Providence, R. I., Rhode Island soldiers and sailors historical society, 1903.

72 p.   19½ cm.   (*Added t.-p.:* Personal narratives of events in the war of the rebellion, being papers read before the soldiers and sailors historical society. 6th series, no. 6)
Inclusive dates: 1864–1865.
Other editions: This pamphlet originally appeared as Pamphlet no. 6 (above). Another edition, much more extended is: The sword of honor; a story of the civil war. Hallowel, Me., Register printing house, 1906.

Hannibal Johnson was captured in the Battle of the Wilderness in May, 1864, and imprisoned at Macon, Charleston, and Columbia. The main part of the narrative relates to his escape from the Confederate prison at Columbia and his subsequent wanderings through South Carolina, North Carolina, and Tennessee until he crossed the mountains to Knoxville and entered the Union lines. His journey as a fugitive, like many others, was assisted by slaves in the plantation regions and bushwhacking mountaineers in the highlands. He seems to have kept some sort of a diary after leaving Charleston, though there is evidence of much subsequent reworking.

Johnson, Richard W., 1827–1897.   261

A soldier's reminiscences in peace and war. By Brig.-Gen. R. W. Johnson ... Philadelphia, Press of J. B. Lippincott company, 1886.

428 p.   front. (port.) pl.   23 cm.
Illustrations: Frontispiece, "Your Obd. Svt. R W Johnson Bv. Maj Genl. U. S. A." [Signature].
Inclusive dates: 1861–1865.

Although this work consists of the author's reminiscences from his earliest remembrances to the date of writing, it is concerned mostly with his Civil War career. He was born in Kentucky, graduated from West Point, and the book mentions briefly his earlier service with the United States Army in the West, principally Texas. He reached Louisville, Kentucky, in 1861, after a trip from Texas by way of Cuba and New York City, and his scene of action was limited to the western area of the Confederacy, through Kentucky and Tennessee and as far southward as Atlanta. The narrative has some travel interest.

Johnston, Isaac N. 262

Four months in Libby, and the campaign against Atlanta. By Capt. I. N. Johnston, Co. H., Sixth Kentucky volunteer infantry. Cincinnati, Printed at the Methodist book concern, for the author, 1864.

191 p. 17½ cm.
Inclusive dates: September, 1863–August, 1864.
Other editions: A reprinting of this book was made in 1893 by the same publishers at the same place with the same number of pages.

The chief significance of this paper-bound booklet lies in the escape journey of the author from Libby Prison to the Federal lines down the Peninsula towards Williamsburg. Captain Johnston was a resident of Henry County, Kentucky, at the outbreak of the war, joined the Sixth Kentucky Volunteer Infantry, and was elected captain of Company H. After various battles in the western area, he was captured at Chickamauga in September, 1863, and taken to Libby Prison in Richmond, going by way of Atlanta, Augusta, Columbia, Charlotte, Raleigh, Weldon, and Petersburg. Johnston was one of the prisoners who succeeded in escaping through the famous Rose tunnel. After entering the Federal lines, he went to Washington and to his home in Kentucky before rejoining the regiment, then a part of Sherman's army. He participated in the campaign against Atlanta, but his three-year enlistment ended in August, 1864. His account of the Atlanta campaign is confined almost entirely to military affairs.

Joinville, François Ferdinand Philippe Louis Marie d'Orléans,

Prince de, 1818–1900. 263

The Army of the Potomac: its organization, its commander, and its campaign. By the Prince de Joinville. Translated from the French, with notes, by William Henry Hurlbert. New York, Anson D. F. Randolph, 1862.

118 p. front. (fold. map) 21 cm.
Maps: "Environs of Richmond." Folding map, 21½ cm. by 25 cm.
Inclusive dates: 1862.
Other editions: This account originally appeared in Revue des deux mondes for October 15, 1862, under the title, "Campagne de l'Armee du Potomac, Mars-Juillet, 1862." In addition

to the edition here used, which was republished by the same publishers in 1863, it appeared as Campagne de l'Armee du Potomac. New York, F. W. Christern, 1862.

The Prince de Joinville, of the French House of Orleans, accompanied General McClellan on his Peninsula campaign in 1862. In this account he gives his impressions not only of military affairs and developments, but now and then of the country and people whom he saw on the march from Yorktown to the environs of Richmond. Before embarking with McClellan's forces, the Prince visited the old battlefield of Manassas and describes what he saw. His sentiments are entirely favorable to the Federals, and being a foreigner his comments on the Confederacy and its people are refreshing and sometimes quite original.

[Jones, Benjamin Washington] 1841–   264

Under the stars and bars; a history of the Surry light artillery; recollections of a private soldier in the war between the states ... Richmond, Everett Waddey co., 1909.

xiii, 297 p.   19½ cm.
Inclusive dates: 1861–1865.

The area of Jones' travels with the Surry Light Artillery was restricted to the lower James River regions except for one move into northern Virginia. His chief service was in the protection of Richmond, where he was stationed on the outskirts most of the time. As his home was in Surry County on the lower James, there was little new for him to see and comment on, except wartime Richmond, which attracted him considerably and led him to make frequent observations. The book is made up of letters which Jones wrote to a friend and therefore has the freshness and reliability of contemporary comment.

Jones, Charles Colcock, 1831–1893.   265

Historical sketch of the Chatham artillery during the Confederate struggle for independence. By Charles C. Jones, jr. Albany, Joel Munsell, 1867.

240 p. maps.   27 cm.
Maps: The Fort Pulaski Region; Plan of the Federal Attack on Fort Sumter, April 7, 1863; Battlefield of Ocean Pond.
Inclusive dates: 1861–1865.

As lieutenant in the Chatham Artillery, the author's army service took him in early 1861 down the Savannah River to Fort Pulaski; to the islands around the mouth of the Savannah River for a year or more; to James Island near Charleston; in 1864 by rail through Valdosta to northern Florida and the minor Battle of Ocean Pond; to the neighborhood of Savannah and into South Carolina to harry Sherman's advance until Johnston's surrender in North Carolina; and finally to Savannah. The account is notably impersonal and only slightly descriptive of regions visited or routes traveled. After the war Jones practiced law and did some historical writing, mainly relating to Georgia.

148

Jones, Jenkin Lloyd, 1843–1918.   266

... An artilleryman's diary. By Jenkin Lloyd Jones ... ₁Madison₁ Wisconsin history commission, 1914.

xviii, 395 p. front., ports., facsim. 22½ cm. (Wisconsin history commission: Original papers, no. 8)

Illustrations: Frontispiece, "Jenkin Lloyd Jones"; "A Group of Comrades in 6th Wisconsin Battery"; "A Group of Officers in 6th Wisconsin Battery"; "Entry in Diary, December 20, 1864" (Facsimile); "The Development of a Soldier" (Three pictures of Jenkin Lloyd Jones); "6th Wisconsin Battery Reunion—Richmond Center, Wis., Aug. 27, 1897."
Inclusive dates: August, 1862–July, 1865.

As Jones was only nineteen years old when he enlisted in the Sixth Wisconsin Battery, his diary was, to begin with, quite annalistic and sketchy, devoted almost entirely to its author's comrades and to military activities. During the last two years, however, the entries were longer and included comments on both the people and the country. This is one of the better diaries of the war, written by a young soldier of high intellectual aspirations and subsequent attainments. Jones was born in Wales but was brought to Wisconsin in 1844 when he was one year old. His army career began in Madison whence he was sent to Cairo and by steamer to Memphis. His fighting began with foraging raids in the country surrounding Memphis and Corinth, Mississippi, followed by the Vicksburg expedition and marches into central Mississippi; it continued up the Mississippi to Memphis and across country to Chattanooga, traversing parts of southern Tennessee and northern Mississippi and Alabama. In 1863–64 he wintered in Huntsville, Alabama, and the following year at Nashville. He participated in Sherman's march into Georgia as far as Etowah Bridge, north of Atlanta. Jones wrote without bitterness, though he detested both the enemy and slavery. After the war he became a well-known Unitarian clergyman and editor of the magazine *Unity.*

Jones, Samuel Calvin, 1828–   267

Reminiscences of the Twenty-second Iowa volunteer infantry, giving its organization, marches, skirmishes, battles, and sieges, as taken from the diary of Lieutenant S. C. Jones of Company A. Iowa City, Ia., 1907.

164, ₁2₁ p. 2 double pl., ports. 22½ cm.
Illustrations: Thirty-one, mostly portraits of soldiers.
Inclusive dates: 1862–1865.

Jones' travels were more extensive than those of most Federal soldiers. Enlisting in 1862 in Iowa City, he saw service first in southeast Missouri, arriving there by railway from Iowa City to Davenport, down the Mississippi by boat to St. Louis, and overland to Rolla, Pilot Knob, St. Genevieve, and other points in that region. Further movements took him by boat down the Mississippi to Vicksburg and after its fall to New Orleans; as far west as New Iberia, returning by boat to the mouth of the Rio Grande, up the coast as far as Indianola, and back by sea to New Orleans. He then went up the Mississippi and Red rivers as far as Alexandria, but was soon on his way to the eastern war area, passing down the Mississippi, through the Gulf, and along the Atlantic coast to the Shenandoah Valley, stopping at Fortress Monroe and Washington. He was captured in September, 1864, and first taken to Richmond, then to Salisbury by way of Danville and Greensboro, and returned to Richmond for exchange. Turning towards the South Atlantic seaboard, he stopped at Newbern on the way to Savannah. When the war ended, he entered the river service between Savannah and Augusta but finally marched from Augusta back to Savannah and went by sea to Annapolis and thence home. Unfortunately Jones was less travel-minded than many others who wrote longer accounts of shorter trips, but there are some comments on scenes and incidents. There is evidence that this diary suffered from changes after the war.

Judson, Amos M. 268

History of the Eighty-third regiment Pennsylvania volunteers. By A. M. Judson ... Erie, Pa., B. F. H. Lynn [1865]

2 p. l., xiii–xv, 17–139, [1] p. 23½ cm.
Inclusive dates: 1861–1864

Because it was written immediately after the war this volume is vivid and reliable. The author was more interested in military affairs than were some other regimental historians, yet he also recorded a few impressions of the Confederacy and its people, including some anecdotes of soldier experiences, such as an agreement with the enemy to divide the casualties in a flock of sheep which got between the firing lines. Judson's marching and fighting were confined entirely to the area from Petersburg to Gettysburg, including most of the famous battles, from 1861 to September, 1864, when the author was mustered out.

Kelley, Daniel George. 269

What I saw and suffered in Rebel prisons. By Daniel G. Kelley ... With an introduction by Major Anson G. Chester ... Buffalo, Printing house of Matthews & Warren, 1866.

86 p. 17½ cm.
Inclusive dates: 1864.

Kelley, sergeant in Company J, Twenty-fourth New York Cavalry, was taken prisoner at the Battle of Cold Harbor in Grant's campaign against Richmond in the summer of 1864. First imprisoned in Libby at Richmond, he was later taken to Andersonville and, when Sherman invaded Georgia, removed to Savannah and to Millen. Near the end of the year he was exchanged, placed aboard a boat at Savannah, conveyed to the mouth of the Savannah River, and turned over to nearby Federal fleet authorities. Kelley gives most of his attention to prison life, but was somewhat observant of general conditions and of the people along the routes he took. He included a generous amount of hatred for Wirz and other prison authorities.

Kellogg, John Azor, 1828–1883. 270

Capture and escape; a narrative of army and prison life. By John Azor Kellogg ... ₍Madison₎ Wisconsin history commission, 1908.

xvi, 201 p. front. (port.) 22½ cm. (Wisconsin history commission: Original papers, no. 2)
Illustrations: Frontispiece, "John Azor Kellogg."
Inclusive dates: 1864–1865.

Kellogg, colonel of the Sixth Wisconsin Volunteer Infantry and finally a brevet brigadier general, was a Pennsylvanian by birth but moved to Wisconsin Territory in 1840 and settled at Prairie du Chien. He enlisted in the Federal Army at the beginning of the war and fought through the campaigns of northern Virginia until his capture in May, 1864, at the Battle of the Wilderness. He was held at Lynchburg and Danville before being taken to Macon, Georgia. While being removed to Charleston he escaped a few miles short of that city but was soon recaptured; during a later transfer to Columbia he jumped from a moving train and wandered northwestward through South Carolina, passing near Abbeville, crossed the Savannah River and prowled through northern Georgia to Calhoun, passing near Elberton, Carnesville, Gainesville, and Jasper. While in northern Georgia he was aided by bands of deserters from the Confederate army, who infested that region. The chief value of this narrative is in its description of the Union population in the mountains of Georgia. Kellogg wrote his first account for the La Crosse *Leader,* which published it serially in 1869–1870, and reworked the story in 1882. After the war he served as a United States Pension Agent at La Crosse. Except for many reconstructed conversations, this narrative may be accepted as a faithful record.

Kellogg, John Jackson, 1837– 271

War experiences and the story of the Vicksburg campaign from "Milliken's Bend" to July 4, 1863; being an accurate and graphic account of campaign events taken from the diary of Capt. J. J. Kellogg, of Co. B, 113th Illinois volunteer infantry. ₍Washington, Ia., Evening journal, c.1913₎

64 p. front. (port.) 17 cm.
Inclusive dates: 1863.

In this pamphlet, Kellogg relates a fragment of his army service, entirely in the environs of Vicksburg. Among the Mississippi towns which he visited were Raymond, Clinton, Jackson, Bolton and Vicksburg after its fall. Kellogg mentions such incidents as stealing cotton from a plantation for bedding and seeing an alligator for the first time.

Life and death in rebel prisons: giving a complete history of the inhuman and barbarous treatment of our brave soldiers by rebel authorities, inflicting terrible suffering and frightful mortality, principally at Andersonville, Ga., and Florence, S. C., describing plans of escape, arrival of prisoners, with numerous and varied incidents and anecdotes of prison life. By Robert H. Kellogg ... Prepared from his daily journal. To which is added as full sketches of other prisons as can be given without repetition of the above, by parties who have been confined therein ... Hartford, Conn., L. Stebbins, 1865.

viii, ₍11₎–400 p. incl. front., pl., plan.   18½ cm.

Illustrations: "The Midnight Storm: Our Miserable Lodgings" (By J. P. Davis); "Capturing the Responsible Party in the Treatment of Union Prisoners" (By J. W. Orr) (Imaginative drawing of Davis' capture); "Rebel Mode of Capturing Escaped Prisoners" (By Brightly); "Prisoners Receiving Rations"; "Execution of Union Prisoners" (By J. P. Davis); "Breaking Away of the Stockade by the Flood" (By J. W. Orr); "Interior View of the Hospital" (By J. W. Orr); "Hanging by the Thumbs" (By J. P. Davis); "View of Libby Prison" (By N. Orr).

Maps: "Andersonville Stockade"; "Andersonville Hospital"; "Florence Stockade."

Inclusive dates: April–November, 1864.

Other editions: Another edition by the same publishers in 1866.

Parallel accounts: The story of another Federal soldier taken prisoner at Plymouth and imprisoned in the same places is Warren Lee Goss, The soldier's story of his captivity at Andersonville, Belle Isle, and other rebel prisons. Boston. I. N. Richardson, 1875.

Hardly as terrifying and biased as its title implies, this account was consciously written for propaganda purposes, as is frankly stated by the publishers: "If you will only spread the facts on this subject through the entire North, it will raise a storm of indignation, the power of which will be felt through the entire South . . . ." (p. 399). Kellogg, sergeant major of the Sixteenth Regiment Connecticut Volunteers, was taken prisoner in April, 1864, at the fall of Plymouth, North Carolina, marched westward to the Wilmington and Weldon Railroad, loaded in box cars with many other prisoners, and taken by way of Wilmington, Charleston, Savannah, and Macon to Andersonville Prison. Part of the journey was made on open flatcars. Kellogg was pleased with the country through which he passed and some of the towns reminded him of New England villages. The people along the way were friendly and generous with gifts of food and water. Kellogg repeats the story of designed cruelty by the prison authorities, but admitted that much trouble was caused by terroristic bands of prisoners, six of whom were hanged at Andersonville after conviction by a jury of prisoners. From Andersonville, Kellogg was taken through Macon, Millen, and Augusta to Charleston, and soon transferred to Florence. He was paroled there in November, taken to Savannah and handed over to a Federal flotilla at the mouth of the Savannah River, whence he proceeded to Fortress Monroe and Annapolis.

Kemper, General William Harrison, 1839–1927. 273

The Seventh regiment Indiana volunteers, three months enlistment. By G. W. H. Kemper ... Muncie, Ind., Press of R. H. Cowan printing co., 1903.

16 p. illus. 24 cm.
Illustrations: Two: one of Kemper and one of the Gettysburg monument to the regiment.
Inclusive dates: 1861.

Responding to Lincoln's call for troops after the fall of Fort Sumter, the regiment left Indianapolis for the area of fighting in western Virginia, passing by rail through Columbus and Bellaire to Grafton. Pushing southward it fought at Philippi, Laurel Hill, and Carrick's Ford and returned over the same route. Kemper has made his short pamphlet largely a travelogue, yet descriptions and comments are brief. He was somewhat interested in the people of this region, who were then in the process of organizing the State of West Virginia.

Kent, Mrs. E. C. 274

"Four years in Secessia." A narrative of a residence at the South previous to and during the southern rebellion, up to November, 1863, when the writer escaped from Richmond. By Mrs. E. C. Kent. 2d ed.—with additions. Buffalo, Franklin printing house, 1865.

35 p. 22½ cm.
Inclusive dates: 1860–1863.
Other editions: First published at a place not given, in 1864. In 1865 it was issued as indicated above, but in an edition previous to the one used here.

This pamphlet is an attack on the South and its kind of civilization, as seen by a native of New York who went from Cincinnati to Yazoo City, Mississippi, in 1859 and engaged in teaching school while her son entered business. After Mississippi seceded she made her way to Virginia, stopping first at Charlottesville, and established residence in Richmond, where she remained until November, 1863, when she made her escape through the lines by way of Harpers Ferry. In this account she devotes most of her attention to conditions in Richmond, wherein she describes Castle Thunder Prison, high prices, the bread riot, a visit to Jefferson Davis, and the people of the city. After Mrs. Kent returned to the North, she traveled widely as a reader, detailing her Southern experiences.

Kerbey, Joseph Orton, 1841?–1913. 275

A boy spy in Dixie. Service under the shadow of the scaffold. Washington, D. C., The national tribune, 1897.

iv, 5–383 p. illus. 20¾ cm.
Illustrations: "A Fence-Corner Office"; "Flag of Truce Boat"; "Eluding the Pickets"; "Back to our Lines"; "Overlooking Harpers Ferry"; "Before Gen. Beauregard's Tent"; "Intercepted by the Orderly"; " 'Keep Still a Minute' "; "Riding behind a Prisoner"; "A Slide for Life"; "Aunt Chloe's Surgery"; "[Jefferson] Davis Reviewing the Cavalry"; "Mike at the Gun"; "Trampling on the Stars and Stripes"; "Miss Brownlow and the Guard"; "What Made Them

Hot"; "Looking into God's Country"; " 'Are You Union or Confederate?' "; "The Business End of a Mule"; "Parson Brownlow on the Locomotive"; "A Statesman in Undress"; "I'll Accept your Resignation, Sir"; "On the War Department Steps." All of these are crude illustrations "By Coffin."

Inclusive dates: February, 1861–Early 1862.

Other editions: Library of Congress lists a book with a slightly different title by the same author: The boy spy; a substantially true record of events during the war of the rebellion. The only practical history of war telegraphers in the field ... thrilling scenes of battles, captures and escapes. Chicago, New York ₁etc.₁ Belford, Clark & co., 1889. Another edition: Chicago, M. A. Donohue & co., c.1890.

A cheap paper-back thriller published in the Old Glory Library, this narrative was written thirty years after the events which it purports to recount. Unreliability is further indicated by an exaggerated style, interlarded with personal exploits and hairbreadth escapes. Yet the book has a certain value, for Kerbey was undoubtedly a Union spy and probably went over the ground he describes. He began his duties by going to Montgomery, Alabama, to report on the organization of the Confederacy in February, 1861, continuing to Pensacola and by ship from Fort Pickens to New York, with a short stop in Key West. He appeared next in the vicinity of Manassas soon after the first battle there, and then moved on to Richmond where he did most of his espionage work, claiming to have met President Davis and to have frequented the Confederate War Office. During this time he represented himself as a Maryland refugee. Being an expert telegrapher, he claimed he could read the tickers by watching their motion when he could not hear the dots and dashes. Kerbey gleaned much valuable news which he sent back in code letters with the real messages embodied in innocent personal correspondence. Enlisting in the Confederate Army he was sent to Knoxville, Tennessee, where he met the famous Parson Brownlow. He deserted to the Federal forces near Cumberland Gap and made his way back to the North through Lexington, Kentucky, and Cincinnati. This account ends with his return to Washington to report to Secretary of War Stanton and to have an interview with Lincoln. Kerbey was born in southern Pennsylvania. After the war he received various Federal appointments, serving in 1890–1891 as consul at Para, Brazil. Besides another volume for boys, dealing with his Civil War experiences, he wrote other books, one being an account of the Amazon River country.

₁Kerwood, Asbury L.₁ 276

Annals of the Fifty-seventh regiment Indiana volunteers. Marches, battles, and incidents of army life, by a member of the regiment. Dayton, O., W. J. Shuey, 1868.

374 p. 19 cm.
Inclusive dates: 1861–1865.

Joining his regiment at Richmond, Indiana, late in 1861, Kerwood went through Louisville and Nashville to the neighborhood of Shiloh, Corinth, and Iuka, passed into northern Alabama, and hurried to Louisville in the autumn of 1862 to intercept Bragg's invasion of Kentucky. Following Bragg's retreating army, he fought at Perryville and Murfreesboro, took part in the Chattanooga-Chickamauga campaign, and marched into East Tennessee as far as Knoxville. In the spring of 1864 the author joined Sherman's campaign against Atlanta, afterward turned northward to intercept Hood's attack on Nashville, and fought at Franklin and Nashville. After wintering at Huntsville, Alabama, he marched back into East Tennessee by way of Chattanooga and Knoxville to Bull's Gap. Kerwood was mustered out in February, 1865, but the narrative continues with the regiment's activities in Texas. The route passed through Chattanooga, Nashville, the Tennessee River, New Orleans, by steamers to Port Lavaca on the Texas coast, and inland as far as Victoria, returning across the Gulf and up the Mississippi River. Kerwood wrote a valuable personal travel account, with pertinent comments on the country, the people, and incidents. For instance, he found much Union sentiment in Kentucky, and at one point in the state noticed a cedar bush decorated with red, white, and blue ribbons. Because it was written soon after the war, this narrative may be accepted as reasonably accurate.

Keyes, Charles M.   277

The military history of the 123d regiment of Ohio Volunteer infantry. Edited by C. M. Keyes ... Sandusky, Register steam press, 1874.

196 p.   19 cm.
Inclusive dates: 1862–1865.

Besides the regimental history Keyes included, apparently from memory, notes on the Southern country and the attitude of its inhabitants towards the war. He writes temperately about the Confederates but gives ample testimony of destruction by soldiers. The regiment was organized at Monroeville, Ohio, in the latter part of 1862, moved to Zanesville by rail, down the Muskingum and up the Ohio rivers on boats to Parkersburg, and over the Baltimore and Ohio Railroad to western Virginia (West Virginia). After some raids in this region it marched across the mountains to fight at Winchester and to surrender to the Confederates. After a short stay in Libby Prison the men were exchanged, sent to City Point, taken to Annapolis on steamers, and back to Ohio. Soon they reappeared in northern Virginia and in 1864 accompanied Hunter on his raid up the Shenandoah Valley to the outskirts of Lynchburg. Forced to retreat, they crossed the mountains to Gauley Bridge in West Virginia, took steamers on the Kanawha and Ohio rivers to Parkersburg, and entrained for the fighting in northern Virginia. Further movements were by steamers down the Potomac and Chesapeake Bay to City Point, fighting around Petersburg and on to Appomattox, by water again from City Point to Annapolis and by rail through Cumberland, Maryland, Bellaire, and Zanesville to Columbus for mustering out.

Kidd, James Harvey, 1840–

Personal recollections of a cavalryman with Custer's Michigan cavalry brigade in the civil war. By J. H. Kidd, formerly colonel, Sixth Michigan cavalry ... Ionia, Mich., Sentinel printing company, 1908.

xiv p., 1 l., 476 p.   front., ports., 3 maps.   22 cm.
Illustrations: Frontispiece, "The Author"; and thirty-three portraits of members of the regiment and others.
Maps: "Route of the Michigan Cavalry Brigade in the Gettysburg Campaign"; "Battlefield of Trevilian Station, June 11–12, 1864"; "Battle Field of Winchester, Va."
Inclusive dates: 1862–1865.

At the outbreak of the war, Kidd was a student in the University of Michigan. In the fall of 1862 he joined the Federal forces and, except for the Gettysburg campaign, operated in the regions of northern Virginia and as far south as Yellow Tavern. His recollections, based on memory, secondary accounts, and official documents, were written at various times from 1886 to 1908, and are mostly about military affairs, with very little travel interest.

Kimbell, Charles Bill, 1839–   279
History of Battery "A" First Illinois light artillery volunteers. By Charles B. Kimbell. Chicago, Cushing printing company, 1899.

viii, [9]–320 p. incl. col. front., illus. (incl. ports.) plates.   22½ cm.
Illustrations: One hundred fourteen, mostly portraits of members of the battery.
Inclusive dates: 1861–1864.

Organized in Chicago in 1861, Battery A fought in western Kentucky, Tennessee, and northern Mississippi. It went by rail to Cairo and by river through Paducah to Fort Henry, across country to Fort Donelson, Shiloh, and Corinth, to Memphis and down the Mississippi to Arkansas Post and the vicinity of Vicksburg. Kimbell was captured near Jackson, Mississippi, and taken by rail to Mobile, by boat up the Alabama River to Montgomery, and by train through Atlanta to Richmond and Andersonville by undesignated routes. He was later taken to Savannah and exchanged in November, 1864. His battery fought with Sherman until the fall of Atlanta, when its term of enlistment expired. Written long after the war without aid of diary or other personal material, this narrative offers very little local color.

Kinnear, John R.   280
History of the Eighty-sixth regiment Illinois volunteer infantry during its term of service. By J. R. Kinnear ... Chicago, Tribune company's book and job printing office, 1866.

viii, [9]–139 p.   18 cm.
Inclusive dates: 1862–1865.

As a soldier in the Federal Army, Kinnear left Peoria, Illinois, for Louisville, Kentucky, reaching there just in time to help expel Bragg from the state. He fought at Perryville, continued south to Nashville, operated for months in Middle

Tennessee, took part in the Chattanooga-Chickamauga campaign, and in the spring of 1864 followed Sherman from Chattanooga to Atlanta. After an excursion up the Western and Atlantic Railway toward Chattanooga, he returned in time to make the march to the sea and on to Washington for the "Grand Review," going home by way of Harrisburg, Pittsburgh, and Chicago. This narrative is little more than military annals until it becomes a valid travel account of Sherman's march, filled with descriptions of the country and rich in local color. Some of the book was written before the end of the war.

Knox, Thomas Wallace, 1835–1896. 281

Camp-fire and cotton-field: southern adventure in time of war. Life with the Union armies, and residence on a Louisiana plantation. By Thomas W. Knox ... New York, Blelock and company, 1865.

524 p. front., plates. 20¼ cm.
Illustrations: Frontispiece, "The Rebel Ram Arkansas Running through our Fleet"; "Hauling down a Rebel Flag at Hickman, Ky."; "The Opening Gun at Booneville" ₍Mo.₎; "Death of General Lyon"; "General Sigel's Transportation in the Missouri Campaign"; "Shelling the Hill at Pea Ridge"; "Nelson Crossing the Tennessee River"; "The Carondolet Running the Batteries at Island No. 10"; "The Rebel Charge at Corinth"; "General Blair's Brigade Assaulting the Hill at Chickasaw Bayou"; " 'Strategy, My Boy!' "; "Running Batteries on the Von Phul." All of these are clear line drawings.
Inclusive dates: 1861–1864.

This book is of outstanding value as a close-up picture of the management of confiscated and abandoned plantations along the Mississippi River which were leased to Northern speculators and managers, and in detailing the ways of Negroes working on them. The author himself made an attempt to manage a plantation near Waterproof, Louisiana, for a year. Knox, born in New Hampshire, went to Colorado in 1860 to dig gold, but turned to newspaper work. On the outbreak of the Civil War, he returned to the East and became a war correspondent for James Gordon Bennett's *New York Herald.* He followed the campaigns in Missouri, going as far as Wilson Creek and Pea Ridge in Arkansas. With the invasion of Tennessee early in 1862 he went with the Federal Army to Shiloh, but became *persona non grata* to Halleck and was banished from that area. Thereafter he was associated with army movements up and down the Mississippi incident to the capture of Vicksburg until he displeased General Sherman, who had him tried by court martial and expelled. It was then that Knox attempted the plantation management previously mentioned. He recorded many experiences, impressions, and conversations with the Southern people in the occupied part of the Confederacy, writing with commendable detachment, but naturally criticizing the Southerners for the slave system and the war. Afterwards he circumnavigated the globe twice and wrote many books, including a series of almost forty travel books for boys.

Langworthy, Daniel Avery, 1832– 282

Reminiscences of a prisoner of war and his escape. By Daniel Avery Langworthy, late captain 85th N. Y. vol infantry ... Minneapolis, Minn., Byron printing company, 1915.

4 p. l., ₍13₎–74 p.   front., plates, ports.   21 cm.
Illustrations: Frontispiece, "Daniel Avery Langworthy"; and seven others relating to prisons and companions.
Inclusive dates: 1864.

This slender volume adds little to the many other prisoner-of-war narratives. Written fifty years after the war, the details, such as reconstructed conversations, are largely imaginary, but the main facts and the routes taken may be accepted. Langworthy was captured at Plymouth, North Carolina, in 1864, taken by rail through Wilmington, Charleston, Savannah, and Macon to Andersonville, soon returned to Macon, transferred to Savannah, to Charleston, and to Columbia, where he escaped and wandered through upper South Carolina and the mountains of North Carolina until he came to the Federal lines at Strawberry Plains in East Tennessee.

Lapham, William Berry, 1828–1894. 283

My recollections of the war of the rebellion. By William B. Lapham ... Privately printed. Augusta, Me., Burleigh & Flynt, printers, 1892.

240 p.   port.   19 cm.
Illustrations: "Lieut. Lapham."
Inclusive dates: 1862–1865.

Joining the Federal Army in 1862, Lapham left Portland, Maine, by railway through Boston to Fall River, by steamer down Long Island Sound to New York City, and by railway to Washington and the operations in northern Virginia. During his first term of service, with the Twenty-third Maine Regiment, he did guard duty along the Potomac from Alexandria to Harpers Ferry. His second enlistment was with the Seventh Maine Battery, with which he fought under Grant from the Battle of the Wilderness to the fall of Petersburg. This account, written from memory fifteen years after the war, contains little description or local color, but offers a few travel observations. After the war Lapham became well known as a physician, journalist, and for books on local history and genealogy.

Larson, James, 1841–1921. 284

Sergeant Larson, 4th cav. By James Larson. San Antonio, Southern literary institute, 1935.

6 p. l., 326 p. incl. plates front. (port.)   23 cm.
Illustrations: Frontispiece, "James Larson"; and six sketches of scenes by the author.
Inclusive dates: 1861–1865.

Larson, born in Wisconsin, joined the United States Army in St. Louis, and for a year or more was attached to the frontier service. Returning to St. Louis, he went by steamer to Louisville and overland into Tennessee where he saw much fighting and was at the Battle of Chickamauga in September, 1863. In the spring of 1864 he followed Sherman to Atlanta but turned off into Middle Tennessee and took part in the engagements around Nashville which dispersed Hood's army in December, 1864. In the spring of 1865 he joined Wilson's raiders in northwestern Alabama and marched to Selma, Columbus, Georgia, and Macon. When the war ended, he went to New Orleans, boarded a boat for Matagorda Bay, and marched to San Antonio. Although Larson states that he wrote the account from rough memoranda made soon after the events, much of it was undoubtedly written from memory and it contains factual errors. Routes are not clearly indicated.

Lathrop, David.   285

The history of the Fifty-ninth regiment Illinois volunteers, or A three years' campaign through Missouri, Arkansas, Mississippi, Tennessee and Kentucky, with a description of the country, towns, skirmishes and battles— incidents, casualties and anecdotes met with on the way; and embellished with twenty-four lithographed portraits of the officers of the regiment. By Dr. D. Lathrop. Indianapolis, Hall & Hutchinson, printers, 1865.

243 p. front., port. 19½ cm.
Illustrations: Twenty-four portraits of officers of the regiment.
Inclusive dates: 1861–1864.

The author considered himself almost as much a traveler as a soldier and took particular pains to describe physical characteristics of the country, natural curiosities, towns and villages, and the sentiments of the inhabitants. His regiment, organized in the summer of 1861, was sent from St. Louis up the Missouri River to Boonville, whence it marched overland to Springfield and on into northwestern Arkansas, where it took part in the Battle of Pea Ridge. Moving again northeastward into Missouri and across the state to Cape Girardeau, the unit took a steamer down the Mississippi, up the Ohio and Tennessee rivers to a landing near Shiloh, and marched to Corinth. During the spring and summer of 1862 it operated in northern Mississippi, and when Bragg invaded Kentucky in the early fall it hurried northward to Louisville. Marching southward through Kentucky, it fought at Perryville in October and continued on to Nashville and the Battle of Murfreesboro at the end of the year, remained in Middle Tennessee for the first half of 1863, then operated in that vicinity until January, 1864, when it received furloughs and the narrative ends. Lathrop wrote this account immediately after the war, basing it on fresh memory and a personal diary.

[Lawrence, George Alfred] 1827–1876.   286

Border and bastille. By the author of "Guy Livingstone." New York, W. I. Pooley & co., [1863]

xii, 291 p.   19 cm.
Inclusive dates: 1863.
Other editions: Second edition, revised, London, Tinsley brothers, 1863.

Lawrence, an English author of some note, arrived in New York early in 1863, intent on making his way into the Confederacy to observe conditions there. He proceeded to Baltimore and Washington and got in touch with various agents who attempted to smuggle him into the Confederacy. After trying to cross at various points along the Potomac, he was arrested west of Harpers Ferry and taken to Wheeling, and then to Washington to the Carroll Prison until the British Government secured his release on the promise that he would leave the country immediately. While bobbing up along the fringes of the Confederacy, Lawrence had opportunities to form opinions of the new nation. Naturally, he looked upon the South with great friendship and came to detest the North.

LeConte, Joseph, 1823–1901.   287

'Ware Sherman, a journal of three months' personal experience in the last days of the Confederacy. By Joseph LeConte; with an introductory reminiscence by his daughter Caroline LeConte. Berkeley, University of California press, 1937.

xxxi, 146 p. incl. front. (port.) illus.   19 cm.
Illustrations: Eighteen crude drawings by Joseph LeConte.
Inclusive dates: December, 1864–March, 1865.
Parallel accounts: Another journal covering part of the route taken by LeConte is: Eliza Frances Andrews, The war-time journal of a Georgia girl, 1864–1865. New York, D. Appleton and company, 1908.

Joseph LeConte's book is one of the most valuable accounts of war experiences in the area overrun by the Federal armies in the period of the war's end. It gives in vivid style, and without a trace of bitterness, the experiences of a highly educated Southerner in the wake of Sherman's march to the sea and up through South Carolina. The author was born in Liberty County, Georgia, and was educated at the University of Georgia. After a few years of teaching at his alma mater he joined the faculty of the College of South Carolina in Columbia. In 1863 he became a chemist in a laboratory in Columbia which manufactured medical supplies for the Confederate Army, and the next year he became consulting chemist for the Confederate States Nitre and Mining Bureau. On Sherman's approach to Savannah, LeConte became much concerned about his kindred in Liberty County, below that city, and set out to bring them away from danger. He went by railway to Charleston and thence to a point a few miles from Savannah but, finding the railroad destroyed, returned to Columbia and set out again by Augusta, Milledgeville, Macon, Albany, and Thomasville, finally reaching Doctortown on the Altamaha River, a few miles below his ancestral home. After many perilous experiences he was able to rescue his kindred and return over the same route. He reached Columbia just in front of Sherman's army and was forced to flee again with all the nitre equipment and personal belongings he could load on wagons. While Sherman's troops were burning and sacking Columbia, LeConte was making his way northward. A few days later his wagon train was pillaged and burned by Federal troops, but the chemist made his escape, wandered around the woods for a few days, and returned to Columbia. After the war LeConte joined the faculty of the newly organized University of California, and developed into one of its most famous scholars and scientists.

Leib, Charles. 288

Nine months in the quartermaster's department; or, The chances for making a million. By Charles Leib ... Cincinnati, Moore, Wilstach, Keys & co., printers, 1862.

vi, 7–200 p. front., pl., port. 19 cm.
Illustrations: Frontispiece, "Truly yours Chas Leib" ₁Signature₁ and eleven other crude drawings of men and buildings.
Inclusive dates: 1861–1862.

Here is a curious mixture of sharp faultfinding and humor. Leib was appointed to the rank of captain in the United States Quartermaster Department and assigned to West Virginia. He made his way to Clarksburg, and the only part of his narrative pertinent to this work relates to the inhabitants of that place. He had little faith in the sincerity of West Virginia Unionism.

Leon, Louis. 289

Diary of a tar heel Confederate soldier. By L. Leon. Charlotte, N. C., Stone publishing company, 1913.

iv, 87 p. front. (port.) 18¾ cm.
Illustrations: Frontispiece, "L. Leon."
Inclusive dates: 1861–1865.

Leon was a New York Jew who went to North Carolina a few years before the war to engage in the dry goods business. He enlisted in the First North Carolina Regiment immediately when the war began and he was sent to the York Peninsula in Virginia. On the expiration of his six-month enlistment he returned to North Carolina and five months later again entered the service. He was sent to Virginia but was soon back in eastern North Carolina around Goldsboro, Kingston, Washington, and Newbern. Returning later to Virginia he was in the Gettysburg campaign, and was captured in the Battle of Spottsylvania in 1864. First imprisoned at Point Lookout, he was sent by water down Chesapeake Bay and up the Atlantic coast to Jersey City, to be held at Elmira until he was paroled in April, 1865. This diary has little value as a commentary on the South.

Leonard, Albert Charles, 1845– 290

The boys in blue of 1861–1865; a condensed history worth preserving ... Lancaster, Pa., A. C. Leonard, ₁1904₁

79 p. incl. front. (port.) illus., plates.   23 cm.
Illustrations: Twenty, relating mostly to prison life.
Inclusive dates: 1864.

Observations of this soldier-author give only a most cursory account of his travels and add nothing new to prison lore. He was taken prisoner in 1864 on the upper Potomac River in West Virginia and was hurried off to Belle Isle Prison in Richmond. He was soon transferred to Andersonville, Georgia, and later taken to Savannah, Charleston, and Florence. Near the end of the year he was returned to Savannah and turned over to the Federals at the mouth of the Savannah River.

Lewis, John Henry, 1834– 291

Recollections from 1860 to 1865. With incidents of camp life, descriptions of battles, the life of the southern soldier, his hardships and sufferings, and the life of a prisoner of war in the northern prisons. By John H. Lewis ... Washington, D. C., Peake & company, 1895.

1 p. l., 92 p.   port.   14¼ cm.
Illustrations: Frontispiece, ₍John H. Lewis.₎
Inclusive dates: 1861–1865.

Lewis became a soldier of the Confederacy in 1861 and reached the rank of lieutenant. He served around Norfolk until the evacuation of that city in the spring of 1862, was sent to Richmond to help repel McClellan, marched northward to the Second Battle of Manassas, and went on to Sharpsburg and Fredericksburg. He missed the Battle of Chancellorsville but participated in the Gettysburg campaign and was taken prisoner in Pickett's charge. He was held at Baltimore, Fort Delaware, and finally on Johnson's Island in Lake Erie. Near the end of the war he was transferred back to Fort Delaware and released in June. The book was written from memory after thirty years and is practically valueless as a commentary on the South during the Civil War.

Lightcap, William Henry. 292

The horrors of southern prisons during the war of the rebellion, from 1861 to 1865. By W. H. Lightcap ... ₍Platteville, Wis., Journal job rooms, 1902.₎

95 p. incl. front. (port.)   21 cm.
Illustrations: Frontispiece, "W. H. Lightcap. From Photo taken at Nashville, Tenn., in 1862."
Inclusive dates: 1864–1865.

This narrative is an excellent travelogue by a Federal soldier from his capture on the Chattahoochee River below Atlanta to his ultimate discharge from the army at Clinton, Iowa. Lightcap's book is filled with details and observations of the country but it was written long after the war and must be the product of a lively imagination stimulated by retelling and embellishing a soldier's experiences. After his capture in 1864 he was taken to West Point, Georgia, and on to Columbus where he was placed aboard the cars (always filthy according to the stock accounts) and dumped off at Andersonville. His transferals thereafter were to Macon, to Savannah (where he was impressed by the kindness of the women), up the railway toward Macon and the prison at Millen, to Savannah and into southern Georgia to Blackshear, back to Savannah, again through Blackshear to Thomasville in southwestern Georgia, northward through Albany, and finally to Andersonville. Near the end of the war he was sent to Vicksburg and turned over to the Federals, who took him by boat up the Mississippi to St. Louis and on to Clinton, Iowa. During most of his wanderings the author traveled on trains.

Livermore, Mrs. Mary Ashton (Rice), 1820–1905.   293

My story of the war: a woman's narrative of four years personal experience as nurse in the Union army, and in relief work at home, in hospitals, camps, and at the front, during the war of the rebellion. With anecdotes, pathetic incidents, and thrilling reminiscences portraying the lights and shadows of hospital life and the sanitary service of the war. By Mary A. Livermore ... Hartford, A. D. Worthington and company, 1888.

700 p. front., plates (part col.) ports. 22½ cm.
Illustrations: Five portraits of women, eight figure illustrations, and eight plates of battle flags.
Inclusive dates: 1861–1865.
Other editions: Another edition published by same company with the same number of pages, 1889.

Hospital scenes and work at the Sanitary Fairs captivated this war observer. Mrs. Livermore's activities were confined almost entirely to Chicago, Washington, and border towns. She made one trip down the Mississippi River and she gives some account of her experiences on the river and in Memphis and Vicksburg.

Livermore, Thomas Leonard, 1844–1918.   294

Days and events, 1860–1866. By Thomas L. Livermore ... Boston and New York, Houghton Mifflin company, 1920.

x p., 2 l., [3]–485, [1] p. front. (port.) illus., fold. pl. 24 cm.
Illustrations: Frontispiece, "Thos. L. Livermore" [Signature]; "Gettysburg Battlefield" (Panorama drawing of the battlefield, 11 inches by 18 inches.)
Maps: Various unlabeled rough sketches of battlefields by the author.
Inclusive dates: 1861–1865.

These reminiscences were written from 1867 to 1870 or slightly later and deal almost entirely with military matters; infrequently Colonel Livermore's prying memory gets outside the military lines. One instance is when he writes of foraging forays in the early part of the war which were made against strict orders by the higher authorities. At the outbreak of war Colonel Livermore went from his native state of Illinois to Washington and volunteered as a private in a New Hampshire unit; he later became colonel of the Eighteenth New Hampshire Volunteers. He served at the head of the Shenandoah Valley with General Patterson at the time of the First Bull Run, participated in the Peninsula campaign, the Sharpsburg campaign, the battles of Fredericksburg and Chancellorsville, the Gettysburg campaign, and the fighting around Richmond and Petersburg in 1864–1865 which led to Appomattox. His best-known literary work is *Numbers and Losses in the Civil War in America, 1861–1865,* published in 1901.

Lloyd, William Penn, 1837–1911. 295

History of the First reg't Pennsylvania reserve cavalry, from its organization, August, 1861, to September, 1864, with list of names of all officers and enlisted men who have ever belonged to the regiment and remarks attached to each name, noting change &c. Philadelphia, King & Baird, printers, 1864.

216 p.   19 cm.
Inclusive dates: 1861–1864.

This reserve cavalry regiment, organized at Harrisburg, Pennsylvania, proceeded to Washington and northern Virginia, and apart from some slight service in Maryland and in the Gettysburg campaign, confined its travels to Virginia. It was in the Shenandoah Valley for a time, and once was close to the northern approaches to Richmond. The narrative is mostly a regimental history practically devoid of personal touches and with only a few travel notes.

Logan, Mrs. Indiana Washington (Peddicord), 1833– *comp.* 296

Kelion Franklin Peddicord of Quirk's scouts, Morgan's Kentucky cavalry, C. S. A.; biographical and autobiographical, together with a general biographical outline of the Peddicord family. By Mrs. India W. P. Logan. New York and Washington, The Neale publishing company, 1908.

170 p.   4 port. (incl. front.)   20½ cm.
Illustrations: Frontispiece, "Kelion Franklin Peddicord, 1863"; "Columbus A. Peddicord"; "Carolus J. Peddicord, Member 1st Kentucky Cavalry"; "Kelion Franklin Peddicord, 1888."
Inclusive dates: 1861–1863.

The major part of this book and the part considered here is a long account written by Kelion Franklin Peddicord in December, 1865, relating to his army career and prison life from 1861 to 1863. In 1863 he was captured a second time but the later period, to the end of the war, is not included in this book except for occasional reference to it in the published letters. Peddicord was born in Ohio in 1833, but in early life the family moved to Virginia and he was thereafter associated with the South. He was in Kentucky at the outbreak of the war, enlisted in 1861 at Glasgow Junction, joined John Morgan's forces, and began operations in Middle Tennessee. In the fall of 1862, back in Kentucky, he was made a prisoner at Shelbyville, taken to Louisville, transferred to Camp Chase at Columbus, Ohio, moved again to Cincinnati, and taken down the Ohio and Mississippi Rivers to Vicksburg to be exchanged. From there he went to Jackson, Mississippi, and by rail through Mobile, Montgomery, Atlanta, and Chattanooga to Knoxville, Tennessee. He was back in Middle Tennessee in time to engage in various local raids and to participate in Morgan's Christmas (1862) raid into Kentucky. In the summer of 1863, he was in Tennessee again and took part in the Kentuckian's famous raid north of the Ohio River through Indiana and to Chester, Ohio, where he was captured and spent the rest of the war in various Northern prisons. Peddicord's story is mostly a personal, straightforward, soldier's narrative of his experiences in battle and in contact with the people he met. Being written immediately after the war, it has the value of a contemporary document.

Long, Lessel. 297

Twelve months in Andersonville. On the march—in the battle—in the Rebel prison pens, and at last in God's country. By Lessel Long ... Huntington, Ind., T. and M. Butler, 1886.

199 p., 1 l., L p. incl. pl. 21½ cm.
Illustrations: Frontispiece, "The Stockade at Andersonville"; "Battle of Chester Station, Va."; "Hospital at Andersonville"; "Prisoners in Camp at Blackshear, Ga."; "Prisoners Hunted Down with Blood-Hounds."
Inclusive dates: May, 1864–May, 1865.
Other editions: No other edition found. Most of this narrative originally appeared in the Andrew (Indiana) Express, under the title of "Army Life."

Lessel Long, a private in Company F, Thirteenth Indiana Infantry, was captured near Richmond in May, 1864, and was first taken to Libby Prison in Richmond. From that point his wanderings from one Confederate prison to another make this account unusual among prisoner-of-war books. He was moved to Andersonville, then by the usual route (after the link of railroad between Danville and Greensboro had been completed in May, 1864) leading through Salisbury, Charlotte, Columbia, Augusta, Millen, and Macon. After the fall of Atlanta most of the prisoners at Andersonville were moved out, Long being taken first to Savannah, by rail to Millen, again to Savannah, and to Blackshear in south Georgia. After an effort to return the prisoners to Savannah had been thwarted by Sherman's cavalry cutting the road, the prisoners were returned to Blackshear and taken by rail to Thomasville, marched across country to Albany, sent by train to Andersonville, and back to Macon. From there Long was sent to Andersonville again, retraced his route to Thomasville, and was taken to Lake City, Florida, and to Baldwin, where he was turned loose to make his way into the Federal lines outside Jacksonville. A few weeks before the prisoner was finally set free, the war had practically closed with Lee's and Johnston's surrenders. Long makes many comments on conditions in the Confederacy in a straightforward matter-of-fact narrative, spiced with a few atrocity stories to make it palatable to prospective readers.

Lothrop, Charles Henry, 1831–1890. 298

A history of the First regiment Iowa cavalry veteran volunteers, from its organization in 1861 to its muster out of the United States service in 1866. Also a complete roster of the regiment. By Charles H. Lothrop ... Lyons, Ia., Beers & Eaton, printers, 1890.

x p., 1 l., ₍13₎–422, v p., 1 l.   front., illus., pl., port.   22 cm.
Illustrations: Frontispiece, "Chas. H. Lothrop, Surgeon"; and 57 other portraits of other members of the regiment with a few exceptions.
Inclusive dates: 1861–1866.

Charles H. Lothrop, surgeon of his regiment, wrote this narrative about twenty-five years after the war. He made use of many official documents, but apparently had no personal material. The account is interrupted by many official reports and documents, and the route taken by the regiment is not clearly designated. Although military affairs predominate, there are some personal observations and comments. The First Regiment left Burlington, Iowa, by steamer for St. Louis, where it disembarked for the area of fighting in southwest Missouri and Arkansas and was most active in the region around Springfield, Fayetteville, and Little Rock. It marched out of Arkansas to Memphis, operated in western Tennessee and northern Mississippi until the end of the war, and was ordered to Texas. It moved down the Mississippi River and up the Red to Alexandria, marched overland to Hempstead, Texas, and proceeded to Austin, where it spent some time before being mustered out in 1866, to return through Galveston, across the Gulf, and up the Mississippi.

Lucas, Daniel R., 1840– 299

History of the 99th Indiana infantry, containing a diary of marches, incidents, biography of officers and complete rolls. By Chaplain D. R. Lucas. Lafayette, Ind., Rosser & Spring, printers, 1865.

iv, (5–179) p.   20½ cm.
Inclusive dates: 1862–1864.
Other editions: Another edition of this work was brought out in 1900 in Rockford, Ind.

Leaving South Bend, Indiana, in 1862 for the scene of operations in northern Mississippi, the 99th Infantry went south to Louisville, down river to Memphis, and marched overland into Tennessee. Returning to Memphis it continued down the Mississippi to the Vicksburg region and, after the fall of that city, went back to Memphis and proceeded eastward through northern Mississippi and Alabama to Chattanooga and Knoxville in East Tennessee. In January, 1864, the author of this work and chaplain of the regiment resigned. His account is extended to include the march of Sherman to the sea and on to Washington. The narrative is surprisingly devoid of travel consciousness.

Lusk, William Thompson, 1838–1897.   300

War letters of William Thompson Lusk, captain, assistant adjutant-general, United States volunteers, 1861–1863, afterward M. D., LL.D. New York, Privately printed, 1911.

x p., 1 l., 304 p.   front., pl., ports., maps.   24 cm.
Illustrations: Frontispiece, "Captain William Thompson Lusk"; and ten other portraits.
Maps: Northeast Virginia, Maryland, and Pennsylvania; Port Royal and the Sea Islands of South Carolina.
Inclusive dates: 1861–1863.

Lusk fought first at Manassas in July, 1861, and was in the expedition which seized Beaufort, South Carolina, and the surrounding country in November, 1861. He remained for about a year in that region and on James Island near Charleson, and returned to Virginia in time for the Sharpsburg campaign and Fredericksburg. This is an excellent series of letters, especially good on conditions in South Carolina.

Lyman, Theodore, 1833–1897.   301

Meade's headquarters, 1863–1865; letters of Colonel Theodore Lyman from the Wilderness to Appomattox, selected and ed. by George R. Agassiz. Boston, The Atlantic monthly press, 1922.

x p., 3 l., 371 p.   front., ports., maps.   24½ cm.
Illustrations: Sixteen portraits of Federal generals and soldiers.
Maps: Thirteen crudely drawn maps relating to Grant's campaign against Richmond.
Inclusive dates: 1863–1865.

Lyman's travels as a Federal officer were restricted to the half circle around Richmond, from the Rapidan-Rappahannock region through the Wilderness, across the lower James, through Petersburg, to Appomattox. In these letters to his wife, and in a journal which he kept, the author has given an excellent picture of conditions in that part of Virginia over which he traveled. He has much to say about people, old homesteads, and towns. Born in Waltham, Massachusetts, and a graduate of Harvard, Lyman was a highly cultured man who after the war became an eminent zoologist and the author of many scientific articles. He was a member of Congress from 1883 to 1885.

Lyon, William Franklin.   302

In and out of Andersonville prison. By W. F. Lyon ... Detroit, Mich., Geo. Harland co., 1905.

3 p. l., [11]–121 p.   illus., plates, ports.   17½ cm.
Illustrations: Frontispiece, "Yours Very Truly W. F. Lyon" [Signature]; "As the author appeared on entering service"; Plan of Andersonville Prison; "Providence Spring as it appears today."
Inclusive dates: 1864.

Lyon was taken prisoner in northern Mississippi in the summer of 1864 while attempting to intercept General Forrest. His captors took him by railway to Meridian, Mississippi, through Montgomery to Andersonville Prison in Georgia, and after a few months he was sent to the Savannah prison and then on to the Millen Prison. At the mouth of the Savannah River he was turned over to the Federals, who took him to Annapolis. The author waited forty years to write his book; it is therefore inaccurate in details and of little historical value.

Lyon, William Penn, 1822–1913. 303

Reminiscences of the civil war; comp. from the war correspondence of Colonel William P. Lyon and from personal letters and diary of Mrs. Adalia C. Lyon. Published by William P. Lyon, jr. ₁San Jose, Cal., Press of Muirson & Wright₁ 1907.

3 p. l., 274 p. front., ports. 23 cm.
Illustrations: Frontispiece, "Judge and Mrs. William P. Lyon, Eden Vale, Cal., 1907"; "Colonel William P. Lyon, Racine, Wisconsin, 1863"; "Mrs. Adelia C. Lyon, Racine, Wisconsin, 1863."
Maps: "Map of Fort Henry, Tenn. Feb. 28, 1863. Drawn by Colonel Lyon."
Inclusive dates: 1861–1865.

Letters and parts of the author's diary, with letters of Mrs. Lyon from the South, make up the body of this narrative. There is no clear continuity of Colonel Lyon's travels but the areas of his chief activities are easily inferred. He was a member successively of the Eightieth and Thirteenth regiments of the Wisconsin Volunteer Infantry, served first in Missouri in 1861, and marched out of St. Louis to Pilot Knob and Greenville in the southeastern part of the state. Later movements were from Memphis to west Tennessee and northern Mississippi, to Fort Henry and Fort Donelson, into Kentucky, and back to Tennessee by way of Nashville. During most of 1863 and 1864 the author was in northeastern Alabama, and campaigned in East Tennessee through Knoxville to Greeneville. At the end of the war, instead of being mustered out he was sent to Texas by steamer down the Mississippi and across the Gulf of Mexico to Matagorda Bay, to be stationed a few miles inland at Green Lake. In the late summer of 1865 he resigned from the army and returned to Wisconsin. The narrative is largely about military matters, with occasional comments on the country and people. He was especially interested in the abnormalities of Texas, detesting everything there except the climate.

M'Bride, Robert Ekin, 1846– 304

In the ranks: from the Wilderness to Appomattox courthouse. The war, as seen and experienced by a private soldier in the Army of the Potomac. By Rev. R. E. M'Bride ... Cincinnati, The author. Printed by Walden & Stowe, 1881.

246 p. front. (port.) 17 cm.
Inclusive dates: 1864–1865.

M'Bride was seventeen years of age when he enlisted in a Pennsylvania unit in December of 1863. Writing in later years from memory he naturally recalled only a boy's experiences and impressions. His first active battle service was in the Wilderness and thereafter he followed the Federal forces in their maneuvers southeastward across the James River to the south side. He was furloughed home for a short time on account of his health, but was back in the fray before Grant made his spring attack on Lee, and was on hand at Appomattox. Despite his years of active service, M'Bride's book is of little importance.

MacCauley, Clay, 1843–1925. 305

Through Chancellorsville, into and out of Libby prison. I. From Chancellorsville into Libby prison. II. In Libby prison, and out of it; home again. By Clay MacCauley, ⟨late lieutenant in One hundred and twenty-sixth infantry, Pennsylvania volunteers.⟩ Providence, Rhode Island soldiers and sailors historical society, 1904.

70 p. front., pl., port. 19½ cm. (*Added t.-p.*: Personal narratives of events in the war of the rebellion, being papers read before the Rhode Island soldiers and sailors historical society. 6th ser., no. 7)

Illustrations: Frontispiece, "Lieut. Clay MacCauley"; "Rev. Clay MacCauley, A. M."; "Libby Prison."

Inclusive dates: 1863.

Other editions: No other edition found. This pamphlet was published as no. 7 in the Sixth Series of Personal narratives of events in the war of the rebellion being papers read before the Rhode Island Soldiers and Sailors historical society.

This reminiscent account, written about forty years after the war, is important only for a description of the march from Chancellorsville, where the author was captured, to the railway at Guinea Station, the train trip to Richmond, and the march through the city to Libby Prison. After exchange arrangements were made, MacCauley was taken to Petersburg and City Point, where he was transferred to Union forces, meeting with a hostile reception along the way.

McCowan, Archibald. 306

The prisoners of war; a reminiscence of the rebellion. By Archibald McCowan ... New York, London ₁etc.₎ The Abbey press, ₁c.1901.₎

187 p. front. (port.) 19½ cm.
Illustrations: Frontispiece, "Archd McCowan" ₁Signature₎.
Inclusive dates: 1864–1865.

This book may be dismissed as of slight if not wholly fictitious value because it is indefinite in details of dates and places and contains imaginary conversations. The author claims to have been captured near Petersburg in the summer of 1864, to have been imprisoned in Libby at Richmond for a short time, and to have been transferred to the Salisbury Prison where he escaped and returned to his regiment. He also claims to have found a great treasure near Wilmington, North Carolina, after the war.

McDonald, Mrs. Cornelia (Peake), 1822–1909.

A diary with reminiscences of the war and refugee life in the Shenandoah valley, 1860–1865. ₍By₎ Mrs. Cornelia McDonald ... annotated and supplemented by Hunter McDonald ... Nashville, Cullom & Ghertner co., ₍c.1935.₎

xvi, 540 p.   col. front., plates (part col.) ports. (1 col.) facsim.   22¾ cm.
Illustrations: Frontispiece, " 'The Sunset of the Confederacy' " ₍Two Confederate flags₎ and thirty portraits of various people mentioned in the diary and others, pictures of houses, and facsimiles of manuscripts.
Maps: "Sketch Map of Lexington, Virginia" (8 by 22 inches); "Sketch Map of Winchester, Virginia and Vicinity from the Earliest to 1864" (8 by 15 inches); "The Valley of Virginia from the Potomac River to Christianburg" (8 by 19 inches).
Inclusive dates: 1861–1865.

Mrs. Cornelia McDonald kept a diary during the war and added reminiscences ten years later. The result is a valuable commentary on conditions in the Confederacy both in the territory occupied by Federal troops and in the Confederate regions. She lived in Winchester, Virginia, until Lee's retreat from Gettysburg, whereupon she became a refugee, going first to Amherst for a few months and then to Lexington, with a few visits to Richmond and Lynchburg. She records the tribulations and rejoicings when Winchester was intermittently occupied by Federals and Confederates. Mrs. McDonald was in Lexington when Hunter devastated that city in 1864 and gives vivid first-hand descriptions of the burning of Governor Letcher's home and the Virginia Military Institute, with comments on the solemn respect these Federal troops showed to the memory of Stonewall Jackson when they marched by the cemetery where he lay buried.

McElroy, John, 1846–1929.

Andersonville: a story of Rebel military prisons, fifteen months a guest of the so-called southern confederacy. A private soldier's experience in Richmond, Andersonville, Savannah, Millen, Blackshear and Florence. By John McElroy ... Toledo, D. R. Locke, 1879.

xxx p., 1 l., ₍33₎–654 p., 1 l. incl. front., illus., plates, maps.   22 cm.
Illustrations: 152 illustrations, most of them small and crudely drawn.
Maps: "Map of Georgia, South Carolina and Part of North Carolina. Showing the Location of Prisons at Andersonville, Savannah, Millen, Blackshear, Charleston, Columbia and Florence" (inaccurate); "Map of Wilmington and Neighborhood."
Inclusive dates: January, 1864–March, 1865.

This book became a standard work on Confederate prisons for Northern readers. Although it was written almost fifteen years after the war, it is utterly biased and fiercely hostile to all things Southern, with a haughty, superior, "holier-than-thou" attitude at all times. McElroy, a member of Company L, Sixteenth Illinois Cavalry, was captured at Jonesville, a small town in southwestern Virginia, in January, 1864. He was marched to Bristol, sent by train to Richmond, and transferred to Andersonville by way of Weldon, Raleigh, Columbia, Augusta, and Macon. When Sherman began his march to the sea,

McElroy was taken to Savannah, back to Millen, returned through Savannah to Blackshear, and finally held at Florence. Near the end of the war he was handed over to the Federals on the outskirts of Wilmington and sent by boat to Annapolis. McElroy was born in Kentucky, but soon left that state for St. Louis and was later employed in newspaper work in Chicago. After the war he was associated first with the *Toledo Blade* and then with the *National Tribune* in Washington. His interest in pensions for Federal veterans explains why he wrote this book.

McGee, Benjamin F., 1834– 309

History of the 72d Indiana volunteer infantry of the mounted lightning brigade ... especially devoted to giving the reader a definite knowledge of the service of the common soldier. With an appendix containing a complete roster of officers and men. Written and comp. by B. F. McGee ... Ed. by William R. Jewell ... LaFayette, Ind., S. Vater & co., printers, 1882.

xviii p., 1 l., 698, 21, ⟨1⟩ p.   front., port.   23 cm.
Illustrations: Five portraits of soldiers.
Inclusive dates: 1862–1865.

McGee left Lafayette, Indiana, with his regiment in 1862 for the scene of war in Kentucky. He marched southward as far as Lebanon and turned back to Louisville with the forces which were being collected to drive Bragg out of the state. The author did not participate in the Perryville fight, but went to Nashville and on to Murfreesboro, and operated in Middle Tennessee for the next few months. In the fall of 1863 he went on the Chattanooga-Chickamauga campaign, and then marched back into Middle Tennessee, northern Alabama, and Mississippi. In the spring of 1864 he went with Sherman as far as Atlanta, returned to the Nashville region, and after Hood's defeat joined the Wilson raid through Selma and Columbus, Georgia, to Macon. The war being over, he returned home by way of Atlanta, Chattanooga, and Nashville. McGee was an untrained writer, but he includes every incident of travel which he could recall or extract from his or his comrades' diaries. The narrative is somewhat garrulous, but it contains much local color and is helpful in assessing conditions in those parts of the Confederacy through which McGee traveled.

McGuire, Judith White (Brockenbrough),
"Mrs. John P. McGuire." 310

Diary of a southern refugee, during the war. By a lady of Virginia ... New York, E. J. Hale & son, 1867.

360 p.   18½ cm.
Inclusive dates: May 4, 1861–May 4, 1865.
Other editions: Second edition, 1868. Same publishers. Third edition "with corrections and additions." Richmond, J. W. Randolph & English, 1889.

Mrs. McGuire was the wife of John P. McGuire, principal of the Episcopal High School at Alexandria, Virginia, and associated with the leading Virginia families. After fleeing from Alexandria at the beginning of the war she also came to know the common folk of Virginia. Thus she had varied experience in wartime conditions at all levels. As a refugee throughout the war she traveled as far southward as Danville and Lynchburg, and northward to Charlottesville and Winchester, but spent most of her time in Richmond and nearby Ashland. Her diary is an interesting and faithful account of conditions as seen by a cultured Virginia lady to whom the war was a tragedy. Though strongly Southern in sentiment and an unswerving supporter of Jefferson Davis's regime, the author showed no bitterness. Her greatest interest was in hospital work and in providing comforts for both the wounded and the well.

McKim, Randolph Harrison, 1842–1920. 311

A soldier's recollections; leaves from the diary of a young Confederate, with an oration on the motives and aims of the soldiers of the South. By Randolph H. McKim ... New York [etc.] Longmans, Green, and co., 1910.

xvii, 362 p. front., 5 port. 21¼ cm.
Illustrations: Frontispiece, "Belvidere, Baltimore, Md."; "Lieut. Gen. Thos. J. ('Stonewall') Jackson"; "Lieut. Randolph H. McKim, 1862"; "Gen. Robert Edward Lee, 1862"; "Gen. Thomas T. Munford"; "The Rev. Randolph H. McKim, D. D., 1904."
Inclusive dates: 1861–1865.

Although these recollections were written about forty-five years after the Civil War, they have been re-enforced with liberal extracts from the author's diary. McKim, a Marylander and a graduate of the University of Virginia, became a notable figure in the religious world after the war. These statements by a scholar, free from all bitterness or bias, may be accepted as authoritative on conditions in the Confederate Army and to a considerable degree on wartime social conditions in Virginia. McKim began his war career by helping to plant a Confederate flag on the rotunda of the University of Virginia; thereafter he served in the Confederate Army successively as private, staff officer, and chaplain. He spent most of his time north of Richmond, especially in the Shenandoah Valley, and as far as Gettysburg. The writer was related maternally to most of the important families of Virginia, visited widely among relatives and acquaintances, and recounts social conditions as he found them. In 1862, on a thirty-day furlough which he stretched into forty, he made a tour among his kin, which led him from Winchester to Richmond, down the James almost to Jamestown, and back northward through Fredericksburg.

McMorries, Edward Young. 312

... History of the First regiment, Alabama volunteer infantry, C. S. A., By Edward Young McMorries ... Montgomery, Ala., The Brown printing co., printers, 1904.

142 p.   23 cm.   (State of Alabama, Department of archives and history ... bulletin no. 2)
Illustrations: Frontispiece, "Yours truly E. Y. McMorries" ₍Signature₎; "Henry D. Clayton"; "Yours truly I. G. W. Steedman" ₍Signature₎; "Farragut's Attack on Port Hudson"; "Richard Williams"; "Alice Whiting Waterman"; " 'Confederate Rest,' Madison, Wis.,"; Steedman "At 30, At 50, At 68"; "U. S. Military Prison on Johnson's Island Ohio"; "Johnson's Island, Ohio. Prison Hospital"; "View of Prison Burial Ground, Johnson's Island, Ohio"; Facsimile of Poem "Farewell to Johnson's Island."
Maps: Frontispiece, "Map of the Movements of the First Alabama Regiment, C. S. A., 1861–1865" (Folding, 12 in. by 12 in.). Four sketch maps illustrative of Pensacola Bay, Island No. 10, Johnson's Island (Lake Erie), and "Defense of Port Hudson Genl. Frank Gardner, Comdg. May 21st to July 8, 1863."
Other editions: Also issued as an independent publication by the same publishers.

In composing this narrative McMorries used various official documents, materials personal to his comrades, and his own memory, "perhaps unfortunate in never forgetting." He served first at Pensacola, was transferred to the Mississippi, traveled by rail from Mobile to Corinth and Memphis, and by boat to Island No. 10, where he was captured and taken to Camp Butler Prison near Springfield, Illinois. On being exchanged, he took part in the defense of Port Hudson, was again captured and exchanged, was sent to Georgia to oppose Sherman's march on Atlanta, and after its fall followed Hood to the gates of Nashville. Afterward he traveled through Montgomery, Columbus, Macon, Milledgeville, and Augusta, en route to North Carolina to join Johnston's forces, with whom he surrendered. Most of the account relates to soldier life; personal comments and travel notes are few but significant.

Macnamara, Michael H.   313

The Irish Ninth ₍Massachusetts₎ in bivouac and battle; or, Virginia and Maryland campaigns. By M. H. Macnamara ... Boston, Lee and Shepard, 1867.

1 p. l., 306 p.   front., pl.   19 cm.
Illustrations: Four crude drawings to illustrate incidents in the text.
Inclusive dates: 1861–1864.

Macnamara, a Boston Irishman, served from 1861 to June, 1864. His comments on the country and people of the Confederacy are prejudiced and many of them do not agree with known facts. For instance, he states that, at Arlington, Lee's mansion, slaves still on the estate told him that Lee was a hard taskmaster and that he had not carried out the Custis will freeing some of the slaves on the estate. All of Macnamara's fighting took place north of the James River including the Sharpsburg and Gettysburg campaigns.

Malet, William Wyndham, 1804–1885.   314

An errand to the South in the summer of 1862. By the Rev. William Wyndham Malet ... London, Richard Bentley, 1863.

viii, 312 p.   front.   17 cm.

Illustrations: Frontispiece, "River Stockade in James River, at Drury's Bluff, Virginia." (Steel engraving). Facsimile Words and music of "Maryland, My Maryland."
Inclusive dates: May 20, 1862–November, 1862.

The Rev. W. Wyndham Malet was Vicar of Ardeley, near Buntingford, Hertfordshire, England. He came to America to visit his sister at Conway, South Carolina, who was married to a Southerner, then a captain in the Confederate Army. He landed at New York, went by train to Washington, and finally got permission to visit the Confederacy. He traveled by steamer from Baltimore to Fortress Monroe, on a British warship to Charleston, by train to Fairbluff, just across the North Carolina line, and finished the journey to Conway in a buggy carrying Confederate mail. Most of his time was spent on his brother-in-law's plantation, but he visited Pawleys Island on the coast, another plantation near Winnsboro, and made trips to Columbia, to Flat Rock, North Carolina, and to Richmond and back by way of Wilmington. He left South Carolina by railway, going through Columbia, Charlotte, Salisbury, Raleigh, Weldon, and Petersburg to Richmond, on a flag-of-truce boat to Fortress Monroe, by boat to Baltimore and by rail to New York, whence he sailed for England. Malet was much interested in the social customs of the Confederacy, and especially in the institution of slavery. Unlike most Englishmen (perhaps influenced by his sister's position), he found slavery a benevolent institution and the slaves wholly contented with their lot. During his six months in the South he saw no beggars and found the people, high and low, unanimously for the war and independence.

Marks, James Junius, 1809–1899.   315

The Peninsula campaign in Virginia; or, Incidents and scenes on the battle-fields and in Richmond. By Rev. J. J. Marks, D. D. Philadelphia, J. B. Lippincott & co., 1864.

xx, 21–444 p.   front., pl.   18½ cm.

Illustrations: Frontispiece, "Battle of Glendale—Contest around General McCall's Cannon"; "The Descent of General Fitz John Porter at Yorktown"; "Contest for the Flag, at the Battle of Glendale, near the Negro House"; "The Sweetest Tears that Heaven Sheds are the Dews that Fall on the Dead Soldier's Face"; "I Will Ask Your Grandmother to Blot Your Name out of the Family Bible"; "Scene among the Wounded at Savage Station, in the Rear of the House"; "Rifling the Knapsacks of our Wounded—Main Street Prison, Richmond"; "German Women Giving Nourishment to our Wounded at the Depot, Richmond."

Inclusive dates: 1861–1862.

Other editions: As this work was copyrighted in 1863 there was probably an edition which appeared that year. The edition used here is not numbered, but in this same year (1864) a Fifth edition appeared.

The chaplain of the Sixty-third Regiment of Pennsylvania Volunteers traveled out of Alexandria, Virginia, down the Potomac to Mount Vernon and with McClellan's expedition down the Chesapeake to the York Peninsula, where he visited Yorktown, Williamsburg, and Richmond as a prisoner of war. His service, as far as detailed in this book, ended with his exchange in July, 1862. He was entranced by the historic parts of Virginia which he visited, described the old mansions around Alexandria and Washington's estate at Mount Vernon at some length, and recorded with shame the desecration of the old Pohick Church, where Washington had worshipped. Marks was also concerned about the careless treatment he thought the medical organization gave the Federal soldiers.

Marshall, Albert O. 316

Army life; from a soldier's journal. By Albert O. Marshall. Incidents, sketches and record of a Union soldier's army life, in camp and field; 1861–64. Joliet, Ill., printed for the author by Chicago Legal News company, 1884.

5–410 p.   19 cm.
Inclusive dates: 1861–1864.
Other editions: First edition, 1883; second edition, used here, 1884; a "Special Edition" appeared in 1886; all published by the author.

Although this purports to be a journal kept by the author during the Civil War, it has the appearance of much working over, including admitted "little changes," "verbal alterations," and evident additions. Yet the book contains interesting comments on the Confederate people and apt descriptions of natural scenery, plantation homes, and a herd of Texas longhorn cattle. Marshall joined an Illinois unit in 1861 and first campaigned in Missouri. He landed in St. Louis and took the train to the end of the line at Pilot Knob, accompanied a foray into Helena, Arkansas, and to the Mississippi, and was returned upstream to Pilot Knob. Later he marched to St. Genevieve, boarded a steamer to be present at the fall of Vicksburg, went to see New Orleans and on by rail to Brashear City and New Iberia in the Teche country. Ordered to Texas, he went by boat from New Orleans to Point Isabel near Brownsville, continued up the coast of Texas to Matagorda Bay, and spent the winter of 1863–1864. The return trip was through Donaldsonville and across country to New Orleans. In the fall of 1864 Marshall went by sea to New York City and was mustered out.

Mason, Frank Holcomb, 1840–1916. 317

The Forty-second Ohio infantry: a history of the organization and services of that regiment in the war of the rebellion; with biographical sketches of its field officers and a full roster of the regiment. Comp. and written for the Veteran's association of the Forty-second Ohio, by F. H. Mason ... Cleveland, Cobb, Andrews & co., 1876.

306 p., 1 l.   front., port.   18½ cm.
Illustrations: Frontispiece, "J. A. Garfield [Signature] Hon. James A. Garfield, Representative from Ohio" (Steel Engraving); "Lionel A. Sheldon"; "Don A. Pardee."
Maps: "Battle-Field of Middle Creek" [Kentucky]; "The Assault at Chickasaw Bluffs"; "The Battle-Field of Thompson's Hill."
Inclusive dates: 1861–1864.

Mason was a private, "promoted to Capt. and A.D.C." in Company A of the Forty-second Ohio Infantry, which was organized in 1861 at Camp Chase, Ohio. He went by train to Cincinnati, by Ohio River steamer to the mouth of the Big

Sandy River on the eastern border of Kentucky, and up that river and across the Kentucky mountains to Pound Gap. Returning to the Ohio River at Greenup, he took a steamer to Louisville, went on an expedition through Lexington and Crab Orchard to Cumberland Gap to wrest that point from the Confederates, retreated with the regiment to the Ohio River, and went to Ohio to recuperate at a rest camp in Jackson County. The regiment then went on an expedition up the Kanawha River to Charleston, West Virginia, embarked on steamers for Vicksburg, fought on both sides of the river until the fall of that city, and was ordered to New Orleans. It floated down the river, camped briefly at Carrollton, and proceeded westward into Louisiana, traveling by rail as far as Brashear City. It marched northward to Opelousas, returned to Brashear City, and moved northward again to Plaquemine on the Mississippi, where it remained for sometime before taking boat for Baton Rouge. From here it went up the Red River a short distance but returned to Morganza. Upon the expiration of his enlistment in 1864, Mason returned to Camp Chase, going by steamer to Cairo and thence by railway. This account is somewhat better than the usual regimental history. Mason frequently describes the country through which he marched, the mountains, the towns and cities, and the people. Neither a diary or letters are mentioned but the narrative, written within a dozen years after the events described, may be accepted as a correct record.

Massie, James William, 1799–1869. 318

America: the origin of her present conflict; her prospect for the slave, and her claim for anti-slavery sympathy; illustrated by incidents of travel during a tour in the summer of 1863, throughout the United States, from ... Maine to the Mississippi. By James William Massie ... London, John Snow, 1864.

viii, 472 p. fold. map. 18½ cm.
Maps: Large folded "Map of the United States, showing the territory in possession of the Federal Union, January, 1864." Lithographed by Bacon & co. ... London.
Inclusive dates: Summer, 1863.

James William Massie, of London, was "One of the Deputation appointed to convey to Ministers in America the Address adopted at the Ministerial Anti-slavery Conference, held in the Free Trade Hall, Manchester, 3rd. June, 1863." His travels were entirely in the North except for two points, St. Louis and Louisville, where he dipped across the line into slave states. Rabid in his opposition to slavery, he was naturally unable to see the slave states as anything but barbaric, but he found St. Louis less objectionable than Louisville. In the latter city he was thoroughly disgusted with all that he saw and hastily retreated across the Ohio into the pure air of the free states. The volume has practically no value as a commentary on the Southern states.

Mathews, Alfred E. 319

Interesting narrative; being a journal of the flight of Alfred E. Mathews of Stark co., Ohio. From the state of Texas, on the 20th of April, and his arrival at Chicago on the 28th of May, after traveling on foot and alone a distance of over 800 miles across the states of Louisiana, Arkansas and Missouri by the most unfrequented routes; together with interesting descriptions of men and things; of what he saw and heard; appearance of the country, habits of the people, &c., &c., &c. [New Philadelphia, Ohio?] 1861.

1 p. l., [7]–34 p. l. l.   22½ cm.
Inclusive dates: 1860–1861.

When the secession movement began in 1860 Alfred E. Mathews, a Northerner, was living in Tuscaloosa County, Alabama. He made his way out of Alabama to Columbus, Mississippi, took a boat down the Tombigbee River to Mobile, and embarked on a coastal steamer for New Orleans. After a short stay he went by steamer up the Mississippi and Red rivers to Shreveport, Henderson, Palestine, Crockett, and Nacogdoches, returned to Shreveport, and set out up the east bank of the Red River. Mathews passed through the Arkansas towns of Lewisville, Washington, Arkadelphia, Hot Springs, Perryville, Batesville, Smithville, and Pocahontas, crossed into Missouri, finally reached Ironton, and proceeded by railway to St. Louis and Chicago. He was one of those Northerners who made himself both conspicuous and subject to suspicion in the South by his occupations as teacher, printer, and jack-of-all-trades. Although his observations and criticisms were generally hostile, this account has distinct value for its descriptions of the country as well as for its comments on the people, who were aroused by the prospects of war and enlisting on both sides.

Maury, Dabney Herndon, 1822–1900.   320
Recollections of a Virginian in the Mexican, Indian, and Civil wars. By General Dabney Herndon Maury ... New York, Charles Scribner's sons, 1894.

xi, 279, [1] p.   front. (port.)   20¼ cm.
Illustrations: Frontispiece, "Very truly yours Dabney H. Maury" [Signature].
Inclusive dates: 1861–1865 (1864–1894).
Other editions: This volume passed through three so-called editions (really printings) during the first year of its publication. No other edition found.

As a graduate of the University of Virginia and of West Point, Maury began his army career in the Mexican War, continued it through the Indian troubles of Texas and New Mexico, and made his main contribution to military history in the Civil War. He was in New Mexico when the secession movement began and, like many other Southerners, hurried eastward through St. Louis and Louisville to Richmond to offer his services to Virginia. He continued immediately to Fredericksburg, but did not participate in the First Manassas battle as his commission had been delayed. In early 1862 he was transferred to the Trans-Mississippi Department, took part in the Battle of Pea Ridge, returned to Mississippi with Van Dorn's army, and spent the latter part of the war as commander of the Department of the Gulf with headquarters at Mobile. After the war he engaged in business in New Orleans and later served as the United States minister to Colombia. The account is well written, scholarly, and reliable, but is interrupted by many evaluations of personalities and fails to state clearly what routes he followed. Yet it is informative on conditions in the Confederacy, especially around Mobile in the latter part of the war.

Merrell, William Howard, d. 1897. 321

Five months in rebeldom; or, Notes from the diary of a Bull Run prisoner, at Richmond. By Corporal W. H. Merrell ... Rochester, N. Y., Adams and Dabney, 1862.

iv, [5]–64 p. front. 21 cm.
Illustrations: Frontispiece, "Rebel Guard Quarters. Prison No. 1. Hospital No. 2."
Inclusive dates: July, 1861–January, 1862.
Other editions: No other edition found. The greater part of this pamphlet originally appeared in the Rochester evening express.
Parallel accounts: Another account of a Bull Run prisoner in the same tobacco warehouse in Richmond is Alfred Ely (Charles Lanman, editor), Journal of Alfred Ely, a prisoner of war in Richmond. New York, D. Appleton & co., 1862.

Merrell's pamphlet is not only one of the best accounts of prison conditions in Richmond during the first year of the war, but it also contains valuable comments on the Southern attitude toward Federal prisoners. It bears evidence of being an honest attempt to tell the truth in a straightforward story. The author, however, seems at times to have felt that his story was becoming too pro-Confederate and interposed explanatory statements that his experiences must undoubtedly have been exceptional. Merrell was color guard in Company E, Twenty-seventh Regiment New York State Volunteers. He was taken prisoner at the First Battle of Bull Run and was sent by train to a tobacco factory in Richmond where he remained until January, 1862, when he was exchanged, taken down the James River on a flag-of-truce boat to a point near Newport News, and transferred to a Federal ship.

Merrill, Samuel, 1831–1924. 322

The Seventieth Indiana volunteer infantry in the war of the rebellion. By Samuel Merrill. Indianapolis, The Bowen-Merrill company, 1900.

4 p. (l)., 372 p. front., pl., port. 23 cm.
Illustrations: Two portraits and a flag illustration.
Inclusive dates: 1862–1865.

As a Federal soldier from the Middle West, Merrill made the convential swing around the circle. He left Indianapolis in 1862 for Kentucky to participate in halting Bragg, was engaged in maneuvers through Nashville, took part in the Chattanooga-Chickamauga campaign, and in the spring of 1864 followed Sherman to the sea and to Washington for the "Grand Review," after which he returned to Indiana. Using various diaries and other personal material of his comrades, Merrill made his narrative more of a composite account than a record of his own observations. It is, therefore, of little value as travel material.

Merrill, Samuel Hill, 1805–1873. 323
The campaigns of the First Maine and First District of Columbia cavalry. By Samuel H. Merrill. Portland, Maine, Bailey & Noyes, 1866.

xv, ₍17₎–437 p.   port.   19 cm.
Illustrations: Three steel engravings.
Inclusive dates: 1861–1865.

Apart from the Sharpsburg campaign in Maryland and the Gettysburg campaign into Pennsylvania, all of Merrill's travels as chaplain in the Federal Army lay in Virginia, principally in the Shenandoah Valley, with Grant's campaign against Richmond, and from the Wilderness to Appomattox. Writing the year after the war ended, Merrill's memory was fresh and apparently aided by personal notes. He was interested in the old homesteads and historic places, especially those associated with Patrick Henry.

Miller, James Newton. 324
The story of Andersonville and Florence. Des Moines, Ia., Welch, 1900.

47 p. incl. front. (port.)   22½ cm.
Illustrations: Frontispiece, James N. Miller in 1865.
Inclusive dates: May, 1864–December, 1864.

Miller's prison experiences, based on an abbreviated diary but strongly fortified by memory thirty-five years after the war, constitute the foundation of this pamphlet. It is singularly free from prejudice and bitterness but is of little importance because there are few comments on the people or the country of the Confederacy. Miller was a Pennsylvanian who joined the Twelfth West Virginia Infantry, Company A, and was captured at Winchester, Virginia, in May, 1864. Unlike most prisoners he was never taken to Richmond, but was taken by prison train through Charlottesville, Lynchburg, Danville, Greensboro, Charlotte, Columbia, Augusta, and Macon to Andersonville. He was later transferred by way of Augusta and Charleston to Florence where he was paroled and handed over to the Federal ships outside Charleston harbor, which conveyed him to Annapolis.

Mixson, Frank M., 1846– 325
Reminiscences of a private. By Frank M. Mixson, Company "E" 1st S. C. Vols. (Hagood's) ... Columbia, S. C., The State company, 1910.

130 p.   19 cm.
Illustrations: Two portraits.
Inclusive dates: 1861–1865.

Beginning service as a Confederate soldier around Charleston, South Caro-

lina, Mixson soon proceeded to Virginia. After Gettysburg he followed Longstreet in the transfer of his army from Virginia by rail through Weldon, Wilmington, and Atlanta to the Chattanooga front. He spent the winter of 1863–
1864 in East Tennessee with Longstreet's army and continued to Virginia in the
spring to help stop Grant's march on Richmond. Since Mixson wrote his account
in old age and from memory his narrative has little value as contemporary travel
literature. The book was first published in *The People*, a Barnwell, South Carolina, newspaper.

Montgomery, Franklin Alexander, 1830–   326

Reminiscences of a Mississippian in peace and war. By Frank A. Montgomery ... Cincinnati, The Robert Clarke company, press, 1901.

xv p., 1 l., 305 p.   front., ports.   22½ cm.

Illustrations: Frontispiece, "Lt. Col Frank A Montgomery, First Mississippi Cavalry, Age 70"
[Signature]; "Lt. Col. Frank A. Montgomery, First Mississippi Cavalry. Age 31" [Signature];
"Col. R. A. Pinson. First Mississippi Cavalry"; "Frank C. Armstrong. Brigadier-General Arm-
strong's Mississippi Cavalry Brigade" [Signature].

Inclusive dates: 1861–1865.

Montgomery was born in Mississippi and, except in the war, remained within
that state. Writing thirty-five years later and largely from memory (some letters
to his wife are included), the account has little travel value. His operations were
largely from Vicksburg to Tupelo and Corinth and southward to Meridian; but
early in the war he marched as far northward as Columbus, Kentucky, and near
the end he joined Gen. J. E. Johnston's forces in the attempt to hold Sherman's
advance on Atlanta. After the fall of that city he returned to Mississippi, but
soon joined the forces of General Forrest, was captured at the Battle of Selma,
taken to Columbus, Georgia, and paroled.

Moore, Edward Alexander, 1842–   327

The story of a cannoneer under Stonewall Jackson, in which is told the
part taken by the Rockbridge artillery in the Army of northern Virginia.
By Edward A. Moore ... with introductions by Capt. Robert E. Lee, jr., and
Hon. Henry St. George Tucker. Fully illustrated by portraits. New York
and Washington, The Neale publishing company, 1907.

315 p.   front., pl., ports. facsim.   20½ cm.

Illustrations: Frontispiece, "General 'Stonewall' Jackson" and sixteen other illustrations of
portraits of soldiers, of a gun, and of a parole.

Inclusive dates: 1862–1865.

Other editions: Lynchburg, J. P. Bell company, inc., 1910.

Mostly about military affairs and personal experiences, this account contains
only a few comments on the desolations of war, such as the destruction wrought
by Hunter in his march up the Shenandoah Valley through Lexington to the

outskirts of Lynchburg. These reminiscences were recorded about forty years after the war, contain improbable details and reconstructed conversations, and are probably unreliable. Moore was a student in Washington College in Lexington, Virginia, when the war broke out. The next year he joined a Confederate artillery unit and remained in service to the end, being present at the Appomattox surrender. Though Moore's chief activities were in the Shenandoah Valley, he participated in the campaigns against McClellan on the Peninsula, in Second Manassas, the Sharpsburg campaign, Gettysburg, and activities around Richmond preliminary to the surrender.

[Morford, Henry] 1823–1881. 328

Red-tape and pigeon-hole generals: as seen from the ranks during a campaign in the Army of the Potomac. By a citizen-soldier ... New York, Carleton, 1864.

318 p. 18½ cm.
Inclusive dates: September, 1862–May, 1863.

Morford participated in the Sharpsburg campaign, in the Battle of Fredericksburg, and at Chancellorsville. His chief purpose in writing this book was to enter complaints against the way the generals were running the war, and to show his dislike of the West Point regime. Though the work borders on travel literature, it gives little aid in assessing the attitude of inhabitants in northern Virginia during the Federal occupation.

Morgan, Julia. "Mrs. Irby Morgan." 329

How it was; four years among the Rebels. By Mrs. Irby Morgan. Nashville, Tenn., Printed for the author, Publishing house, Methodist Episcopal church, South, 1892.

204 p. front., ports. 18½ cm.
Illustrations: Frontispiece, "Gen. N. B. Forrest"; "Gen. Frank Cheatham"; "Gen. Geo. G. Dibrell"; "Faithful Old Joe"; "Gen. John H. Morgan."
Inclusive dates: 1861–1865.

This is a trustworthy account which does not attempt to record minute details, conversations, and exact dates. Mrs. Irby Morgan was married to a brother of General John H. Morgan and was living in Nashville when the war broke out. When General Albert Sidney Johnston retreated southward out of Kentucky, Mrs. Morgan left Nashville before the Federal troops arrived, going first to Fayetteville and Shelbyville and then to Lookout Mountain near Chattanooga. She later retreated to Marietta, Georgia, remained there until Sherman headed for Atlanta, and removed to the Sand Hills near Augusta. During this time Mrs. Morgan made herself useful in hospital work and, while living in the Sand Hills, her children worked in the Augusta Arsenal, making cartridges. The narrative is a valuable and vivid record of a wartime refugee's experiences.

Morgan, William Henry, 1836–   330

Personal reminiscences of the war of 1861–5; in camp—en bivouac—on the march—on picket—on the skirmish line—on the battlefield—and in prison. By W. H. Morgan. Lynchburg, Va., J. P. Bell company, inc., 1911.

> 4 p. l., 7–286 p.   front. (port.)   19¾ cm.
> *Illustrations:* Frontispiece, "W. H. Morgan."
> *Inclusive dates:* 1861–1865.

Written nearly fifty years after the Civil War, these reminiscences contain little new or contemporaneous material. Morgan enlisted at Lynchburg in May, 1861, and was sent by railway to Manassas Junction in time to participate in the first battle. He believed that the rebel yell was first used there and that it helped to rout the Federal troops. Thereafter he served on the Peninsula against McClellan, at Second Manassas, Sharpsburg, Fredericksburg, in eastern North Carolina around Newbern and Washington, in the Battle of Plymouth, and in the opening campaign against Richmond in 1864. He was captured in May of that year and taken first to Old Capitol Prison in Washington, then down Chesapeake Bay and out through the capes to Fort Delaware in the Delaware River. A little later he was one of the Confederate officers transported to Morris Island near Charleston, South Carolina, to be exposed to Confederate fire. After a short stay he was removed to Fort Pulaski near the mouth of the Savannah River, returned to Fort Delaware, and paroled in May, 1865.

Morris, George W.   331

History of the Eighty-first regiment of Indiana volunteer infantry in the great war of the rebellion, 1861 to 1865. Telling of its origin and organization; a description of the material of which it was composed; its rapid and severe marches, hard service and fierce conflicts on many bloody fields. Pathetic scenes, amusing incidents and thrilling episodes. A regimental roster. Prison life, adventures, etc., by Corporal Geo. W. Morris. [Louisville, Ky., The Franklin printing company, 1901.]

> 202 p.   21 cm.
> *Inclusive dates:* 1862–1865.

The regiment was formed at New Albany, Indiana, in the late summer of 1862. After a short encampment, it went to Louisville and took part in Buell's campaign against Bragg, which culminated in the Battle of Perryville in October, 1862. After this battle the regiment marched to Nashville, took part in the Battle of Murfreesboro, and leisurely raided and skirmished in Middle Tennessee until it marched on Chattanooga late in 1863 to engage in the Battle of Chickamauga and the subsequent engagements around Chattanooga. The unit followed Sherman to Atlanta in the spring of 1864, marched back to Nashville that fall to intercept Hood, and after the Battle of Franklin near the end of the year it raided southward into Alabama and thence to Chattanooga, Knoxville, and across the mountains to Asheville, North Carolina. With Lee's surrender it returned to Nashville, was mustered out in the early summer, and returned by rail to Louisville.

₁Morse, Charles Fessenden₁ 1839–   332
Letters written during the civil war, 1861–1865. ₁Boston, Mass.₁ Privately printed. T. R. Marvin & son, printers, 1898.

3 p. l., ₁5₁–222 p.   front. (port.)   22½ cm.
Illustrations: Frontispiece, "C. F. Morse" ₁Signature₁.
Inclusive dates: 1861–1865.

Lieutenant Colonel Morse of the Second Massachusetts Infantry volunteered at the beginning of the Civil War. He served first with General Patterson's forces around Harpers Ferry at the time of the First Battle of Manassas, and until the fall of 1863 his activities were confined to northern Virginia, Maryland, and the Gettysburg campaign. Transferred to Middle Tennessee, he remained until the spring of 1864 when he became a part of Sherman's march. He was wounded at the Battle of Averasborough in North Carolina and was sent north to recuperate. His letters were mostly about marches and other military activities, but there are occasional notes on the country and hints of the colonel's opinion of the Confederate population. At first he was opposed to pillaging but by the time he had followed Sherman through Georgia and into South Carolina he had ceased to pity the Southern population.

Morse, Francis W.   333
Personal experiences in the war of the great rebellion, from December, 1862, to July, 1865. By F. W. Morse ... Albany, Printed but not published ₁Munsell, printer₁ 1866.

iv, ₁5₁–152 p.   22¼ cm.
Inclusive dates: December, 1862–July, 1865.

The author expressly states that this work, based on a "meagre diary," was printed only for his immediate family. Yet it was written from fresh memory and has considerable merit for comments on other than military matters. From the beginning of 1863 to the summer of 1864 Morse operated first in the East, including Chancellorsville, Gettysburg, and Grant's early battles against Richmond. He then went to Louisville, Kentucky, for service in the West, made a short trip by rail to Nashville and returned just in time to be a guest of the famous Galt House when it burned down, traveled by an Ohio River steamer to the mouth of the Tennessee and up that river to the bend on the boundary of northeastern Mississippi, participated in Wilson's Raid across Alabama through Selma, which was burned, and continued eastward through Columbus. The Wilson raiders were fast devastating the country preparatory to entering Macon, Georgia, when a courier arrived from Sherman announcing Johnston's surrender.

Morse went on to Macon and Atlanta, which he describes as being in fearful ruins, and to Augusta. There he took a steamer down the Savannah River to Savannah and a small boat to Hilton Head, South Carolina, where he boarded a steamer for New York City. This volume's chief value lies in its description of Wilson's Raid, which has engaged the attention of fewer writers than many other expeditions.

Morton, John Watson. 334

The artillery of Nathan Bedford Forrest's cavalry, "the wizard of the saddle." By John Watson Morton ... Nashville, Tenn., Dallas, Tex., Publishing house of the M. E. church, South, Smith & Lamar, agents, 1909.

374 p. front., plates (1 fold.) ports., facsims. 23 cm.

Illustrations: Frontispiece, "John Watson Morton"; "Nathan Bedford Forrest"; "General Forrest and Staff"; "General Forrest at Brice's Crossroads"; "Beautiful Lines Found on Back of Confederate Note"; "Captain Morton's Parole"; "Only Written K.K.K. Order"; "Captain W. H. Coley"; "Mrs. John W. Morton"; "Confederate Notes"; "John W. Morton, Secretary of State 1901–09."

Inclusive dates: 1861–1865.

Morton, as chief of artillery in Forrest's cavalry, was most interested in military matters, but he included some travel observations. He was present on most of Forrest's expeditions throughout western Tennessee, northern Mississippi, Alabama, and the western part of Kentucky. He was taken prisoner at Fort Donelson, conveyed first to Camp Chase in Columbus, Ohio, and thence to Johnson's Island in Lake Erie. He was soon exchanged and turned over to the Confederates at Vicksburg. At the end of the war he was mustered out at Gainesville, Alabama. His book, written more than forty years after the war, and largely from memory, except for much checking of facts in documentary sources, has slight value as travel literature.

Mowris, James A. 335

A history of the One hundred and seventeenth regiment, N. Y. volunteers, (Fourth Oneida,) from the date of its organization, August, 1862, till that of its muster out, June, 1865. By J. A. Mowris, M. D., regimental surgeon. Hartford, Case, Lockwood and company, printers, 1866.

xi, ₍13₎–315 p. 20½ cm.

Inclusive dates: 1862–1865.

As a travel narrative, written immediately after the war, this work is notable among regimental histories for freshness in its treatment of men and events and for a relatively unbiased attitude. Mowris served first around Washington and the Suffolk Region of Virginia; later at Folly Island near Charleston he was plagued more by fleas than by Confederate soldiers. Back in Virginia in the summer of 1864 he fought around Petersburg and was present at the famous Crater explosion. He then went on Butler's expedition to reduce Fort Fisher at the mouth of the Cape Fear River, and was there when the fort was captured and blown up. Mowris marched into Wilmington, Kenansville, and Raleigh, and after Johnston's surrender went by train to City Point and by steamer to New York City. The best travel comments are in that part of the narrative which pertains to North Carolina and in lengthy descriptions of the nature of the country and of contacts and conversations with the people.

Neese, George Michael, 1839–   336
Three years in the Confederate horse artillery. By George M. Neese ... New York and Washington, The Neale publishing company, 1911.

4 p. l., 3–362 p.   20 cm.
Inclusive dates: 1861–1865.

The war diary reproduced in this volume was evidently edited into smooth writing. The account contains minute details of military movements, is an excellent picture of soldier life, and is equally satisfactory as comment on the country and on civilians with whom Neese became acquainted. He was a native of the northern part of the Shenandoah Valley and wrote with characteristic eloquence on the beauties of that region. His .military activities were confined entirely to the Valley, to other parts of northern Virginia, and to Maryland and southern Pennsylvania. In October, 1864, he was captured and taken by rail to Baltimore and thence by water to Point Lookout prison, where he remained until the latter part of June in the following year.

₍Newcomb, Mary A., "Mrs. H.A.W. Newcomb"₎ 1817–1893?   337
Four years of personal reminiscences of the war. Chicago, H. S. Mills & co., 1893.

vii, ₍9₎–131 p.   front. (port.)   19 cm.

Mrs. Newcomb was one of those "mothers" in the Federal armies who traveled extensively and administered to sick and dying soldiers in the hospitals throughout the war. The locale of her activity was the Mississippi River Valley; at one time or another she was at Bird's Point, Island No. 10, Fort Henry, Fort Donelson, Nashville, Shiloh, Corinth, Memphis, Vicksburg, Natchez, New Orleans, Helena, and Little Rock. Neither a quarter century, nor a head of hair "white as the paper on which I write" mellowed her memories or softened her prejudices. Slavery had contaminated everything in the South, and so depraved were some of the planters that they held in slavery people of white skin and in whose veins coursed their masters' blood. Mary Newcomb met "poor whites" who were so ignorant that they neither knew their own names nor how many children they had. Manifestly the contents of this book should be accepted with due caution.

Newcomer, Christopher Armour.   338
Cole's cavalry; or, Three years in the saddle in the Shenandoah Valley.

By C. Armour Newcomer ... Baltimore, Cushing and co., booksellers and stationers, 1895.

x, [9]–165, [1] p. front., port. 23 cm.
Illustrations: Frontispiece, "Yours truly, C. Armour Newcomer"; "Colonel Henry A. Cole."
Inclusive dates: 1861–1864.

The main reasons for inclusion in this bibliography are that the book was written by a Marylander in the Federal Army and that it describes personal associations of the author with natives of Maryland and northern Virginia. Newcomer was tricked into making a social visit to a Virginia family and while there was taken prisoner. His captors conveyed him to Richmond where he was imprisoned in Libby and on Belle Isle for a short time before being paroled and sent into the Union lines. His military activities were confined mostly to Maryland and the Shenandoah Valley in northern Virginia.

Newlin, William Henry. 339

An account of the escape of six federal soldiers from prison at Danville, Va.: their travels by night through the enemy's country to the Union pickets at Gauley Bridge, West Virginia, in the winter of 1863–64. By W. H. Newlin. Cincinnati, Western Methodist book concern print, 1889.

136 p. plates, 22 cm.
Illustrations: "Foiled at Seven-Mile Ferry"; "Left Alone"; "Trouble at Lewis's House"; "Out of the Woods [Inset:] L. B. Smith, W. H. Newlin, W. C. Tripp, W. Sutherland."
Inclusive dates: September, 1863–April, 1864.
Other editions: The first edition appeared in 1870 under the same imprint as the one used here. There was another edition in 1889, under the same imprint.

W. H. Newlin was captured at the Battle of Chickamauga in September, 1863, and was immediately sent by rail over an undesignated route through Georgia, South Carolina, North Carolina, and Virginia to Richmond. Soon he was removed to the Danville prison where he, with five other prisoners, escaped in February, 1864. They moved southward into North Carolina, heading for East Tennessee, but turned northwestward and back into Virginia by way of Rockymount, and across the mountains into West Virginia. They reached Federal pickets at Gauley Bridge, and went on to Charleston. Here they boarded a Kanawha River boat for Point Pleasant, Gallipolis, and Cincinnati. As was unanimously stated by escaping war prisoners, they were aided by Negroes in the plantation country and by Union Southerners in the hills and mountains. This is a paper-back book which seems to have been a popular seller as this particular printing is the "Fifteenth Thousand." Actually it adds little or nothing to prisoner-of-war stories, except for description of some new territory.

[Newsome, Edmund.] 340

Experience in the war of the great rebellion. By a soldier of the Eighty-first regiment Illinois volunteer infantry. From August 1862, to August 1865. Including nearly nine months of life in southern prisons, at Macon, Savannah, Charleston, Columbia and other places. Carbondale, Ill., E. Newsome, 1879.

1 p. l., 137, ₍4₎ p.   14½ cm.
Inclusive dates: 1862–1865.

This narrative, issued as a poorly printed diary, seems to have been little changed from its original form. It is a straightforward account of an Illinois volunteer who entered the Federal Army in 1862 and rose to the rank of captain. He trained at Camp Anna, Union County, Illinois, proceeded to Cairo, boarded a steamer for Columbus, Kentucky, and went by rail to the scene of action in western Tennessee and northern Alabama. After marching as far south as Oxford, Mississippi, he returned northward to Memphis, took a steamer to the vicinity of Vicksburg, and operated in that region until some time after the fall of that city. After marching as far west as Monroe, Louisiana, he joined the Red River expedition down the Mississippi and up the Red into northern Louisiana. Afterward he proceeded up the Mississippi to Memphis and into northern Mississippi where he was captured in the summer of 1864. As a prisoner he was taken down the railway to Meridian and eastward to Selma, up the Alabama River by steamer to Montgomery, and by rail through Columbus and Fort Valley, Georgia, to Macon, to be held for a time and then transferred successively to Savannah, Charleston, and Columbia. In early 1865 Newsome was taken northward by rail through Charlotte, Salisbury, Greensboro, Raleigh, and Goldsboro to a point near Wilmington, and turned over to Federal authorities. He proceeded to Annapolis by steamer, and by way of Baltimore, Harrisburg, Pittsburgh, and Cincinnati to his home in Illinois. This narrative is of considerable value as its author was interested in the country and people he saw on his travels and took pains to record his observations.

Nichols, G. W., *of Jesup, Ga.* 341

A soldier's story of his regiment (61st Georgia) and incidentally of the Lawton-Gordon-Evans brigade, Army northern Virginia. By Private G. W. Nichols ... Jesup? Ga., 1898.

xi, ₍1₎ ₍13₎–291 ₍2₎ p. incl. ports.   18 cm.
Illustrations: Nine crude drawings of the author and of various officers.
Inclusive dates: 1861–1865.

Thirty-three years after the war, G. W. Nichols reworked and added to an account of his war experiences which he had written in 1887 and published in the *Pioneer and Eagle,* a newspaper in Bullock County, Georgia. Nichols enlisted in 1861 and stopped briefly at Brunswick before going to Savannah. His unit, the Seventh Georgia Battalion, afterwards the Sixty-first Georgia Regiment, went from Savannah to Charleston, by rail to Richmond, and was assigned to Stonewall Jackson's army in the Shenandoah Valley. Nichols participated in Jackson's famous Valley campaign, followed his commander to the Peninsula to help drive McClellan to the protection of his gunboats on the lower James

River, fought through Second Manassas, and took part in the Sharpsburg campaign. Becoming sick on this march, he was sent to hospitals in Lynchburg, Richmond, and Danville, but recovered in time to fight at Chancellorsville in May, 1863, and to join the Gettysburg campaign. Thereafter he fought in Virginia, including Lee's holding operations against Grant in the summer and fall of 1864, returned to Georgia on furlough in January, 1865, and engaged in no further fighting. The book is crudely printed but written in a lively style without a trace of bitterness, and its value is above average.

Nichols, George Ward, 1837–1885. 342

The story of the great march. From the diary of a staff officer. By Brevet Major George Ward Nichols ... 26th ed. New York, Harper & brothers, 1866.

xii p., 1 l., [15]–456 p. incl. front., illus., plates. fold. map.   18½ cm.

Illustrations: Half-title page, "Badge of General Sherman's Headquarters"; Frontispiece, "Sherman and his Generals"; "Allatoona Pass"; "Atlanta in Ruins"; "Sports of the Army" (Vignette); "Rice-mill on the Ogeechee"; "Fort McAllister"; "Treasure Seekers"; "Destruction of Columbia"; "Corduroying at Lynch's Creek"; "Army Mule"; "Refugee Train"; "Headquarters Camp of General Sherman"; "The Heroes that are not Gazetted"; "A 'Bummer' "; "Battle of Bentonville"; "The Conference between General Sherman and General Johnston"; "The Graves of our dead Comrades"; "The End."

Maps: "Map Showing the Routes Traversed by each Corps of Genl. Sherman's Army, in the Two Campaigns of Georgia & the Carolinas, from Rome to Savannah, Georgia and thence to Raleigh, North Carolina. Expressly prepared for 'The Great March' by Brt. Maj. Geo. Ward Nichols ... Endicott & Co. Lith ..." 8½ x 15 in.

Inclusive dates: September, 1864–April, 1865.

Other editions: First edition, New York, Harper & brothers, 1865. There were at least twenty-six editions of this work. It was reprinted in English newspapers and was said to have been translated into Spanish, French, and German. Setting this material in a fictionalized form, Nichols brought out: The sanctuary: a story of the civil war. New York, Harper & brothers, 1866.

Major Nichols' book was one of the best accounts of Sherman's march and tremendously popular. It records conversations with Southern people and describes the citizens, the conflagration, the work of the "bummers," and the movements of the army. Though a valuable narrative, it is marred by the inevitable fault in wartime writings, in which the enemy is always evil and the author consistently honest and upright. Descriptions of harrowing war scenes and civilian suffering offer no pity on the ground that the people were the sole cause of the war and were being justly punished. This volume was undoubtedly important propaganda in promoting Radical Congressional reconstruction of the South, especially as its program related to the Negroes, whom Nichols rated higher than common Southern whites. After the war George Ward Nichols promoted music and art education, principally in Cincinnati, and wrote several books on art and music.

Nichols, James Moses, 1835–1886. 343

Perry's saints; or, The fighting parson's regiment in the war of the rebellion; by James M. Nichols. Boston, D. Lothrop and company, [1886.]

299 p. incl. illus., plates, map, plans. fold. map, plan.   17¾ cm.
Illustrations: Thirty-seven clearly drawn pen and ink sketches of forts, ships, camps, and various other Southern scenes such as landscapes.
Maps: "Map of a Portion of 'Sea Islands,' Showing 'Port Royal' "; "Plan of the Battle at Port Royal Harbor"; "Fort Walker"; "Siege of Charleston"; "Outline of the Crater and Magazines."
Inclusive dates 1861–1865.
Parallel accounts: Another history of this regiment, which has practically no observations apart from military affairs but which contains many of the same illustrations, is Abraham J. Palmer, The history of the Forty-eighth regiment New York state volunteers, in the war for the Union. 1861–1865. Brooklyn, N. Y., Published by the Veteran association of the regiment, 1885.

Diaries of the author and other members of the regiment were used as sources for this well-written and temperate book. Nichols was born in Haverhill, Massachusetts, and was educated at Phillips Academy and Williams College. Apart from service around Petersburg late in 1864 and in the reduction of Fort Fisher in 1865, Perry's Saints operated in the seaboard of South Carolina, Georgia, and Florida. More particularly Nichols was concerned with the capture of Port Royal early in the war and with raiding from that point up the coast to James Island off Charleston, the reduction and occupation of Fort Pulaski, two trips to Florida, one to Jacksonville, westward as far as the battle of Olustee, southward on the St. Johns River to Palatka and vicinity, and on the St. Augustine. This soldier, with the instinct of a traveler, noted all the unusual sights which met his eye and his associations with the population. This book is one of the best regimental histories, measured as a travel account.

Nisbet, James Cooper. 344
Four years on the firing line. By Col. James Cooper Nisbet. Chattanooga, The Imperial press, c.1914.

2 p. l., 445 p.   front. (port.)   19¼ cm.
Illustrations: Frontispiece, "Col. James Cooper Nisbet."
Inclusive dates: 1861–1865.

Colonel Nisbet's memoirs are more trustworthy than the usual Civil War reminiscences. He avoided improbable details and anecdotes but frequently inserted personal estimates of men and events, with observations on people, places, and regions. No diary is mentioned but there are many references to contemporary documents and later works. At the outbreak of the war he joined a Georgia unit and proceeded by rail through Chattanooga to Richmond and northern Virginia, but arrived too late for the First Battle of Manassas. He took part in Jackson's campaign in the Shenandoah Valley, marched with him to Richmond to repel McClellan in the summer of 1862, and returned northward to fight at Second Manassas, Sharpsburg, and Fredericksburg. Shortly after the latter battle Nisbet returned to Georgia and raised a regiment which was attached to the Army of Tennessee. He took part in the Battle of Chickamauga and continued in Johnston's army before Sherman's advance on Atlanta. In the fighting near Atlanta he was captured, taken by railway through Chattanooga, Nashville, and Louisville to Johnson's Island, and held prisoner until September of 1865. He returned by way of New York to Georgia, landing at Savannah, and thence by Macon and Atlanta to Lookout Valley in northern Georgia.

Noel, Theophilus, 1840–
345

A campaign from Santa Fe to the Mississippi; being a history of the old Sibley brigade from its first organization to the present time; its campaigns in New Mexico, Arizona, Texas, Louisiana and Arkansas, in the years of 1861–2–3–4. By Theo. Noel, 4th Texas cavalry. Shreveport, La., Shreveport news printing establishment—John Dickinson, proprietor, 1865.

152 p.   front. (fold. tab.)   21½ cm.
Inclusive dates: 1861–1864.

The author was primarily interested in the military activities of the Sibley brigade but also observed the country traversed and described its striking aspects. The brigade assembled in San Antonio, Texas, in 1861 and went west to New Mexico by way of El Paso. It passed up the Rio Grande valley and was engaged at Val Verde and Glorietta, occupying both Albuquerque and Santa Fe on the way. Being defeated at Glorietta, it retreated down the Rio Grande valley and across Texas to San Antonio, was reorganized at Hempstead, campaigned against Galveston, and marched into Louisiana to fight from Mansfield on the north to Brashear City on the south.

North, Thomas.
346

Five years in Texas; or, What you did not hear during the war from January 1861 to January 1866. A narrative of his travels, experiences, and observations, in Texas and Mexico. By Thomas North. Cincinnati, Elm street printing co., 1871.

viii, ₍9₎–231 p.   16½ cm.
Inclusive dates: 1861–1866.

This account of Texas during the Civil War, by a Northern merchant turned preacher to evade the Confederate draft law, is written in a friendly spirit but contains some sharp criticism and incisive observations on the manners and customs of Texans. In January, 1861, he left his home in Freeport, Illinois, went by train to Cairo and on a Mississippi River steamer to New Orleans. Crossing the river, he went by train to Brashear City (Berwick Bay), embarked for Galveston on a ship of the Morgan Line, went into Texas to Houston, and established himself as a merchant at Brenham. Driven out by violence near the end of the war, he went to Matamoras, Mexico, until Lee's surrender when he embarked with his family for New Orleans, returned to Galveston, continued on to Brenham, and finally left Texas.

Northrop, John Worrell. 347

Chronicles from the diary of a war prisoner in Andersonville and other military prisons of the South in 1864. ... An appendix containing statement of a Confederate physician and officer relative to prison condition and management. By John Worrel Northrop ... Wichita, Kans., The author, 1904.

228 p. 16¾ cm.
Inclusive dates: May–December, 1864.

The author devotes a great deal of space to his travels from the battlefield where he was captured to one prison after another. Northrop, a New Yorker, was impelled by a writing instinct and intellectual ambition which took form at times as less than mediocre poetry and in the war period as a diary. The narrative is evidently expanded from those notes. As a member of the Seventy-sixth New York Infantry, he fought through the war until he was captured in May, 1864, near Culpeper in northern Virginia. He was taken by rail to Andersonville by the route through Charlottesville, Lynchburg, Burkeville, Danville, and Greensboro. Between Danville and Greensboro he walked across a six-mile gap in the railroad not yet completed and continued by train to Charlotte, Columbia, Augusta, Millen, and Macon. From Andersonville he was later transferred to Florence, retracing the route through Augusta to Branchville. After some time at Florence Northrop was paroled in December, 1864, sent directly to Charleston, transferred to a Federal ship off Fort Sumter, and carried to Annapolis. He made many comments on the people he saw and recorded many conversations. As an observer he was better than the average, and free from bitterness.

Norton, Oliver Willcox. 348

Army letters, 1861–1865. Being extracts from private letters to relatives and friends from a soldier in the field during the late civil war, with an appendix containing copies of some official documents, papers and addresses of a later date. By Oliver Willcox Norton, private Eighty-third regiment Pennsylvania volunteers; first lieutenant Eighth United States colored troops ... Chicago, Printed by O. L. Deming, 1903.

355 p. incl. front., plates (1 col.) ports. 22½ cm.
Illustrations: Frontispiece, "O. W. Norton ₍Signature₎ Chicago, 1903"; "O. W. Norton, April, 1861, In Uniform of Girard Guards"; "Brigade Headquarters Flag. Third Brigade, First Division, Fifth Army Corps, Army of the Potomac"; "Strong Vincent. Colonel Eighty-third Pennsylvania Volunteers. Brigadier General U. S. Volunteers"; "Lieutenant Oliver W. Norton. December, 1863"; "Escutcheon"; "Monument of Eighty-Third Pennsylvania Volunteers. Little Round Top, Gettysburg"; "Position of Eighty-Third Pennsylvania Volunteers on Little Round Top, Gettysburg."
Inclusive dates: 1861–1865.

As a private from 1861 and a first lieutenant from late in 1863, Norton served in all the major engagements in the East after the First Battle of Manassas. During the first half of 1864 he campaigned in Florida and took part in the fight at Olustee; after Lee's surrender he was sent to Brazos Santiago at the mouth of the Rio Grande and later up the river to Ringgold Barracks at Rio Grande City. Throughout his service Norton's letters home contained intelligent observations on the country and the people wherever he happened to be. In Virginia he noted the widespread use of the white flag by the inhabitants of the York Peninsula to protect their homes and property, and was attracted by evidences of beauty and culture in some of the old homes. In Florida, poverty and palmettoes attracted his attention; in Texas he was interested in the landscape, the Mexican population and their customs, tarantulas, snakes, and wolves.

Nott, Charles Cooper, 1827–1916.   349

Sketches in prison camps: a continuation of sketches of the war. By Charles C. Nott, late colonel of the 176th New York vols. ... Third edition. New York, Anson D. F. Randolph, 1865.

204 p.   18½ cm.
Inclusive dates: 1863–1864.
Other editions: The "Third Edition" is used here. There were two other editions (really printings) in 1865.

This is an excellent account not only of the two Texas prison camps in which the author was incarcerated, but also of the country traversed and of the people seen. (The first part of Nott's army career was detailed in his book *Sketches of the War. A Series of Letters to the North Moore Street School of New York, q.v.*). In the summer of 1863 he was captured at Brashear City, Louisiana, marched across country to Niblett's Bluff on the Sabine River, sent by boat to Beaumont and by train to Houston and Hempstead, and imprisoned in Camp Groce for a few months before being taken across country to Camp Ford near Tyler. The author had a happy disposition and was willing to give credit to the Confederates whenever he could, including a wholesome respect for the "wild Texans" who captured him. Hence, this account of prison life differs from those which described only the worse side. In 1864 he was taken by way of Shreveport and exchanged at the mouth of the Red River. Later Nott became colonel of the 176th New York Volunteers.

Nott, Charles Cooper, 1827–1916.   350

Sketches of the war: a series of letters to the North Moore street school. Revised and enlarged edition. By Charles C. Nott ... New York, William Abbatt, 1911.

xvii, 201 p.   18½ cm.
Inclusive dates: 1862.
Other editions: The "Revised and Enlarged Edition" is here used. The first edition was: New York, C. T. Evans, 1863. Second edition: New York, A. D. F. Randolph, 1865. In 1883, Hermann von Hoff, a Prussian officer, translated it into German and published it under the title Krieg Scenen.

Although these letters were addressed to school children, they are not "written down" to an imaginary mental level, but give a close-up view of the country and inhabitants of northwestern Tennessee and western Kentucky. There is also a good, simple discussion of military activities leading to the capture of Fort Donelson. Nott, a resident of New York City at the outbreak of the Civil War, went to St. Louis and became captain of the Fifth Iowa Cavalry. He found much Unionism among the Southern people he visited on foraging raids, became quite friendly with them, and reproduces conversations that seem to be authentic. Nott was later taken prisoner and wrote about those experiences in *Sketches in Prison Camps: A Continuation of Sketches of the War* (New York, A.D.F. Randolph, 1865), *(q.v.)*. After the war he was appointed to the United States Court of Claims, which he served for the next forty years.

Noyes, George Freeman, 1824–1868. 351

The bivouac and the battlefield; or, Campaign sketches in Virginia and Maryland. New York, Harper & brothers, 1864.

xii, 13–339 p.   19¼ cm.
Inclusive dates: 1862.
Other editions: The first edition (or printing) of this work appeared in 1863 by the same publishers.

Captain Noyes, of the United States Volunteers, writes of a year's service in the Army of the Potomac. He traveled down the Potomac, was at Fredericksburg, turned northwest to Cedar Mountain and the battle of Second Bull Run, continued northward across the Potomac by way of Frederick, Maryland, and participated in the Battle of Sharpsburg. Afterward he went to Harpers Ferry and then back into Virginia to Fredericksburg, where the account closes. Noyes was interested in the towns and villages and in all the people whom he met, and gives interesting descriptions of the "contrabands," of Southern women's contempt for Federal soldiers, of·mansion headquarters he occupied, and of what he thought about the Confederate soldiers' ability to fight. He admitted that his soldiers did some pillaging, though not as much as the papers claimed.

Olmstead, Charles H. 352

Reminiscences of service with the First volunteer regiment of Georgia, Charleston harbor in 1863. An address delivered before the Georgia historical society, March 3, 1879. Savannah, Ga., Printed and presented by J. H. Estill, 1879.

15 p.   23½ cm.
Inclusive dates: 1863.

In this record of military service confined to the Charleston harbor region, Olmstead gives some attention to his trip over the Charleston and Savannah railroad from Savannah to Charleston, and to a description of Morris Island.

Opie, John Newton.   353
A rebel cavalryman with Lee, Stuart, and Jackson. By John N. Opie.
Chicago, W. B. Conkey company, 1899.

336 p.   front., illus., plates, ports., facsim.   19½ cm.
Illustrations: Sixty-two illustrations of Confederate soldiers and civilians, battle scenes, and
pen and ink sketches relating to military activities.
Inclusive dates: 1861–1865.

As a Confederate soldier, Opie traveled extensively in the eastern theater of
the war. Besides taking part in the major Virginia campaigns he raided in West
Virginia, was at Sharpsburg and Gettysburg, and followed Early to the outskirts
of Washington. He was captured in the Shenandoah Valley on his return and
was imprisoned at Elmira, New York, until the end of the war. Writing many
years later, Opie did not mention a diary or other personal records; though he
wrote in a light vein, he was not unmindful of facts. His account is not first-
rate travel literature, yet it is colorful, as in the instance when he asked a Marylander where a road went and was given the well-known reply of the "Arkansas
Traveler."

Osborn, Hartwell.   354
Trials and triumphs; the record of the Fifty-fifth Ohio volunteer infantry.
By Captain Hartwell Osborn and others; with eighty portraits, four views,
and ten maps. Chicago, A. C. McClurg & co., 1904.

364 p.   front., plates, ports., maps.   22½ cm.
Illustrations: Eighty portraits of officers and soldiers, three views of monuments, and one
group picture, "Company H, Mess."
Maps: Ten maps of various battles: McDowell, Cross Keys, Second Manassas, Chancellors-
ville (Two), Gettysburg, Resaca, Peach Tree Creek, Averasborough, and Bentonville.
Inclusive dates: 1861–1865.

The volume is severely military, but merits inclusion in a bibliography of
travel books on account of the generally clear indications of routes taken by the
author, and for a few comments on objects likely to interest a traveler. The unit
was organized at Norwalk, Ohio, and sent to the area of war in western Virginia (West Virginia). Eventually it became a part of Fremont's forces and was
roughly handled by Stonewall Jackson in his Valley campaign. Thereafter it
participated in the various engagements in Virginia, except Fredericksburg, until
the Gettysburg campaign. It followed Meade to Gettysburg and back again,
later going west to fight around Chattanooga in the fall of 1863. It went by
train over the customary route: Wheeling, Columbus, Indianapolis, Louisville,
and Nashville. In the spring of 1863 it followed Sherman on his march through
Georgia and the Carolinas to ultimate victory at Durham Station, and marched
to Washington for the "Grand Review."

Osborne, William H.   355
A history of the Twenty-ninth regiment of Massachusetts volunteer in-

fantry, in the late war of the rebellion. By William H. Osborne ... Boston, Albert J. Wright, printer, 1877.

393 p.   23 cm.
Inclusive dates: 1861–1865.

The Twenty-ninth Massachusetts Regiment saw service first on the York Peninsula in Virginia, around Norfolk, and as far south as Suffolk. After the McClellan campaign ended, this unit went by boat to the lower Potomac and took part in the fighting in northern Virginia preceding the Sharpsburg campaign. Crossing the Potomac, it participated in this campaign and then returned to northern Virginia. In the spring of 1863 it was ordered to the western area and went over the Baltimore and Ohio Railway to Parkersburg, on the Ohio, and by boat to Cincinnati. From here it went by rail to Paris and Lexington, and on various expeditions southward to Somerset and Cumberland Gap and over into East Tennessee to Knoxville and vicinity. The regiment returned to Cincinnati and went by rail to Cairo where it embarked for Vicksburg. After that city fell it returned up the river to northern Virginia to engage in Grant's campaign against Richmond and remained with Grant until Lee's surrender at Appomattox. Although it is primarily military, the narrative includes a few incidents and observations relative to the country through which the author passed.

Otto, John. 356

History of the 11th Indiana battery, connected with an outline history of the Army of the Cumberland during the war of the rebellion, 1861–1865. By John Otto ... Fort Wayne, Ind., W. D. Page, 1894.

109, (2) p.   21½ cm.
Inclusive dates: 1861–1865.

This narrator's service as a Federal soldier was confined to the war in the West. Setting out in 1861 from Fort Wayne, John Otto proceeded to Louisville, down the Ohio and up the Cumberland rivers to Nashville, and on to Shiloh, Corinth, and northern Mississippi. Marching northward to intercept Bragg's invasion of Kentucky, he returned with Bragg's retreat, passing through Nashville to the battlefield of Murfreesboro. He later fought in the Chattanooga-Chickamauga campaign and was with Sherman on his march to Atlanta. After the fall of that city Otto returned to Chattanooga and was mustered out on December 31, 1864. Written long after the events described, this narrative has little value as a contemporary travel account.

Owen, William Miller, 1832– 357

In camp and battle with the Washington artillery of New Orleans. A narrative of events during the late civil war from Bull run to Appomattox and Spanish fort ... By William Miller Owen ... Boston, Ticknor and company, 1885.

1 p. l., xv p., 1 l., 467 p.   front., pl., maps.   21½ cm.

Illustrations: Four military scenes.

Maps: First Manassas; Second Manassas; Antietam; Fredericksburg; Marye's Heights, May 3, 1863; Gettysburg; Drewry's Bluff; Petersburg.

Inclusive dates: 1861–1865.

Owen left New Orleans in 1861 for the fields of northern Virginia, traveled by way of Lynchburg and Richmond, and arrived in time to participate in the First Manassas battle. Thereafter he fought in the principal campaigns of Virginia, and extended his travels far beyond the movements of most Confederate soldiers. In 1863 he passed down the railroad through southwestern Virginia and East Tennessee to Chattanooga, participated in the Battle of Chickamauga in September, returned to Virginia by way of Charleston, South Carolina, and fought to the surrender at Appomattox. This excellent work of travel is filled with local color, pertinent comments, and observations. For instance, the author describes the twenty-one-car train on which he traveled from New Orleans to Richmond in 1861, and how the engineer deserted his train in East Tennessee, refusing to haul "rebels."

Owens, John Algernon.   358

Sword and pen; or, Ventures and adventures of Willard Glazier, (the soldier-author,) in war and literature; comprising incidents and reminiscences of his childhood; his chequered life as a student and teacher; and his remarkable career as a soldier and author; embracing also, the story of his unprecedented journey from ocean to ocean on horseback. Philadelphia, P. W. Ziegler & company, 1882.

xvi p., 1 l., 21–436 p.   front. (port.) plates.   18½ cm.

Illustrations: Frontispiece, "Willard Glazier" ₁Signature₁ (steel engraving by H. B. Hall & Sons, 13 Barclay St., N. Y.); "Birth-Place of Willard Glazier"; "The First Battle"; "Race with the Schoolmaster"; "Tragic Experience with an Ox-Team"; "The Young Trapper of the Oswegatchia"; "Cavalry Column on the March"; "Night Attack on Falmouth Heights"; "Illicit Trading on the Rappahannock"; "Burial of Captain Walters at Midnight, During Pope's Retreat"; "Sergeant Glazier at Aldie"; "Lieutenant Glazier at Brandy Station"; "Cavalry Fight at New Baltimore"; "Libby Prison"; "The Hole in the Floor"; "Tunneling—The Narrow Path to Freedom"; "Charleston Jail—Charleston, South Carolina"; "The Escape from Columbia—Crossing the Dead Line"; "The Escape—Fed by Negroes in a Swamp"; "The Pursuit of Knowledge under Difficulties"; "Uncle Zeb's Prayer"; "The Escape—Crossing the Savannah at Midnight"; "A Mutual Surprise"; "Recaptured by a Confederate Outpost"; "The Escape and Pursuit"; "The Escape From Sylvania, Georgia"; "Interview with John Munsell"; "Cavalry Foraging Party Returning to Camp"; "A Cavalry Bivouac"; "Battle of Gettysburg"; "Captain Glazier at Tremont Temple, Boston"; "Boston to Brighton—First Day of Journey"; "A Night Among Wolves"; "Captured by Indians near Skull Rock, Wyoming"; "Pursued by the Arapahoes"; "Riding into the Pacific—Near the Cliff-House, San Francisco." All of these are clear pen and ink drawings.

Inclusive dates: 1861–1876.

Other editions: The same publishers issued editions in 1881 and 1883.

Owens merely combined two accounts by Glazier which are evaluated elsewhere in this bibliography. This author undoubtedly had the close collaboration of ebullient Captain Glazier. Additional matter relates to Glazier's life before the Civil War and to a horseback ride he made from Boston to San Francisco as a part of the celebration of the Centennial of 1876.

Ozanne, T. D.   359

The South as it is, or Twenty-one years' experience in the southern states of America. By the Rev. T. D. Ozanne, M. A. London, Saunders, Otley, and co., 1863.

v, ₍1₎, 306 p.   19½ cm.
Inclusive dates: 1861–1862.

Most of this book is concerned with factual discussion of the South; only the last three of its sixteen chapters deal with the author's personal experiences. The Reverend Ozanne was an Englishman who became a resident of the South in 1841 as an Episcopal rector on the Gulf coast of Mississippi. In 1862 he decided to remove from this exposed region and settle for a time in the interior of the state, but after a few weeks at Terry, near Jackson, he determined to return to England. He took the New Orleans, Jackson, and Great Northern Railroad to a point near Lake Pontchartrain where the railway had been destroyed, crossed the lake on a leaky boat, continued on to New Orleans and waited there under the Butler regime for an opportunity to go by sea to New York. In September he sailed for England. This narrative gives an interesting picture of conditions in that part of the Confederacy which the author visited and especially of New Orleans under Butler.

Page, James Madison, 1839–   360

The true story of Andersonville prison: a defense of Major Henry Wirz. By James Madison Page, late 2d lieut. Company A, Sixth Michigan cavalry, in collaboration with M. J. Haley. With portraits. New York and Washington, The Neale publishing company, 1908.

248 p.   front., ports.   18¼ cm.
Illustrations: Frontispiece, "Major Henry Wirz"; "James Madison Page, 2d Lieutenant Company A, Sixth Michigan Cavalry" (second frontispiece); "W. J. W. Kerr, M.D."
Inclusive dates: September, 1863–November, 1864.

Although Page was imprisoned in Libby and Belle Isle prisons and in Andersonville, and therefore made the trip from Richmond to Andersonville and, when exchanged, from Andersonville to Savannah to board a Federal ship, he writes practically nothing about either the country or the people. Yet the book is a valuable contribution to an understanding of prison life in the Confederacy and is unique among prisoner-of-war accounts because it defends the Confederate prison regime and Major Wirz in particular. It is therefore a powerful antidote to the stereotyped horror accounts. Page was born in Pennsylvania but had moved to Michigan where he joined the Sixth Michigan Cavalry, to serve as second lieutenant in Company A until his capture in northern Virginia in September, 1863. After the war he moved to Montana.

Palfrey, Francis Winthrop, 1831–1889. 361
Memoir of William Francis Bartlett. Boston, Houghton, Osgood and company, 1879.

1 p. l., 309 p.   front. (port.) facsim.   17¾ cm.
Illustrations: Frontispiece, "W. F. Bartlett" ₍Signature₎.
Maps: Rough sketch of the battlefield and vicinity of Ball's Bluff.
Other editions: Other printings of this work were made in 1878 and in 1881.

Basing his story on letters and a diary kept by William Francis Bartlett, the author adds enough material of his own to make a continuous narrative. The last half of the book relates to Bartlett's life in the North after the war. He was a student in Harvard College when the Civil War began, and sympathetic to the South, but he enlisted and became captain of the Twentieth Regiment Massachusetts Volunteer Infantry. He served first in the Battle of Ball's Bluff, later participated in McClellan's Peninsula campaign, in Banks' unsuccessful attempt to take Port Hudson on the Mississippi River (reaching that region by ship from New York to Baton Rouge), and finally in Grant's attempt in 1864 to take Richmond. He was taken prisoner in the Battle of the Crater at Petersburg, sent to the Danville prison, and a few weeks later was transferred to Libby preparatory to exchange on a flag-of-truce boat in September. Bartlett's letters and diary were mostly about military affairs, but he had some experiences with the native Southerners. He was opposed to vandalism and sternly controlled his unit in such activities. He found prison conditions disagreeable in both Danville and Libby, but sensed that he was singled out because he had been captured while fighting with Negro soldiers at the Crater.

Palmer, Abraham John, 1847–1922. 362
The history of the Forty-eighth regiment New York state volunteers in the war for the union, 1861–1865. By Abraham J. Palmer ... Brooklyn, Published by the Veteran association of the regiment, 1885.

xvi, 314 ₍2₎ p.   front., illus., pl., port., maps.   21 cm.
Illustrations: Forty-five illustrations of soldiers, battle scenes, countryside, etc., many of them taken from B. J. Lossing, *Pictorial History of the Civil War.*
Maps: Fort Walker; Ft. Beauregard; Plan of battle of Port Royal; Map of Sea Islands; Fort Pulaski and Environs; Richmond and Petersburg.
Inclusive dates: 1861–1864 (1865).

This Northerner's travels were confined to the Atlantic seaboard. He went by rail from New York City to Annapolis, and by steamer to Port Royal, South Carolina. At various times he was at Morris Island, Fort Pulaski, St. Augustine, and points around Norfolk, and he participated in the Battle of Olustee, in Florida. This narrative is composed of much personal material, mostly from the author's comrades; a diary is not indicated. It is of little value as a travel account.

Palmer, Donald McN. 363

Four weeks in the Rebel army. By Don McN. Palmer. New London, ₁Conn.₁ D. S. Ruddock, 1865.

40 p. 21½ cm.
Inclusive dates: 1864.

This well-written, half humorous pamphlet describes the experiences of a Connecticut Yankee in Missouri, who found himself in the fall of 1864 an unwilling member of General Price's Confederate Army, then on its famous raid through the state. Palmer, captured at Potosi, was forced to join the Confederate Army and to continue with those forces through Jefferson City, Lexington, and various intervening places, until he made his escape at Price's defeat near the Kansas line. He went on to Leavenworth and back through northern Missouri to Hannibal and down the Mississippi to St. Louis. His narrative gives interesting glimpses into the social conditions prevailing in the state and presents a few sketches of Confederate officers.

Palmer, Mrs. Sarah A. 364

The story of Aunt Becky's army-life. By S. A. Palmer. New York, John F. Trow & co., 1867.

xix, 215 p. front. (port.) plates. 13½ cm.
Illustrations: Frontispiece, "Sincerely Yours, S. A. Palmer" ₁Signature₁; "A. E. Burnside" ₁Signature₁; and seven other hospital and battle scenes, unlabeled.
Inclusive dates: 1862–1863.

"Aunt Becky" Palmer's writings constitute a book of lamentations for the sick, wounded, dead, and dying Federal soldiers on the battlefields and in the hospitals of Virginia. Infrequently her mind gets beyond the unfortunate Federal troops. Her chief centers of operation were around Fredericksburg, on the Peninsula, at City Point, and in the battle area south of Richmond.

Parker, Francis Jewett, 1825–1909. 365

The story of the Thirty-second regiment Massachusetts infantry. Whence it came; where it went; what it saw, and what it did. By Francis J. Parker, colonel. Boston, C. W. Calkins & co., 1880.

xi, 260 p. 20 cm.
Inclusive dates: 1861–1862.

Parker joined the Union forces in 1861 and resigned at the end of 1862, but continued his account to the end of the war, though he was not a participant after the Battle of Fredericksburg. His first service was garrison duty at Fort Warren, in Boston harbor; early in 1863 he went by train from Boston to Fall River, Massachusetts, where he boarded a steamer for New York and went from there to Washington by rail. After a short term around the capital city Parker went by boat down the Potomac and Chesapeake Bay to Fortress Monroe and served in

McClellan's Peninsula campaign, returned by boat to Aquia Landing, marched to the field of Second Bull Run and into Maryland to participate at Sharpsburg. After the engagement he returned to Virginia and took part in the Battle of Fredericksburg in December, 1862. After he left the regiment it fought at Chancellorsville, Gettysburg, and with Grant against Richmond. This narrative, despite its title, actually contains little travel material; the author was mainly interested in army life and other military matters.

Parker, Thomas H. 366

History of the 51st regiment of P. V. and V. V., from its organization, at Camp Curtin, Harrisburg, Pa., in 1861, to its being mustered out of the United States service at Alexandria, Va., July 27th, 1865. By Thomas H. Parker ... Philadelphia, King & Baird, printers, 1869.

xx, [9]–703 p. front., ports. 20 cm.

Illustrations: Frontispiece, "J. F. Hartranft" [Signature]; "Thomas S. Bell" [Signature]; "Yours &c Edwin Schall" [Signature]; "Wm. J. Bolton" [Signature].

Inclusive dates: 1861–1865.

This account is almost as much a travel narrative as a regimental history and is therefore one of the best commentaries on wartime conditions in the South. It was based on copious daily notes which the author made throughout the war and also contains verbatim many letters the author wrote to newspapers from the scenes of military operations. Parker was not carried into extreme statements by over-zealous patriotic exuberance, but was frank in his observations whether they discredited Federal troops or favored the Confederacy. The account is especially valuable because his travels were extensive. In early 1862 the author sailed with the Fifty-first Pennsylvania Regiment, of which he was captain, from Annapolis to Hatteras Inlet, calling on the way at Fortress Monroe. After crossing the bar his forces landed on Roanoke Island, conquered it, and went to Newbern to operate in that region and northward around Albermarle Sound, especially in Currituck County. In the late summer of 1862 he returned to northern Virginia and took part in the battles of Second Manassas, Sharpsburg, and Fredericksburg. In March, 1863, he was sent west, going by rail through Harrisburg, Pittsburgh, Columbus, and Cincinnati, thence southward into Kentucky through Paris, Lexington, and Nicholasville to Lancaster, until his forces were recalled by way of Cincinnati and Cairo to aid in the reduction of Vicksburg. After operating around Vicksburg and eastward to Jackson, Parker retraced his journey by river to Cairo and by rail to Cincinnati. From there he was sent to assist Burnside's invasion of eastern Tennessee which resulted in the seizure of Knoxville, arriving there through eastern Kentucky by way of Cumberland Gap. At the beginning of 1864 he returned to the eastern area and participated in Grant's campaign against Richmond. Many interesting descriptions and observations enliven and enrich this book, such as grave robbing in eastern North Carolina, turning out the convicts at Currituck Courthouse, crops and cornfields in Mississippi, Negro ministrels in Kentucky, and Horace Maynard and Parson Brownlow making their way across the mountains back to Knoxville.

Payne, Edwin Waters, 1837– 367

History of the Thirty-fourth regiment of Illinois volunteer infantry, September 7, 1861, July 12, 1865. By Edwin W. Payne ... Clinton, Ia., Allen printing company, printers, 1903.

viii, 370 p. front. illus., ports., maps. 23 cm.
Illustrations: One hundred and three, mostly portraits of soldiers.
Maps: Battlefield of Stone's River; Chattanooga and Vicinity; Atlanta Campaign; Kennesaw Mountain; Jonesboro, Ga.; Savannah to Goldsboro; Bentonville, N. C.; Large folding map of the Complete Route of the Unit from 1861 to 1865; From Atlanta to the Sea.
Inclusive dates: 1861–1865.

Payne joined his regiment at Decatur, Illinois, in 1861, and went first to Kentucky, passing through Indianapolis and Cincinnati to Lexington, westward through Frankfort and Louisville, and southward to Shiloh and northern Alabama. In the late summer he returned northward through Nashville into Kentucky on the campaign against Bragg, went as far as Louisville and followed the Confederate retreat, passing through Crab Orchard, Perryville, Nashville and on to the Battle of Murfreesboro. Thereafter he operated in Middle Tennessee and in the fall of 1863 was in the Chattanooga-Chickamauga campaign, followed by a short excursion into East Tennessee as far as Loudon and a quick return westward into northern Alabama. In the spring of 1864 he marched with Sherman through Atlanta and the Carolinas to Goldsboro, where he was discharged. He continues the account of the regiment to Washington. Payne used a great mass of personal notes and material from his comrades and the work is, therefore, more a composite account (poorly organized) than a travel narrative by one man.

Peet, Frederick Tomlinson. 368

Civil war letters and documents. Newport, R. I., Privately printed, 1917.

285 p. 28 cm.
Inclusive dates: 1861–1863.

Written by a Seventh New York Regiment Sharpshooter who later became a lieutenant in the United States Marines, this collection relates to the Peninsula campaign, the Battle of Fredericksburg, and service on Folly and Morris islands on the South Carolina coast. It has little value as a picture of conditions in the Confederacy, for Peet was not much concerned with anything apart from military affairs and soldier life. On the Peninsula he felt that the Negroes were helping the Confederates and the rumor was out that a couple of regiments of slaves were fighting for their masters. The author was sure that the Federals would take no prisoners wherever they found Negroes with arms in their hands.

Pepper, George Whitfield, 1833–1899.   369
Personal recollections of Sherman's campaigns in Georgia and the Carolinas. By Capt. George W. Pepper. Zanesville, O., Hugh Dunne, 1866.

522 p.   21½ cm.
Inclusive dates: 1863–1865.

George Pepper's work might be characterized as a travel narrative with a military background. Its author, a captain in a Sherman regiment and incidentally a correspondent for a few newspapers, wrote about the country and people of the Confederacy more as traveler than soldier. He was especially interested in the towns he visited, almost all of which are described in both contemporary setting and historical background. Though highly hostile to the people and their institutions, he was, nevertheless, frank in describing the wanton destruction visited upon them. He left Ohio in the fall of 1863 and went by rail through Cincinnati, Indianapolis, Louisville, Nashville, and Murfreesboro to Chattanooga, where he joined Sherman's army. He raided across Georgia to Savannah and up through the Carolinas to the surrender near Durham Station, marched northward across Virginia, passing through Richmond and Fredericksburg, to Washington and the "Grand Review."

₁Perry, John Gardner₁ 1840–1926.   370
Letters from a surgeon of the civil war; compiled by Martha Derby Perry; illustrated from photographs. Boston, Little, Brown, and company, 1906.

xii p., 1 l., 225 p.   6 pl., 2 port. (incl. front.)   20 cm.
Illustrations: Frontispiece, "John G. Perry, March, 1864"; "View of Fredericksburg from above the Town of Falmouth. From a Sketch by Surgeon Hayward"; "The Post Office"; "Winter Quarters of the Twentieth Massachusetts"; "The Country through which the Battle of the Wilderness was Fought—A Pontoon Bridge"; "An Ambulance Removing the Wounded"; "Major-General Bartlett"; "Sketch of the Hut of an Officer of the Twentieth Massachusetts."
Inclusive dates: 1862–1864.

Without bitterness or bias John Gardner Perry referred to the enemy as Confederates, ignoring the almost universal term of "rebel" used by other Northern writers. These letters relate to the area of northern Virginia, giving special attention to Fredericksburg, Warrenton, the Peninsula, and to the regions around City Point and Petersburg. Perry, a surgeon in the Twentieth Massachusetts Regiment, was interested not only in telling of conditions in the Federal hospital service but also in describing the character of both the Confederate civil population and soldiers. He thought the pillaging of private residences was indefensible and whenever possible he strongly repressed it.

Peyton, John Lewis, 1824–1896.   371
The American crisis; or, Pages from the note-book of a state agent during the civil war. By John Lewis Peyton ... London, Saunders, Otley and co., 1867.

2 v. I, xii, 340 p.; II, vi, 329 p.   front. (port.)   19¾ cm.
Inclusive dates: 1861.

When Peyton, a Virginian living in the Jackson River country west of Staunton, was visiting in Raleigh in the fall of 1861, the governor of North Carolina appointed him state agent to England, where he remained throughout the war. He went first to Richmond to make arrangements for running the blockade, but finally selected Charleston and the blockade runner *Nashville* for his exit. Most of this work is devoted to his English experiences. The part relating to the Confederacy is largely concerned with descriptions of the country through which he passed and the personalities of men he met, especially the high government officials in Richmond. Peyton weakened the account by exaggeration, as in the statement that on the trip to Charleston he saw no groves beneath which there were not pitched the tents of drilling Confederate recruits, nor a building or post from which the Confederate flag did not fly.

Pike, James, 1834–   372

The scout and ranger: being the personal adventures of Corporal Pike, of the Fourth Ohio cavalry. As a Texan ranger, in the Indian wars, delineating western adventure; afterward a scout and a spy, in Tennessee, Alabama, Georgia, and the Carolinas, under Generals Mitchell, Rosecrans, Stanley, Sheridan, Lytle, Thomas, Crook, and Sherman. Fully illustrating the secret service. Twenty-five full-page engravings. Cincinnati & New York, J. R. Hawley & co., 1865.

xi, 19–394 p. incl. 24 pl.   front. (port.)   20½ cm.
Illustrations: A frontispiece portrait of the author and twenty-four imaginary sketches of scenes and incidents described in the narrative.
Inclusive dates: 1859–1865.
Other editions: A reprint of the Texas portion of this narrative is: Scout and ranger; being the personal adventures of James Pike of the Texan rangers in 1859–60, with introduction and notes by Carl L. Cannon. Princeton, Princeton university press, 1932.

Born in Ohio, James Pike dabbled in printing for a few years but in the spring of 1859 he drifted to Missouri where he was employed by a drover taking a herd of horses to Texas. They passed through Missouri by way of Springfield and crossed the Indian Territory into Texas, locating finally at Waco. Pike soon became a Ranger in the Indian service and for the next two years he roamed through central and western Texas chasing Indians. When Texas seceded from the Union he went to Little Rock, Arkansas, where he took passage on a river boat to Memphis. From then to the end of the war he traveled extensively in the Confederacy as soldier, scout, and spy. His routes are not always clear, but he operated mainly in northern Alabama, middle and eastern Tennessee, and northern Georgia. He was taken prisoner, incarcerated in Libby Prison at Richmond, exchanged, captured again and held in Charleston and Columbia, and finally escaped when Sherman arrived at the latter place. This is a remarkable narrative, surprisingly true in its main discussions but undoubtedly embellished in details. It is peppered with characteristic travel incidents, local customs, and descriptions of the country traversed. Soon after the war Pike was killed in California.

Pittenger, William, 1840–1904. 373

Capturing a locomotive: a history of secret service in the late war. By Rev. William Pittenger. Washington, The National tribune, 1885.

354 p. front., plates, ports. 18 cm.

Illustrations: Frontispiece, "A Railroad Chase"; "General O. M. Mitchel"; "Midnight Consultation"; "William Pittenger"; "Capture of a Train"; "William A. Fuller"; "D. A. Dorsey"; "A Terrible Descent"; "Liberty or Death"; "W. W. Brown"; "Dorsey and Hawkins in the Cumberland Mountains"; "Saved at Sea."

Maps: "Chattanooga and Railroad Connections."

Inclusive dates: March, 1862–March 18, 1863.

Other editions: First edition: Philadelphia, J. B. Lippincott & co., 1881. The next edition was in 1882 by the same publishers. The 1885 edition by new publishers is here used. Another edition by these publishers appeared in 1905, without the illustrations (except a sketch portrait of Pittenger as a frontispiece) and without an appendix which was included in earlier editions. The page numbering is the same. Another edition of this work appeared under this title: The great locomotive chase: a history of the Andrews railroad raid into Georgia, by William Pittenger, a member of the expedition. New York, J. B. Alden, 1889. This was the third edition under this title. Other editions under this same title appeared as follows: Philadelphia, The Penn publishing company, 1910, and another edition in 1917. The story first appeared in an abbreviated form under the title: Daring and suffering ... Philadelphia, J. W. Daughaday, 1863 and in 1864. Also under the same title: New York, The War publishing co., 1887.

William Pittenger, born in Jefferson County, Ohio, volunteered in the Federal Army at the outbreak of the Civil War. He took part in the First Battle of Manassas, re-enlisted, and was assigned to Buell's army in the West. In March, 1862, he became a member of the well-known "Andrews Raiders" who, going from Middle Tennessee by Chattanooga and over the Western and Atlantic Railroad to Marietta, Georgia, seized an engine at Big Shanty, a small station north of Marietta and hoped to burn the railroad bridges between Big Shanty and Chattanooga. But the twenty-two members of this party were captured; eight were hanged as spies, eight escaped from prison, and the remaining six were exchanged. They were imprisoned successively in Chattanooga; Madison, Georgia; Knoxville; Atlanta; and in Castle Thunder, Richmond. This thrilling story is embellished somewhat with hairbreadth escapes and adventures but the account is valuable for descriptions of prison life and details of the Confederate railroad equipment used in his railroad exploits. Pittenger rejoined the army but was mustered out in 1863 after having been promoted to a lieutenancy; in 1864 he entered the Methodist ministry.

Pollard, Edward Albert, 1828–1872. 374

Observations in the North: eight months in prison and on parole. By Edward A. Pollard. Richmond, E. W. Ayres, 1865.

vii, [9]–142 p. 20½ cm.
Inclusive dates: 1864–1865.

An editor of the Richmond *Examiner* and bitter critic of Jefferson Davis, Edward Pollard went to Wilmington, North Carolina, and ran the blockade for England on the British steamer *Greyhound.* A short distance out, the vessel was intercepted by a Federal warship and taken to Fortress Monroe, to New York, and finally to Boston for adjudication. In the meantime Pollard was temporarily imprisoned in Fort Warren and released on parole. In November, 1864, he was ordered to New York for exchange, sent by train to Baltimore and by ship to Fortress Monroe, and again allowed freedom on parole. Soon, however, the parole was revoked, and he was placed in solitary confinement, but in January, 1865, General Benjamin F. Butler sent him through the lines to Richmond for exchange. In this account Pollard gives an excellent description of the Negroes in and around Fortress Monroe, where he claimed the Federal Army was fast deteriorating. This little volume seems to have been written principally to steel the hearts of the Confederates and to convince them that they could yet win if they made the best use of their materials and opportunities.

Polley, Joseph Benjamin, 1840–   375

Hood's Texas brigade, its marches, its battles, its achievements. By J. B. Polley ... New York, and Washington, The Neale publishing company, 1910.

347 p. front., pl., ports. 22 cm.
Illustrations: Facing half-title, "Monument to Hood's Texas Brigade"; Frontispiece, "J. B. Hood" [Signature]; "Hon. John H. Kirby"; "Albert Sneed"; "John M. Pinckney"; "Billy Pearce"; "E. K. Goree"; "George S. Qualls"; "John Coleman Roberts"; "Lieutenant Ben M. Baker"; "Dick Pinckney"; "Captain L. P. Hughes"; "General William R. Hamby"; "Lieutenant B. Eldridge"; "Lieutenant W. W. Henderson"; "Colonel R. M. Powell"; "John D. Murray"; "Captain J. T. Hunter"; "W. H. Burges"; "J. B. Polley"; "Captain W. T. Hill"; "Dr. Sam R. Burroughs"; "Captain Frank Bowden Chilton"; "George W. Littlefield"; "Frank Bowden Chilton."
Inclusive dates: 1861–1865.
Other editions: No other edition found. An unreliable account of a private in Hood's Brigade, based entirely on memory more than forty years after the war, is W. A. Fletcher, Rebel private, front and rear. Experiences and observations from the early fifties and through the civil war. Beaumont, Texas, The Greer print, 1908. In the summer of 1864 Private Fletcher transferred to the Terry Texas rangers, and thereafter pursued a course different from that of the Hood Brigade. After the battle of Franklin, Tennessee, in December, 1864, he turned up in South Carolina, retreating before Sherman's onrush. He surrendered with Johnston's army and then made his way back to Texas, by boat from Natchez down the Mississippi and up the Red to Alexandria, and thence overland to Texas. Another work covering the route of the Hood Brigade, made up of letters purported to have been written by one of the members, is J. B. Polley, A soldier's letters to charming Nelly. New York, The Neale publishing company, 1908. A narrative by a member of Hood's Texas Brigade covering a part of the marches of this unit is Nicholas A. Davis, The campaign from Texas to Maryland (Houston, Texas, 1863), listed in this bibliography.

Although much of this narrative appears to be a composite account of excerpts from letters and reminiscences of members of the Hood Brigade, it is nevertheless a consecutive story of the marches of that unit, to which the author belonged. It has little of a personal element and therefore lacks the characteristics of the usual travel account. Hood's Texas Brigade, to a great extent, was organized in Virginia by Texans who had gone eastward by the later summer of 1861. During the rest of the war it participated in most of the marches and battles of the Army of Northern Virginia. After Gettysburg, it was sent with Longstreet to re-enforce Bragg around Chattanooga, following the customary route of that time through Wilmington, Augusta, and Atlanta. Soon after Chickamauga (where the brigade arrived too late to take part in the battle) this unit was detached to proceed with Longstreet into East Tennessee to drive the Federals out of Knoxville. After failing to accomplish that purpose it marched back into Virginia and joined Lee in the campaign which ended at Appomattox. The brigade made its way back to Texas, traveling in detached, informal groups by way of Montgomery, Mobile, New Orleans, and Galveston. The men walked most of the way southward to Montgomery, but from that place they traveled by boat.

Porter, David Dixon, 1813–1891.   376

Incidents and anecdotes of the civil war. By Admiral Porter ... New York, D. Appleton and company, 1885.

357 p.   front. (port.)   22 cm.
Illustrations: Frontispiece, "David D. Porter" [Signature].
Inclusive dates: 1861–1865.

This book was written twenty years after the war and much of it is made up of supposed conversations, but as the Admiral had some literary pretensions, and as he wrote in a spirit of fairness to both sides in the Civil War, his work is of some importance. The main facts which he presents may be accepted as trustworthy, and the conversations, though not verbatim, convey reliable details. Admiral Porter had occasion in his various assignments to know intimately much of the Confederacy. He participated in naval operations around Pensacola, Mobile, Wilmington, and Richmond; and for a year or more he was in command of the Mississippi Squadron which took him up and down the Mississippi River, and made him a critical participant in Banks' Red River expedition. He gives interesting glimpses of the people in the Mississippi Valley and presents close-up details of the fall of Richmond and of Lincoln's visit there. He had a high admiration for the endurance of Confederate soldiers and was thankful that the Federal troops were never called on to bear such hardships.

Powers, Elvira J.   377

Hospital pencillings; being a diary while in Jefferson general hospital, Jeffersonville, Ind., and others at Nashville, Tennessee, as matron and visitor. By Elvira J. Powers. Boston, Edward L. Mitchell, 1866.

viii, 211 p.   front.   18¾ cm.
Illustrations: Frontispiece, "Jefferson General Hospital, Jeffersonville, Ind."
Inclusive dates: April–October, 1864.

The book is less an account of scenes inside hospital walls than its title indicates. Although the author details many conversations with patients in hospitals, her story is about equally divided between her observations in Nashville, Tennessee, her experiences in the hospital in Jeffersonville, Indiana, and her travels between these places, down the Ohio River to Louisville and by train to Nashville. She was a friendly person and a close observer, who kept her diary filled with notes and interviews. She met old Judge Joseph R. Underwood in Louisville and elicited from him much information about his early life and the history of the country through which they passed as they rode southward on the Louisville and Nashville Railroad. When she arrived at Nashville she acquainted herself with the principal mansions, estates, and objects of historical interest in the city and vicinity, such as the Hermitage and the estates of Isaac Franklin's widow and Mrs. James K. Polk. She also visited various institutions such as the penitentiary, the camp for refugees, and the hospitals. This book is a first-rate account of that part of the Confederacy which was within the Federal lines. While on her Nashville assignment, Miss Powers made a visit to Quincy, Illinois, going all the way by steamer down the Cumberland and Ohio and up the Mississippi.

Powers, George Whitefield, 1834–1903. 378

The story of the Thirty eighth regiment of Massachusetts volunteers. By George W. Powers. Cambridge, Dakin and Metcalf, 1866.

x p., 1 l., 308 p.   18½ cm.
Inclusive dates: 1862–1865.

The regiment, of which Powers was a member, embarked from Baltimore in the latter part of 1862 for the fighting in Louisiana. Stopping first at Ship Island off the coast of Mississippi, the unit proceeded to the mouth of the Mississippi and up river to Carrollton, on the outskirts of New Orleans. For a year or more it operated up and down the Mississippi as far as Port Hudson, westward from New Orleans to Berwick City, and northward to Opelousas and to Alexandria on the Red River, with further operations up the Red River as far as Cane River and Grand Ecore. The regiment finally returned to New Orleans and embarked for Alexandria, Virginia. For the rest of the war (with Powers absent because of protracted illness) the unit operated for a time in the Shenandoah Valley and later went to Savannah, Georgia, to engage in raiding activities on the coast of South and North Carolina. Powers' account is based on a diary and may be considered a first-hand narrative. After he left the regiment he depended on diaries and letters of others. He was interested in the Louisiana countryside, its people and their mansions, and he gives some insight into general conditions in that part of the Confederacy.

Price, Isaiah, 1822– 379

History of the Ninety-seventh regiment, Pennsylvania volunteer infantry, during the war of the rebellion, 1861–65, with biographical sketches of its field and staff officers and a complete record of each officer and enlisted man. Prepared at the request of the regiment, by Isaiah Price ... Philadelphia, Published by the author for the subscribers, B. & P. printers, 1875.

viii, ₍3₎–608 p., 1 l. front., illus., ports. 26½ cm.
Illustrations: Sixty-two steel portrait engravings and wood cuts and one page of music.
Maps: Eight maps and plans, illustrative of the campaigns engaged in by the regiment.
Inclusive dates: 1861–1865.

Apart from the great number of regimental names and maneuvers, this book has occasional descriptions of the country traversed by the regiment, especially of the southern country from James Island near Charleston to St. Augustine. There are fewer descriptions of the Virginia and North Carolina areas. The regiment operated first along the South Atlantic coast, making raids into the interior from Beaufort and Fernandina, especially; it was then transferred to the lower James country for the fighting around Bermuda Hundred and Petersburg; afterward it was sent to the Cape Fear River in North Carolina to engage in the reduction of Fort Fisher and the capture of Wilmington; and finally the Ninety-seventh marched into the interior of the state and joined forces with Sherman's command. It was mustered out at Weldon, North Carolina, at the end of the war. The book was written from diaries, letters, and official accounts.

Price, William N. 380

One year in the civil war. A diary of the events from April 1st, 1864 to April 1st, 1865. No place, publisher or date. Printed for private distribution.

59 p. 23½ cm.
Inclusive dates: April, 1864–April, 1865.

Private Price, of Company D, Sixth Tennessee United States Volunteer Infantry, was most interested in the weather and the day-by-day marching, yet he commented now and then on other matters. He believed the war was a scourge sent upon the people for their sins, in which apparently Northerners and Southerners were equally blameworthy, and lamented the senseless destructions of property. The author of this paper-backed booklet began his travels and diary in East Tennessee, marched southward to Decatur, Georgia, northward to Chattanooga, and westward to Nashville. Then he went down the Cumberland and up the Ohio to Cincinnati, to Washington by rail, to Fortress Monroe by boat and on to Wilmington, North Carolina, where he arrived in March, 1865. He was at Goldsboro when the war ended, returned by boat from Newbern to Baltimore, by train to Pittsburgh, Indianapolis, Louisville and Nashville, and was discharged.

Prutsman, Christian Miller. 381

A soldier's experience in southern prisons. By C. M. Prutsman ... a graphic description of the author's experience in various southern prisons. New York, Andrew H. Kellogg, 1901.

80 p. front. (port.) 18 cm.
Illustrations: Frontispiece, C. M. Prutsman.
Inclusive dates: October, 1863–July, 1865.

C. M. Prutsman was a lieutenant in the Seventh Regiment Wisconsin Volunteers, who enlisted in August, 1861. The account begins with his capture in northern Virginia in October, 1863, and deals with the author's prison experiences. After short stays in Libby and Danville he was sent to Macon, Georgia, and was there when Sherman invaded the state. Before Sherman's army could block the road to Charleston, Prutsman was sent there and then on to Columbia. After a few attempts he finally escaped about the time Sherman reached Columbia. He was picked up by Sherman's army north of the South Carolina capital and was later in Fayetteville, North Carolina, where he took a boat down the Cape Fear River to Wilmington, to Baltimore, and thence to the army in northern Virginia. He was near Appomattox about the time of the surrender. This account is brief and of little value. It is marred by the customary tales of atrocities and bad treatment in prisons, attempts at escape with a few successes and recaptures, and the invariable tribute to the helpful services of Negroes.

Putnam, George Haven, 1844–1930. 382

A prisoner of war in Virginia, 1864–5. By George Haven Putnam, adjt. and bvt-major 176th N. Y. S. vols. Reprinted with additions, from the report of an address presented to the N. Y. commandery of the U. S. loyal legion, December 7, 1910 ... New York and London, G. P. Putnam's sons, 1912.

v, 104 p. incl., plates, front. (port.) plates. 20½ cm.
Illustrations: Frontispiece, "Geo. Haven Putnam 1st Lieut. and Adj. 176th Reg., N. Y. Vols.";
"Mosby's Raiders Attack a Commissary Train"; " 'And Sheridan, fifteen miles away!' ";
"Libby Prison, Richmond, Va. From a photograph taken in 1865"; "Morning Toilet."
Inclusive dates: 1864–1865.
Other editions: A second edition with additions appeared in 1912, brought out by the same publishers.

Major Putnam wrote his account forty-eight years after the events which he describes, but he was still convinced that Jefferson Davis should be held personally responsible for the death of prisoners of war in Southern prison camps. In this staunch belief the old Union soldier believed Davis guilty of murder. Apart from this adamant opinion Major Putnam writes an account worthy of his intelligence and literary attainment. As a prisoner of war he was marched to Staunton, placed aboard a train, and taken to Libby Prison in Richmond. He was later transferred to the prison in Danville, but was returned to Richmond and paroled for a few weeks in a restricted area before being exchanged in early 1865. He was taken to Annapolis and re-assigned to his old regiment, at that time in North Carolina. He went by boat down Chesapeake Bay, through the Dismal Swamp Canal and on to Morehead City, thence by train to Newbern, Goldsboro, and Durham Station, where he witnessed Johnston's surrender.

Major Putnam's volume deals principally with prison life but includes observations on the country and people of the Confederacy.

Putnam, Samuel Henry. 383

The story of Company A, Twenty-fifth regiment, Mass. vols. in the war of the rebellion. By Samuel H. Putnam. Worcester, Putnam, Davis and co., 1886.

> 1 p. l., 324 p.   front. (port.) maps.   23½ cm.
> *Illustrations:* Frontispiece, "J. Pickett ₍Signature₎ Brevet Brigadier-General, U. S. V."
> *Maps:* "Roanoke Island"; "Topographical Map of Newberne, N. C."; "Dept. of North Carolina" (double-page); "Map of Bermuda Hundreds and Vicinity" (double-page); "Battlefield of Drewry's Bluff, May 16, 1864."
> *Inclusive dates:* 1861–1864.

This travel commentary is worth-while principally for its descriptions of the countryside, of the various North Carolina towns such as Newbern, Plymouth, Goldsboro, Tarboro, Kingston, and Washington, and of the people, especially the Negroes. The regiment set sail from Annapolis with Burnside, engaged in the Battle of Roanoke Island in February, 1862, and in the subsequent fighting around Newbern, Plymouth, and Goldsboro. Putnam was transferred to Butler's forces at Bermuda Hundred, and later sent across the Dismal Swamps by canal steamer to re-enforce the troops at Plymouth, but his unit arrived too late to prevent the fall of that place to the Confederates. His enlistment expired in October, 1864, and he was mustered out. The book shows evidence of having been composed from contemporary personal material.

Quincy, Samuel Miller, 1833–1887. 384

History of the Second Massachusetts regiment of infantry. A prisoner's diary. A paper read at the officers' reunion in Boston, May 11, 1877, By Samuel M. Quincy ... Boston, George H. Ellis, printer, 1882.

> 24 p.   24 cm.
> *Inclusive dates:* 1862.

For the most part this brief pamphlet is the diary of Samuel M. Quincy, who was a captain in the regiment and who was captured at Cedar Mountain in Northern Virginia in 1862. He was taken first to Staunton and later to Libby in Richmond. He was soon paroled and turned over to the Federal authorities down the James River. There is some slight comment on conditions he found in the Confederacy.

Quint, Alonzo Hall, 1828–1896. 385

The Potomac and the Rapidan. Army notes from the failure at Winchester to the reenforcement of Rosecrans. 1861–3. By Alonzo H. Quint ... Boston, Crosby and Nichols; New York, O. S. Felt, 1864.

407 p. front. (fold. map) 19 cm.
Maps: "Map of Parts of Pennsylvania, Maryland and Virginia referred to in this Volume. Published by Permission from the Map of the Coast Survey Office. Boston, Crosby & Nichols." Folding map in front of book, 12 by 8½ in.
Inclusive dates: July, 1861–January, 1864.
Other editions: No other edition found. A more consecutive account, but entirely rewritten, in which the history of the Second Massachusetts regiment is detailed, and to which is added Quint's experiences on Sherman's march to Atlanta, Savannah and northward, is Alonzo H. Quint, The record of the Second Massachusetts infantry, 1861–65. Boston, James P. Walker, 1867.

Despite Quint's pronounced views on the evils of slavery, the low state of civilization among Southerners, and the blood and iron policy which he advocated for the South, this book is of considerable value. Quint was well-educated, having graduated from Dartmouth College, and was a close observer of the Southern scene, whether military, social, or political. He carefully noted sentiment among the people of Maryland and northern Virginia, and concluded that there was practically no Unionism in the communities which he visited. Hence his program for more civilized Northerners to colonize the country and develop its resources. Quint, attached to the Second Massachusetts Infantry as chaplain, spent the first two years of the war in Maryland and northern Virginia where he visited and commented critically upon such communities as Frederick, Maryland, and Harpers Ferry, Charlestown (where he was impressed by the John Brown episode), Winchester, New Market, Harrisonburg, and Fredericksburg. In October, 1863, he accompanied forces sent to re-enforce Rosecrans around Chattanooga, going over the Baltimore and Ohio Railroad through Wheeling, across Ohio and Indiana to Louisville, and southward over the Louisville and Nashville and the Nashville and Chattanooga railroads. Quint was born in New Hampshire, and became a Congregational clergyman; after the war he wrote other books and edited the *Congregational Quarterly*. This book is made up of letters, with later additions and changes, which originally appeared in the religious publication *Congregationalist*.

Quint, Alonzo Hall, 1828–1896.   386

The record of the Second Massachusetts infantry, 1861–65. By Alonzo H. Quint, its chaplain. Boston, Joseph P. Walker, 1867.

viii p., 1 l., 528 p. front., port. 19¾ cm.
Illustrations: Frontispiece, "Brevet Maj. Gen. George H. Gordon"; "Capt. Edward G. Abbott"; "Brevet Maj. Gen. George L. Andrews"; "Capt. Richard Cary"; "Lieut. Col. Wilder Dwight"; "Lieut. Col. James Savage"; "Lieut. Col. Charles R. Mudge"; "Brevet Brig. Gen. William Cogswell"; "Rev. A. H. Quint, Chaplain"; "Capt. William B. Williams"; "Capt. Thos. B. Fox, Jr." All of these illustrations are steel engravings.
Inclusive dates: July, 1861–June, 1865.

This should be considered as supplementary to the author's *The Potomac and the Rapidan (q.v.)* which, despite its limitations, is a more valuable account. It repeats in abbreviated form, the observations in the first volume but has more extensive accounts of regimental organization and military movements, and adds new material about the campaign of Sherman to Atlanta, to the sea, and northward through the Carolinas.

Quintard, Charles Todd, bp., 1824–1898.   387

Doctor Quintard, chaplain C. S. A. and second bishop of Tennessee; being his story of the war (1861–1865). Edited and extended by the Rev. Arthur Howard Noll ... Sewanee, Tenn., The University press of Sewanee Tennessee, 1905.

> 5 p. l., 183 p., 1 l., vi p.   front. (port.)   19½ cm.
> *Illustrations:* Frontispiece, "C. T. Quintard" ₍Signature₎.
> *Inclusive dates:* 1861–1865.

Although not written until 1896, this book was drawn from the author's war diary and seems to be reliable. Quintard, born in Connecticut in 1824, was identified with the Episcopal Church in Tennessee some years before the outbreak of the Civil War, and was serving a church in Nashville when Tennessee entered the war. At the beginning of hostilities he became chaplain of the First Tennessee Regiment and served throughout the war in various units as chaplain and surgeon, being equipped for the latter by a medical degree. He went first to Virginia and was in the Cheat Mountain, West Virginia, campaign. Thereafter he traveled extensively over the Confederacy, frequently going to Richmond, Lynchburg, Winchester, Staunton, and Norfolk. After 1862 his chief activities were with the Army of Tennessee, including Bragg's campaign into Kentucky in the fall of 1862. He was present at Chickamauga, and later in the fighting north of Atlanta incident to Sherman's march on that city. He saw service in various parts of Alabama, Mississippi, Georgia, and middle and western Tennessee. This account not only gives impressions of the difficulties of travel during the war, but naturally centers attention on the religious work both in the army and in the southern cities visited. After the war Quintard was elected second bishop of Tennessee, succeeding Bishop Otey.

Ransom, John L.   388

Andersonville diary, escape, and list of the dead, with name, co., regiment, date of death and no. of grave in cemetery. By J. L. Ransom ... Auburn, N. Y., The author, 1881.

> 304 p. incl. port.   18 cm.
> *Illustrations:* "John L. Ransom"; "George W. Hendryx"; "Battese, the Minnesota Indian"; "Michael Hoare"; "David Buck"; "John L. Ransom. (From a photograph taken three months after escape)"; "James A. Garfield."
> *Inclusive dates:* November, 1863–December, 1865.
> *Other editions:* No other edition found. This text, almost in its present form, was first published in the *Jackson* (Michigan) *Citizen.*

This book was published in its original diary form with some additions. Ransom was a sergeant in the Ninth Michigan Cavalry, who was taken prisoner in

East Tennessee near Rogersville in November, 1863. He was marched to Bristol, conveyed by railway to Richmond and imprisoned on Belle Isle and in the Pemberton warehouse before he was transferred to Andersonville. He does not make plain the route he took, but it was probably the customary one (before the gap between Danville and Greensboro was completed) by way of Petersburg, Weldon, Wilmington, Branchville, Augusta, Millen, and Macon. In early fall, 1864, he was removed to Millen, to Savannah, and escaped and was recaptured while en route to Blackshear in southern Georgia. When Sherman began his march to the sea, the Confederacy began concentrating its prisoners at Columbia and Florence; while Ransom was being conveyed northward to Charleston he escaped near Savannah and reached the near-by Federal lines. His account, tempered by good feeling and with few extreme statements, is mostly of life within prison walls, with occasional comments on conditions among the Southern people, and is one of the better prisoner-of-war travel accounts.

Rauscher, Frank. 389

Music on the march, 1862–'65, with the Army of the Potomac. 114th regt. P. V. Collis' zouaves. By Frank Rauscher. Philadelphia, Press of Wm. F. Fell & co., 1892.

vii, 9–270 p. front., pl., port. 18½ cm.
Illustrations: Frontispiece, Frank Rauscher.
Inclusive dates: 1862–1865.

Written more than a quarter century after the war, this narrative was substantiated by a diary and a few personal letters. Rauscher, an Alsatian German, joined the One Hundred and Fourteenth Regiment Pennsylvania Volunteers in 1862. He was sent to Washington, up and across the Potomac near Leesburg, and marched to Fredericksburg where he and his military band were made prisoners. After a few weeks in Libby Prison he was paroled, sent to Annapolis, and later exchanged. He participated in the Gettysburg campaign and returned southward through Williamsport, Harpers Ferry, and Warrenton to the Fauquier White Sulphur Springs to stay for some weeks. In the spring of 1864 he followed Grant's army through various battles and crossed the James at City Point. From then to the end of the war he operated south of the James. After Appamottox he marched through Richmond and on to Washington for the "Grand Review." Rauscher included a description of the Sulphur Springs and observations on the landscape, some of which reminded him of his native Alsatian hills, and the temper of Southern women.

Reed, William Howell. 390

Hospital life in the Army of the Potomac. By William Howell Reed. Boston, William V. Spencer, 1866.

199 p. 17½ cm.
Inclusive dates: May, 1864–April, 1865.

Besides an account of hospital life among Federal soldiers, this is somewhat a travel book, for the author moved with the Army of the Potomac from Fredericksburg to City Point and Petersburg. In his travels Reed observed many matters of interest, such as the Negroes and their ways, topography and fauna, and the horrors of the battlefields. He also noted, not without compassion, the condition of wounded Confederate soldiers who were captured and taken into Federal hospitals.

Reid, Jesse Walton. 391

History of the Fourth regiment of S. C. volunteers, from the commencement of the war until Lee's surrender. Giving a full account of all its movements, fights and hardships of all kinds. Also a very correct account of the travels and fights of the Army of Northern Virginia during the same period. This book is a copy of the letters written in Virginia at the time by the author and sent home to his family. Containing an account of the author's services in the First regiment of engineer troops in the latter part of the war. With a short sketch of the life of the author. By J. W. Reid. Greenville, S. C., Shannon & co., 1892.

143 p. front. (port.) 22½ cm.
Illustrations: Frontispiece, "Yours truly, J. W. Reid."
Inclusive dates: 1861–1865.

Chiefly significant in this booklet are the impressions of a South Carolinian seeing Virginia for the first time. The contrasts between the two states were so great that Reid naturally noticed them. He found more beautiful landscapes in Virginia than in South Carolina and there he saw a richer farming country. The letters and some later reminiscences indicate the thoughts of a Confederate soldier on such subjects as conscription, which he felt was tyranny, and on President Davis, whom he considered to be a dictator. Reid wrote with a sense of humor, positive convictions, and unusual candor and naivete. He volunteered at the beginning of the war and served to the end. He went immediately to Leesburg on the Potomac, took part in the First Battle of Manassas, advanced almost to the Potomac opposite Washington, and took part in the Peninsula fighting in the early summer of 1862. Since he was beyond the original conscription age of thirty-five he was mustered out in 1862 but was conscripted in 1863 when the age limit was raised. Therefore he fought in Virginia until Appomattox.

Richardson, Albert Deane, 1833–1869. 392

The secret service, the field, the dungeon, and the escape ... By Albert D. Richardson ... Hartford, Conn., American publishing company; Philadelphia, Jones bros. & co.; ⌈etc., etc.⌉ 1865.

512 p. incl. facsim. front., plates, ports. 22 cm.
Illustrations: "Albert D. Richardson" (Signature, "Photo by Brady. Engd. by Geo. E.

Perine, N. Y." steel engraving); "A Group of Army Correspondents," Charles C. Coffin of Boston Journal, Junius H. Browne of New York Tribune, Thomas W. Knox of New York Herald, Richard T. Colburn of New York World, L. L. Crounse of New York Times; William E. Davis of Cincinnati Gazette, William D. Bickham of Cincinnati Commercial (Steel engraving by H. B. Hall, New York); "The Mississippi Convention Viewed by a Tribune Correspondent"; "Opening of the Battle of Antietam—General Hooker"; "Fac-Simile of an Autograph Letter of President Lincoln"; "The Capture, while Running the Rebel Batteries at Vicksburg"; "Interior View of a Hospital in the Salisbury Prison"; "The Massacre of Union Prisoners Attempting to Escape from Salisbury, North Carolina"; "Escaping Prisoners Fed by Negroes in their Master's Barn"; "Fording a Stream"; "Portrait of Dan. Ellis"; "Portrait of 'Nameless Heroine' [Melvina Stevens]"; "'The Nameless Heroine' Piloting the Escaping Prisoners out of the Rebel Ambush." Most of the above are drawings by J. P. Davis.

Inclusive dates: February, 1861–January 13, 1865.

Other editions: A cheaper printing without the illustrations (though the page listing them is included) came out the same year—1865. A German edition was: Feld, gefangniss und flucht. Hartford, Conn., 1865.

Parallel accounts: Accompanying Richardson and covering much the same topics is Junius Henri Browne, Four years in Secessia (*q.v.*).

Albert D. Richardson was born in Franklin, Mass., and was assassinated at his desk in New York City thirty-six years later. He early became interested in newspaper work and associated himself with papers in Pittsburgh, Cincinnati, and Kansas. In 1859 he became a correspondent of the New York *Tribune* and remained in this position until his death. After the war he journeyed into the Rocky Mountain country and wrote his famous book *Beyond the Mississippi*. Richardson's Civil War book relates almost entirely to his newspaper activities, prison life, and escape in the Confederacy. At the beginning of the secession movement he went to New Orleans as a *Tribune* correspondent incognito, visited the Louisiana Convention and the Mississippi Convention in Jackson, and returned to Washington by way of Mobile, Montgomery, Atlanta, Charleston, and Richmond. At the beginning of the war he reported military activities in Missouri, and after various other assignments joined Grant's expedition against Vicksburg in 1863. In attempting to run the river blockade at this place Richardson's flotilla was demolished and he was taken prisoner. He was sent to Richmond, imprisoned in Libby and Castle Thunder, removed to the Salisbury Prison, and escaped in the latter part of 1864. As a fugitive he made his way through the "deserter country" of western North Carolina and East Tennessee and early in 1865 reached the Union lines near Knoxville. Richardson recounts the terrors of Confederate prison life and the tricks used to effect escapes, and reports many conversations with Unionists who by 1863 were beginning to make themselves known in the Confederacy. The particular value of this work lies in its description of the "deserter country"; it is written clearly with occasional lapses into unbiased observations.

Ripley, Mrs. Eliza Moore (Chinn) McHatton.   393

From flag to flag. A woman's adventures and experiences in the South during the war, in Mexico, and in Cuba. By Eliza McHatton Ripley. New York, D. Appleton and company, 1889.

296 p.   18 cm.
Inclusive dates: 1861–1865.
Other editions: No other edition found, though there was probably a printing in 1888 as the work was copyrighted in that year.

Mrs. Ripley and her husband lived on a Mississippi River plantation four miles below Baton Rouge, Louisiana. After the fall of New Orleans and the fighting around Baton Rouge, the Ripleys fled to Texas with whatever they could take in a wagon and hack. Sending some of their slaves ahead, they set out across Louisiana late in 1862, crossed the Sabine, took a train at Beaumont for Houston, and after some time continued to Laredo. Then they went up the Rio Grande on the Mexican side to Piedras Negras, remained for a while and finally settled in San Antonio. During the course of the war they sought refuge in various parts of the state, often camping out on the prairie. Near its end they returned to Laredo, crossed the river and continued down the Mexican side to Matamoras, remained for a period, took a boat to Havana, and eventually returned to the United States. Although this account was composed more than a quarter century after the war, it is a valuable commentary on the trials of refugees and the destruction in and around Baton Rouge, on life, society, towns, and the countryside of Texas, and on the cotton trade which passed out of Texas into Mexico. There are touches of natural history in stories of prairie wolves (coyotes) sitting on their haunches around a dying campfire, held by the scent of cooked meat, and of a rattlesnake charming and nearly swallowing a bullfrog until interrupted by a pistol shot.

Roach, Alva C.   394

The prisoner of war, and how treated. Containing a history of Colonel Streight's expedition to the rear of Bragg's army, in the spring of 1863, and a correct account of the treatment and condition of the Union prisoners of war in the rebel prisons of the South, in 1863–4. Being the actual experience of a Union officer during twenty-two months' imprisonment in rebeldom. With personal adventure, biographical sketches, and history of Andersonville prison pen. By Lieutenant A. C. Roach ... Indianapolis, Ind., The Railroad city publishing house, 1865.

244 p.   19 cm.
Inclusive dates: April, 1863–March, 1865.

Lieutenant Roach's book is among the most bitter of prisoner-of-war accounts. The author confesses that it was written to bring "the guilty leaders of treason to just punishment, for their enormous crimes against humanity" (p. 4). He was a member of the Streight expedition organized in Nashville to move in behind Bragg's army and cut the Western and Atlantic Railroad in Georgia. It moved some miles down the Cumberland River and disembarked, the flotilla continuing down to the Ohio River in order to ascend the Tennessee River and pick up the expedition near Fort Henry. It continued up the Tennessee into Alabama, where Streight's forces rushed across country to the vicinity of Rome, Georgia, only to suffer capture of the whole command by General Forrest, and to be sent to Libby Prison (probably following the railroad through East Tennessee, which was still in Confederate hands). In May, 1864, Roach was transferred to the Macon prison by way of Danville, Charlotte, and Augusta. He was later moved to Charleston, then to Columbia, and escaped from the train while being sent to Charlotte in February, 1865, to avoid Sherman's army. He wandered around a few days, being aided by South Carolina Unionists, before he rejoined the Federal forces and went with Sherman's army to Fayetteville, took a Cape Fear steamer to Wilmington, and an ocean vessel to Washington. This account is prejudiced and inaccurate. For instance, Roach claims that the Sansom person who aided Forrest was a man instead of Emma, who was later recognized for this exploit as the outstanding Confederate heroine.

Roe, Alfred Seelye.   395

The Ninth New York heavy artillery. A history of its organization, services in the defenses of Washington, marches, camps, battles, and muster-out, with accounts of life in a rebel prison, personal experiences, names and addresses of surviving members, personal sketches, and a complete roster of the regiment. By A. S. Roe. Worcester, Mass., 1899.

615 p.   front. illus., plates, ports. diagrs.   23½ cm.
Illustrations: Sixty-nine portraits of soldiers, battle scenes, landscapes, etc.
Maps: Ten plans of battles and maps.
Inclusive dates: 1862–1865.

Thirty years after the war Alfred Seelye Roe produced a work of unusual excellence from painstaking researches among his comrades' diaries and papers, historical documents, and his own enriched memory. He saw much more than the marching of armies and the smoke of battle. People, the countryside, and historical scenes attracted him. He remembered the soldier who remarked that he had just seen a document from an old Virginia courthouse, which bore the signature of George II. Roe enlisted in 1862 at Auburn, New York, and was soon in Washington where he and his comrades spent considerable time guarding the city. In the spring of 1864 he joined Grant's march on Richmond. When Early made his famous raid on Washington, Roe was among the forces sent by Grant to save the city. Thereafter he operated in the Shenandoah Valley until the latter days of the war, when he was transferred back to Petersburg. After Lee's surrender, he went on the raid to Danville and retraced his steps northward, passing through Richmond and on to Washington. After the war, he attended Wesleyan University in Middletown, Conn., taught school for some years in Massachusetts, and was elected to that state's legislature. He wrote various ous books dealing with the war.

Roemer, Jacob, 1818–1896.   396

Reminiscences of the War of the rebellion, 1861–1865. By Bvt.-Maj. Jacob

Roemer ... Ed. by L. A. Furney ... Flushing, N. Y., Estate of Jacob Roemer, 1897.

316 p., 1 l. front. (port.) 20 cm.
Illustrations: Frontispiece, "J. Roemer" ₍Signature₎.
Inclusive dates: 1862–1865.

Like scores of other Civil War authors, Roemer did not begin to organize his memoirs until three decades after the war. No diary is mentioned; therefore details, such as the exact hour at which a certain operation began, and certain incredible personal exploits, may be suspect. Nevertheless this book is a well-written, straightforward account unencumbered with bitterness or invective. He relates many experiences with civilians but seems to have respected their rights. He enjoyed campaigning, and the country, especially Kentucky, looked good to him. Roemer, a native of Germany, migrated to America in young manhood and settled in New York state. Upon joining the United States Army he became captain of Battery L, Second New York Artillery, and later was transferred to the Thirty-fourth New York Independent Veteran Volunteer Light Battery in which he ultimately became brevet major. He served first at the Second Battle of Manassas and fought at Sharpsburg and Fredericksburg before being transferred to the West. To reach that theater he went by rail to Cincinnati and southward over the Kentucky Central to Lexington. He maneuvered in that vicinity for some weeks, passing through Nicholasville and Crab Orchard. Later he went to Louisville and by boat to Vicksburg, and was present in the operations leading to the downfall of that city and the sacking of Jackson. He then returned to the eastern theater of the war and fought with Grant from the Wilderness to Petersburg. Being wounded a few days before Appomattox he was on his way North when he heard of Lee's surrender.

Rogers, Edward H. 397

Reminiscences of military service in the Forty-third regiment, Massachusetts infantry, during the great civil war, 1862–63. By E. H. Rogers. Boston, Franklin press: Rand, Avery & co., 1883.

210 p. plates (incl. front.) 23 cm.
Illustrations: Frontispiece, "Camp Rogers. Headquarters of the Forty-Third Regiment, M. V. M. at Newbern N. C. With the Field and Staff"; "Camp Rogers. Encampment of the Forty-Third Regiment, M. V. M. Newbern N. C., March 12th, 1863"; "Capture of Kingston"; "Battle of Goldsborough."
Inclusive dates: November, 1862–July, 1863.

Rogers re-enforced his reminiscences with various letters written during the war and other contemporary material. Some of this narrative was first published in the *Boston Journal* and all of it originally appeared in the Chelsea, Massachusetts, *Pioneer*. The Forty-third Massachusetts enlisted for nine months, and at the end of its service retired from the war. Its field of activity lay in eastern North Carolina around Newbern, Kingston, Trenton, and Goldsboro. Rogers gives interesting descriptions of these towns and of the people in eastern Carolina, with especial criticism of the "poor whites." He frankly described some wanton pillaging of private residences, mentioning one instance in which a soldier broke into a physician's office and carried away in mock triumph a beheaded skeleton. Rogers set sail from Boston for Newbern and returned to Baltimore by way of Chesapeake Bay, where he was encamped at the time of the Battle of Gettysburg.

Rose, Victor M.   −1893.   398

Ross' Texas brigade. Being a narrative of events connected with its service in the late war between the states. By V. M. Rose. Louisville, Ky., The Courier-journal book and job rooms, 1881.

185 p.   front., port.   20 cm.
Illustrations: Frontispiece, "General L. S. Ross"; "General John S. Griffith"; "Colonel Jack Wharton"; "Lieutenant-Colonel John H. Broocks"; "Lieutenant-Colonel P. F. Ross."
Inclusive dates: 1861–1865.
Other editions: No other edition found; but another work on this same brigade is: Samuel Benton Barron, The Lone star defenders *(q.v.).*

This work was composed from a variety of sources, including the author's memory. Victor Rose was a member of the Ross Brigade and, although he was primarily concerned with its military exploits, he included many details interesting to an intelligent traveler. His statements about Confederates capturing and pillaging the Federal supplies in Holly Springs, Mississippi, are frank and graphic. The Ross Brigade was formed in Dallas, Texas, in the first year of the war, and moved northward through Indian Territory into northern Arkansas and southwestern Missouri. It also made an expedition back into the Indian country before marching down the Arkansas River to Little Rock and on to Duvall's Bluff on the White River, where it embarked for Memphis, down the White and up the Mississippi. It continued to Corinth and for the next year or more operated in west Tennessee, northern Mississippi, and southward to the capture of Vicksburg; marched into Middle Tennessee and in the spring of 1864 was with General Joseph E. Johnston on his retreat southward toward Atlanta. After the fall of that city it followed Hood across Alabama and back through Middle Tennessee to the outskirts of Nashville where it participated in the battles which practically destroyed the Confederate army.

Ross, Fitzgerald.   399

A visit to the cities and camps of the Confederate states. By Fitzgerald Ross. Edinburgh and London, William Blackwood and sons, 1865.

x, 300 p.   front. (map)   18½ cm.
Maps: Frontispiece, "Map of the Seat of War in the United States. The Red line denotes the Author's route." (Folding map, 11 x 14 in.)
Inclusive dates: May, 1863–Early spring, 1864. (Exact dates not evident.)

Fitzgerald Ross, "Captain of Hussars in the Imperial Austrian Army," was evidently a Scotsman. In May, 1863, he made his way across the military lines in northern Virginia and went directly to Richmond. Finding easy access to military and civil leaders of the Confederacy, he had an opportunity to accompany the Confederate Army in its invasion of Pennsylvania and into the Battle of Gettysburg. Afterwards he spent some time in Charleston and went by way of Augusta and Atlanta to the environs of Chattanooga about the time of the Battle of Chickamauga. Retracing his way to Charleston, he went by rail to Savannah and on to Macon, Montgomery, and Mobile, returning on a steamer up the Alabama River to Montgomery and back over the same road to Charleston. In the early spring of 1864 he ran the blockade to Nassau and proceeded to Havana and New York. Captain Ross gave considerable attention to military affairs but he also made many comments on the life of the people. He had a friendly attitude towards everybody and everything and, without making any predictions, evidently believed that the Confederacy could never be conquered. This account first appeared in *Blackwood's Magazine*.

Runyan, Morris C.   400

Eight days with the Confederates and capture of their archives, flags, etc., by Company "G" Ninth New Jersey vol. Written by Capt. M. C. Runyan. Princeton, N. J., Wm. C. C. Zapf, printer, 1896.

44 p. front. (port.) 22¼ cm.
Illustrations: Frontispiece, "Morris C. Runyan" ₍Signature₎.

An account of the march of a small Federal detachment from Raleigh to Charlotte and the seizure there of many United States flags which the Confederates had captured during the war, together with many boxes of Confederate archives, constitutes an interesting part of this pamphlet. Captain Runyan also gives a picture of the ragged, dispirited Confederate soldiers making their way southward. While in Charlotte he met General Joseph E. Johnston.

Russell, David E.   401

Seven months in prison; or, Life in rebeldom. Details of real prison life in Richmond and Danville, with a list of Wisconsin men who died in the Andersonville prison, in perfect order, by regiments. By D. E. Russell. Milwaukee, Godfrey & Crandall, 1866.

104 p. 19 cm.
Inclusive dates: 1863–1864.

Written in an inflated and grandiloquent style, spiced with bitterness, this narrative describes the prison life of the author, a Wisconsin volunteer. He was captured in the Battle of Chickamauga and was taken to Richmond for safekeeping. He went by rail, passing through Atlanta, Augusta, Columbia, Raleigh, and Petersburg. He describes the people along the route, finding them degraded and generally bitter towards Federal prisoners, though at a few places, notably Augusta, they were more kind-hearted. After some months of imprisonment in Richmond he was taken to Danville for a time and finally was returned to Richmond and paroled, passing down the James River to a Federal flag-of-truce vessel which transported him to Annapolis.

Russell, George G. 402

Reminiscences of Andersonville prison. A paper read by Comrade Geo. G. Russell, before Post 34, G. A. R. Tuesday evening, June, 22. Salem, Mass., Observer steam book and job print, 1886.

8 p.   23 cm.
Inclusive dates: 1864.

George Russell was captured at the Battle of the Wilderness in 1864 and was taken first to Lynchburg and then to Danville. In each place he was imprisoned only a few days. From Danville he was taken to Andersonville by way of Greensboro, Charlotte, Columbia, Augusta, and Macon. Russell gives some attention to the journey southward, relating the reception he received from the population at the various railway stations through which he passed. Only at Columbia did he find the people kindly disposed toward the prisoners.

Russell, Sir William Howard, 1820–1907. 403

My diary North and South. By William Howard Russell. Boston, T. O. H. P. Burnham; New York, O. S. Felt; Toronto, C. W. Rollo and Adam, 1863.

xxii, 602 p.   20 cm.
Inclusive dates: March 16, 1861; April 12, 1861–June 19, 1861; April, 1862.
Other editions: London, Bradbury and Evans, 1863. 2 vols. The letters to the *Times* which he wrote on this trip follow closely the *Diary* but are more restrained in language and hostile criticisms, and more valuable in generalisations. They are published in *The Civil War in America.* Boston, Gardner A. Fuller, 1861. Omitting the first five letters they were also published as *Pictures of Southern Life, Social, Political, and Military.* New York, J. G. Gregory, 1861.

William Howard Russell was born in County Dublin, Ireland, and received a legal education, but devoted his chief interest to newspaper reporting. He set the pace for the special correspondent when he reported the Crimean War and the troubles thereafter in India, and in March, 1861, he arrived in the United States as a special correspondent for the London *Times.* Landing in New York, he entered the South in April and traveled by train to the Alabama River and thence to Mobile, Pensacola, and Fort Pickens; back to Mobile, by steamboat to New Orleans and Columbus, Kentucky, and by boat to Cairo, Illinois. Leaving the South, he went to Chicago, Niagara Falls, Philadelphia, and Washington, with various trips thereafter. Russell was a caustic and penetrating critic of both the North and South, and succeeded in stirring up a storm of hostility in both sections by his continuous faultfinding with hotels and travel facilities. He irked the North especially by his account of the rout of the Federals at First Manassas. He stirred up hostility in the South by his phobia against slavery, which he denounced time and again as barbarism. Yet he found much to praise in the South, where he met all the principal officials, civil and military, thought highly of them, and felt that the South would probably never be conquered. He found universal acclaim of the Confederacy, saw none of the Union feeling which Seward and Lincoln had talked so much about, and seemed to enjoy the planters' hospitality that was showered upon him wherever he went. Discounting his bias and highly critical attitude toward all things American, one may get a remarkably vivid picture of life in the South during three months in the early period of the Confederacy. He wrote without restraint, scruples, or delicacy in describing his association with individual Southerners.

Sabre, Gilbert E. 404

Nineteen months a prisoner of war. Narrative of Lieutenant G. E. Sabre, Second Rhode Island cavalry, of his experience in the war prisons and stockades of Morton, Mobile, Atlanta, Libby, Belle Island, Andersonville, Macon, Charleston, and Columbia, and his escape to the Union lines. To which is appended, a list of officers confined at Columbia, during the winter of 1864 and 1865. New York, The American news company, 1865.

207 p. plates incl. front. 18¼ cm.
Illustrations: Frontispiece and repeated in text, "The Chain Gang"; "Carrying out the Dead."
Inclusive dates: July, 1863–March, 1865.
Other editions: Another printing of this book was made in 1866.

Differing from the stories of most other traveling prisoners of war, this account covers some new territory. Sabre was captured near Jackson, Louisiana, in August, 1863, and was marched northward through Louisiana and Mississippi to Morton, a small town on the railroad between Jackson and Meridian. After a short imprisonment there he was transferred to Mobile by railway and by an undesignated route to Atlanta, held briefly there, in Libby at Richmond, and Belle Isle, whence he was taken by train to Andersonville, going southward through Danville, Greensboro (the railroad from Danville to Greensboro had not been completed by this time), and by Salisbury, Charlotte, Columbia, Augusta, Millen, and Macon. From Andersonville he was sent to Charleston and then back to Columbia, where he made his escape into Sherman's lines. Sabre sprinkled a considerable number of atrocities through the account, but he did not consider everything he saw in the Confederacy wholly bad. He declared that the people shouted epithets at the Federal prisoners as they passed, but that the slaves were cordial and tossed bread and bacon into the cars.

Scheibert, Justus. 405

Sieben monate in den rebellen-staaten, wahrend des nordamerikanischen krieges 1863. von Scheibert. Stettin, Germany, Verlag von Th. von der Nahmer, 1868.

vi, 126 p. maps. 21 cm.
Maps: "Uebersichts-Plan des Feldzuges 1863 am Potomac" (Folding map, 28½ cm. by 37 cm.); "Plan der Schlachten von Chancellorsville u. Wilderness (1–3. Mai 1863)" (Folding map, 34 cm. by 41 cm.); "Schlacht bei Gettysburg" (Folding map, 17 cm. by 25 cm.); "Belagerung u. Blokade v. Charleston 1863" (Folding map, 28 cm. by 35 cm.)
Inclusive dates: 1863.

Scheibert, a major of engineers in the Prussian army, was sent by his government to the Confederacy early in 1863 to observe military operations. He came by way of London and ran the blockade at Charleston. After becoming acquainted with conditions in this region, he went by rail to Richmond where he was cordially received. Becoming imbued with uncontrollable military ardor he volunteered in the Confederate Army, went northward to join the forces around Fredericksburg, and was present at both Chancellorsville and Gettysburg. He returned southward and observed further conditions around Charleston. After spending seven months in the Confederacy, he ran the blockade out of Wilmington and landed in Liverpool. This account makes interesting comments on Confederate military operations, general conditions in the Confederacy, and some of the outstanding leaders such as Lee, Jackson, and Stuart.

Schwartz, Stephan. 406

Twenty-two months a prisoner of war. A narrative of twenty-two months' imprisonment by the Confederates, in Texas, through General Twiggs' treachery, dating from April, 1861, to February, 1863. By Stephan Schwartz. St. Louis, A. F. Nelson publishing co., 1892.

221 p. front. (port.), illus. 19 cm.
Illustrations: Frontispiece, "Yours truly, Stephan Schwartz" ₍Signature₎ and six sketches of incidents described in the narrative.
Inclusive dates: 1861–1863.

Experiences, incidents, and scenes in and around San Antonio, Texas, during the imprisonment of a Federal soldier constitute the body of this narrative. Since he wrote the book from memory about thirty years after the events, minor details and extensive conversations must be discounted sharply, but the main impressions and movements mentioned may be taken as trustworthy. Schwartz was one of a group of Federals seized by Texas troops after the Fort Sumter affair and was imprisoned at five different places around San Antonio; Camp Verdee, sixty miles away, being the farthest. In early 1863 he was marched across Texas by an undisclosed route to Shreveport, taken on a ship to New Orleans and turned over to the Federal authorities. On the way he stopped at Alexandria, Port Hudson, Baton Rouge, and Carrollton.

Scott, John, 1820–1907.   407
    Partisan life with Col. John S. Mosby. By Major John Scott ... with por-
traits and engravings on wood ... New York, Harper & brothers, 1867.

   1 p. l., [vii]–xvi p., 1 l., [19]–492 p.   front., illus., ports., fold. map, facsim.   23½ cm.
   Illustrations: Forty-three illustrations, mostly pen and ink sketches of incidents and scenes
connected with Mosby's operations.
   Maps: "Map of 'Mosby's Confederacy'."
   Inclusive dates: 1863–1865.

Written in the form of letters, this narrative was composed the year after the
war, from fresh memory aided by Mosby's military papers, documents, and the
reminiscences of various individuals. The author, a member of Mosby's Rangers,
crisscrossed the so-called "Mosby's Confederacy" (the northern Virginia counties) in every direction. There are many personal touches in the descriptions of
this country and its people.

Scribner, Benjamin Franklin, 1825–1900.   408
    How soldiers were made; or, The war as I saw it under Buell, Rosecrans,
Thomas, Grant and Sherman. By B. F. Scribner, late colonel Thirty-eighth
Indiana veteran volunteers, and brevet brigadier-general, commanding
brigade, First division, Fourteenth army corps, Army of the Cumberland.
New Albany, Ind. [Chicago, Donohue & Henneberry] 1887.

   2 p. l., iii–iv, 5–316 p.   19½ cm.
   Inclusive dates: 1861–1864.

There is little to recommend this work as a travel account beyond a straightforward style and its author's good temper as indicated in incidental comments
on the subjugated population of the Confederacy. Scribner fought southward
from Louisville in the fall and spring of 1861–1862 and helped occupy Nashville.
Apart from his retreat northward to intercept Bragg on his invasion of Kentucky in the late summer of 1862 and his participation in the Battle of Chickamauga and Sherman's subsequent campaign against Atlanta, Scribner's army
service was confined to Middle Tennessee. Soon after the battle of Kennesaw
Mountain he resigned from the army on account of ill health.

SeCheverell, John Hampton.   409
    Journal history of the Twenty-ninth Ohio veteran volunteers, 1861–1865.
Its victories and its reverses. And the campaigns and battles of Winchester,
Port Republic, Cedar Mountain, Chancellorsville, Gettysburg, Lookout
Mountain, Atlanta, the march to the sea, and the campaign of the Carolinas
in which it bore an honorable part. By J. H. SeCheverell ... Cleveland, Ohio,
By a Committee of the regiment, 1883.

   2 p. l., [9]–284 p.   front. (port.)   18½ cm.
   Illustrations: Frontispiece, "Lewis P. Buckley, Late Colonel 29th O. V. V. I."
   Inclusive dates: 1861–1865.

This annalistic and choppy account is little more than a brief narrative of military movements. The first part up to the fall of Atlanta was written by SeCheverell, although he was not with the regiment after May, 1862. The latter part from Atlanta to Washington was written (largely from his diary) by Col. Jonas Schoonover, a member of the regiment. The unit was organized at Ashtabula, Ohio, in the latter part of 1861 and early in 1862 it went by rail through Columbus, Wheeling, and Cumberland, Maryland, to the scene of fighting around Winchester, Virginia. Thereafter it fought in northern Virginia, at Sharpsburg, and at Gettysburg. After Gettysburg it boarded steamers on the Potomac for New York to help put down the draft riots there. Returning by water, it entrained on the Baltimore and Ohio Railway and proceeded by Wheeling, Columbus, Indianapolis, Louisville, and Nashville to participate in the fighting around Chattanooga after the Battle of Chickamauga and to join Sherman's march. After the "Grand Review" it went by railway to Parkersburg, West Virginia, and by steamer down the Ohio to Louisville where it was mustered out.

Shaver, Lewellyn Adolphus.   410
A history of the Sixtieth Alabama regiment, Gracie's Alabama brigade. By L. A. Shaver. Montgomery, Ala., Barrett & Brown, 1867.

111 p.   front. (port.)   20 cm.
Illustrations: Frontispiece, "Brig. Gen. A. Gracie."
Inclusive dates: 1862–1865.

Shaver began his military career at Montgomery, Alabama, in 1862 and continued to the surrender at Appomattox. He left Montgomery by rail for Chattanooga, going by way of Atlanta, and then marched into East Tennessee and on through Cumberland Gap into central Kentucky in support of Bragg's invasion of that state. Returning through Cumberland Gap he operated widely over East Tennessee, took part in the Battle of Chickamauga, went back to East Tennessee to support Longstreet's attack on Knoxville in the fall of 1863, and wintered in the neighborhood of Morristown. In the spring of 1864 he marched to Bristol and boarded a train for Lynchburg and Richmond, operated in that region and down the James as far as Drewry's Bluff, and went to Petersburg for the winter of 1864–1865, being on hand the next spring for the surrender at Appomattox. This narrative has some travelogue quality, with descriptions of routes taken and things seen.

Shaw, William H., 1833–   411
A diary as kept by Wm. H. Shaw, during the great civil war, from April, 1861 to July, 1865. No place, publisher or date.

76 p.   front. (port.)   21¾ cm.
Illustrations: Frontispiece, "William H. Shaw, 1863."
Inclusive dates: 1861–1865.

Shaw, a native of Massachusetts, joined the Third Connecticut Volunteer Infantry, Company B, and fought in the First Battle of Manassas. Returning to

Massachusetts at the expiration of his three-month enlistment, he joined the Thirty-seventh Regiment of Massachusetts Volunteers in 1862. He was at Fredericksburg, Chancellorsville, and Gettysburg, accompanied Grant's forces in the assault on Richmond and was in the vicinity when it fell, and later marched to Danville to entrain for the North. The diary was augmented for publication but is undistinguished, with few comments beyond trivialities, descriptions of army movements, and occasional glimpses of both white and black people in the Confederacy.

Sheldon, Winthrop Dudley. 412

The "Twenty-seventh". ₁Connecticut₁ A regimental history. New Haven, Morris & Benham, 1866.

144 p. front., ports. 18 cm.
Illustrations: Frontispiece, "Henry C. Merwin" ₁Signature₁; "Addison C. Taylor"; "Jedediah Chapman, Jr."
Inclusive dates: 1862–1863.

This New Haven, Connecticut, Yankee enlisted in 1862 and went by rail to Washington. After helping to man a fort protecting the city, he marched down the Potomac River and across country to participate in the Battle of Fredericksburg. After a period of idleness in winter quarters he was captured at Chancellorsville, taken to Richmond and imprisoned for a few months, paroled and sent to City Point, and forwarded by Federal authorities up Chesapeake Bay to Annapolis. That part of the regiment which was not captured, fought at Gettysburg, which battle Sheldon briefly describes. This work, written soon after the war, gives some meager descriptions of the country and the people but is tinged with considerable bitterness and contempt for the Confederates.

Shelton, W. H. 413

"A Hard Road to Travel out of Dixie," *in* Famous adventures and prison escapes of the civil war. New York, The Century co., 1893.

Inclusive dates: May, 1864–March 4, 1865.

There is evidence that the author checked his memory against the reminiscences of native Southerners involved in the escape which he described many years later. Shelton was captured in the Battle of the Wilderness in northern Virginia and was taken by an indefinite route to Lynchburg and then to Macon, Georgia. On Sherman's invasion of Georgia the prisoners at Macon were removed to Columbia where Shelton escaped. He reached the coast above Charleston but found no sign of Federal ships, gave himself up to the Confederates, and was returned to Columbia. He escaped again and wandered through the mountains of western North Carolina until he was recaptured and taken to the Greenville, South Carolina, jail, to escape once more and to wander through much the same country he had traversed previously. He continued westward through North Carolina, passing across the Great Smoky Mountains to the upper Tennessee River Valley. This account is interesting for the description it gives of the life of the mountaineers, who gladly aided Federal prisoners to escape.

Sheridan, Philip Henry, 1831–1888. 414

Personal memoirs of P. H. Sheridan. New York, Charles L. Webster & company, 1888.

2 v.; I, xiv, 500; II, xii, 486 p.   front. (port.) illus., maps.   23 cm.

Illustrations: Frontispieces, "P. H. Sheridan. Brevet 2d Lieutenant 1st Regiment Infantry" ₍Signature, Steel Engraving₎ and "P. H. Sheridan Lieut General" ₍Signature, Steel Engraving₎ and fifteen other illustrations, consisting of portraits of people, facsimiles of manuscripts, and pictures of buildings.

Maps: Twenty-seven maps, most of them folding and relating principally to the Civil War. These maps are badly executed and not clear.

Inclusive dates: 1854–1870 with emphasis on 1861–1865.

Other editions: "New and Enlarged Edition": New York, D. Appleton and company, 1902.

General Sheridan's personal memoirs deal with his travels and military experiences from 1854, beginning at Fort Duncan, Texas, and including his visit to Europe during the Franco-Prussian War. After the Texas assignment he was transferred to the Pacific Coast where he remained until the latter part of 1861. His first active service in the Civil War was in Missouri at the Battle of Pea Ridge, followed by transfer to the Mississippi theater around Corinth and southward. Further movements were to Louisville, Kentucky, in the fall of 1862 for the expulsion of Bragg's army and the Battle of Perryville; southward to fight at Murfreesboro and Chickamauga; and into East Tennessee to remain for a time around Knoxville. In the spring of 1864 he was transferred to the war in the East and put at the head of the cavalry of the Army of the Potomac. Here he won his greatest renown, defeating and killing Stuart at Yellow Tavern and later ravaging the Shenandoah Valley and scattering Early's army. During the last stages of the war he was operating around Petersburg and westward and he was an important factor in bringing about the final collapse of Lee's army at Appomattox. After the war he was sent to command in Texas and Louisiana and with the coming of Military Reconstruction he was placed in charge of the Fifth Military District, embracing those two states. He was soon (1867) transferred to the Department of the Missouri and sent into the west to fight the Indians. In 1870 he went to Europe to view the Franco-Prussian War. This narrative contains many valuable comments and descriptions, covering his experiences in Texas and the West, both before and after the Civil War. His activities during that conflict give especial value to his commentaries on cavalry exploits and the territory over which he operated. It is generally free from bitterness, though Sheridan condemned the burning of Chambersburg, Pennsylvania, by the Confederates as "ruthless" and accepted his own devastation of the Shenandoah Valley as normal warfare.

Sherman, William Tecumseh, 1820–1891. 415

Memoirs of General William T. Sherman. By himself. New York, D. Appleton and company, 1875.

2 v.; I, 405; II, 409 p.   maps.   21½ cm.

Maps: "Military Map Showing the Marches of the United States Forces under Command of

Maj. Genl. W. T. Sherman, U. S. A. during the Years 1863, 1864, 1865. Compiled by Order of Maj. Genl. W. T. Sherman, U. S. A. at Head Quarters Military Division of the Mississippi under the Direction of Bvt. W. L. B. Jenney, Capt. A. D. C., U. S. A. Drawn by Capt. William Kossak, Addl. A. D. C., U. S. A. and John B. Muller, Draughtsman. St. Louis, Mo. 1865."

Inclusive dates: (1846–1865) 1861–1865.

Other editions: Three others, brought out by the original publishers, appeared in 1876, 1886, and 1889. Another is: Memoirs of Gen. W. T. Sherman, written by himself, with an appendix, bringing his life down to its closing scenes, also a personal tribute and critique of the Memoirs by Hon. James G. Blaine. Fourth, revised, corrected, and complete edition. New York, C. I. Webster & co., 1891.

This well-known work is confined to General Sherman's military career except for a few years of civil life in the 1850's. The author devotes considerable space to what may be called travel notes. Sherman's unusual character, in which frankness and impetuosity were outstanding, led him to record much that a quieter personality would have overlooked. This narrative, therefore, should not be neglected in evaluating wartime conditions in the South. The second volume, devoted entirely to his famous march, is much richer in personal reactions than the first. Sherman's travels were so varied and continuous that they cannot be segregated from the other details in his memoirs, but the routes of his main campaigns are so well known as to call for little delineation. St. Louis was a focal point in the first years of his war career, and the Mississippi Valley was the area of his larger operations. During the last year and a half of the war he was engaged in the famous march to Atlanta, to the sea at Savannah, and through the Carolinas and Virginia to Washington for the "Grand Review." This work, written a decade after the war, is temperate and trustworthy.

Shotwell, Randolph Abbott, 1844–1885. 416

The papers of Randolph Abbott Shotwell, edited by J. G. de Roulhac Hamilton, with collaboration of Rebecca Cameron. Raleigh, The North Carolina historical commission, 1929–37.

I, 2 p. l., ix–xxv, 511 p., front. (port.); II, 2 p. l., vii–x, 581 p.; III, 3 p. l., 466 p. 22½ cm. (Publications of the North Carolina historical commission.)

Illustrations: Frontispiece, "Randolph Abbott Shotwell."

Inclusive dates: 1861–1865.

Other editions: No other edition found. The third volume deals with his troubles in North Carolina relative to the Ku Klux Klan troubles, his conviction, and imprisonment in Albany, New York.

These volumes are a mixture, none too clearly labeled, of a diary which Shotwell kept during the Civil War and of reminiscences written years afterwards. Shotwell was high-strung and sensitive, with almost a martyr complex. He writes with extreme bitterness against the enemy for their treatment of the Confederacy, and particularly of himself after he was captured. Many of his descriptions of battlefields and hospitals are realistic to the extent of being morbid. Shotwell was a schoolboy in Mifflin and later in Media, Pennsylvania, in 1861. Being a native of Virginia and the son of a Presbyterian minister, he determined to follow his predestined course by making his way southward through Delaware and Maryland and across the Potomac to join the first Confederate troops he met. He took part in most of the fighting north of the James River, including Sharpsburg and Gettysburg, until his capture near Richmond in the summer of 1864. He was sent as a prisoner of war to Point Lookout first and later to Fort Delaware. Despite the extreme bitterness there is no reason to distrust the factual part of the narrative.

Simmons, Louis A.   417

The history of the 84th reg't Ill. vols. By L. A. Simmons. Macomb, Ill., Hampton brothers, 1866.

345 p., 1 l. 18½ cm.
Inclusive dates: 1862–1865.

Giving an excellent view of the country traversed, this narrative is written in good temper and contains apt descriptions of various Southern towns and other objects of interest. Simmons was appointed quartermaster of the regiment, which was organized in the fall of 1862 and arrived at Louisville in time to help drive Bragg out of Kentucky. It fought at Perryville and marched southeastward to Somerset before turning westward to Tennessee. At the end of 1862 it took part in the Battle of Murfreesboro, later marched through Manchester to Chattanooga, and fought at Chickamauga and the subsequent battle in that vicinity. Early in 1864 it proceeded southward with Sherman and after the fall of Atlanta turned northward to Chattanooga, westward through northern Alabama, and back into Tennessee in pursuit of Hood. After helping to destroy Hood's army at the gates of Nashville it returned to northern Alabama, proceeded to East Tennessee, going by train to Knoxville and northeastward to Bull's Gap. Hearing of Lee's surrender, it returned to Nashville, where it was mustered out in the summer of 1865, and returned to Illinois by way of Louisville.

Sipes, William B.,   –1905.   418

The Seventh Pennsylvania veteran volunteer cavalry; its record, reminiscences and roster; with an appendix. By William B. Sipes. [Pottsville, Pa., Miners' journal print, 1905?]

1 p. l., iv, 6, 169, [1], 60, 143 p., 3 l. pl., ports. 24 cm.
Illustrations: Forty-six illustrations, mostly portraits of soldiers.
Inclusive dates: 1861–1864

William B. Sipes organized the Seventh Pennsylvania Cavalry in 1861 at Harrisburg and remained with it until November, 1864, when he resigned. He continues the narrative, however, to the end of the war. In this account he gives some observations and comments on the country, people, and institutions of the Confederacy, but quotes much material from published works. For this reason, and because it was not written until 1906, apparently without the aid of contemporary notes, it is mediocre in value. The unit left Harrisburg late in 1861, going by rail to Pittsburgh and by steamers down the Ohio to Louisville. During the next few months it marched southward with Buell's army and participated in the capture of Nashville. Thereafter it operated widely through Middle Tennessee and into northern Georgia for the Battle of Chickamauga, was stationed for some time at Huntsville, Alabama, followed Sherman to the fall of Atlanta, and marched northward to ward off Hood in his march against Nashville. After Sipes resigned, the Seventh Pennsylvania became a part of Wilson's Raiders, who captured Selma and marched eastward to Macon, Georgia, before the war ended.

Small, Abner Ralph, 1836–1910. 419

The road to Richmond. The civil war memoirs of Major Abner R. Small of the Sixteenth Maine volunteers. Together with the diary which he kept when he was a prisoner of war. Edited by Harold Adams Small. Berkeley, Calif., University of California press, 1939.

xiv, 314 p. front. (port.) illus., map. 21½ cm.

Illustrations: Frontispiece, "Abner R. Small as Adjutant, 16th Maine Volunteers"; "The Dunker Church at Antietam"; "A Field Hospital"; "Leaving Winter Quarters"; "Pontoon Bridge, Jerico Mill"; "In the Trenches at Petersburg." These are all clear contemporary photographs.

Maps: "Reference Map [Eastern Theatre of War]."

Inclusive dates: 1861–1865.

Other editions: The narrative is "based upon material ... collected in writing a regimental history of the Sixteenth Maine" regiment. (American historical review v. 45, p. 479. Jan. 1940) The Sixteenth Maine regiment in the war of the rebellion, 1861–1865, by Major A R. Small ... Portland, Me., 1886.

The Road to Richmond is a well-written account containing many observations on life and conditions in the Confederacy. Though Major Small did not record his memoirs until forty years or more after the war, they were checked against records he had made earlier and against a prison diary, which is here published. His military activities were confined to the eastern theater of war, where he fought in the principal battles from First Manassas until his capture south of the James River in July, 1864. He was imprisoned in Libby, Danville, Salisbury, and again in Libby just before his exchange in early 1865. The memoirs contain such items as his unsuccessful attempt to visit Mount Vernon, which Federal pickets guarded against all intrusion except by commissioned officers, his being quartered in Virginia mansions and his acquaintance with the owners, and the early rules of the Federal Army against pillaging.

Smith, A. P. 420

History of the Seventy-sixth regiment New York volunteers; what it endured and accomplished; containing descriptions of its twenty-five battles; its marches; its camp and bivouac scenes; with biographical sketches of fifty-three officers, and a complete record of the enlisted men. Cortland, N. Y., Printed for the publisher. Truair, Smith & Miles, Printers, 1867.

429 p. incl. port. front., pl.   21 cm.
Illustrations: Frontispiece, "Yours Truly A. P. Smith" [Signature]; "Head Quarters, 76th Regt. N. Y. S. V. Camp Doubleday"; and forty-eight pen and ink sketches of officers.
Inclusive dates: 1861–1865.

Smith and his regiment, in which he was quartermaster and later first lieutenant, participated in most of the marching and fighting in the war in the East, except that in the Shenandoah Valley. This account is the product of memory, diaries, and various official records. Naturally it is concerned mostly with military affairs, yet Smith includes impressions and observations of the scene which presented itself along the line of march. Pillaging the countryside, "Secession ladies," slaves, and other related subjects find a place in this narrative.

Smith, Adelaide W., 1831–   421

Reminiscences of an army nurse during the civil war. By Adelaide W. Smith. New York, Greaves publishing company, 1911.

263 p.   front. (port.) pl.   18½ cm.
Illustrations: Frontispiece, "Adelaide W. Smith" [Signature] and forty-three other illustrations, mostly of well-known characters as Lincoln, Lee, and Grant, or of insignificant persons.
Inclusive dates: 1864–1865.

The author of this book was a Federal Army nurse who, apart from service in hospitals in the North, administered to the wounded around City Point and Petersburg, Virginia. At Petersburg when the war ended, she saw triumphant Federal troops march through that city to take possession of Richmond. She made a few trips out into the country in the lower James River country and describes in this book what she saw. She waited forty years to write her book, and it is of little value.

Smith, George Gilbert, 1825–   422

Leaves from a soldier's diary; the personal record of Lieutenant George G. Smith, Co. C., 1st Louisiana regiment infantry volunteers (white) during the war of the rebellion; also a partial history of the operations of the army and navy in the Department of the Gulf from the capture of New Orleans to the close of the war. Putnam, Conn., G. G. Smith, 1906.

5, 151 p.   front. (port.) pl.   17 cm.
Illustrations: Frontispiece, "G. G. Smith."
Inclusive dates: 1861–1865.

This New Englander went from New Haven, Connecticut, through New York City and by boat to New Orleans. He operated up the Mississippi River around Donaldsonville, Baton Rouge, and Port Hudson before going on the Red River expedition. Returning he went up the Mississippi and Ohio rivers to Paducah and back to New Orleans, where he was mustered out. He returned to Connecticut up the Mississippi River by boat to St. Louis and from there by rail. Though this narrative purports to be a Federal soldier's diary, it has the appearance of having been recast later, if, indeed, it was ever a contemporary document, and has little value for local color or description.

Smith, James E., 1831?– 423

A famous battery and its campaigns, 1861–'64. The career of Corporal James Tanner in war and in peace. Early days in the Black Hills with some account of Capt. Jack Crawford, the poet scout. By Captain James E. Smith. Washington, W. H. Lowdermilk & company, 1892.

237 p.   front. (port.) pl., maps.   18½ cm.
Illustrations: Frontispiece, "James E. Smith"; "Edward Kearney"; "J. Harvey Hanford"; "James Tanner"; "J. W. Crawford."
Maps: "Plan of the Battle of Williamsburg. From Sketch Made by the Author at the Time"; "Plan of the Battle of Gettysburg. From Sketch Made by the Author at the Time."
Inclusive dates: 1861–Dec. 23, 1863.

Smith enlisted in New York for three months' service in the early days of the war, sailed for Annapolis, passed through Washington and across the Potomac, and encamped at the foot of Arlington Heights. He marched as far as Cub Run but did not participate in the Battle of Manassas. When his term of enlistment expired he returned to New York and re-enlisted, became captain of the Fourth New York Independent Battery, and returned to Washington. First stationed down the Potomac at Budd's Ferry on the Maryland side, he marched with McClellan from Yorktown for the Peninsula campaign and returned to Washington too late for Second Manassas, but fought later in Burnside's Fredericksburg campaign. In the summer of 1863 the battery marched northward into Pennsylvania to fight at Gettysburg and was mustered out in December. This account is of no great value, as it was written more than a quarter century after the events and there is no evidence of contemporary sources except for some quotations from official reports. Smith was mostly concerned with army matters, but occasionally mentions the countryside.

Smith, Mrs. Susan E. D. 424

The soldier's friend; being a thrilling narrative of Grandma Smith's four years' experience and observation, as matron, in the hospitals of the south, during the late disastrous conflict in America. Revised by Rev. John Little … Memphis, Tenn., Printed by the Bulletin publishing company, 1867.

300 p.   front. (port.)   18 cm.
Illustrations: Frontispiece, "Grandma Smith."
Inclusive dates: April, 1861–August, 1865.

By design this book was published to show the horrors of war and to discourage any repetition. Nevertheless, it is more concerned with traveling from one hospital to another, with discussing the general progress of the war, and with recording a great many conversations with patients in hospitals, townspeople, and acquaintances. Susan Smith was a native of Tennessee, and at the outbreak of the war she immediately interested herself in the welfare of the Confederate soldiers and found that she could make her greatest contribution in hospital service. She spent more time in the Cuthbert, Georgia, hospital than in any other—a period of two years. She also served in hospitals at Chattanooga, Tunnell Hill, Griffin, and Covington, Georgia, and Columbus, Mississippi.

Smith, William B. 425

On wheels and how I came there. A real story for real boys and girls, giving the personal experiences and observations of a fifteen-year-old yankee boy as soldier and prisoner in the American civil war. By Private W. B. Smith. Edited by Rev. Joseph Gatch Bonnell. New York, Hunt & Eaton, 1893.

338 p. front. (port.) pl. 18¼ cm.
Illustrations: Frontispiece, "The Author: 'On Wheels' "; "Andersonville Prison."
Inclusive dates: 1864–1865.
Parallel accounts: A book that closely parallels Private Smith's travels as a prisoner of war is: Lessel Long, Twelve months in Andersonville ... *(q.v.).*

Here is a thread of fact, embellished after more than twenty-five years with details of adventure and experience designed to interest boys and girls; yet it need not be discounted except for the hazards of memory. In early 1864, when Smith was fifteen years old, he joined the Fourteenth Illinois Volunteer Infantry, Company K, and went down the Mississippi from Cairo to Vicksburg to participate in Sherman's raid through Jackson and Meridian. By the time he had returned up river to Cairo and up the Ohio and Tennessee rivers to northern Alabama, Sherman was on his way to Atlanta and Private Smith operated behind the Federal lines in northern Georgia until he was captured. He was marched southward to West Point, Georgia, on to Columbus, taken by train to Fort Valley, Georgia, and southwestward to Andersonville. When the Confederates transferred prisoners eastward before Sherman's approach, Private Smith was taken to Millen and Blackshear in southern Georgia, then to Thomasville and northward to Albany, and entrained for Andersonville. After Lee's surrender he was returned to Thomasville and sent into Florida to the railroad running from Tallahassee towards Jacksonville. At Baldwin he and his comrades were turned loose to make their way into the Federal lines at Jacksonville. Thence he was taken to Annapolis by sea, to St. Louis by rail, and finally sent to an Illinois camp to be mustered out. With due allowance for the nature of this book and the age of its author, it gives some interesting glimpses into a considerable part of the Confederacy.

Spangler, Edward Webster, 1846– 426

My little war experience. With historical sketches and memorabilia. By Edward W. Spangler. York, Pa., York daily publishing company, 1904.

xv, 202, [3] p. front., plates, incl. illus., ports. facsims. 22½ cm.
Illustrations: Frontispiece, "[Edward W. Spangler] 1863–1903" and sixty-three illustra-

tions of people, battle scenes, and landscapes. Also two facsimiles of York, Pa. Revolutionary War Troop roster and Muster Roll of York Revolutionary Troops.
Inclusive dates: 1862–1863.

As the author admits, this book is a sort of "medley or hodge-podge"; yet as Private Spangler, a member of the 130th Regiment of Pennsylvania Volunteers, participated in the marches and battles associated with Sharpsburg, Fredericksburg, and Chancellorsville, he had occasion on his travels to offer some observations and comments. He was more interested in strictly military matters and particularly stresses the terrible carnage at Sharpsburg and Fredericksburg. He believed the turning point in the war was not Gettysburg but the death of Stonewall Jackson, whom he considered a great general.

Sprague, Homer Baxter, 1829–1918. 427

Lights and shadows in Confederate prisons. A personal experience, 1864–5. New York, G. P. Putnam's sons, 1915.

x, 163 p. front. 18½ cm.
Illustrations: Frontispiece, "Portraits of Fellow Officers in Prison."
Inclusive dates: 1864–1865.
The author also wrote: History of the 13th regiment of Connecticut volunteers, during the great rebellion. By H. B. Sprague, Hartford, 1867. v, 353 p.

Sprague gives more than usual attention to the journeying of captives between prisons. He was an officer in the Thirteenth Connecticut Volunteers, and was captured at the Battle of Winchester in September, 1864. He was marched a great part of the distance to Richmond before he was finally put aboard a train for the remainder of the journey. After a short stay in Libby Prison he was sent to the Salisbury Prison by rail through Danville and Greensboro, but was returned to spend some time at Danville before going to Richmond, where he was turned over to the Federal authorities down the James River in February, 1865. Sprague was a graduate of Yale and after the war he taught in various institutions of higher learning, including Cornell, and from 1887 to 1891 he was president of the University of North Dakota. This work is written in good temper and is re-enforced factually by public documents, secondary accounts, and particularly by the author's diary.

Stafford, David W. 428

In defense of the flag. A true war story (Illustrated). A pen picture of scenes and incidents during the great rebellion.—Thrilling experiences during escape from southern prisons, etc. By David W. Stafford. Kalamazoo, Mich., Ihling Bros. & Everard, 1904.

88 p. front. (port.) illus. 22 cm.
Illustrations: Frontispiece, "David W. Stafford"; "Henry Lederer" and four pen-and-ink sketches of incidents mentioned in the narrative.
Inclusive dates: 1864–1865.

This lugubrious story of a Pennsylvania soldier who was captured south of Petersburg in the autumn of 1864 is peppered with self-pity. The narrative is confused as to time, distance, and geography, and is therefore practically worthless except as a sample of senile reminiscence. He was taken to Macon, Georgia, where he was imprisoned "about two weeks" (in a later statement "about three weeks"), before being taken to Andersonville "about ten miles distant"—in reality nearer seventy-five miles. He was then taken to Charleston and on to Florence Prison, where he escaped. Most of the narrative is made up of his experiences while traveling from Florence to Knoxville. He was so vague in his ideas of where he was at any given time that it is impossible to trace his wanderings.

Stearns, Amos E.   429

Narrative of Amos E. Stearns, member of Co. A, 25th regt., Mass. vols., a prisoner at Andersonville. With an introduction by S. H. Putnam. Worcester, Mass., Franklin P. Rice, 1887.

> 57 p. front. (port.) 23½ cm.
> *Illustrations:* Frontispiece, "A. E. Stearns" [Signature].
> *Inclusive dates:* 1864–1865.

Stearns was captured in 1864 near Richmond and sent to Libby Prison aboard a James River steamer. After a short stay he was sent by train to Andersonville, by way of Danville, Greensboro, Charlotte, Columbia, Augusta, and Macon. From Andersonville he was transferred to Charleston and then to Florence. In early 1865, on the approach of Sherman, he was sent to Wilmington and on to Goldsboro, moved around in this region a number of times, finally paroled at Goldsboro, and sent into the Federal lines near Wilmington. Thence he went by boat to Annapolis, and eventually to his home in Worcester, Massachusetts. In his brief narrative Stearns devotes considerable space to his traveling experiences between prisons.

Stevens, Charles Augustus, 1835–   430

Berdan's United States sharpshooters in the Army of the Potomac, 1861–1865. By Capt. C. A. Stevens ... St. Paul, Minn. [The Price-McGill company] 1892.

> xxiii, 555 p. front., plates, ports. 23 cm.
> *Illustrations:* Forty-eight illustrations, principally portraits of soldiers.
> *Inclusive dates:* 1861–1865.

This work is largely a military record, with some descriptions of people and countryside scenes. The route taken is not always clearly indicated. Stevens joined the Sharpshooters, a New York unit, and rose to the rank of first lieutenant. After the war he settled in Minnesota and became a newspaper editor. His unit fought in all the principal campaigns of the Army of the Potomac including the Peninsula, Second Bull Run, Sharpsburg, Fredericksburg, Chancellorsville, Gettysburg, and in Grant's campaign against Richmond.

Stevens, George T. 431

Three years in the Sixth corps. A concise narrative of events in the Army of the Potomac, from 1861 to the close of the rebellion, April, 1865. By George T. Stevens. New York, D. Van Nostrand, 1867.

xii, 441 p. front. (port.) ports., map. 21¼ cm.
Illustrations: Frontispiece, "John Sedgwick [Signature] Maj.-Gen. John Sedgwick"; and fourteen other portraits and well-executed drawings by the author and Captain J. Hope.
Maps: "Charge of the Sixth Corps, Which Broke the Rebel Line, April 2, 1865."
Inclusive dates: 1861–1865.
Other editions: First edition: Albany, N. Y., S. R. Gray, 1866.

A well-written book which includes, in addition to the military narrative, highly observant comments on that part of the country and the people of the Confederacy visited by the author. For instance he writes a great deal about the Negroes who fled northward into the Union lines, the devastated villages and countryside of northern Virginia, the embittered Southern women, old mansions, one of which was John Tyler's, and other topics such as Sulphur Springs near Warrenton. It thus has many characteristics of a travel book and is reliable because it was written largely from notes taken during the war and is not marred by unseemly bitterness. Stevens started out in the Seventy-seventh Regiment of New York Volunteers, but when this unit became a part of the Sixth Corps, he broadens the account. He fought through the principal campaigns in the East from the Peninsula to Appomattox, and was among the troops which Grant sent in the summer of 1864 to protect Washington against Early's raid into Maryland. Afterwards he participated in the Shenandoah Valley activities which laid waste much of that region.

Stevenson, Benjamin Franklin 432

Letters from the army. By B. F. Stevenson, surgeon to the Twenty-second Kentucky infantry. Cincinnati, W. E. Dibble & co., 1884.

vi, [7]–311 p. 19 cm.
Inclusive dates: 1862–1864.
Other editions: Another edition: Letters from the army, 1862–1864. Cincinnati, Robert Clarke & co., 1886.

These letters relate to the Mississippi and Ohio valleys, and more particularly to Kentucky, West Virginia, Mississippi, and Louisiana. Stevenson, a Kentuckian, began his army service in the Big Sandy Valley around Louisa and Pikeville, moved down the Ohio to Louisville and across to Lexington and southeast to the Cumberland Gap region, and up the Ohio and Kanawha valley to Charleston, West Virginia. He spent the latter part of the war around Vicksburg and Jackson, and in Louisiana around Brashear City, New Iberia, Donaldsonville, Opelousas, Plaquemine, and Baton Rouge. Besides descriptions of hospital service and army movements, there are frequent comments on scenery and inhabitants. He was greatly attracted to Louisiana, believing that its fertile lands could support the whole Confederacy. Though a strong Unionist, he showed no unreasonable bitterness against the enemy.

Stevenson, Thomas M. 433

History of the 78th regiment O.V.V.I., from its "muster-in" to its "muster-out"; comprising its organization, marches, campaigns, battles and skirmishes. By Rev. T. M. Stevenson. Zanesville, O., Hugh Dunne, 1865.

vii, ₍9₎–349, ₍2₎ p. 21½ cm.
Inclusive dates: 1862–1865.

Though choppy in organization, this work carries a narrative of travel through the Confederacy, written in the style of a peace-time traveler. The author, chaplain of the regiment, was much interested in the towns and cities he visited, and in most instances gave sketches of their physical appearance and of their inhabitants. He was frank in describing the ravages of war, though most of the destruction he saw was by his own regiment. Interspersed through the narrative are letters which Stevenson wrote home as well as some written to newspapers by his comrades. The regiment was formed in early 1862 at Zanesville, Ohio, went by rail to Cincinnati, by steamer to Paducah, and up the Tennessee River to a point near Pittsburg Landing, arriving in time to take part in the battle. Thereafter it fought through western Tennessee and into Mississippi to Oxford, returned to Memphis, took steamers down the Mississippi to Lake Providence, continued its activities around Vicksburg on both sides of the river, and participated in the siege and capture of that city and in the devastating march eastward to the frontiers of Alabama. After a visit home on furlough, the regiment went down the Ohio and up the Tennessee again and marched across northern Alabama to Rome, Georgia, where it joined Sherman in his drive against Atlanta, followed him to Savannah, shipped by boat to Beaufort, South Carolina, and rejoined the main forces at Columbia. It was present at the burning of that city, continued into North Carolina and, after the surrender of Johnston, on to Washington and the "Grand Review." Going by rail to Parkersburg, West Virginia, and on down the Ohio to Louisville the 78th was mustered out in the summer of 1865.

₍Stevenson, William G.₎ 434

Thirteen months in the Rebel army: being a narrative of personal adventures in the infantry, ordnance, cavalry, courier, and hospital services; with an exhibition of the power, purposes, earnestness, military despotism, and demoralization of the south. By an impressed New Yorker. New York, A. S. Barnes & Burr, 1862.

232 p. front. 17 cm.
Illustrations: Frontispiece, "Council of War before the Battle of Pittsburg Landing."

Inclusive dates: 1861–1862.

Other editions: Another edition in French: Treize mois dans l'armée des rebelles; aventures d'un engagé volontaire malgré lui, par William G. Stevenson. Genéve, Imprimierie Ramboz et Schuchardt, 1863.

Stevenson's highly personal narrative is in the nature of both a tall tale and propaganda. The author was in Arkansas in the lumber business when the war broke out. Being regarded as uncertain on the slavery issue and suspected of being a Northerner he was brought before a Vigilantes Committee, and though acquitted he fled to Helena and on to Memphis, where he was forced to join the Confederate army. He was sent up the Mississippi to Columbus, Kentucky, and from there he operated eastward and southward, ultimately arriving at Bowling Green before he became a part of Albert Sidney Johnston's retreating forces at Shiloh. After that battle Stevenson was sent to Corinth to help in the hospital service and soon found himself at Mobile in charge of a contingent of wounded Confederates. He was then sent up the Alabama River to Selma to engage in hospital service there. After an unsuccessful trip to Richmond (by a route not indicated) to collect back pay he returned to Selma, and a little later set out for Chattanooga, where he obtained a horse and rode through the country, with many personal adventures, to the Union lines at Murfreesboro. He then went on to Nashville, Louisville, and back to New York. Stevenson found the South determined in the most extreme degree to fight on for its independence—he could discover no Unionism in the Confederacy. He probably overstated this point in order to stir up the North to greater effort in the war. With due allowance for Stevenson's character and purposes, his observations may be accepted as suggestive of the truth.

Stewart, Alexander Morrison. 435

Camp, march and battle-field; or, Three years and a half with the Army of the Potomac. By Rev. A. M. Stewart. Philadelphia, Jas. B. Rodgers, 1865.

x, 413 p.   front. (port.)   19 cm.
Illustrations: Frontispiece, "A. M. Stewart" ₍Signature₎.
Inclusive dates: 1861–1864.

This collection of contemporary war sketches appeared originally in an undesignated newspaper (probably the Pittsburgh *Chronicle*). Stewart was chaplain in the Thirteenth Regiment Pennsylvania Volunteers, later reorganized into the One Hundred and Second. His activities were confined to the war in the East and principally to northern Virginia, on the Peninsula with McClellan, and around Richmond and Petersburg in 1864. He was much interested in the country, the natives, the historical spots, and the old mansions. He gave particular attention to Charlestown with its John Brown associations, Warrenton, Aquia Creek, Williamsburg, Yorktown, and some communities in Maryland. He noted such items as soldiers chipping away completely the monument marking the spot where Cornwallis surrendered; the great increase of rabbits and small game in the devastated country; and the fierce patriotism of Southern women, who, he averred, would not permit a man able to bear arms to remain in their vicinity.

Stillwell, Leander 436

The story of a common soldier of army life in the civil war, 1861–1865. By Leander Stillwell. ⌈Erie, Kansas?⌉ Franklin Hudson publishing co., 1920.

278 p.   front. (port.) pl.   19½ cm.
Illustrations: Frontispiece, "Judge Leander Stillwell. December, 1909"; and eleven photographs of inconspicuous people, mostly Illinois troops.
Inclusive dates: 1862–1865.
Other editions: The copy examined is labeled "Second Edition." The first was: Erie, Kan., Press of the Erie record, 1917.

Writing fifty years after the Civil War, the author used many letters he had written home from the army and also a diary he kept in the latter part of the struggle, both of which strengthen the reliability of his account. Stillwell, born in Illinois, joined troops from his state and went to St. Louis early in 1862 for a short time before going to the theater of war in southwestern Tennessee. He went by boat down the Mississippi and up the Ohio and Tennessee rivers to Pittsburgh Landing where he took part in the near-by battle of Shiloh. Afterwards he served at Corinth and around Jackson and Bolivar, Tennessee, went down the Mississippi by way of Memphis, and participated in the campaign against Vicksburg in 1863. Soon he was sent up river to Helena, only to be returned down stream to the mouth of White River and then to Duvall's Bluff. He marched overland to Little Rock where he spent some months engaging in short expeditions to surrounding points. His last service was around Nashville, Tennessee, going there by steamer up the Cumberland River. The account is largely personal, with few comments or generalizations on conditions in the Confederacy. Yet Stillwell was good at straggling and foraging, and these activities brought him in close touch with the natives. He gives numerous accounts of such experiences.

Stubbs, Charles H., *ed.* 437

Life in southern prisons; from the diary of Corporal Charles Smedley, of Company G, 90th regiment Penn's volunteers, commencing a few days before the "Battle of the Wilderness," in which he was taken prisoner, in the evening of fifth month fifth, 1864: Also, a short description of the march to the battle of Gettysburg, together with a biographical sketch of the author. Fulton, Pa. The Ladies' and gentlemen's Fulton aid society, 1865.

60 p.   front. (port.)   19 cm.
Illustrations: Frontispiece, "Your Friend Chas. Smedley" ⌈Signature⌉.
Inclusive dates: 1864.

This straightforward account in diary form was written by a Pennsylvania Quaker, who was captured at the Battle of the Wilderness in 1864. He was taken by rail for short stays at Lynchburg and Danville and as far as the new railroad was completed toward Greensboro, North Carolina. After walking across a gap of a few miles he entrained again for the south, passing through Greensboro,

Charlotte, Columbia, Augusta, and Macon to Andersonville. Here he spent a few months and then continued to the Florence prison where he died in November, 1864. The narrative is particularly valuable for the description it gives of the journeys between prisons.

Stuber, Johann.   438

Mein tagebuch uber die erlebnisse im revolutions-kriege von 1861 bis 1865. By Johann von Stuber. Cincinnati, Druck von S. Rosenthal & co., 1896.

206 p.   23½ cm.
Inclusive dates: 1861–1865.

Stuber was a member of an Ohio unit in the Federal Army which, having gone through training at Camp Chase in Columbus, embarked at Cincinnati down the Ohio and up the Tennessee to participate in the engagements against Forts Henry and Donelson. Thereafter he fought in the battles of Shiloh, Corinth, Vicksburg, and in the surrounding territory, and at Fort Morgan, Alabama. This account is notable as a German's viewpoint, though it is mostly about military and naval affairs.

Surby, Richard W., 1830–   439

Grierson raids, and Hatch's sixty-four days march, with biographical sketches, and the life and adventures of Chickasaw, the scout. By R. W. Surby. Chicago, Rounds and James, 1865.

396 p.   ports., illus.   18½ cm.
Illustrations: "Brevt Maj. Genl. B. H. Grierson"; "Edward Prince, Col. 7th Reg. Ill. Vol. Cav."; "Federal Cavalry on a Foraging Expedition"; "Brevt. Maj. Genl. Edward Hatch"; "Brevt. Brig. Genl. Datus E. Coon"; "2nd Brigade 5th Cav. Div. Charging Rebel Works at Nashville Dec. 15th 1864"; "Charge of 2nd Brigade 5th Cav. Div. on Rebel Forts at Nashville, 1864"; "L. H. Naron or Chickasaw the Scout"; "This is the Spot and this is the Tree."
Inclusive dates: 1863–1864.

Other editions: Another edition (enlarged): Two great raids. Col. Grierson's successful swoop through Mississippi. Morgan's disastrous raid through Indiana and Ohio. Vivid narratives of both these great operations, with extracts from official records. John Morgan's escape, last raid and death. Washington, The National tribune, 1897.

Surby was born in Canada, a son of a British soldier, but at the outbreak of the Civil War he was in Illinois, where he immediately enlisted in the United States Army. In April, 1862, he joined the Grierson raiders on their march from La Grange, Tennessee, through the heart of Mississippi to Baton Rouge, and saw further service with them around Port Hudson, near which he was captured. He was sent by slow stages to Libby Prison in Richmond, traveling by railway except where the track had been torn up or where water connections were necessary as from Selma, Alabama, to Montgomery. He went by way of Jackson, Meridian, Selma, Montgomery, West Point (Georgia), Atlanta, Augusta, Columbia, Charlotte, Raleigh, Weldon (North Carolina), and Petersburg. He remained in Richmond only a short time before being taken to City Point and exchanged, to go up Chesapeake Bay to Annapolis, to Baltimore, by railway through Pittsburgh and Columbus to St. Louis, and by river to Memphis. He had also served with a force sent from Memphis in the fall of 1864 to intercept Hood on his march against Nashville. The work is decidedly a travel book, based in part on the author's war diary. On the Grierson raid he noticed plantations and their inhabitants, and on the trip to Libby Prison he was specific in describing railway accomodations and the route traveled.

Swiggett, S. A., 1834–   440

The bright side of prison life. Experiences, in prison and out, of an involuntary sojourner in rebeldom. By Captain S. A. Swiggett. Baltimore, Fleet, McGinley & co., 1897.

254 p.   front. (port.) ports.   19 cm.
Illustrations: Frontispiece, "Capt. S. A. Swiggett"; "Gen. F. M. Drake"; "Lieutenant Walter S. Johnson"; "Adjutant S. K. Mahon"; "Capt. J. B. Gedney"; "Capt. Thomas M. Fee"; "Capt. Charles Burnbaum"; "Capt. J. P. Rummel"; "Capt. B. F. Miller"; "Sergeant E. B. Rocket."
Inclusive dates: 1862–1865.

Thirty years after the war Captain Swiggett wrote calmly and with some humor of his incarceration at Camp Ford, near Tyler, Texas, and of incidents in his two attempts to escape. He found prison life no worse than the lot of many people in ordinary life. Swiggett was born in Maryland and moved to Iowa about twenty years later. In 1862 he joined the United States army at Keokuk, proceeded to St. Louis, and floated down the Mississippi to Helena, Arkansas, before marching to Camden in the southwestern part of that state. On an expedition from that point he was captured and taken to Camp Ford. There he remained until the end of the war, with the exception of two escape attempts, one of which was foiled before he was able to get out of Texas, and the other coming to grief in Arkansas. Swiggett gives a close-up view not only of life in prison but of the country over which he traveled as soldier, prisoner, and fugitive. Barring reconstructed conversations and minor imaginary incidents, this narrative may be accepted at face value.

Tafel, Gustav.   441

"Die neuner." Eine schilderung der Kriegsjahre des 9ten regiments Ohio vol. infanterie vom 17, April, 1861 bis 7, Juni, 1864. Mit einer Einleitung von Oberst Gustav Tafel. Cincinnati, S. Rosenthal & co., 1897.

v–ix, 11–290 p., 1 l.   front., illus., ports.   19½ cm.
Illustrations: Frontispiece, "General W. S. Rosecrans, Oberst Gustav Kammerling, Oberst Robt. L. McCook, General August Willich, General Geo. H. Thomas"; "Camp Harrison"; Graves at Mill Springs, Ky., "Sergeant-Major Raimund Herrmann"; Dr. Beatty's House, New Market, Ala.; and six other illustrations of men, monuments, and scenes.
Inclusive dates: 1861–1864.

The Ninth Ohio Infantry Volunteers was composed entirely of Germans. It was organized in Cincinnati and in 1861. Soon after completion of training, it went to the area of fighting in western Virginia (West Virginia), participating in the Battle of Rich Mountain and in other engagements. It steamed down the Kanawha and Ohio rivers to Louisville and into Kentucky to Lebanon before returning to Louisville to move on and fight at Shiloh and Corinth. It moved eastward into northern Alabama and hurriedly marched northward through Tennessee and Kentucky in the summer of 1862 to intercept Bragg's attempt to take Louisville. It fought at Perryville, marched back into Tennessee, took part in the operations in Middle Tennessee, and marched to Chickamauga where it lost over half of its strength. After the battles around Chattanooga in the fall of 1863 it went into winter quarters and the next spring followed Sherman on his march to Atlanta, reaching the Etowah River when the term of its enlistment expired. Tafel, a lieutenant in the regiment, was born in Munich, Germany, had been city editor of the Cincinnati *Volksblatt,* and after the war served in the Ohio Legislature.

Tarrant, Eastham. 442

The wild riders of the First Kentucky cavalry. A history of the regiment in the great war of the rebellion, 1861–1865, telling of its origin and organization; a description of the material of which it was composed; its rapid and severe marches, hard service, and fierce conflicts on many a bloody field. Pathetic scenes, amusing incidents, and thrilling episodes. A regimental roster. Prison life, adventures and escapes. By Sergeant E. Tarrant ... Published by a committee of the regiment. ₁Louisville, Press of R. H. Carothers, c.1894.₁

x, 503 p.   front., port.   21 cm.
Illustrations: Nineteen pen-and-ink sketches of officers and men.
Inclusive dates: 1861–1864.

A combination of the author's reminiscences and personal memoranda from other sources, tempered by a lapse of thirty years and mature judgment, this work contains many comments on men, events, and territories in wartime. The regiment was a Union aggregation from the divided state of Kentucky and most of its operations were in that region, but it reached Chattanooga and East Tennessee and penetrated Georgia as far south as Macon. It is conglomerate as travel literature but contains definite indications of a traveler's impressions of strange territory.

Taylor, Benjamin Franklin, 1819–1887. 443

Mission ridge and Lookout mountain, with pictures of life in camp and field. By Benj. F. Taylor. New York, D. Appleton & co., 1872.

vi, (7)–272 p.   20½ cm.
Inclusive dates: 1863–1865.
Other editions: Pictures of Life in Camp and Field. Chicago, S. C. Griggs & co., 1875.

This author, who later became a well-known poet, journalist, and lecturer, was a correspondent for the *Chicago Evening Journal* during the last two years of the war. Although his narrative is episodical rather than a continuous travelogue, he was with the Army of the Cumberland for a time and later observed conditions around Alexandria, Virginia, and in Washington. His descriptions of the Tennessee landscape and the desolation of war there, of towns such as Chattanooga, Nashville, and Stevenson, Alabama, and of life as he saw it, are written with poetic sensitivity and matter-of-fact realism. It is an unusual narrative, which first appeared as letters to the newspaper he represented.

Taylor, Mrs. Susie King, 1848– 444

Reminiscences of my life in camp with the 33d United States colored troops late 1st S. C. volunteers. By Susie King Taylor. Boston, Published by the author, 1902.

xiv, 82 p. front. (port.) ports. 18¾ cm.
Illustrations: Frontispiece, "Susie King Taylor" ₍Signature₎; "Capt. A. W. Heasley, Capt. Walker, Capt. W. W. Sampson, Capt. Charles E. Parker"; "Thomas Wentworth Higginson"; "Major H. A. Whitney, Lieut. J. B. West, Henry Batchlott"; "Lieut. John A. Trowbridge, Lieut. Eli C. Merriam, Lieut. James M. Thompson, Lieut. Jerome T. Furman"; "Capt. L. W. Metcalf, Capt. Miron W. Saxton, Capt. A. W. Jackson, Corporal Peter Waggall"; "C. T. Trowbridge"; "My Schoolhouse in Savannah."
Inclusive dates: 1862–1865.

Susie King Taylor, a Negress, born in Liberty County, Georgia, joined the unit for hospital service in 1862. She was first stationed on St. Simons Island, off the coast of Georgia, but was soon transferred to the coast of South Carolina and stationed at various times at Hilton Head and Beaufort, Morris Island, and Folly Island. The account is somewhat vague about the order in which trips were made, and it gives only slight insight into conditions in that part of the South.

Tharin, Robert Seymour Symmes, 1830– 445

Arbitrary arrests in the South; or, Scenes from the experience of an Alabama Unionist. By R. S. Tharin ... New York, John Bradburn, 1863.

245 p. 17½ cm.
Inclusive dates: 1861.

A highly emotional account of Tharin's experiences in Alabama in connection with his arrest and trial by a Vigilantes Committee and his subsequent escape to the North. Much of it must be discounted as the product of a highly-wrought imagination. Tharin was born in Charleston, South Carolina, and was educated at the College of Charleston. He migrated to Alabama to engage in teaching, but soon turned to the law, and seems to have had for a short time a legal partnership with William L. Yancey. Being unjustly suspected of Abolition and Union sentiments Tharin was tried and sentenced to the lash by a committee in Collirene, a small settlement in Lowndes County, and advised to leave the community immediately. He went by stage to Montgomery and by train to Chattanooga, presumably going on to Louisville by train and probably by boat to Cincinnati. This book gives an insight into the excitement that swept the South on the advent of the secession movement.

Thatcher, Marshall P. 446

A hundred battles in the West, St. Louis to Atlanta, 1861–65. The Second Michigan cavalry, with the armies of the Mississippi, Ohio, Kentucky and Cumberland, under Generals Halleck, Sherman, Pope, Rosecrans, Thomas and others; with mention of a few of the famous regiments and brigades of the West. By Captain Marshall P. Thatcher ... Detroit, Published by the author, L. F. Kilroy, printer. 1884.

xiv, ₍15₎–416, 15, ₍63₎ p. incl. front., illus., port., maps, pl., port. 21½ cm.
Illustrations: Twenty portraits of soldiers and landscapes.
Maps: "New Madrid"; "Booneville ₍Miss.₎"; "Perryville"; "Chicamauga"; "Dandridge"; "Franklin"; "Nashville."
Inclusive dates: 1861–1865.

More observant than the average soldier who wrote about the war, Marshall P. Thatcher included more travel minutiae about landscapes, especially mountain scenery, and people seen on the way. Constructed largely on the author's journal, and checked by other documents, this temperate narrative may be accepted as faithful contemporary observation. Thatcher enlisted in Michigan, went from Grand Rapids to Detroit and thence to St. Louis, where his military service actually began. He was sent down the Mississippi River to New Madrid and Shiloh, passing up the Mississippi, Ohio, and Tennessee rivers. After subsequent operations in northern Mississippi he went northward in 1862 to intercept Bragg's invasion of Kentucky, went to Columbus, Kentucky, and boarded a steamer for Cincinnati. Returning to Louisville, he fought through the Battle of Perryville and followed the retreating Confederates almost to Cumberland Gap. Before the end of the year he raided through eastern Kentucky into East Tennessee and on into southwestern Virginia, and returned to Louisville and Nashville to operate in Middle Tennessee for some time before continuing into East Tennessee again. He took part in Sherman's march on Atlanta, followed Hood into Middle Tennessee for the Battle of Franklin, returned to northern Mississippi, and was following Wilson in his raid on Selma and Macon, when the war ended.

Tilney, Robert 447

My life in the army. Three years and a half with the Fifth army corps, Army of the Potomac, 1862–1865. By Robert Tilney. Philadelphia, Ferris & Leach, 1912.

247 p. front. (port.) 20½ cm.
Illustrations: Frontispiece, "Robert Tilney" ₍Signature₎.
Inclusive dates: 1862–1865.

Tilney was an Englishman who landed in New York in November, 1861, and joined the Federal Army early in 1862. He served first in the Twelfth New York Volunteers and from July, 1864, to the end of the war was chief clerk in the office of the assistant adjutant general at the Fifth Corps Headquarters. He was in the Peninsula campaign, and in the operations culminating at Fredericksburg, Chancellorsville, and Gettysburg. There is little value in that portion of the book containing experiences recalled by a dimming memory forty-five years later. Beginning with March, 1864, when he was preparing for Grant's campaign against Richmond, and continuing to the end of the war, Tilney had a diary and many letters which he had written from the field, and he wisely reproduces that material here. This portion has considerable merit as a description of the country and the pillaging, including *literary* raids which consisted in robbing the libraries of Virginia mansions, a practice he deplored. He gives a good description of the raid against the Weldon Railroad in December, 1864; he also notes that by summer, 1864, considerable numbers of Confederate troops were deserting to the Federal lines.

Todd, William, 1839/40– 448

The Seventy-ninth Highlanders New York volunteers in the war of rebellion, 1861–1865. By William Todd ... Albany, Press of Brandow, Barton & co., 1886.

xv, 513 p. incl. front., illus., pl., maps.   24 cm.

Illustrations: Frontispiece, "Fort Sanders"; "Highlanders at Bull Run.—Death of Colonel Cameron"; "Highlanders at Tower Battery"; " 'Want to go in for the Union' "; "Foraging"; "Charge of the Highlanders at Spottsylvania." All of these are rough pen-and-ink sketches.

Maps: Twenty clearly drawn maps of battles and campaigns in Virginia, South Carolina, Kentucky, Tennessee, and Mississippi.

Inclusive dates: 1861–[1864]–1865.

Written twenty years after the war from a diary, personal letters, and historical works and documents, this narrative has a personal touch which gives it a marked travel flavor. Indeed, Todd and his regiment traveled much more extensively than most units. Its first services were around Washington before the First Battle of Manassas, after which it was sent to Annapolis and embarked for Port Royal. It participated in the capture of Beaufort and the occupation of that region, made a short expedition up the coast to James Island near Charleston, took part in the battle at Secessionville, and returned to Virginia in time to fight at Second Manassas, followed by service in the battles of Sharpsburg and Fredericksburg. In the spring of 1863 it was sent westward by rail through Baltimore to Parkersburg, West Virginia, by steamer to Louisville, and on foot into the interior of Kentucky as far as Jamestown near the Cumberland River, before it was ordered to Vicksburg, reached by rail and boat from Louisville. As part of its activities around Vicksburg, it marched on Jackson and helped to sack that place. Ordered up river to Cincinnati, it went by rail to Lexington and Nicholasville and began a march overland through Cumberland Gap to Knoxville. After campaigning for some time in East Tennessee it returned across the mountains to Lexington and by rail through Cincinnati, Columbus, and Pittsburgh to Baltimore and Washington. In the spring of 1864 it followed Grant on his Richmond campaign as far as Spottsylvania Courthouse, where most of the regiment was mustered out. Todd gives a due amount of attention to conditions in the Confederacy as he sensed them, with special notice of customs, such as snuffdipping, loyalty or disaffection among the inhabitants, and foraging. He mentions such simple things as the great liking of soldiers on the march for blackberries and honey.

Toombs, Samuel 449

Reminiscences of the war, comprising a detailed account of the experiences of the Thirteenth regiment New Jersey volunteers in camp, on the march, and in battle. With the personal recollections of the author. By Samuel Toombs. Orange, N. J., Printed at the Journal office, 1878.

2 p. l., ₍4₎, 232, 47 p.   16¾ cm.
Inclusive dates: 1862–1865.

The author worked from letters he had written home, published histories and documents, and memory mellowed but still dependable after a dozen years. Toombs gives many interesting glimpses into conditions in the Confederacy as he observed them during extensive travels. His first fighting was at Second Manassas and thereafter he participated in the Sharpsburg, Chancellorsville, and Gettysburg campaigns before being sent to the West over the Baltimore and Ohio Railroad through Harpers Ferry, to Bellaire, Ohio, through Indianapolis to Louisville, and over the Louisville and Nashville to Nashville and the vicinity of Chattanooga. After participating in the Tullahoma campaign he became part of Sherman's army and followed him through Atlanta, Savannah, the Carolinas, and Richmond to the "Grand Review" in Washington.

Torrey, Rodney Webster, 1836– 450

War diary of Rodney W. Torrey, 1862–1863. ₍No place, no publisher, 19–₎

93 p. incl. port. front.   20 cm.
Illustrations: Frontispiece, "Rodney Webster Torrey at the age of 68"; "Colonel William Francis Bartlett of the Forty-Ninth Mass. Vol. Inf."
Inclusive dates: 1862–1863.

This brief but straightforward diary, although primarily attentive to the weather, records various observations of the country through which its author passed. Torrey enlisted in the Federal Army at Pittsfield, Massachusetts, in 1862 trained near New York City, and boarded a steamer for New Orleans, going by way of Key West. All of his activities in Louisiana lay between New Orleans and Port Hudson. He was stationed longest at Baton Rouge, but spent some time in and around Donaldsonville. He returned up the Mississippi River to Cairo, Illinois, and by rail to his home in Pittsfield.

Tourgee, Albion Winegar. 451

The story of a thousand. Being a history of the service of the 105th Ohio volunteer infantry, in the war for the union from August 21, 1862 to June 6, 1865. By A. W. Tourgee. Buffalo, N. Y., S. McGerald & son, 1896.

8 p. l., 409 p., 1 l., xiv p. incl. illus., port. maps. 22 cm.
Illustrations: Seventy-seven illustrations, mostly portraits of officers and men of the regiment (including Albion W. Tourgee).
Maps: "Map of the Battle of Perryville, October 8th, 1862"; "Battle of Milton, Tenn.";
"Chattanooga and Vicinity"; "Map of the Atlanta Campaign."
Inclusive dates: 1862–1865.
Other editions: No other edition found but this material was published in the Cosmopolitan volume XVIII.

The regiment was organized in Cleveland in the summer of 1862, crossed the Ohio from Cincinnati to Covington, and proceeded to Lexington. As Bragg was moving northward to threaten Louisville, the unit was sent there by way of Frankfort. It took part in the Battle of Perryville in October, 1862, moved southward in a futile effort to capture John Morgan's raiders, continued into Middle Tennessee, and at the end of the year took part in the Battle of Murfreesboro. Remaining in that region it marched against Chattanooga in the fall of 1863 and fought in the Battle of Chickamauga and the engagements around Chattanooga. In the spring of 1864 it joined Sherman's campaign and followed him to the "Grand Review" in Washington, returning home by rail through Baltimore and Pittsburgh to Cleveland. This author, after the war, became a well-known Carpetbagger in North Carolina and the author of various novels on Reconstruction, *The Fool's Errand* being the best known. Tourgee was with the 105th Ohio Regiment, except for a short time in captivity, until he resigned in December, 1863. To that point the narrative is interesting and observant of the country, the people, and conditions among the Federal soldiers. The latter portion, dealing with the march from Chattanooga to Savannah and northward, of which Tourgee could have had no personal knowledge, is made up of military discussions and some extracts from diaries kept by Federal soldiers.

Trobriand, Philippe Régis Denis de Keredern, Compte de, 1816–1897. 452

Four years with the Army of the Potomac. By Regis de Trobriand. Translated by George K. Dauchy. Boston, Ticknor and company, 1889.

xx, 757 p. front. (port.) maps. 21 cm.
Illustrations: Frontispiece, "Yours very truly R. de Trobriand" [Signature].
Maps: "Williamsburg"; "Fredericksburg"; "Chancellorsville, May 3–4–5, 1863"; "Gettysburg—Second Day"; "Action of Boydton Road Oct. 27th, 1864"; "Map of Virginia" (10¼ by 7¾ inches).
Inclusive dates: 1861–1865.
Other editions: Original edition: Quartre ans de campagnes à l'Armée du Potomac. Paris, Librairie internationale, A. La-croix Verboeckhoven et cie, 1867, 1868. 2 vols.

De Trobriand became colonel of the Fifty-fifth New York Regiment, a French unit, in July, 1861, and before the end of the war had been made brevet major general of United States Volunteers. His services were confined to the battle area north of the James with the exception of the Petersburg-Richmond campaign which resulted in the final overthrow of the Confederacy at Appomattox. He took part in the principal campaigns within the region indicated, including the Peninsula, Second Manassas, Sharpsburg, Fredericksburg, Chancellorsville, Gettysburg, and in Grant's drive against Richmond, except for a short period in the summer of 1864 when he commanded the garrison and district of New York City. De Trobriand kept a diary during the war and prepared his narrative very soon after Appomattox. Naturally his principal interest was in military activities, but he gave many descriptions of the country and people of Virginia, especially the old Virginia homesteads and their occupants. The most sustained comment on the countryside related to his march up the Peninsula as part of McClellan's army.

Trollope, Anthony, 1815–1882. 453
North America. By Anthony Trollope. Philadelphia, J. B. Lippincott & co., 1863.

2 vols. I, i–iv, 5–335; II, i–iv, 5–334. 18½ cm.
Inclusive dates: 1861–1862.
Other editions: London, Chapman & Hall, 1862; New York, Harper & brothers, 1863.

Anthony Trollope, the well-known English author, made a trip to America in August, 1861. He spent most of his time in the North and in Canada, but he dipped into the South along the northern border on a trip from Baltimore to Missouri. He went by rail through Harrisburg and Pittsburgh to Cincinnati, crossed the Ohio River into Kentucky, visited Lexington, Frankfort, and Louisville, and continued to St. Louis and to Rolla in central Missouri. On the way back he stopped at Louisville again, made a side trip southward to visit a Federal army camp on Green River, and eventually retraced his route through Cincinnati eastward. Though Trollope was frank in what he had to say about Americans and American institutions, his criticisms, descriptions, and observations were penetrating and enlightening. He did not believe in either secession and slavery or abolition. He was entranced with the natural beauty of Kentucky.

Trumbull, H. Clay. 454
The knightly soldier; a biography of Major Henry Ward Camp, Tenth Conn. Vols. By Chaplain H. Clay Trumbull. Boston, Noyes, Holmes & co., 1871.

i–xii, 13–335. front. (port.) pl. 17 cm.
Illustrations: Frontispiece, "Henry W. Camp" [Signature]; "Camp of 10th Connecticut Volunteers, Annapolis, Md."; "Jail Yard, Columbia, S. C."; "Interior Columbia Jail, Officers' Quarters"; "Rebel Earthworks, Darbytown Road."
Inclusive dates: February, 1862–October, 1864.
Other editions: The first edition: Boston, Nicholas and Noyes, 1865 and New York, O. S.

Felt, 1865. The edition used here is "Sixth Edition, Revised." Another "New and Revised Edition"; Philadelphia, J. D. Wattles, 1892.

Letters from Henry Ward Camp and parts of his diary form the principal text of this narrative. A native of Connecticut and educated at Yale College, Camp joined the Tenth Connecticut Volunteers and became a major in the unit. First encamped at Annapolis, he was sent to the coast of North Carolina to participate in the capture of Roanoke Island and to engage in military actions around Newbern and Plymouth. He was then sent to Port Royal and subsequently to James Island off Charleston, where he was captured. While he was imprisoned in Columbia he escaped and almost reached the North Carolina line before being recaptured and transferred to Libby Prison in Richmond. He was then paroled, sent down the James on a flag-of-truce boat, and exchanged, after which Camp participated in the fighting around Petersburg in the summer of 1864 and was killed in the following October. In his letters and diary he was concerned mostly with military activities and army life, but he also recorded observations on the country and the people. This book is free from extreme bias and unseemly bitterness.

Tunnard, William H.   455

A southern record. The history of the Third regiment Louisiana infantry. Containing a complete record of the campaigns in Arkansas and Missouri; the battles of Oak Hills, Elk Horn, Iuka, Corinth; the second siege of Vicksburg, anecdotes, camps, scenery, and description of the country through which the regiment marched, etc., etc. By W. H. Tunnard. Baton Rouge, La., Printed for the author, 1866.

xx, [21]–393, [1] p. front., ports. 19 cm.
Illustrations: Frontispiece, "Truly Yours &c Willie H. Tunnard" [Signature].
Inclusive dates: 1861–1865.

A Southern Record is an exceptionally valuable commentary on conditions in the Civil War South, written by a Confederate soldier soon after the end of the conflict. Considerable portions of the narrative are transcriptions of notes kept by Tunnard, and the rest is based on fresh memory and on documents and papers provided by his comrades; the work is almost as much a travel book as a military narrative. He was interested in almost everything and everybody he saw, whether they were Indians on the western borders of Arkansas, lead miners in southwestern Missouri, swamps, mountains, farm lands, country frolics, or a Mississippi or Arkansas backwoodsman. He gives one of the few descriptions of a Confederate parole camp and of a football game among the soldiers. The author joined the regiment at Baton Rouge in the beginning of the war, and was sent down the Mississippi and Arkansas rivers to Little Rock and Fort Smith. After camping there for some weeks he went into the regions of northwestern Arkansas and southwestern Missouri and took part in the campaign leading up to the Battle of Pea Ridge or Elkhorn Tavern. Early in 1862 he was transferred to

Corinth in northern Mississippi, by boat down the Arkansas and up the Mississippi rivers to Memphis and across country. He operated through northern Mississippi before becoming part of the garrison defending Vicksburg where he was captured and paroled, and ultimately reached a parole camp at Alexandria, Louisiana. A year later he was exchanged and sent to Shreveport, where he was stationed when the Trans-Mississippi Department collapsed more than a month after Lee's surrender.

Tyler, Mason Whiting, 1840–1907.   456

Recollections of the civil war with many original diary entries and letters written from the seat of war, and with annotated references. By Mason Whiting Tyler, edited by William S. Tyler. New York, G. P. Putnam's sons, 1912.

xviii, 379 p. front. (port.) ports., maps. 22 cm.

Illustrations: Frontispiece, "Mason Whiting Tyler" ₍Signature₎; "Mason W. Tyler in 1907"; "Samuel C. Vance, Rufus P. Lincoln, and Mason W. Tyler (group) From a tintype, March, 1863"; "Captain Mason W. Tyler. From a photograph, 1863 or 1864"; "Captain Mason W. Tyler. From a photograph, 1864."

Maps: "The Salient at Spottsylvania. From Two Sketches Drawn by Colonel Tyler to Explain the Text" (5½ by 5¾); "The Battle Field of Spottsylvania C. H. May 9 to 21–1864" (4¾ by 5¾); "Field of Operations of the 37th Mass. Regiment From Spottsylvania to Petersburg" (4¾ by 8); "Field of Operations of the 37th Mass. Regiment as Far South as Spottsylvania Court House" (8¾ by 12½).

Inclusive dates: 1862–1865.

The first part of this book was composed by Colonel Tyler shortly before his death in 1907, from a war diary and many letters written home from the battlefields. The latter portion was put together by other hands almost entirely from the original text and is much more valuable because it includes many interesting comments and observations which were ironed out in the earlier version. Tyler, a native of Massachusetts, was graduated at Amherst in 1862 and immediately joined the Federal Army, rising by the end of the war to the rank of brevet colonel of the Thirty-seventh Regiment Massachusetts Volunteers. Colonel Tyler's service led him across Maryland to Gettysburg and back again to various places in Maryland, across most of northern Virginia, and also to the region around Richmond and Petersburg. The latter part of the book is confined almost wholly to military affairs; only in his letters are such items as the raiding of ex-President Tyler's home, the scattering of his library and theft of his manuscripts, the many desertions of Confederate soldiers into the Federal lines near the end of the war, and the thought in February, 1865, that General Lee must be a great man because he seemed utterly unperturbed though he knew the end was virtually at hand. After the war Colonel Tyler became a prominent lawyer in New York City.

Upson, Theodore Frelinghuysen, 1845–1919.   457

With Sherman to the sea; the civil war letters, diaries & reminiscences of

Theodore F. Upson, edited with an introduction by Oscar Osburn Winther ... University Station, Baton Rouge, La., Louisiana state university press, 1943.

xxii, 181 p. front., plates, port. 21 cm.

Illustrations: Frontispiece, "Atlanta in Ruins"; "Howe (Lima), Indiana, Today"; "Theodore F. Upson in Later Life"; "Allatoona Pass"; "The 'Bummer' "; "Captured Confederate Fort 'D', Atlanta, 1864"; "Sherman's Soldiers Destroying Railroad Emplacements, 1864"; "A Union Encampment, Atlanta, 1864"; "Union Troops Southeast of Atlanta, 1864"; "The 100th Indiana Crossing the Catawba River"; "Treasure Seekers." Mostly contemporary.

Maps: End paper map of the route taken by the author.

Inclusive dates: November, 1862–May, 1865.

The author, born in Steuben, Indiana, was brought up under the care of staunch Presbyterian foster parents. He joined the United States Army in 1862 as a member of the 100th Regiment of Indiana Infantry Volunteers. In November, 1862, his regiment reached Memphis, coming down the Mississippi River, and remained for some time. Later he took part under Grant in the Vicksburg campaign and was among the first to enter the city on its surrender. He was then assigned to Sherman's army and campaigned against Jackson, Mississippi, before returning up the Mississippi to Memphis and overland to Chattanooga to participate in the battles around that city in the fall of 1863. Upson was sent to Knoxville but returned to join, from Savannah to Richmond, Sherman's invasion of Georgia and his March to the Sea. This account, though essentially contemporaneous, was somewhat amended by Upson in the years following the war, but there is no evidence of fundamental changes. It is one of the better accounts of soldiers' observations in the South, and is not marred by unseemly bitterness or bias.

Urban, John W.   458

Battle field and prison pen; or, Through the war, and thrice a prisoner in Rebel dungeons. A graphic recital of personal experiences ... By John W. Urban. Philadelphia, Hubbard brothers, 1882.

xii, ₁13₁–422 p. front., plates, ports., plans. 18½ cm.

Illustrations: Frontispiece, "John W. Urban" ₁Signature₁; "Battle-Field of the Seven Pines"; "Ruins of Gaines's Mill"; "Hand to Hand Fighting at Mechanicsville"; "Field Hospital"; "Death in the Trenches"; "Gen. George G. Meade"; "Gen. Robert E. Lee"; "Chapel in the Camp"; "Prisoners Entering Andersonville Prison-Pen"; "Hanging of Six Thieves by the Regulators in Andersonville Prison"; "Prisoner Shot for Dipping Water too near the Dead Line"; "In 'God's Country' Again."

Maps: "Battle of Seven Pines and Fair Oaks"; "Battle of Gaines's Farm."

Inclusive dates: 1862–1865.

Other editions: Hoping to make the most of this story in retailing it to the public, Urban had it published under two other titles: My experiences mid shot and shell and in rebel den; a graphic recital of personal experiences throughout the entire war. Lancaster, Pa., For the author, 1882; Through the war and thrice a prisoner in rebel dungeons. A graphic recital of personal experiences throughout the whole war period of the late war of the union. Philadelphia, J. H. Moore & co., 1892.

Urban, a member of Company D, First Regiment Pennsylvania Reserve Infantry, was first taken prisoner on the Peninsula in July, 1862, and was imprisoned in Libby at Richmond for a short time before being exchanged and sent from Fortress Monroe to Annapolis. He was soon back in service and was captured again in Grant's campaign against Richmond but escaped almost immediately. Later in the summer of 1864 he was captured a third time and held until near the end of the war. He was first taken to Libby for a few days and then to near-by Pemberton prison. When the prisoners were removed from Richmond, Urban was sent to Andersonville in central Georgia, going by way of Danville, Greensboro, Charlotte, Columbia, Augusta, Millen, and Macon. In the fall of 1864 he was removed to Savannah, then to Millen, back to Savannah, and finally to Blackshear, for a short time before being transferred to Charleston and then to Florence. Near the end of the war he was paroled, sent to Charleston, and delivered to a Federal fleet waiting outside the harbor. Urban's book is extremely bitter, giving no credit to Confederate authorities for their attempts to take care of prisoners and claiming omission of information about the worst side of prison conditions. This book became a classic with those who read the lurid accounts written by the Federal prisoners of war. Urban, like many of his fellows, thoroughly believed his charges of inhumanity against the Confederate authorities were true, and was unable to recognize the psychosis which took possession of his judgment.

A voice from rebel prisons: 459
Giving an account of some of the horrors of the stockades at Andersonville, Milan [Millen], and other prisons. A returned prisoner of war. Boston, Press of Geo. C. Rand & Avery, 1865.

16 p. 23½ cm.
Inclusive dates: 1864.

The anonomyous author begins a lurid account with his marching westward out of Jacksonville, Florida, to the Battle of Olustee where he was captured. After walking a few miles to the railroad he was taken to Tallahassee and imprisoned for a few months before being sent westward by rail to Quincy, by wagon to the Chattahoochee River, northward by steamer to Fort Gaines, and by train to Andersonville. Leaving this prison camp late in 1864 he went by rail through Macon to Millen for a short stay and by rail to Savannah. At this point he was taken by steamer to the mouth of the Savannah River and turned over to the Federal fleet, which took him by way of Port Royal to Annapolis. This account, written immediately after the war, is valuable for descriptions of the routes taken by the author.

Waddle, Angus L. 460
Three years with the Armies of the Ohio and the Cumberland. By A. L. Waddle. Chillicothe, Scioto gazette book and job office, 1889.

iv p., 1 l., [7]—81 p.   22½ cm.
Inclusive dates: 1861–[1862]–1864.

These war reminiscences first appeared in the periodical *Ohio Soldier* from January to October, 1888. They were written entirely from memory, but since they relate more to general impressions than to minute details, their trustworthiness may be accepted with greater confidence. Waddle, an adjutant in the Thirty-third Ohio Veteran Volunteer Infantry, was more interested in the people he saw in the Confederacy than with purely military details. For example, he noted warmth of friendly feeling or cold hostility towards the Federal troops as they marched through the South, gave glimpses of life among the lowly snuff-dipping women of the Tennessee mountains, and related how he used counterfeit Confederate money to buy whiskey in Robertson County, Tennessee. He began the narrative in camp at Bacon Creek, south of Louisville, Kentucky, and continued it throughout all his marching southward to Nashville and into Alabama, back north into Tennessee in the summer of 1862 in the race to beat Bragg to Louisville, passing through Nashville and on to the Ohio River, back through Kentucky to fight at the Battle of Perryville and on into Tennessee and again to Murfreesboro by the end of that year, thence to fight at Chickamauga in the early fall of 1863, and finally to march with Sherman in the late spring and summer of 1864 to Atlanta. He was honorably discharged late that summer at Big Shanty, Georgia.

Walcott, Charles Folsom   461

History of the Twenty-first regiment Massachusetts volunteers in the war for the preservation of the union 1861–1865 with statistics of the war and of rebel prisons. By Charles F. Walcott. Boston, Houghton, Mifflin and company, 1882.

xiii p., 1 l., 502 p.   front., illus., ports., maps.   21½ cm.
Illustrations: Frontispiece, "J. L. Reno" [Signature]; "A. E. Burnside" [Signature].
Maps: "Field of Operations in North Carolina"; "Roanoke Island Surroundings Feb. 7, 1862"; "Charge of the Battery Roanoke Island Feb. 8, 1862"; "Sketch of Field of Operations in Northern Virginia. Summer of 1862"; "Last Fight at Second Manassas, by Reno's Old Brigade and Graham's Battery, 7 to 9 P. M., August 30, 1862"; "Sketch Map of McClellan's Maryland Campaign"; "Sketch Map of Surroundings of Knoxville"; "Sketch of the Union and Rebel Lines in Front of Petersburg"; "Retreat of the Rebel Army from Richmond and Petersburg April 2d to 9th 1865"; "Andersonville Prison Pen, as it Appeared in June, 1864."
Inclusive dates: 1861–1865.

Walcott traveled widely with the Twenty-first Massachusetts and another unit but the account is almost entirely about military affairs, with infrequent incidental notes on Confederate sentiment in the conquered regions. He served first in the Battle of Roanoke Island on the coast of North Carolina, then around Newbern and Elizabeth City, and was transferred to Virginia to fight at Second Manassas, Sharpsburg, and Fredericksburg. In March, 1863, he was sent by rail through York, Pittsburgh, Columbus, and Cincinnati to Paris, Kentucky, and later went with Burnside on the expedition to capture Knoxville, finally returning to Virginia to fight with Grant until Appomattox. The book contains a chapter on Andersonville Prison based on diaries of inmates.

Walker, Aldace Freeman 462
The Vermont brigade in the Shenandoah Valley. 1864. By Aldace F. Walker. Burlington, Free press association, 1869.

191 p. front. (map) plans. 19½ cm.
Maps: "Plan of the Battle of the Opequan, 19th September, 1864"; "Plan of the Battle of Fisher's Hill. 22d September, 1864"; "Plan of the Battle of Cedar Creek. 19th October, 1864."
Inclusive dates: 1864.

Walker left City Point, Virginia, by steamer for the defense of Washington against General Early's attack in the summer of 1864. After service in one of the forts defending the city, he followed Early into the Shenandoah Valley and served there until the Confederate commander was driven out. Walker narrates the route taken and gives some description of the country. He was entranced with the beauty of the Valley.

Ward, Joseph Ripley Chandler. 463
History of the One hundred and sixth regiment Pennsylvania volunteers, 2d brigade, 2d division, 2d corps, 1861–1865. By Joseph R. C. Ward ... Philadelphia, Grant, Faires & Rodgers, 1883.

viii, 351 p. front., pl., port. 22¼ cm.
Illustrations: Frontispiece, "Fraternally Yours &c Jos. R. C. Ward" ₍Signature₎ and eleven additional plates of portraits of officers, four of which contain groups.
Inclusive dates: 1861–₍1864₎–1865.
Other editions: Philadelphia, F. McManus, Jr. & co., 1906.

This book is restricted to the area between Gettysburg and Petersburg, including an account of those battles along with Ball's Bluff, McClellan's Peninsula campaign, Sharpsburg, Fredericksburg, Chancellorsville, and the conflicts between Grant and Lee up to July, 1864, when Ward was mustered out. The author based his composition on a diary and personal letters. Besides military matters he was interested in such subjects as cemeteries (with a long inscription copied from a tomb near New Kent Courthouse), plantations, pillaging, and the sacking of Fredericksburg.

Ware, Eugene Fitch, 1841–1911. 464
The Lyon campaign in Missouri. Being a history of the First Iowa infantry and of the causes which led up to its organization, and how it earned the thanks of congress, which it got. Together with a birdseye view of the conditions in Iowa preceding the great civil war of 1861. By E. F. Ware. Topeka, Kan., Crane & company, 1907.

xi, 377 p.   front. (facsim.) maps, ports.   19 cm.

Illustrations: "Capt. Thomas W. Sweeny, Second U. S. Infantry, as he appeared on the Forsyth Campaign"; "Thomas W. Sweeny, as Brigadier-General U. S. A. 25 years after the Battle of Wilson Creek, where he was Wounded."

Maps: "Map of the Route of the 1st Iowa Infantry, from Keokuk, Iowa to Boonville, Missouri, June 13, 1861 to June 21, 1861"; Map of March from Boonville to Little York; "Map of the Routes of the First Iowa Infantry to Dug Springs and McCulla's Store, and to Wilson Creek, Mo., July 20, 1861 to August 10, 1861."

Inclusive dates: 1861.

Writing forty-six years after the war, the author intimated that he used a campaign diary but there is little evidence of it. Ware, a private in the First Iowa Regiment, gives a wealth of details of the regiment's life and marches, as well as many comments on the country and people of Missouri. Only a fertile imagination coupled with a garrulous memory, or a rich and full diary could produce the many descriptions and experiences recounted. It is difficult, therefore, to determine how trustworthy this narrative is; yet it was written by a man who became a responsible citizen and lawyer in Kansas after the war. He was born in Hartford, Connecticut, but volunteered in the First Iowa Regiment early in the war, and moved with it to Keokuk, down the Mississippi to Hannibal, and across country by rail to Macon, Missouri. Thence the regiment marched to Boonville on the Missouri, continued on the move until after the important Battle of Wilson Creek, south of Springfield, and then went by way of Rolla to St. Louis.

Wash, W. A. 465

Camp, field and prison life; containing sketches of service in the south, and the experience, incidents and observations connected with almost two years' imprisonment at Johnson's Island, Ohio, where 3,000 Confederate officers were confined. With an introduction by Gen. L. M. Lewis, and a medical history of Johnson's Island by Col. I. G. W. Steedman, M. D. By W. A. Wash. Saint Louis, Southwestern book and publishing company, 1870.

i–xvi, 382 p.   18¼ cm.
Inclusive dates: May, 1863–July, 1865.

Captain Wash was from Kentucky and early in the war was stationed in East Tennessee. Later he was moved to the Vicksburg region and in May, 1863, was captured in an engagement on the Big Black River. He was marched around Vicksburg, which had not yet fallen to the Federals, and was sent by steamer, and by train from Cairo, Illinois, to Johnson's Island in Lake Erie. Early in 1865 he was paroled and sent by way of Pittsburgh and Harrisburg to Baltimore, transferred to a steamer for Harrison's Landing on the James, turned over to a Confederate flag-of-truce boat, and taken to Richmond. After spending a few days in the Confederate capital, he traveled by rail to Lynchburg and Bristol, and later almost to Jonesboro, Tennessee. Retracing his steps he visited in southwestern Virginia for the next two months. After the war ended and he attempted to pass into East Tennessee, he was arrested by bitter East Tennesseeans and imprisoned in the Jonesboro jail. In July, 1865, he was released, and made his way to the Bluegrass region in Kentucky through Cumberland Gap. Wash gives a mild account of his sufferings in the Federal prison and is very considerate in his comments on the enemy. He describes the ravages of war along the Mississippi, and there are some intimate observations on the people of southwestern Virginia among whom he visited before he was arrested.

Watkins, Sam R. 466

1861 vs. 1882. "Co. Aytch," Maury grays, First Tennessee regiment; or, A side show of the big show. By S. R. Watkins. Nashville, Tenn., Cumberland Presbyterian publishing house, 1882.

236 p. 21 cm.
Inclusive dates: 1861–1865.
Other editions: Second edition: Chattanooga, Times printing co., 1900.

There is a touch of humor in this personal and intimate narrative; probably Watkins occasionally let his desire to tell a good story lead him away from strict truth. His account is not of the tall tale variety, however, and may be accepted cautiously as depicting the lives of Confederate soldiers and also what civilians were doing and thinking. At least he states that he wrote from memory alone what he honestly believed at the time and what he saw. His military movements led him over most of the Confederacy south of the Ohio and east of the Mississippi. His unit was organized in Columbia, Tennessee, early in 1861 and was sent to Nashville, then by way of Chattanooga, Knoxville, and Bristol to Staunton, and into western Virginia to participate in Jackson's Romney expedition. Returning to Tennessee it was at Shiloh and Corinth. From northern Mississippi it went by rail to Mobile and on to Montgomery, Atlanta, Chattanooga, and across country with Bragg's invasion of Kentucky in the summer of 1862, retreating by way of Cumberland Gap and Knoxville to Chattanooga. After Murfreesboro came Chickamauga and the other battles around Chattanooga. In the spring of 1864 Watkins and his unit were part of Johnston's attempt to stop Sherman's march on Atlanta. After the fall of that city he followed Hood to the battles of Franklin and Nashville, and thereafter was able to reach North Carolina in time for the surrender in April, 1865.

Watson, William, of Skelmorlie, Scotland. 467

Life in the Confederate army, being the observations and experiences of an alien in the South during the American civil war. By William Watson. London, Chapman and Hall, limited [Aird and Coghill, printers, Glasgow] 1887.

xvi, [17]–456 p. 18½ cm.
Inclusive dates April, 1861–Summer, 1863.
Other editions: New York, Scribner & Welford, 1888.

Watson was a Scotsman who came to America some years earlier and at the beginning of hostilities was engaged in a trading business in Baton Rouge, Louisiana; he was also an expert mechanic and sometimes made use of his skill in the sugar works of the surrounding country. Though a British subject, the contagion of war led him to enlist in the Confederate forces. He was sent to a camp of instruction in New Orleans, transferred to northwestern Arkansas, and sent up the Mississippi and Arkansas by steamer to Little Rock and Fort Smith. He engaged in the campaign resulting in the battles of Wilson's Creek and Pea Ridge and afterwards fought around Corinth in northern Mississippi. Being an alien, he was mustered out when his enlistment expired even though conscription forced his comrades to remain in the army. He returned to Baton Rouge and was in New Orleans under the Butler regime; his description of that period is worth noting. He re-enlisted in the Confederate Army a short time later, was wounded and captured, and soon paroled. In the summer of 1863 he and some associates secured control of a small ship and made their way out of the Confederacy down the Mississippi River. Watson later engaged in blockade-running. He wrote with facility and at times with a sense of humor. He gives an excellent description of soldiers' life in camp, on the march, and in battle. The account was not written until 1887, when he was in Skelmorlie, Scotland, and there is no evidence of a diary or notes. Yet this work has the essence of reliability and may be rated among the best descriptions of a Confederate soldier's experiences.

Weiser, George. 468

Nine months in rebel prisons. By George Weiser. Philadelphia, John N. Reeve & co., 1890.

54 p. front. (port.) pl. 20½ cm.
Illustrations: Frontispiece, "Yours Truly George Weiser" [Signature]; "The Author, from a daguerreotype taken three months before his capture"; "The author just before he made his escape."
Inclusive dates: 1864–1865.

This pamphlet is of little value for any purpose, travel or otherwise. The author was not clear in his mind about the route taken from one prison to another and sometimes located towns incorrectly. He was captured in May, 1864, at the Battle of Spottsylvania Courthouse and taken immediately to Andersonville Prison. Later he was removed to the Florence Prison, in South Carolina, and in early 1865 was transferred to Wilmington to be turned over to Federal authorities. While he was in that vicinity the Federals captured the city, and Weiser was put aboard ship and taken to Annapolis.

West, John Camden, 1834– 469

A Texan in search of a fight. Being the diary and letters of a private soldier in Hood's Texas brigade. By John C. West ... Waco, Tex., Press of J. S. Hill & co., 1901.

189, 8 p., 1 l., incl. port. 19½ cm.
Illustrations: "John C. West."
Inclusive dates: 1863–1864.

A diary kept by West from April 12 to June 13, 1863, and February 28 to April 20, 1864, with various letters written during his term of service comprise the text of this book. The diary gives a minute account of routes and means of travel, and includes comments on matters of interest to a traveler. The letters are devoted more to the author's life as a soldier and to family acquaintances. West was born in Camden, South Carolina, and was educated at the College of South Carolina in Columbia. He moved to Texas in 1855 and settled in Waco. For the first two years of the war he served as Confederate attorney for the Western District of Texas, but feeling impelled to enlist, he made his way to Virginia and joined Hood's Brigade. He went from Waco through Palestine and Marshall to Shreveport and as far as Natchitoches where he found it impossible to proceed further. Returning to Shreveport he went to Monroe and across the state to Natchez, Jackson, Meridian, and Selma to Montgomery. Thence his journey was entirely by rail through Atlanta, Augusta, Columbia, Charlotte, Raleigh, Weldon, and Petersburg to Richmond. He reached his unit on the Rapidan shortly before Gettysburg, in which he took part. Returning to Virginia, he joined Bragg's army around Chattanooga, taking the indirect route by Wilmington, Augusta, and Atlanta (since the railway through East Tennessee was now in the hands of the enemy). After fighting at Chickamauga, he went into East Tennessee with Longstreet, and in early 1864 was honorably discharged. Retracing his eastward route through Lynchburg and Columbia to Meridian, Mississippi, he found the enemy in possession of much of this region, detoured to cross the Mississippi River in a skiff between Natchez and Vicksburg, and continued through Shreveport to Waco.

Weygant, Charles H. 470

History of the One hundred and twenty-fourth regiment. [N. Y. S. V.] By Charles H. Weygant. Newburgh, N. Y., Journal printing house, 1877.

2 p. l., vi, [7]–460 p. front. (port.) fold. tab. 23¾ cm.
Illustrations: Frontispiece, "A. Van Horne Ellis" [Signature].
Inclusive dates: 1862–1865.

Throughout his narrative the author concerns himself with the Confederate population. He based his account on memory, documents, historical writings, and diaries of other soldiers in the regiment. Like nearly all soldier authors Weygant mentioned pillaging and irate women trying to protect their meager belongings. He also reports such experiences as finding a bin of corn in an old mill and forcing the unwilling miller to grind it. Weygant and his regiment fought in all the principal battles from Sharpsburg to Appomattox, so the narrative relates principally to Virginia and incidentally to Maryland and Pennsylvania.

Wheeler, William.   471

In memoriam. Letters of William Wheeler of the class of 1855, Y. C. Cambridge, Mass., Not published. Printed for private distribution by H. O. Houghton and company, 1875.

vi, 468 p.   front. (port.)   21½ cm.
Illustrations: Frontispiece, William Wheeler (unlabeled.)
Inclusive dates: 1861–1864.

These letters were written by a highly intellectual and cultured soldier, who was twenty-five years old when he joined the Federal army at the outbreak of the war. Wheeler was a graduate of Yale College and had traveled extensively in Europe. He was in two areas of operations in the Confederacy; first, in northern Virginia, embracing operations in the Shenandoah Valley under Fremont and Sigel, and in the campaigns culminating in the Battles of Fredericksburg, Chancellorsville, and Gettysburg; secondly, in Sherman's march from Chattanooga against Atlanta until his death near Marietta. He was transferred to the West in the fall of 1863 with Hooker's forces, to aid Rosecrans, and traveled by Columbus, Ohio, Indianapolis, Louisville, and Nashville to Chattanooga. Wheeler was strongly Abolitionist, but actual fighting and associating with the conquered population sobered rather than embittered him. He visited with many Confederate families within the occupied country, attended their religious services and sang their songs, and disapproved of pillaging. He repelled the idea that these normal human relations made him less patriotic or less determined to fight the war to a successful conclusion.

Wheelock, Julia S.   472

The boys in white; the experiences of a hospital agent in and around Washington. By Julia S. Wheelock. New York, Lange & Hillman, 1870.

x, 9–274 p.   front. (port.) port.   18 cm.
Illustrations: Frontispiece, "Julia S. Wheelock" ₍Signature₎; "Orville Wheelock" ₍Signature₎.
Inclusive dates: 1862–1865.

Miss Wheelock was an army nurse in Federal hospitals and this narrative is largely a condensation of her journal. Her headquarters were in Alexandria, Virginia, from which place she made numerous journeys to the battlefields of northern Virginia; once as far south as Yorktown and City Point. She was interested in the "rebel people," whom she detested, in the historic places such as Mount Vernon and Fredericksburg, and in general conditions in the Confederacy, all of which she describes.

White, William S.   473

"A diary of the war, or what I saw of it," being Pamphlet no. 2, Contributions to a history of the Richmond howitzer battalion. Richmond, Va. Carlton McCarthy & co., 1883.

p. 87–304.   22½ cm.
Inclusive dates: 1861–1865.

This diary gives an excellent close-up account of the experiences of a member of the Richmond Howitzers, a unit of the First Virginia Artillery. White naturally gives most attention to military matters, but had much to say about the people he met. On the march he often approached a nearby house, visited with the occupants, took meals with them, and sometimes remained over night. His operations were mostly confined to Virginia, but once he dipped down into North Carolina south of Suffolk, Virginia, where he was stationed for a time, and he crossed Maryland into Pennsylvania on the Gettysburg campaign. The diary shows some signs of having been reworked after the war, but the changes are mostly stylistic and do not affect its first-hand importance.

Whitney, J. H. E. 474

The Hawkins zouaves: (Ninth N. Y. V.) their battles and marches. By J. H. E. Whitney. New York, Published by the author, 1866.

x, [11]-216 p.   18½ cm.
Inclusive dates: 1861–1863.
Other editions: No other edition found. Another history of this same regiment, but written thirty-five years after the war, is: Matthew J. Graham, The Ninth regiment New York volunteers (Hawkins' Zouaves) being history of the regiment and veteran association from 1860 to 1900. New York, 1900 (E. P. Coby & co., printers.)

Traveling with the Hawkins Zouaves, Whitney went from New York City to Fortress Monroe to take part in the campaign up York Peninsula in the summer of 1861, participated in the capture of Roanoke Island, and for the next few months engaged in raiding along the northern shore of Albermarle Sound and the rivers flowing into it. In one of these expeditions his troops fired the little town of Winton, said to be the first town burned by the Federals in the war. In the summer of 1862 his unit went to Fredericksburg, marched into Maryland for the Sharpsburg campaign, returned to Virginia, and later marched into southeastern Virginia to operate around Suffolk until the unit was mustered out in May, 1863. Whitney gives considerable attention to the people of the Confederacy, finding those on Roanoke Island woefully ignorant, and the inhabitants generally less intelligent than New Yorkers. He admits that his troops were first-class pillagers of the countryside. Whitney makes no mention of a diary but there was little lapse of time to affect his memory. It is, however, a biased account by one who refused to find anything commendable in the Confederacy.

Wilkeson, Frank. 475

The soldier in battle. Or, Life in the ranks of the Army of the Potomac. By Frank Wilkeson. London, Bellaire & co., 1896.

xii, 196 p.   18¾ cm.
Inclusive dates: 1863–1864.
Other editions: Published as: Recollections of a private soldier in the Army of the Potomac. New York, G. P. Putnam's sons, 1887, 1893, 1898.

Written in a lively, peppery style, this book is filled with barbs directed against army discipline and officers, especially West Pointers. Wilkeson seems to have had a grudge against almost everything that came to his attention. He enlisted from the state of New York in 1863 and was soon in the battle area of northern Virginia. He was with Grant's army in its campaign against Richmond in 1864 and until the investment of Petersburg. After a short term as guard at the Elmira, New York, prison camp he reached Nashville, Tennessee, by an undesignated route, unsuccessfully tried to find his unit in the vicinity of Chattanooga, and returned by Nashville and up the Tennessee to Eastport, Mississippi. In seeming disgust he resigned his commission and went home. The account is somewhat improbable, yet it contains comments which may be balanced against some more prosaic statements by other Northerners. For example, he saw no slaves running away from their masters to join the Federal Army, and he was sure that Confederate prisoners at Elmira were treated little better than Federal prisoners in Confederate camps.

Wilkie, Franc Bangs, 1832–1892. 476

Pen and powder. By Franc B. Wilkie. Boston, Ticknor and company, 1888.

383 p. 19 cm.
Inclusive dates: 1861–1863.

The book consists of sketches by a war correspondent, interspersed with penetrating word pictures of personalities, evidently worked over from pieces which appeared during the war. Wilkie, born in West Charlton, New York, was engaged in newspaper work at Davenport, Iowa, when the war began. He was soon in the Missouri area of military operations, attached to both Lyon's and Fremont's forces, whose activities he considered a fiasco. He then went to Cairo and followed Grant's army to Forts Henry and Donelson and on to Nashville. The remainder of his service as a correspondent was spent in Mississippi across the river from Helena, Arkansas, and around Vicksburg and Jackson. He considered the pillaging in Mississippi unequaled anywhere and thoroughly outrageous. He believed everybody connected with the army and a horde of speculators who swarmed down from the North were reaping fortunes from the cotton trade—even war correspondents could not keep out of it. After the fall of Vicksburg he went on to New Orleans and soon left military service to assume editorship of the *Chicago Times,* with which paper he remained for a quarter of a century. He was the author of many other books.

Williams, Edward Peet. 477

Extracts from letters to A. B. T. from Edward P. Williams during his service in the civil war, 1862–1864. New York, For private distribution, 1903.

122 p. 20 cm.
Inclusive dates: 1862–1864.

The author of these letters was a person of education and refinement who wrote without bitterness or bias. Williams entered the Federal military service in 1862 as first lieutenant and adjutant of the One-hundredth Indiana Volunteer Infantry and went down the Mississippi River to Memphis; from there he raided through northern Mississippi and southwestern Tennessee and went on to the Vicksburg region. Afterwards, until the latter part of 1864 when he resigned from the army, Williams operated from Nashville (arriving there by railway from Louisville) to Chattanooga and northwestern Georgia. Williams commented on such topics as the Hebrew merchants who took over business in Memphis when the Federals occupied that city, foraging parties in Mississippi, the Confederate woman who was discovered with a pair of boots hidden under her clothing, and the great numbers of slaves making their way into the Federal lines.

Williams, George Forrester. 478

Bullet and shell. War as the soldier saw it; camp, march, and picket; battlefield and bivouac; prison and hospital. By Geo. F. Williams. Illustrated by Edwin Forbes. New York, Fords, Howard, & Hulbert, 1882.

454 p. illus. 21½ cm.
Illustrations: Sixty-two pen-and-ink sketches by Edwin Forbes.
Inclusive dates: 1861–1865.
Other editions: Subsequent editions of this work are: Under the same title in 1883 by same publishers; Bullet and shell: a soldier's romance, 1895, by same publishers.

Bullet and Shell is a fictional account of army service beginning at Big Bethel on the York Peninsula; continuing through McClellan's drive on Richmond; the campaigns culminating in the battles of Fredericksburg, Chancellorsville, and Gettysburg; some minor activities around Winchester; and Grant's assault which resulted in Appomattox. During this time Williams was twice taken prisoner but never remained in captivity long enough to be taken to a Confederate prison camp; he was also in hospital for a time. The value of a work in this conversational style, except for atmosphere and definite descriptions of events, landscapes, and beliefs, is questionable. But it is not marred by bitterness against the enemy or by conviction of Northern superiority.

Williamson, James Joseph, 1834–1915. 479

Prison life in the old capitol and reminiscences of the civil war, by James J. Williamson ... illustrations by B. F. Williamson. West Orange, N. J., 1911.

x, 11–162 p. front., illus. 19½ cm.
Illustrations: Frontispiece, "Old Capitol Prison"; "Exemption Certificate"; "Pass Through Confederate Lines"; "Carroll Prison (Duff Green's Row)"; "Arch Window in Room No. 16"; "Colonel William P. Wood, Superintendent"; "James J. Williamson"; "Stove in Room No. 16"; "John H. Barnes"; "Lieutenant Albert Wreen"; "Colonel John S. Mosby"; "Lieutenant Frank Fox"; "Brigadier-General Edwin H. Stoughton"; "Certificate of Membership" [in Mosby's Rangers]; "Major Henry Wirz"; "Rev. F. E. Boyle"; "Rev. Bernardin F. Wiget, S. J."; "Gunnell House (General Stoughton's Headquarters)."
Maps: "Map of James River, from Fortress Monroe to Richmond."
Inclusive dates: April, 1861–April, 1863.

The writing is significant for its descriptions of life in Federal prisons in Washington, of a Confederate parole camp near Petersburg, and of his travels through northwestern Virginia to join Mosby's Partisan Rangers. Williamson was born in Baltimore, but was a resident of Washington at the outbreak of war. He entered the Confederate service but was taken from the army to aid in civilian work in Richmond. Returning to Washington in August, 1862, he was arrested and imprisoned there in the following January. In March he was paroled, transported down the Potomac and up the James to City Point, and turned over to the Confederate authorities. He went by railroad to Petersburg and entered a parole camp where he remained until he was exchanged shortly thereafter. He then joined Mosby's Rangers who were operating in northwestern Virginia. The author describes his trip up to the point of entering active service.

Wills, Charles Wright, 1840–1883. 480

Army life of an Illinois soldier, including a day by day record of Sherman's march to the sea; letters and diary of the late Charles W. Wills. Compiled and published by his sister [Mary E. Kellogg.] Washington, D. C., Globe printing company, 1906.

383 p. incl. front. (port.) 22¾ cm.
Illustrations: Frontispiece, Portrait of C. W. Wills.
Inclusive dates: April 28, 1861–May 19, 1865.

Charles Wright Wills was born in Illinois, and died in Louisiana. He enlisted in the Federal Army as a private in 1861 and was promoted to a lieutenant-colonelcy before the end of the war. The scene of his military activities until 1864 lay in western Tennessee and northern Mississippi and Alabama; in 1864–1865 he participated in the Atlanta campaign and Sherman's March. Letters from the author containing many interesting comments on the country and its population, are the most valuable part of this work; the latter portion, relating to his march with Sherman, is in sketchy diary form and mostly about military matters. He was much opposed to the "nigger war" nature which the struggle assumed, thoroughly detested both slaves and free Negroes, and was sure that they must be removed from the country when they were freed. Wills condemned wholesale pillage of private homes and robbery of personal belongings and livestock. Most of his comments on such matters related to Tennessee, Mississippi, and Alabama. He found the people, despite their sociability, extreme secessionists in sentiment. Southern women entertained soldiers at dances and parties but insisted on singing "rebel songs" and playing "rebel music" as well as arguing in the most rebellious fashion. Yet the account is singularly free from bitterness and is written in a lively style, interspersed here and there with sly humor.

Wilson, John A. 481

Adventures of Alf. Wilson. A thrilling episode of the dark days of the rebellion. Washington, D. C., The national tribune, 1897.

xiv, 15–237 p.   illus.   21½ cm.

Illustrations: "Good-By to Gen. Mitchel"; "Tearing up Tracks"; "A Close Pursuit"; "Jumping from the Engine"; "Halt there, You"; "Going down into Darkness"; "Prison at Chattanooga"; "Bids his Comrades a Final Farewell"; "Racing for the Woods."

Inclusive dates: March, 1862–January, 1863.

Other editions: This work was evidently first published in book form in 1880, but no printing earlier than 1897 has been found.

Parallel accounts: Another account of the same episode up to Wilson's escape from the Atlanta prison is Rev. William Pittenger *(q.v.)*, Capturing a locomotive: a history of secret service in the late war. Washington, The national tribune, 1885.

Born in Ohio, and living near the town of Haskins, the author joined the Federal Army in 1861 and in March, 1862, volunteered to accompany J. J. Andrews in his well-known raid to disrupt the Western and Atlantic Railroad by seizing an engine at Big Shanty, Georgia, and running it northward to Chattanooga to burn the principal bridges on the way. The expedition failed and Wilson escaped into the woods north of Dalton, Georgia, only to be captured a few days later and imprisoned at Chattanooga, Madison, Georgia, and Atlanta. In Atlanta he and a companion escaped and made their way to the Chattahoochee River nearby, floated down that river in a boat to its mouth, and joined the Federal blockade squadron. Wilson soon shipped to Key West, suffered an attack of yellow fever, and went by ship to Port Royal, South Carolina, and to New York City; thence to Washington, to his Ohio home, and back to join his original company on Stone's River, Tennessee, arriving there soon after the battle of Murfreesboro. The account is highly personal and spiced with adventure, but of little value. It was first written about 1880 and published in the *Wood County Sentinel*.

[Wise, George.]   482

History of the Seventeenth Virginia infantry, C. S. A. [By George Wise] Baltimore, Kelly, Piet & company, 1870.

312 p.   18½ cm.
Inclusive dates: 1861–1865.

Naturally this narrative deals principally with affairs of the regiment and considerably with the life of the soldiers composing it. To a lesser degree it contains the ordinary observations of a person marching through a country with which he was fairly well acquainted. Whenever possible the author visited with admiring civilians, and his description of the Unionism of Maryland women, the hunger of the soldiers, and other matters suggests a traveler's viewpoint. Wise began his military activities around Alexandria at the outbreak of the war and operated mostly in Virginia, except for the Sharpsburg campaign, one journey into East Tennessee, and a trip into eastern North Carolina.

Wood, George L.   483

The Seventh regiment: a record. By Major George L. Wood. New York, James Miller, 1865.

304 p. 18½ cm.
Inclusive dates: 1861–1864.
Other editions: Another edition under another title: Famous deeds by American heroes. A record of events from Sumter to Lookout Mountain. New York, James Miller, 1865.

The Seventh Ohio Regiment was organized in 1861 in Cleveland and, after training at Camp Dennison, entrained for western Virginia (West Virginia), going by way of Columbus, Bellaire, and Grafton, and operated in the central mountain country around Gauley Bridge and on down to Charleston. Being ordered to the northern Virginia region, it moved down the Kanawha and up the Ohio rivers to take a Baltimore and Ohio train for a point near Romney. It was active, until the fall of 1863, up and down the Shenandoah Valley, across into eastern Virginia around Fredericksburg and Chancellorsville, and took part in the Sharpsburg and Gettysburg campaigns. Immediately after Gettysburg it was sent by steamer down the Potomac and Chesapeake Bay to New York to help check the draft riots. Soon returning by the same route, the regiment was ordered to re-enforce the Federal armies around Chattanooga, went by rail through Columbus, Indianapolis, Louisville, and Nashville, and arrived in time to take part in the battles of Missionary Ridge and Lookout Mountain. The next spring it went with Sherman on his march against Atlanta, arriving at Allatoona just as its term of enlistment expired, when it returned by rail to Nashville and by steamers down the Cumberland and up the Ohio to Cincinnati. This account is based almost entirely on memory but was written before the end of the war and may be accepted as trustworthy. The author was somewhat sharp in his feelings against the Confederates, and against the institution of slavery. He forgot these dislikes, however, as he passed through the beautiful mountainous country of western Virginia (West Virginia), which he frequently describes.

Woodbury, Augustus, 1825–1895.   484

A narrative of the campaign of the First Rhode Island regiment, in the spring and summer of 1861. Providence, Sidney S. Rider, 1862.

4 p. l., 260 p. front. (port.) map. 19 cm.
Illustrations: Frontispiece, "A E. Burnside ₍Signature₎ Col. First Regt. R I D. M."
Maps: "The Battle Fields of Blackburn's Ford and Bull Run."

The only significance this book has as a travel account is its description of pillaging by the first Federal troops who visited the Confederacy. He wrote of a time before the bitterness of war and bloodshed had colored the attitude of the invaders. In Fairfax, where the Federal forces were encamped on their way to First Manassas, some of them looted houses in the town, which the author rated as lower than ordinary burglary. He also noted the attitude of people in the country through which he traveled. The unit marched from Washington up through Maryland to Harpers Ferry and thence through Virginia to take part in the First Manassas battle.

Woodruff, William Edward, 1831–   485

With the light guns in '61–'65. Reminiscences of eleven Arkansas, Missouri and Texas light batteries, in the civil war. By W. E. Woodruff. Little Rock, Ark., Central printing company, 1903.

> 115 p.   front. (port.) map.   19½ cm.
> *Illustrations:* Frontispiece, "First Lieut. Omer R. Weaver."
> *Maps:* "Field of Battle of Oak Hill, August 10, 1861."

Woodruff, reaching the rank of major in the Confederate Army, fought through southwestern Missouri, Arkansas, and into the Indian Territory. He made a trip to Texas during the war, going as far as Dallas in the north and Austin in the south. This account, written from memory almost forty years after the events, has the defects of such narratives and mentions few subjects other than military affairs.

Woodward, Evan Morrison.   486

Our campaigns; or, The marches, bivouacs, battles, incidents of camp life and history of our regiment during its three years term of service. Together with a sketch of the Army of the Potomac, under Generals McClellan, Burnside, Hooker, Meade and Grant. By E. M. Woodward, adjutant, Second Pa. reserves. Philadelphia, The Keystone publishing company, c.1865.

> vii, 9–362 p.   18½ cm.
> *Inclusive dates:* 1861–1864.
> *Other editions:* First edition: Philadelphia, John E. Potter, 1865.

This volume has some merit in that the author now and then gives interesting descriptions of the desolated towns of northern Virginia as well as glimpses into the countryside through which he marched. In other respects, and apart from its military matter, it should be used with caution, for it was first-rate propaganda designed to embitter the Northern people against the Confederates and thereby aid recruiting. Woodward recounted many gruesome episodes, including a story of Southern soldiers sawing Yankee leg bones into finger rings and a report of Confederate ambulance drivers remarking that corduroy roads were "bully to haul wounded Yankees over." Woodward joined the Second Regiment of Pennsylvania Reserve Volunteers and fought from 1861–1864 in the principal engagements, excluding Manassas and Chancellorsville, from the Peninsula to Gettysburg. In July of the latter year his enlistment expired and he returned to Pennsylvania.

Worsham, John H.   487

One of Jackson's foot cavalry; his experiences and what he saw during the war 1861–1865, including a history of "F" company, Richmond, Va., 21st regiment Virginia infantry, Second brigade, Jackson's division. Second corps, A. N. Va. By John H. Worsham ... New York, The Neale publishing company, 1912.

353 p.   front., plates, ports.   20 cm.
Illustrations: Frontispiece, "[Soldier] 1861"; "First Captain R. Milton Cary"; "[Soldier] 1862"; "Second Captain Richard H. Cunningham, Jr."; "Third Captain William H. Morgan"; "Fourth Captain William A. Pegram"; "[Soldier] 1863"; "[Soldier] 1864"; "Fifth Captain Reuben J. Jordan"; "1865."
Inclusive dates: 1861–1865.

A well-written account with many plausible details. There is nothing to indicate that it was not composed immediately before publication (forty-seven years after the war) or that its author had access to a diary or other contemporary material, yet there is little in the story that is improbable. It is concerned mostly with the life of a soldier in camp and on the march, but gives an insight into conditions inside the Confederacy. Worsham developed friendly relations with the people of regions through which he marched and found them glad to open their dining rooms to Confederate soldiers, sometimes for a price and sometimes on the bounty of the household. All of the author's military activities took place north of the James River, and included most of the important battles and campaigns of that area, with the exception of Gettysburg. Worsham was wounded at the Battle of Winchester, in September, 1864, and was disabled for the rest of the war.

Wright, Henry H., 1840–1905.   488

A history of the Sixth Iowa infantry. By Henry H. Wright. Iowa City, Iowa. The State historical society of Iowa, 1923.

xii, 539 p.   22½ cm.
Inclusive dates: 1861–1865.

Wright, who was a sergeant in the Sixth Iowa Regiment, began this narrative in 1898. The general impressions and atmosphere came from his memory, the more substantial military information from official records and regimental data. He used neither diary nor other personal papers, though he did make use of a diary kept by another member of the regiment. The work is almost wholly military but there are intelligent comments on conditions in the Confederacy. Wright wrote without bitterness, and in his description of the destruction of Columbia, South Carolina, he was inclined to blame the drunken Federal soldiers. The regiment was formed in Burlington, proceeded down the Mississippi by boat and later by train to Keokuk, and went westward to the Missouri border to engage in its first fighting near Athens, Missouri. It then returned to Keokuk, embarked for St. Louis, went by train to Jefferson City, and marched across country to Springfield in the southwestern part of the state. Returning to St. Louis over practically the same route, it took boats to Cairo and up the Ohio and Tennessee rivers to Shiloh. After that battle it proceeded to Corinth and Memphis, operated in West Tennessee and northern Mississippi during the remainder of 1862 and early 1863, and embarked down the Mississippi for Vicksburg. After the fall of that city it went with Sherman on the Jackson (Mississippi) raid, returned to Vicksburg and by river to Memphis, and marched eastward to Chattanooga to arrive after the Battle of Chickamauga. It then went into East Tennessee as far as Knoxville to ward off the blows of Longstreet. In the spring of 1864 it marched with Sherman through Atlanta and on to Washington for the "Grand Review." It returned to Iowa by the Baltimore and Ohio Railroad to Parkersburg, West Virginia, and by steamer for Louisville, where it was mustered out in the summer of 1865 and finished the journey by rail through Chicago.

Wright, Thomas J. 489

History of the Eighth regiment Kentucky vol. inf., during its three years campaigns, embracing organization, marches, skirmishes, and battles of the command, with much of the history of the old reliable Third brigade, commanded by Hon. Stanley Matthews, and containing many interesting and amusing incidents of army life. By Capt. T. J. Wright. St. Joseph, Mo., St. Joseph steam printing co., 1880.

286 p., 1 l. 17 cm.
Inclusive dates: September, 1861–November, 1864.

Captain Wright's book is one of the best of the regimental histories. Written fifteen years after the close of the Civil War, it is temperate and, since it was composed from the author's diary, is reliable and worthwhile. Wright enlisted in the regiment at Estill Springs in September, 1861, and the unit went to Louisville to embark on river steamers for Nashville. It soon saw action around Murfreesboro and Wartrace, and in the early fall, 1862, raced back to Louisville in General Buell's command to head off Bragg's invasion of Kentucky. After the Battle of Perryville, the army continued back into Tennessee and ultimately took part in the Battle of Chickamauga and the subsequent union victories at Lookout Mountain and Missionary Ridge. Wright's unit remained in the Chattanooga region when Sherman set out for Atlanta and in November, 1864, it returned to Kentucky and was mustered out. This work contains many interesting comments on the population of Middle Tennessee, especially on the Confederate and Union elements and the slaves. This may be accepted as a fair account by an officer who was not influenced by a burning hatred of the Confederates and whose later feelings, mellowed by time, were even milder.

Wynn, William O. 490

Biographical sketch of the life of an old Confederate soldier, also Three years as a cowboy on the frontier of Texas. By W. O. Wynn. Greenville, Texas, Greenville printing co., inc., 1916.

159 p. port., illus. 19 cm.

Illustrations: "W. O. Wynn" and twenty-eight rough sketches of scenes described in the narrative.
Inclusive dates: 1862–1865 (1859–1865).

A frank and artless narrative written half a century after the events. The author had no formal education, and as a result his book is practically worthless, except as indicating the informality and simplicity of the author and the majority of the people he mentions. He has misspelled many names of men and battles and, without desiring to misstate facts, has badly confused his war career. He enlisted in 1862, went first to Galveston and then to Arkansas, was captured and taken to Camp Douglas in Chicago, removed to City Point, Virginia, and exchanged. Wynn made his way to Middle Tennessee to join Bragg's army and subsequently fought at Chickamauga and around Chattanooga. He made a raid into Kentucky and on his return to northern Georgia was again captured and taken to Rock Island where he escaped and made his way back southward through St. Joseph, Missouri, Leavenworth, Kansas, and across the Indian Territory into Arkansas. In the summer of 1864, Wynn returned to the fighting near Atlanta and later followed Hood to the outskirts of Nashville. When the war ended he returned to Texas.

[Young, William Henry.]   491
Journal of an excursion, from Troy, N. Y., to Gen. Carr's head quarters, at Wilson's landing, (Fort Pocahontas,) on the James River, Va. during the month of May, 1865. By one of the party. Troy, N. Y., Privately printed, 1871.

59 p.   front.   25 cm.
Illustrations: Frontispiece, "Spotswood Hotel, Corner of Main & Eighth Streets, Richmond, Va."
Inclusive dates: May, 1865.

Immediately after hostilities ended in 1865, a party from Troy, New York, made a sightseeing trip to Richmond and the lower James River Valley. They went by boat down the Hudson to New York, by train to Baltimore, and again by boat to Fortress Monroe. After a short visit in Norfolk, the party went up the James, stopping at such places as Harrison's Landing to see the old Harrison mansion and at Westover to enjoy the Byrd home surroundings. From City Point the New Yorkers went on to Petersburg, and along this route they saw the devastations of war. Returning the same day to City Point they continued by boat up the James to Richmond and stayed for a few days at the Spotswood House. In Richmond the visitors reveled in all the sights made famous by the war as well as those objects of earlier historic interest. They viewed Castle Thunder and were delighted to see some Confederate prisoners in Libby Prison. They visited the old Virginia capitol, saw the halls where the Confederate Congress had sat, and viewed the statues and monuments in and around the building. Curios were collected everywhere. Chips from the old William Byrd monument in the gardens of Westover, ancient documents found scattered in old country estates, rifles and fragments of shells, and $500.00 packages of Confederate money which were bought for fifty cents each. This account has specific value as a picture of the wreckage of war before it could be cleaned away, and as indicating the psychology of the conquerors.

## Zettler, Berrien McPherson, 1842–	492
War stories and school-day incidents for the children. By B. M. Zettler. New York, The Neale publishing company, 1912.

168 p.   18½ cm.
Inclusive dates: 1861–1865.

Zettler was a native of the Salzburger community in Georgia, living near Springfield in Effingham County. At the outbreak of war he was a student in the Lutheran college at Newberry, South Carolina, but the war fever impelled him to join the local Vigilantes Committee and then to join Bartow's regiment in Savannah. Soon he was on his way to Harpers Ferry, and was in the First Battle of Manassas. Breaking winter quarters in the spring of 1862 he retreated with his unit to the Peninsula to repel McClellan's attack on Richmond, and returned northward to engage in Second Manassas, where he was wounded and permanently disabled. Zettler was then assigned as a collector of the Confederate tax-in-kind for his home community and remained there until Sherman appeared and disrupted the economic and social life of the people. Near the end of the war he made a wagon trip to Augusta to trade hides and tallow for provisions and merchandise. This is a brief account, but it contains some interesting insights into the social history of the Confederacy. After the war Zettler became superintendent of public schools in Macon, Georgia.

INDEX

461 (map), 488; see also Ambrose E.
Burnside

Magruder, John B.: 120
Mail carrier: 203
Mammoth Cave: 69
Manassas, first Battle of: 22, 30, 32, 34, 38, 46, 63, 67, 79, 96, 102, 126, 150, 152, 154, 155, 173 (map), 179, 223, 243, 263, 300, 321, 330, 357 (and map), 373, 391, 403, 411, 419, 448, 484 (and map), 492
Manassas, second Battle of: 32, 38, 48, 55, 68, 75, 90, 101, 103 (illus.), 113, 116, 117, 138, 149, 179, 214, 223, 231, 241, 291, 327, 330, 341, 344, 354 (map), 357 (map), 365, 366, 396, 430, 448, 449, 452, 461 (and map), 492
Manassas Junction: 18, 150
Mansfield, La. (including battle): 201, 345
Marching through Georgia (Hedley): 225
Marching with Sherman (Hitchcock): 235
Marietta, Ga.: 329, 373
Marshall, Texas: 136, 224
Marshall House, Alexandria, Va.: 32, 38, 85
Martinsburg, W. Va.: 140
Maryland: 3, 6, 15, 18, 20–22, 24, 26, 29, 32, 33, 36–39, 45–48, 51, 54, 55, 66–68, 72, 74–76, 78–80, 83, 85, 90, 94, 95, 97, 98, 100, 101, 103, 105–108, 111–13, 115–17, 120, 122, 124–26, 130, 132, 134, 137, 138, 142–46, 149–52, 155, 158, 160, 162, 163, 165, 166, 170, 172–75, 179, 180, 182, 183, 185, 186, 191–93, 195, 196, 198, 204, 209, 212–15, 217, 222, 223, 231, 233, 239, 241, 243, 248–51, 253, 259, 268, 275, 277, 278, 283, 286, 289, 291, 294, 300, 308, 311, 313, 314, 323–25, 327, 328, 330, 332, 333, 336, 338, 341, 343, 344, 347, 348, 351, 353–55, 357, 358, 360–62, 364–66, 375, 378, 380–83, 385, 386, 389, 392, 395–97, 399, 403, 405, 407, 409, 411, 412, 414, 416, 419, 420, 423, 425, 426, 429, 430, 431, 435, 439, 447–49, 452–54, 456, 458, 461, 463, 468–71, 473, 474, 478, 479, 482–84, 486, 487, 490, 491
Maryland line in the Confederate States army (Goldsborough): 192
Maryville, Tenn.: 229
Mason, George: 106
Matagorda Bay: 27, 45, 219, 258, 284, 303, 316
Maynard, Horace: 366
Meade's headquarters, 1863–1865 (Lyman): 301
Mechanicsville, Battle of: 458 (illus.)
Medical service: *see* Hospitals
Mein tagebuch uber die erlebnisse im revolutions-kriege (Stuber): 438
Memoir of William Francis Bartlett (Palfrey): 361
Memoirs: historical and personal; including the campaigns of the First Missouri Confederate Brigade (Anderson): 7
Memoirs of a veteran who served as a private (Hermann): 227

Memoirs of chaplain life (Corby): 95
Memoirs of General William T. Sherman: 415
Memoirs of life in and out of the army in Virginia during the war between the states (Blackford, comp.): 36
Memoirs of the civil war between the northern and southern sections of the United States of America, 1861–1865 (Chamberlaine): 74
Memoirs of the Confederate war for independence (Borcke): 47
Memoirs of the rebellion on the border, 1863 (Britton): 52
Memorials of William Fowler: 169
Memories. A record of personal experience and adventure during four years of war (Beers): 24
Memories of the southern states (Collins): 86
Memphis, Tenn.: 7, 12, 13, 15, 27, 30, 58, 68, 71, 83, 84, 135, 137, 143, 157, 171, 177, 199, 202, 204, 218, 258, 266, 293, 298, 299, 303, 337, 340, 372, 398, 434, 439, 457, 477, 488
Meridian, Miss.: 178, 194, 244, 326, 340, 425
Mexico, Mo.: 15
Middleburg, Battle of: 47
Military history of the 123d regiment of Ohio Volunteer infantry (Keyes): 277
Military reminiscences of Gen. Wm. R. Boggs, C. S. A.: 43
Mill Springs, Ky., graves at: 441 (illus.)
Milledgeville, Ga.: 30, 49, 141, 163, 194, 252, 287
Millen Prison (Ga.): 15, 114, 235 (illus.), 269, 292, 297, 302, 308, 388, 425, 458, 459
Milton, John: 239
Milton, Tenn., Battle of: 451
Mission ridge and Lookout mountain (Taylor): 443
Mississippi: 4, 5, 7, 8, 13, 15–20, 25, 27, 30, 34, 35, 45, 50, 56, 58, 59, 64, 65, 68, 70, 71, 73, 75, 78, 79, 81–84, 87, 97, 104, 110, 116, 118, 128–31, 133, 135, 137, 139, 141, 143, 157, 164, 171, 175–78, 181, 184, 194, 199, 202–205, 208, 210, 211, 218, 219, 221, 224, 226, 227, 230, 234, 237, 242, 244, 247, 255, 257, 258, 261, 266, 267, 271, 274, 276, 279, 281, 284, 285, 292, 293, 296, 299, 302, 303, 309, 312, 316, 317, 319, 320, 326, 334, 337, 340, 355, 356, 359, 366, 367, 376, 378, 387, 392 (secession convention [illus.]), 396, 398, 403, 404, 414, 415, 422, 424, 425, 432–34, 436, 438, 439, 441, 446, 448 (map), 455, 457, 465–67, 469, 476, 477, 480, 488
Mississippi River: 5, 7, 8, 13–17, 19, 27, 30, 45, 51, 56, 58, 64, 65, 68, 70–73, 81, 84, 87, 97, 110, 129, 130, 133, 137, 141, 143, 146, 157, 171, 177, 195, 198, 199, 202–204, 218, 219, 224, 226, 234, 237, 242, 244, 255, 256, 258, 261, 266, 267, 276, 281, 284, 292, 293, 296–99, 303, 312, 316, 317, 319, 326,